Flesch, Carl. 1873-1944. Hungarian violinist and teacher. Studied at Vienna (1887-1889) and Paris (1890-94). Professor, Bucharest (1897-1902), Amsterdam (1903-08); to Berlin (1908); head of violin department at Curtis Inst., Philadelphia (1924) and founder of Curtis String Quartet (1925); settled in Baden-Baden (1926). Auther of Urstudien for violin (1911) and Die Kunst des Violinspiels (2 vols., 1923-28).

CARL FLESCH

The ART *of* VIOLIN PLAYING

Book One

Technique in General
Applied Technique

8.00

Second Revised Edition

Book Two

Artistic Realization
and Instruction

8.00

English Text by
FREDERICK H. MARTENS

CARL FISCHER, INC.
COOPER SQUARE, NEW YORK 3
Boston • Chicago • Dallas

Copyright, 1924
by
CARL FISCHER, Inc.
NEW YORK

International Copyright Secured

Revised Edition Copyright 1939
by
CARL FISCHER, Inc.
New York

International Copyright Secured

Printed in U. S. A.

N1404

THE ART OF VIOLIN PLAYING

FOREWORD

TO THE FIRST EDITION

The present work is not meant to be a "School of Violin-Playing" in the current meaning of the term. It is broadly conceived, from the pedagogic standpoint, its intention is not only to advise the teacher how to train his pupils most advantageously, on the basis of the most modern acquisitions in the domain of violin technique, but also—by leading him to think logically, and by cultivating analytical investigation of the problems of violin technique—to bring the violinist to a plane of development which, in time, will enable him to be his *own teacher*. Hence this work is not addressed to violin beginners, nor to advanced students; but to *reasoning* violinists, or those who wish to become reasoning violinists. It represents an attempt to raise the art of violin-playing from mere crude experience to a higher plane of a *logically* formed experience. Yet abstract theory, in the violinistic profession, has a right to exist only to the degree in which its validity is justified by experience, and the way is shown for its practical utilization. For the final aim and end of violin study is the *public performance* of a composition as the intermediary between its creator and its audience. Therefore, the validity of a theory cannot be regarded as proven until it has been *publicly* tested. Who among us has not had the experience that some improvement or novelty which, tried out in the privacy of a small room, seemed epochal, collapsed completely in the concert-hall, or even seemed the very opposite of that for which it was intended! Hence it is very much to be deplored that all the great violinists of the preceding century have not allowed us a peep into their workshop, and that, in the main, the theory of violin-playing has been developed by men who were not in a position to put theory to a practical test in the *concert-hall*. The ghost of charlatanism will only be laid when artists will not be satisfied merely to reproduce an art-work in the most perfect manner, but will also undertake the task, as the most competent interpreters, of disclosing the secret of how it was accomplished.*

Until some fifty years ago, the incipient violinist's course of study was based on one of the numerous violin schools, later supplemented by the customary etude material (*Kayser*, *Kreutzer*, *Gavinies*, *Fiorillo*, *Rode*),

---

* Even the violin methods by *Baillot*, *Beriot*, *Spohr*, *Leonard* and *Joachim*—in spite of valuable practice material and occasional precious aesthetic considerations (Joachim)—merely contain generalized, impersonal presentations of purely technical problems.

Not until quite recently has *Karl Klingler* broken this spell by the publication of his essay (which will be discussed in detail in the proper place) on the fundamentals of violin-technique. The "School of Bowing," by *Lucien Capet*, that admirable French violinist, considers the problem from too limited a point of view—that of bow *division*. *Steinhausen*, again, with his physiology of bowing, has the merit of being the first who has plainly shown the German violin-playing world the nonsense of an exclusively exaggerated development of the wrist. In consequence of his imperfect preparatory violinistic training, however, he has been mislead into an announcement of certain principles (theory *of rolling elbow-joint movements*, etc.) the use of which not only does not stand any serious test, but would absolutely ruin a bowing, good in itself. Consideration and discussion of pedagogic works published in the United States and England within the last few years was made impossible, as same were unknown to me at the time of writing this work.

while at the same time the concertos of *Viotti*, *Kreutzer*, *Rode*, *Bériot*, *Vieuxtemps* and *Spohr* served to teach the student the art of phrasing in accordance with the spirit of the time. Teacher and pupil gave little thought to the means to be acquired and the goal to be reached. On the contrary, in most cases the former was satisfied to train the average pupil to be able to meet the requirements of a theater or concert-orchestra, as well as might be, or as a teacher to promulgate the established traditions as an unassailable legacy, and hand them on without further thought. Those who strove for higher things were compelled, by reason of their special individual talent, to seek their path *alone*. All in all, it was a rather mechanical activity, which conditioned the permanent retention of the great majority of violinists on a low plane of technical ability and expressive power. The few who succeeded in shining as stars of the first magnitude in the heavens of art owed their position to their own genius, i.e., creative gifts.

The appearance of *Sevčik*'s study works were responsible for a fundamental change in this respect, since, using them properly, the technique of every violinist may be raised to a level making it possible for him to solve difficult technical problems, which previously only a few had been able to overcome. Yet all depends on the proper use of these studies. Neither in *Sevčik* nor in other works, so far as I know, is it possible to find adequate directions for discovering possible *hindrances* or *impediments* which may develop, or how to analyze and dispose of them. The seductive convenience and comfort of the "guaranteed" successful, ready-made extracts offered leads the pupil to shirk the trouble of investigating their components.

In most cases he is content to go through his daily allotment of work without any mental activity whatever. Then, when difficulties arise, he has no competent guide at his disposal. Yet those who lack foresight are not the only ones who are mislead, and who are overtaken by this misfortune—for *all* of us there comes a time when we can go no further, when we are confronted by seemingly insurmountable physical or psychical impediments. This critical moment may occur at the most widely separated periods in the artist's life. Yet *only* in old age is decline a law of nature. When it occurs *before*, it is his own fault. If those whose development was arrested or whose advance was checked prematurely had been taught in their youth to render themselves a mental accounting for all they carried out mechanically, if a *reasoning* teacher had accustomed them to regard their failings first of all as errors of *motive* power and then shown them a way to overcome them, later, as their own teachers, they would have been able to discover the road which would lead them once more into the open.

Not infrequently teachers are satisfied to announce traditional principles as incontrovertible truths. However: "Tradition is slovenliness!" as Gustav Mahler once said in his drastic fashion. A great violinist is prone to form habits which, technically or psychically, are in any event grounded in purely personal characteristics.* A generation later they already have become "traditions." This is a very serious matter, for a school should rest on the laws of *universal validity*.

For my own part, I should like to aid the violinist clearly to understand that which he thus far has deduced only under the ban of tradition or by means of instinct. He would then be so placed that he would be able to remove obstacles which might be opposed to his development. The distance between the insufficient violinistic accomplishments of the rank and file, and the vanishing number of surpassing talents that need no guide, should be lessened so far as possible. It is the duty of a *reasoning* body of teachers to raise the artistic level of the average violinist.

I am quite well aware of the fact that the usefulness of the present work will be limited, inasmuch as it cannot materially further the development of those psychic qualities which may be collectively summed up under the head

---

* *Fritz Kreisler* is a case in point: he has arranged for himself a technique of tone-production which is uniquely calculated to lend authority to his personality. He uses but little of the bow, strong pressure, and a continuous, most intensive *vibrato* (even during runs) when he plays, and with these most individual means achieves the highest measure of expression. Yet what results might not a "Method" bring about which raised Kreisler's purely personal means of expression to a generally current law?

of *original* talent. Yet one should be careful not to regard too many things as gifts of nature. Colour and volume of tone, bowing and finger technique, an ear for proper intonation—all these may be acquired and improved, because the functions of the organs which participate in them are susceptible to verification, and are accessible to external influences. On the other hand, a man's nature and mode of feeling are given qualities, and can only be altered when his inner consciousness, as a consequence of one or another influence, undergoes a change. Hence the teacher, first of all, must not consider a want *congenital* and difficult to rectify until he has convinced himself that it is rooted in the *psychic* peculiarity of the individual.

The reader cannot fail to notice that no special place has been assigned to *instructions for beginners* (with the exception of some considerations of a general nature contained in Book II of this work, to appear at some future time), although every one is convinced of their fundamental importance. But the instruction of beginners is a science in itself, and the most intimate knowledge of the sum total of the result to be attained is a preliminary necessity. Possibly the present work may induce specialists in this field to establish the basis of the most adequate course of elementary instruction, by the aid of the principles it advances.

I have tried to employ as clear and generally understandable a manner of writing as possible, and have used foreign words only where they were unequivocally demanded in the interests of general comprehensibility.

Only in certain specific cases have I indicated sources and literary references. Aside from the unnecessary overloading of the text with notes, it is of little importance for the non-historian to know who may or may not have been the first to have recommended one or another mode of procedure. For the same reason, so far as at all possible, I have avoided discussions with regard to authors whose opinions differ from my own.

It would hardly have been possible for me to have completed this work—which represents a vital necessity to me—while continuing to be active as a solo violinist and teacher, had I not found a faithful aid in my friend, *Prof. Dr. Max Dessoir* to whom I am expressing the cordial thanks so justly due him. (*Berlin*—1924)

FOREWORD

To the Second Edition

If a pedagogic work is to exercise a lasting influence in its particular sphere, it should be kept up to date by the inclusion of references to all matters of recent investigations and research. Twenty years have elapsed since I began to outline the general plan of this book, and although neither the technical foundations of our art nor its purely musical components have undergone any important changes, I nevertheless felt the desirability of altering certain details, of eliminating involuntary errors and of clarifying many definitions which might have been misunderstood by the average student.

For reading through the proofs and for his most valuable suggestions thereon, I am much indebted to Mr. Rowsby Woof of The Royal Academy of London.

CARL FLESCH.

(*London. March* 1939.)

GENERAL INDEX

I. Technique in General

The theory of the general technique of violin-playing falls naturally into the following sub-divisions:

1. The Instrument and its Component Parts (pages 8 to 14)

2. The Position of the Body (pages 14 to 17)

		PAGE
(*a*)	Position of the Legs	14
(*b*)	Direction in which the Violin is Held	15
(c)	Position of the Violin	15
(*d*)	Position of the Head	16

3. The Left Arm

(*a*)	Manner in which the Left Arm is Held	17
(*b*)	Intonation	19
(c)	Basic Movements of the Left Hand	23
(*d*)	Change of String, (to the Left)	25
(*e*)	Positions and Change of Position	25
(*f*)	The Vibrato	35
(*g*)	Basic Forms of Left-Hand Technique	40

4. The Right Arm (pages 50 to 80)

		PAGE
(*a*)	Remarks in General	50
(*b*)	How the Bow Should be Held	51
(c)	Bowing	54
(*d*)	Change of Bow	58
(*e*)	Change of String, (to the Right)	61
(*f*)	Division of the Bow	63
(*g*)	Long Bowings	64
(*h*)	Short Bowings	68
(*i*)	Thrown Strokes and Springing Strokes	73
(*j*)	Mixed Strokes	78

5. Tone Production (pages 81 to 103)

(*a*)	Remarks in General	81
(*b*)	Point of Contact Between Bow and String	81
(c)	Defects of Tone Production	84
(*d*)	Dynamics	90
(*e*)	Dynamic Faults	96
(*f*)	Tonal Studies	97
(*g*)	Tone Colors	99
(*h*)	Tone as a Means of Expression	100

II. Applied Technique

		PAGE
1.	General Remarks as to Practicing	104
2.	Practice of General Technique	108
(*a*)	Daily Exercises (System of Scales)	109
(*b*)	Etude Material	114
3.	Practice of Applied Technique	118
(*a*)	Fingering in General	118
(*b*)	Fingering as a Technical Means	119
(c)	Fingering as a Means of Expression	144
(*d*)	Fingering and the Tone Colors	146
(*e*)	The Bowing	148
4.	Practice as a Means of Learning	157
5.	Musical Memory	167

SUMMARY.

The art of violin-playing calls for control of three factors, which are closely interrelated.

1. *Technique In General.* Under this term I include the most practicably perfected cultivation of the mechanism of both arms for the purpose of securing all tonal effects possible of production on the violin, in a dependable and impeccable manner. One might call it: violin-playing as a *craft.*

2. *Applied Technique.* When I apply the general technical facility acquired to technical difficulties occurring within a *composition,* then it is a question of "Applied Technique." It is violin-playing as a *science.**

3. *Artistic Realization.* Not until I control a perfect mechanism and am able to apply it in the right way, am I free enough, physically, to give myself up entirely to the spirit of the music, and to allow *expression* to rule a technique which now merely *serves.* This is violin-playing as an *art.*

The theory of general as well as applied technique forms the contents of Book I of the present work, while Book II is devoted to "Artistic Realization," as well as to violin-pedagogics in general.

Before we concern ourselves with the fundamentals of violinistic ability, it seems advisable to raise the question whether there are in our art such things as immovable, unchangeable elementary principles, which defy the passage of ages. In general this must be denied. Many roads lead to Rome—our art contains no magic formulas—the only difference being that some roads lead to Rome more quickly and with less expenditure of effort than others. At the same time one demand may be acknowledged as a fundamental law: This law reads: *A perfect technique consists in producing all tones with purity of intonation, tonal beauty, and with the shadings and the rhythm as required by the composer.* Every technical error, without exception, offends this fundamental law or one of its parts. This ideal which floats before us is the aim we follow when studying the technique of the violin. Ideals are probably unattainable, yet we must try to realize them as closely as possible.

* For instance, the correct execution of scales in thirds, on the violinist's part, by no means guarantees that when playing the F Sharp Minor Concerto by *Ernst,* he will produce the two well-known scales in thirds in a brilliant manner, i.e., that he will be able to apply in the right way the technical raw material at his disposal.

1. The Instrument and its Component Parts**

Italian Violins

With the passing of time the expressions *"an Italian violin"* and *"a good violin"* have become synonomous. Now, it cannot be denied that the majority of good instruments are of Italian origin; yet all Italian instruments by no means sound as well as they might. Other violins, too, may be excellent. The experience of years, and a certain natural tonal instinct are necessary in order to discriminate as to the tonal qualities of a violin. The principal qualities of a good instrument are: an easy responsiveness (readiness in "speaking"), carrying quality of tone, equalized sounding of the four strings, and an agreeable tone-color. These advantages depend upon the way in which it has been built, the strength of the wood, the quality of the varnish, and the instrument's state of preservation.***

** It has not been my intention here to present an exhaustive consideration of the instrument as a tone-producing body or a discursive characterization of its component parts. The following remarks only touch concisely upon certain details which, as experience has shown, are not explained in accordance with their importance in teaching.

Lining of Violins

*** One should ascertain the exact conditions inside the violin, above all whether, and to what extent, it has been "lined." Although a small lining where the sound-post fits at either the top or back hardly affects it adversely, (the tone of an instrument being otherwise good, and may in course of time become absolutely necessary in order to strengthen the belly, because of the unrelieved pressure on the bridge) a lining inside of the belly (top) or other lining even more extended, especially when the weather is damp, unquestionably makes the instrument sadly unreliable.

ill- ne lins

It is due to J. B. Vuillaume that we have so few perfect concert instruments, for he rendered some 3,000 violins unfit for concert purposes by "baking" them.*

If the same number of violins "baked" by his emulators and admirers be added, we have at least 6,000 admirably built examples, captivating in appearance, which have been withdrawn from artistic use owing to Vuillaume's obsession, and which are greatly missed. Incidentally, in his very first and in his last period Vuillaume manufactured normal violins which have a splendid tone, and drive home the loss we have suffered in consequence of his unfortunate mania.

e of tru- nts

In general, the *smaller* instruments are to be preferred to the larger for normally proportioned as well as for small hands. In particular, when buying an instrument of the Brescian school (*Maggini*), one should make sure in advance that its proportions place no excessive demands upon the hands. One should also pay attention to the fact that many violins, despite normal proportions, are more difficult to play on than others, because of a circular rather than elliptic rounding of their upper right-side curve. In the case of *children* the size of the instrument should always be in due proportion to the development of the hands. If a child, in order to favor development of a big tone, is given a violin disproportionate for his age, the future invariably takes its revenge.

Testing an Instrument

The purchase of a violin is one of those acts in an artist's life productive of the most far-reaching consequences. If it so seldom happens that he is able to find a medium corresponding to his abilities and his taste in the matter of tone, this is due principally to the fact that in the choice of an instrument (in nearly every case) *subjective* impressions almost always, and *objective* conclusions hardly ever determine his choice. The testing of an instrument is influenced too greatly by the player's own firmly established characteristics, his disposition at the moment, the weather, surroundings, personal taste, and upon the more or less prejudiced auditory impressions of the advising listener, to permit of clear judgment with regard to the inner, unalterable qualities of the object. Violinists who have a mode of tone-expression altogether individual, that is to say, in most cases, the best violinists, are quite useless in such instances, since the individuality of the instrument is thrust into the background by that of the player. To this must be added a blunting of the auditory nerves consequent upon repeated comparisons made between two instruments, which often leads to the most fantastic of false conclusions.**

New Violins

In our own day, as a result of the extraordinary increase in price of old Italian instruments, which makes it impossible for young violinists who are not wealthy enough to obtain them, numerous inventors have endeavored to substitute new instruments for old through processes of tonal perfection. Hitherto none of these processes have been able to secure unqualified rec-

---

*"Baking" is an artificial preparation of the wood, which consists in exposing it to a high temperature, which kills the wood fibres, a process taking place *naturally* only after a very long period of time.

lin -s

** During past years, in Paris, various experimental contests have been inaugurated between new and old instruments of different origin, the results of which turned out to be very favorable for various contemporary violin-makers. Subsequent tests in private or in the concert-hall, however, have not confirmed such verdicts. The reason for this contradiction is that, although the attempt was made to eliminate certain subjective moments during the contest (such as, above all else, any influence due to sight of player and instrument), by securing complete darkening of the hall, the fact remained that the player's personal tone-production, his mood, and that of his audience could not be eliminated. *Vidal*, in his "Les instruments à l'archet" (Paris, 1876), narrates the following characteristic occurrence: At the beginning of the nineteenth century the physicist *Savart* addressed a petition to the French Academy to take into consideration a novelty which he had developed in the field of violin-making, and to compare the tonal results he had secured with those of old, recognized instruments. A committee of investigation comprising the most prominent French musicians, among them Cherubini, Kreutzer, Rode and Baillot, was appointed to compare Savart's new violins with well-preserved examples by Stradivarius and Guarnerius. Here, too, certain moments of personal susceptibility to influence were eliminated by the fact that the player was in an adjacent room. In the committee's opinion Savart's violins were unquestionably superior to those of Stradivarius and Guarnerius.

This verdict, which posterity cannot be said to have endorsed, is well adapted, in view of the standing of the judges, permanently to discredit similar attempts. It is not sufficient for an instrument to give satisfaction at the moment when it is tested; it must also retain its qualities during the entire time it endures, something which cannot be verified until many years have passed.

ognition. The estimation of tonal qualities will remain on a vacillating basis so long as no scientific method for their *objective*, uninfluenced verification has been discovered.

The way to this end is the following: first of all, an investigation must be made to discover wherein a "beautiful" tone differs from an "unbeautiful" one in a *physical* sense. (Number and kind of the overtones, vibratory breadth, anti-vibratory moments, combination-tones, etc.) This should be followed by the discovery of a procedure which would cause all those physical qualities of a tone which either give us pleasure or gains our disapproval, to register themselves graphically, by their own spontaneous action. Only in this manner would it be possible to arrive at an incontrovertible, scientific and objective estimate of the tonal qualities inherent in an instrument. It would be desirable were the inventors in our field content to concern themselves with the solution of this problem, instead of disseminating their energies in fruitless experiments the value of which will always remain questionable so long as their working-out cannot be objectively controlled. Incidentally, it seems remarkable that no one hitherto has thought of employing the *grammophone record* as a nonpartisan and incorruptible judge in this connection. At least it would have the advantage of eliminating personal influence of the player by reproduction on the machine, and the tonal result could at any moment be drawn upon for comparison.

Care of the Violin

Quite as important as the excellence of the instrument is its *care*. What sins are not commited in this respect! One hesitates to believe that many violinists, and not the worst either, regard the thickest possible layer of rosin dust as an indispensable attribute of their instrument. Is it possible that they follow the same principle with regard to the care of their own persons? Whenever it has been used the violin should be cleaned. At the same time, the *strings* also should be freed from the loose rosin-dust clinging to them by means of a soft cloth, since otherwise hard crusts form in the course of time, preventing them from speaking freely. Also *inside* of the instrument dust- and rosin-particles collect in large quantities, of which, as a rule, the player is not aware until the instrument has to be opened for some reason or other. In my opinion every instrument in constant use should be cleaned from the foreign bodies which may have gathered in its interior *several times a year*, by means of a handful of dry but roasted rice grains, poured into the violin through the F-holes, and vigorously shaken—the tonal improvement of the instrument when it has been subjected to this quite harmless process is surprising. When great demands are made upon a violin, especially in warm concert-halls, it may sound weary and *feeble*. In such case it is worth while to diminish the pressure of the strings on the belly for twenty-four hours, by tuning the strings down an octave. The instrument seems to take a fresh breath when temporarily relieved of the pressure of the strings and repays one with an unaccustomed freshness of tone. Furthermore, the *thickness* of the strings plays a great part with regard to the tone. The normal ratio of the thickness of strings, compared to each other, in millimeters, is as follows:* E-string (gut) 63/100; A-string, 82/100; D-string, 190/100; G-string, 82/100. When the proportion is wrong the fifths will seldom sound in tune; and the bow pressure may be too weak in the case of strings which are too thick, and *vice versa*. A good Italian violin demands individual stringing, its peculiarities can be determined only after repeated experiments.**

Size of Strings

Once this has been done the measurement is recorded on the *string-gauge*. This apparent pedantry is necessary, since otherwise the defects mentioned will occur again and again. When the *pitch purity* of the strings is tested, by making them sound together, the use of minor *sixths*

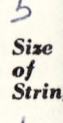

* A millimeter is equivalent to 0.0394 of an inch.

** That our ancestors played on strings much thinner than our own is proven by the following occurrence. Some thirty years ago the owner of the firm of Schott showed the celebrated violinist *Hugo Heermann* one of Paganini's letters, wherein the latter begged the head of the firm of his day to procure strings for him like the samples enclosed. *Heermann* obtained the loan of these strings, measured them on a string-gauge, and found to his astonishment that the D-string had the strength of the A-string used to-day, the A-string the thickness of our E-string, and that the latter was not unlike a strong thread. Probably another proof that the older violinists did not lay any special stress on the production of a "big" tone. A fact known only to a few experts is the possibility of fixing the *tonal capacity* of the G-string by means of the string-gauge. The thinner the winding and the thicker its so-called "gut foundation" (E-string), the thickness of which is controllable at the extreme end of the G-string, the better the string will "speak."

is preferable to that of the fifths ordinarily used, since every violinist knows through experience how closely he must press his fingers together, for instance, at 

in order to produce perfect intervals. Any departure at once betrays to him the string which is out of tune, especially if he plays the parallel interval on the other strings. A *fifth*, on the other hand, may be played in so many different ways, that it is far more difficult to obtain a clear idea of the correct interrelation of the strings.

It was during the world war, that a century-old tradition was gradually undermined till its definite demolition brought about a most important change in conditions of violin playing—I mean the substition of gut strings by wire strings.* It would look like carrying coals to Newcastle to enumerate the manifold advantages of metal strings. But in any way there is no doubt, that public performance has become not only much more reliable from the technical side but also more enjoyable from the musical standpoint, since the chances of string-sagging or breaking have become so remote. With gut strings the smooth performance of the Chaconne of Bach for instance always remains a gamble. Nowadays an artist, whose instrument is provided with a steel E, an aluminum-covered steel A and an aluminum-covered gut D may step on the concert platform with the comfortable feeling, not to be at the mercy of the too capricious gut strings, whereas in former days a violin recital looked sometimes very much like a circus show, the performance being suspended a few times, the artist rushing from the platform to the green room and the artistic impression of the public being irremediably destroyed. The difference in tone colour between gut and metal is hardly noticeable and the only disadvantage of the metal A consists in its somewhat higher pitch in relation to D and E which may endanger the intonation of double stops. Let us hope, that research work in this line will soon find a remedy for this inconvenience.

As regards *tuning* in general, I believe that the strings should invariably be tuned with the *left hand*. Aside from the impression of awkwardness and inconvenience produced when the peg is turned by the right hand, this procedure makes it impossible to tune *while* playing. For instance, in the Bach *Chaconne*, which takes about 17 minutes to play, the E-string frequently drops half a tone lower, and if the performance of the composition is not to be interrupted, it is necessary to tune at the following places:

When playing the D major Concerto by *Paganini*, in the *Wilhelmj* edition, the E-string, as a rule, is also in a deplorable condition before the second entrance of the *Cantilena*: here the violinist has only a very brief space of time to devote to tuning:

Above all things, one must be sure that the peg is so firmly set that it cannot slip back. For this reason the string should be mounted in a special way. The extreme end of the string first must be firmly laid down (see Ill. No. 1, in Appendix), after which it is simply rolled up. At the same time the string leans against the inner wall of the peg-box, which supports it and prevents it from rolling back again (Ill. No. 2). The tuning should be done by the left hand, using the index finger as a lever, while the thumb (Ill. No. 3) in the case of the A- and E-strings, and in that of the G- and D-strings, the ring-finger and little finger, should be used for the counter-pressure (Ill. No. 4). I would never allow a pupil to appear in public unless I were assured that he could adjust his strings in the manner as above described, and possessed the necessary skill to tune with his left hand.

Tuning with Piano Accomp.

Many violinists are in the habit of tuning *too high* when playing with *piano accompaniment*. The difference of intonation between the two instruments lies in the fact that the violin must be tuned in perfect fifths while, owing to the tempered tuning of the piano, each of its fifths is lower by a few vibrations. Hence, if I accept the exact A of the piano, the two lower violin strings, in comparison

* I can remember only two violinists, who on account of excessive perspiration, had the courage already at the beginning of this century, to use wire E-strings, when playing in public—Willy *Burmester* and Anton *Witek*.

to the keyboard instrument, are too low from the very start. Personally, I prefer to tune according to the open G, and have the pianist strike this triad: [bass-clef triad] Thus it is possible for me to secure the following result: the other strings become immaterially higher than the corresponding tones of the piano, and just sufficiently so to equalize the usual drop in the intonation. In the *orchestra* it is usually the *oboe* which sounds the A for the soloists. Yet, woe to him if he tunes his strings in exact accord with it! In less than a quarter of an hour, especially if the temperature be warm, he will find himself differing from the first violins—which in nearly all cases are tuned higher than the wind instruments at the very beginning—by a quarter tone. He is, therefore, confronted by the dilemma of either having to play too high on the open strings at the beginning of the composition, or else of playing too low later on.

Tuning with Orchestra Accomp.

Of these two evils he will have to choose the lesser, that of *tuning somewhat higher*, which, as a rule, does not affect the ear as unpleasantly as the opposite. Yet here it is imperatively necessary to preserve a happy medium. The temperature of the concert-hall, the age of the strings and length of the first solo are the chief factors which determine the necessary deviation from the pitch of the normal A.*

In general one should avoid tuning down the strings by violent *pulling* or drawing out, or raising the pitch by means of pressure on the part before the nut. However, when the time available for tuning may be counted only by seconds, we are compelled to resort to such means. Furthermore:

4.

* Unfortunately, in the last decades, the agreement between the wind and strings in the orchestra—usually owing to inadequate control on the part of the conductor—has been anything but satisfactory, and the soloist has to make his choice between two different pitches. *Lamoureux* himself did not shirk the toil of personally dictating the normal A to each one of his 120 orchestra players, violin in hand!

Owing to the left-hand *pizzicati* (+), the strings get out of tune in the very first measures, which materially and disadvantageously affects the collective performance. Hence it is my custom, at the beginning af this composition, to "pull out" the D-string and A-string in a forceful manner, securing an otherwise unattainable stability of intonation in the case of both strings. It may also be taken for granted, generally speaking, that in the case of new, unused strings, this "drawing out or pulling" represents the sole means of making them quickly serviceable.

Bridge

Of the *parts* of the instrument which do not belong actually to the *body* of the violin, the bridge is undoubtedly the most important. Practical experience has taught us the following lines of orientation: The *bridge* must be high enough on the *left* side to prevent the vibrations of the G-string from touching the fingerboard, so that the string does not "rattle." On its *right* side the bridge may be much lower, and in consequence the pressing down of the strings calls for less exertion. It must be so *rounded* that even when a stronger pressure is applied, the middle strings may be attacked without the bow touching their neighbors. (The German violin-makers favor the flatter bridge, the Romanic ones the more rounded form.) When the bridge is too *high* the strings, as a result, "speak" with greater difficulty. The height of the bridge, however, is often conditioned by the position of the fingerboard with regard to the violin-neck. When the neck has been fitted in too *straight*, the fingerboard will lie too low, calling, in turn, for too low a bridge, and imparting a certain pressed quality to the tone. When the neck is fitted in too *obliquely* the fingerboard will be too high, and will call for too high a bridge. In addition, experience teaches us that high bridges correspond to flat violin-bellies, and low bridges to rounded ones. The thickness of the bridge, in a way, is conditioned by the inner qualities of the instrument itself: a violin, lacking in responsive qualities and which has a sombre tone calls for a *thinner* bridge, a bright-sounding violin for a *thicker* one. Its *position* depends on the position of the F-holes, and the proportionate measurements according to which the instrument is built, as well as on the position of the sound-post. Only an expert is qualified to determine what is right in this instance. When the bridge is not correctly placed, the intonation may be rendered incorrect; if it be too far from the sound-post the tone will sound hollow. When the bridge is too near the sound-post the E-string sounds shrill. The relation of the bridge to the top of the violin should be a more or less rectangular one, in accordance with

Sound-post

the way in which the feet of the bridge are fitted to the body of the violin. Views differ with regard to this, as to whether a straight bridge is to be preferred to one cut in a backward direction. In any case the tonal character of the instrument is most unfavorably affected when the bridge inclines towards the fingerboard.

#4915
Pernambuco
Bow
Prager
Model
ea 29.00
length stick 28½" (28¼")
height head & nut from stick 3/4" (3/4")
uniform thickness "1/16" (10/16") length on nut end
D @ Nut end 3/8" (5/16")
@ tip 3/16" (3/16")
hair length 25-3/4" (25½")
Center of gravity from nut 7¼" (7 3/8")
wt = 2 oz with hair
(2 oz)

at it is
oo far
niddle
ight is
widely
e pro-
old the
ts, and
of the
violin
ess the
ar. If
violin
levelop,
are thus
ned see
heir own
hiefly to
om this,
t humid-
(steam
impon-
trument.
the sur-
, so one
to one's
on with a
te in per-
e best of
struments
a *transi-*
ortions as
such care
alities.

Repairings

The Bow

Whereas, in the case of a violin, the inherent qualities of its tone, independent of the player, can be said to exist, the qualities of a *bow* cannot be objectively defined. Their consideration depends on the type and school of bow technique used, and hence are the player's personal affair. At all events, the stick must be neither too stiff nor too flexible, since tone production is unfavorably influenced by both extremes. Whether the bow should be stretched with a *strong* or *weak* tension is a matter of personal preference (See p. 51). The *weight* of the bow varies between 52 and 62 Gramm (1). I regard 58 Gramm (2) as the most advantageous weight. A bow which is too light (weighing under 54 Gramm (3) should be unconditionally discarded, because of the needless amount of exertion called forth by pressure at the point. The substitution of a long-drawn *India-rubber cover* for the silver-wire lapping is something which, personally, I do not like, especially when it is extended to the edge of the nut, and prevents actual contact of wood and fingers. The custom, generally observed up to about thirty years ago, of filing off the rectangular *edge of the nut* is something I regard as absolutely injurious. It is just this sharp edge which provides a sure hold for the thumb while the latter, when resting on an abruptly declining edge, is in danger of sliding off as soon as the player perspires ever so little. The old bow-makers, beginning with *the older Tourte*, made many bows one to two centimeters (4) shorter than normal. Contemporary bow-makers have given up this habit and have not been justified in so doing, in my opinion, for when the right arm is too short, and this frequently is the case with women, a shorter bow seems an absolute necessity, since otherwise, when the player wishes to move the bow parallel with the bridge even when playing at the point, the arm must be stretched too far, or (as is usually the case) the arm moves in a backward direction with the bow gliding along the fingerboard and in this way causing a sudden break of tone during *forte*, or a lack of all consistency during *piano* passages.* (See p. 57)

(1) Approximately 1⅞ and 2 1/16 ounces.
(2) Approximately 2 ounces.
(3) Less than 2 ounces.
(4) Approximately ⅜ to ¾ of an inch. A centimeter is 0.3937 of an inch.

An immoderate use of *rosin* is to be avoided, since the tone (even when the bowing is good in itself) grows scratchy. A threefold application, over the hair and back again, is entirely sufficient.

The bow-hair, when used on the average for three or four hours daily, should be renewed every month. Playing with worn-out bow hair is exceptionally injurious, since it leads to exaggerated pressure.

(4 hrs)(30 days) = 120 hrs = c. 4 mos @ 1 hr

2. Position of the Body.

Position of Legs

(a) Position of the Legs. Let us endeavor, first of all, to determine the most advantageous *position of the legs.* Although this question, superficially considered, seems to be one of slight account, it is in reality very important. Even the simplest movements of the arms can be carried out properly only when the position of the legs is correspondingly correct. When we *saw* wood, the left foot must be advanced; we *chop* wood with spread legs; a coffee-mill is *ground* with the least expenditure of energy when the operator is seated. Hence it should be taken for granted that in so complex a procedure as that represented by violin-playing only *one* position of the legs is valid as being the most practical: as a matter of fact, however, *three* different positions are used.

1. *The Joined Together, Rectangular Leg-Position* (Ill. No. 5). This, the "position of the industrious pupil," which is still recommended in many older violin methods, must, above all, be rejected from the anatomical standpoint, because it deprives the body of the possibility of a free balance. It is a position which causes the player, when technically difficult passages occur, to feel that his freedom of movement is greatly impeded, and usually he instinctively moves over into Position 2.

2. *The Acutangular Leg-Position* (Ill. No. 6). This position, unquestionably preferable to the one just discussed, nevertheless has the disadvantage that at the moment the right or left foot is advanced some 4 inches the upper part of the body automatically swings some 75 degrees to the left or right, producing an accidental posture out of relationship to the music-stand or the listener confronting the player. Furthermore, three-quarters of the entire weight of the body now rests on the leg farthest back, which easily may cause curvature of the leg or a protrusion of the hip, that is to say, a lasting disfigurement. When the player shifts the dead weight to the *right* leg, (advancing the left one) the body, in addition, assumes that unaesthetic, frontally inclined position which immediately arouses a certain mistrust in the listener with regard to the expected performance; and rightly so, for in violin-playing just as in life generally it is necessary to stand firmly upright on *both* feet in order to accomplish something worth while.

3. *The Spread or Straddling Leg-Position* (Ill. No. 7). This position has been accepted by nearly all the concert artists during the last decade, as though by a mute agreement among themselves, because it offers the body a broad foundation and the necessary stability and unhampered freedom in movement. Aesthetically, perhaps, it is not free from censure, especially when exaggerated, yet it comprises so many practical advantages in itself that the visually more graceful "dance" position is willingly abandoned for it.*

Position of Body

The movements of the *upper part of the body* while playing are in themselves so violent that it is impossible for the lower part of the body to be unaffected by them. The latter reacts to them with corresponding movement during the temporary shifting of the dead weight, by balancing and "swinging." There are teachers who demand a quiet position from their pupils even in moments of the greatest inward emotion. This, above all, contradicts the fundamental psychological law, in consequence of which every emotion seeks to express itself in movement. A yoke of the most insupportable kind is implied if, during a powerful effect, the player is supposed to maintain a stiff position. (The quasi-"professional" movements of the arms do not count in this connection.) On the other hand, the *swaying* of the body as a result of *habit*, accompanying each up or down stroke of the bow, is unquestionably *injurious*, since the amount of energy expended for this purpose is withdrawn from the artist's collective playing power, and remains unproductive. The only movement which makes a pleasant impression, even optically, is the

* Women players using this position may, for aesthetic reasons, rather stay sideways than directly opposite to the public.

one *unconsciously* generated by an irresistible inner compulsion; indeterminate swaying to and fro, on the other hand, is neither more nor less than a bad habit.

In general, I am strongly in favor of the pupil's learning to play even during the earlier stages of his studies *seated* as well as standing, and for the following reasons: first and mainly, there is the danger that young people may be stunted in their growth when compelled to stand too long, and may be afflicted with permanent curvature of the legs.

Again, the majority of players *sit* when they are working professionally—in the orchestra, when playing chamber music and when teaching—and some time must elapse before one accustoms one's self to playing while seated, something which calls for a balance of its own.

Whether it is tonally advantageous to stand before an audience *facing* it or in profile is a question difficult to decide. It is generally believed that the vibrations are flung back most perfectly by the walls of a hall when the instrument is held parallel to the rows of seats which the hall contains.

rec- n of olin

(b) Direction in which the Violin is held. The *direction* in which the instrument should be held may be seen in the example given (Ill. 8); only thus is it possible to draw the bow on a line parallel with the bridge. When the instrument is held too far to the left, the proportionate position of the bow with regard to the bridge, at the point, is somewhat as follows:

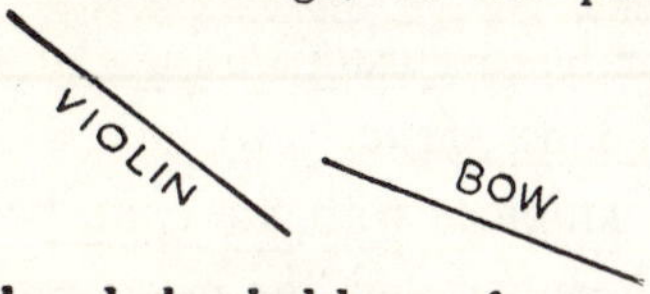

If the bow, on the other hand, be held too far to the right, the following line-picture results:

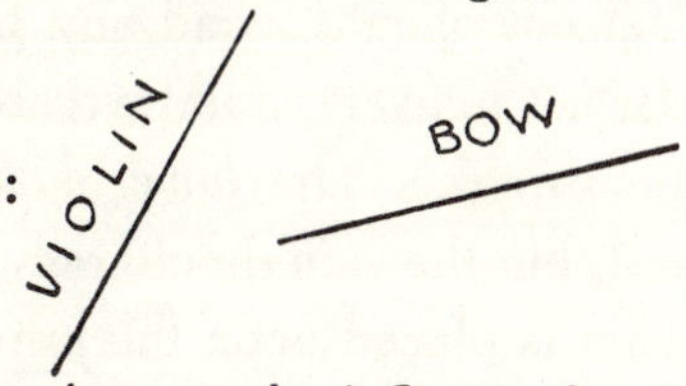

It is easy to see how the bowing may be influenced to its disadvantage when the violin is held in the wrong direction.

si- n of olin

(c) Position of the Violin. As regards the position of the violin, it is placed on the collar-bone, held by the left lower jaw and is only *supported* by the left hand which, above all, must retain the greatest possible freedom in change of position. It should be considered, however, that the sides of the violin are only from two to three centimeters (1) high, while the distance between the lower jaw and the collar-bone, usually called the "length of a neck," is from four to eight centimeters (2). Hence we must

(1) Approximately 4/5 to 1 1/5 inches.

(2) Approximately 1⅝ to 3¼ inches.

either raise the shoulder or fill the empty space by means of a small *cushion* or pad. It is a very decided advantage not to be obliged to use a cushion, since in that case, first of all, the back of the violin is in far more intimate contact with the player's body, which promotes the spread of the vibrations. Drawing up the shoulder, however, is to be avoided in any case: muscular contractions which result in consequence cannot help but affect the entire left-arm technique disadvantageously. Long-necked players, therefore, must resign themselves to using the cushion as a necessary evil with which they cannot dispense. The *raised chin-rest* (the so-called "Prague" chin-rest) is something to which, hitherto, I have found it impossible to accustom myself. Nor have the spring cushions so frequently used by ladies justified their use, for some one or another reason. The size of the cushion should conform to the space which must necessarily be filled in, and hence is altogether an individual matter. Not until the player is able to hold the violin without the aid of the left hand, with relative lack of effort, for the space of half a minute, may the cushion be regarded as having proved itself to be of the correct form and size. When the cushion is too *thick* it results in a position as shown in Ill. 9, one vacillating between vertical and horizontal, and admittedly permitting a less tiring use of the lower strings (hence much favored by second violins in orchestra or quartet), but bringing the arm too close to the body when the E-string is used, and also making it easy for the finger to slip on the E-string. Every violinist, therefore, must continue to experiment and modify his cushions until he has found one the size of which makes it possible for him to hold the violin most firmly in the correct position (Ill. 10 (3)). *Cushion*

Level of Violin

With regard to the height at which the violin should be held, we know that when the latter is too low the bow has a tendency to slide to the fingerboard, and that pressure exerted in this place greatly impairs the tone quality. When the violin is held too low a flat, non-resonant quality of tone results. Yet the exact opposite—holding the violin too high—though not so injurious, should be avoided because, even

(3) Many violinists, among them *Kreisler*, develop an artificial cushion for themselves by allowing their coat to remain unbuttoned and turning back the left side, which makes their support twice as strong. Others again, can only play with their coats buttoned, because of the fear that the bow may catch in one of the buttons arouses in them a kind of nervous restlessness.

then the bow, when it is to approach the fingerboard, will have a natural tendency to remain near the bridge, which easily causes the tone, especially the *détaché*, to become scratchy. The whole secret of an impeccable tone consists in bringing bow and strings into contact in the narrowly limited space conditioned by the necessity of shading, duration of stroke and tonal pitch, as is explained in detail on p. 81. Hence the bow must possess the necessary freedom of movement needed in order to be able to travel a middle course between bridge and fingerboard on a *level* and not on an ascending or descending plane.

Chin-rest

The *chin-rest*, too, is a necessary evil. Without it the lower left side of the top at the point where it comes in contact with the lower jaw would be destroyed by friction and perspiratory emanations in a relatively short time, and in addition, prevented from taking part in vibration during tone production. Hence every instrument sounds considerably more powerful *with* a chin-rest. One of its disadvantages is that it prevents the immediate contact between head and violin. Personally, therefore, I have always regretted, because of the reasons given, that I had to play with a chin-rest.*

Its most practical form is represented by a rather broad model, arching slightly over the tailpiece, which prevents direct pressure on the tailpiece, and in addition allows the player to move the violin a little to the left if necessary.

Position of Head

(d) Position of the Head. This is either:

(1) *erect*, or (2) *inclined*, or (3) *recumbent*. Which is the most advantageous? The importance of the question lies in the fact that with each we receive a different acoustic impression of the tone. In the first case the tone is not directly received by the ear, but is partly reflected by the walls, in the way a listener receives it, i.e., *objectively*. The more closely our ear approaches the violin, the more powerful and *subjective* is the tonal effect produced: the vibrations are directly communicated to the auditory nerves. The further our ear is removed from the violin, the more *critical* we become with regard to tone-production, the more distinctly we hear its imperfections, its accompanying noises. When our ear approaches the tonal body we have a tendency to listen to ourselves, to *luxuriate* in mere tonal beauty, without criticism. Hence the tendency of most violinists is to approach their ear to the instrument in *cantilenas* and, contrariwise, in the case of difficult passages, demanding control, to maintain a certain distance. These movements, in nearly all cases, are instinctive, unpremeditated expressions of the most intimate feeling, frequently of genuine fervor. Hence one must guard against trying to subject them to regulation. One should confine one's self to seeing that they are not mis-used. When, for instance, a violinist *habitually* lays his head on the violin while *studying* difficult passages, and thus is prevented from criticizing *objectively* what he produces, he is guilty of a species of self-deception, which must necessarily result in an unreliable technique. The same thing happens when the player forcibly prevents every expression of impulse on the part of his *subconscious* inner self by a stiff retention of the erect head position, and the resulting uninterrupted technical control connected with it. Hence I advocate the retention of the erect position of the head during *study*, and a suspension of control when making *music*.

It is advisable to touch the *tailpiece* with the *chin*, because in this way a heightened contact with the instrument is obtained. Yet one should avoid any *pressure* on the tailpiece, in order not to exert an unfavorable influence on the pitch of the strings. The *lower jaw* should *press* upon the chin-rest, but the *chin* should only *touch* the tailpiece. If the chin is placed upon the instrument *too far* from the tailpiece, the contact between player and instrument is too indirect, on the one hand; while on the other hand the ear, also, is too widely removed from the body of the violin, and therefore receives impressions which are too *objective*.

Skin diseases

The *inflamed, sore places* and *abcesses* which occasionally develop at the points of contact between violin and neck may be counted among the violinist's professional maladies. Above all, any excessive pressure on a wounded surface should be avoided, by shifting the point of contact somewhat to the right or left, upward or downward; and by trying to ***shift the skin of the neck***, hence creating

* In the eighteenth century the chin-rest was unknown and the violinist laid his chin against the *right* side of the violin. When we try this to-day, for mere curiosity's sake, we find that we play more lightly on the high strings and more heavily on the low ones; furthermore, that the power of the tone is doubled for our own ear and becomes unendurable in the long run. How were our predecessors able to support such a condition? In all probability by producing a minimum of tone. This explains the fact that the small, sweet-toned Amati models were preferred to the larger-form Stradivarius and Guarnerius types up to the beginning of the nineteenth century.

a new, unused point of contact in an artificial double chin. In case of necessity a thin cloth may be interposed, but a silk cloth, which is too heating, should not be used. In addition, the inflamed place should be rubbed, especially at night, with a very mild salve. The greatest care should be observed while shaving. In case of a turn for the worse a physician should be called in as a matter of course.

3. The Left Arm.

osition ' Left rm, ingers d humb

(a) Manner in which the Left Arm is Held. A reasonable development of the technical capacities of both arms must be founded on the mechanical peculiarities with which they have been endowed by nature. Unfortunately, we are compelled to do violence to nature in respect to one of the most important functional prerequisites in the case of the left hand. I refer to the *unnatural* position due to the outward rolling of the left lower arm in the elbow-joint, which departs from the normal position of the hand (at the seam of the trousers) by approximately 90-100 degrees. Moreover in shifting into high positions the upper arm has to take a marked inward turn. How much better off the cellists are in this respect, or even the pianists, whose arms are active in an unforced position. So long, however, as a violin with a fingerboard ending in the direction toward the right arm does not come into use, we shall be obliged to put up with this evil.

he humb

*The Positions of the Arm, Fingers and Thumb** are closely interconnected and interdependent. One cannot be changed without the others participating in the change. Let us begin with the *thumb*. What is its position in the customary activities of daily life? When I hold any object lightly between thumb and forefinger, the thumb is neither completely bent nor entirely stretched, but *slightly bent*. It has the same shape in a state of rest; this may be defined as a "natural" position in the best sense of the word, the only one corresponding to its violinistic functions (light and uncramped support of the neck by the thumb on one side and the end of third joint of the index finger on the other). The point, however, at which the thumb comes in contact with the neck, depends less upon itself than upon the remaining fingers, or, to be more exact, upon their length; and here the proportions vary in every case. *M. P. Marsick* recommended in oral instruction the following procedure to verify the natural thumb and finger position in individual cases:

The violin is held only by means of the lower jaw and collar-bone, the left arm is lowered, the four fingers lightly curved, the thumb rests against the third joint of the index finger, counting from the end of the finger (See Ill. 11). Thereupon the left arm slowly draws near the violin neck, which thrusts itself between index finger and thumb. *The index finger touches the right side of the violin neck at the lower end of its third joint, so that it still may move freely in the carpal joint.* The fingers are laid upon the A-string, and the position which the thumb now assumes, its slight curvature, its relation to the other fingers, the point at which it touches the neck, all now are adapted to the individual conformation of the hand. (See Ill. 12.)

Besides the lateral position just described, there is still another *lower thumb-position* recommended by various teachers (Ill. 13). In it the thumb *carries* the neck, the latter rests upon it, but the index finger does not rest against the neck, the elbow is turned inward still more, the fingers are *compelled* to drop *squarely* upon the strings. In fact the thumb in this lower posture *permanently* assumes a place which it takes only *temporarily* (when preparing to move to higher positions) in the lateral position. Rapid ascending into the higher positions is facilitated thereby, it is true, but on the other hand, it is impossible for the hand to feel comfortable in one and the same position while playing, if only because the turning inside of the arm as a whole is greatly exaggerated. In addition, in this position counter pressure and support are eliminated on the part of the third joint of the index finger, which, compelled by the exaggerated inward turning of the elbow, can no longer touch the neck. The thumb hereby is given a burden which it is unable to assume without injuring its technical sureness. On the other hand, the lower thumb position becomes an indisputable necessity under the following conditions:

(1) In the case of three- and four-note chords demanding wide interval stretches:

13a. 

(2) As a preparatory movement when *ascending* into the higher positions.

(3) As a momentary point of support when *descending* from the third or fourth to the first or second position.

To summarize: the *thumb* has three duties to perform: it provides a light support for the violin, held between collar-bone and lower jaw; supplies a counter-pressure for the pressure of the four other fingers; and acts as an intermediary in the transfer from the middle register (third and fourth) to the lower (first and second), and upper (from the fifth on), by carrying out the movement shown in Ill. 13a.

Position of Fingers

It is impossible to set up a uniform rule regarding the manner in which the *fingers should be placed on the strings.* The player who has a long fourth finger will have to *curve* it when placing it on the string; while a finger that is too short necessarily must be *stretched.* In any event I reject the curvature shown in Ill. 14, in view of the following reasons: The lower arm is unnecessarily rolled still further inward, exaggerated curving is synonymous with unnecessary waste of strength, the danger of slipping is far greater, and the finger-nails touch the strings, which makes the tone more brittle. But above all the three articulations connecting the three joints of each finger are no longer able to move freely. These disadvantages are counterbalanced by no advantages. On the other hand, the exaggerated *flat* application of the fingers, though I am opposed to it, still has the advantage that, as a consequence of the contact with the little fat-cushions of the lower part of the finger-tip, the tone grows noticeably softer. This mode of playing is one I can recommend only in two cases: when the fingers are very short or when (mainly in the case of very slender girls) they are so sharp and bony that a flat finger-touch is needed in order to create an artificial cushion of fat.*

The fact that the *index finger* must rest against the neck, not with the *upper* part of its third joint, but with its *root,* is of the very greatest importance. In the former case the first half-tones on the four strings (A flat, E flat, B flat and F) will always be *too* high, since the bending back of the index finger, with the elimination of the lowest joint, represents a most awkward, unnatural movement, which the player instinctively avoids making. The consequent technical hindrance it develops—the stiffness of the lowest joint of the index finger—is sufficient in itself to jeopardize a healthy development of left hand technique. In addition, this fettering of the third joint of the index finger destroys the freedom of the wrist during *vibrato.* Furthermore, the index finger should only touch the neck *sideways,* yet by no means with the inner surface of the third joint, since this, as a consequence, would entail an outward rolling of the lower arm, making the arm-position still more strained than it already is owing to the shape peculiar to the violin.

Raising of Fingers

Every finger should drop elastically on the string with its own naturally inherent motive power. I regard exaggerated *raising* of the fingers as well as "flinging" them on the strings as needless, a waste of strength, and consequently injurious. The *knocking* which results from this practice is a decidedly disturbing accompaniment, and, together with the involuntary *pizzicati* resulting from the sidewise raising of the fingers, belongs to the group of disturbing noises.**

Finger-Pressur

Then, too, *excessive finger pressure* is injurious, giving the tone a somewhat brittle quality, and carrying with it the danger of overirritating the nerves at the point of pressure. *Sarasate,* the father of modern "conscientious" violin technique, dropped his fingers so lightly on the strings that no indentation of his finger-tips was noticeable.

The *finger-nails* should be kept trimmed so short that they do not touch the strings. The violinist must take the greatest care of his *finger-tips.* Callouses, in consequence of the lack of a soft fat-cushion, impair the tone quality in the highest degree, and too deep indentations are often followed by nervous irritation.

---

* *Thibaud* and *Enesco* for a time played in this manner, and with excellent tonal results.

** Both varieties are most annoying in phonograph recording. Since at present (and presumably in the future) recording represents a by no means inconsiderable part of the artistic activity of the concertizing violinist, teachers are expressly cautioned to guard against these faults.

Use 2 bandaides, 3/4" wide. Wrap one around finger near the end; the other, over the tip of the finger

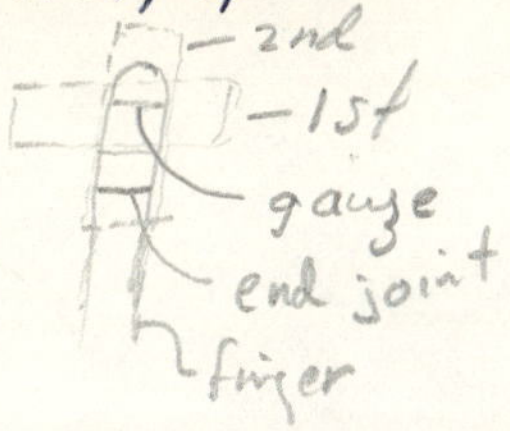
2nd
1st
gauze
end joint
finger

The most efficient hygiene in this regard consists of subjecting the fingertips to a thorough, massage-like cleansing *after* (not before) playing, using a stiff brush, warm water and soap. Removing the callous skin with scissors may cause permanent injury for then the finger-tip is robbed of its natural protection. If the ramifications of the main nerves at the finger-tips have grown supersensitive the irritation may be diminished by covering temporarily the tip with a finger-guard of soft kid; the latter being held in place by two soft bands tied about the wrist.* Only too frequently it happens that supersensitiveness of the finger-tip leads to nervous pains in the whole finger. In such cases it is well to try alternate bathing of the left hand (i.e., alternately dipping it in hot, then in cold water for a minute at a time). Excessive perspiration of the left hand is one of the least welcome gifts of Mother Nature, occasionally so cruel. Treatment by some experienced specialist in skin diseases, as well as the use of a metal-string, is all that can be recommended in such cases.

Among the professional violinist's diseases must be counted the cramped *contraction of the ball of the thumb*, only curable when its cause—cramped pressure of the thumb on the violin neck—is removed. This is best done by means of light finger exercises in the first position, without using the thumb, which meanwhile hovers freely in the air. (In case the player finds it difficult to hold the violin during this exercise, the scrolled-end of the instrument may be rested against a wall.) The great majority of hand troubles is due to the fact that the player regards his incipient *weariness* as a difficulty which must be overcome, instead of one of nature's warnings not to continue working. When he is tired he should rest, and allow his arm to drop for half a minute. Frequent, and even permanent *muscular pains* in the arm may be fought by health-treatment or by massage. Sometimes the tonsils may be held responsible for it. One should not hesitate to apply to a specialist for advice.

"Relaxation"

In the course of the past few years we find that many a pedagogic work of greater or lesser merit insists upon a *relaxed* motive apparatus. But this well-sounding, rather nebulous generalization is usually of absolutely no practical use to the pupil. Such directions only gain a definite value when more concretely expressed, and accompanied by generally comprehensive examples for application. Hence, for instance, the advice given by *Barmas*, in *Die Lösung des geigentechnischen Problems* ("The Solution of the Problem of Violin Technique"), to drop the left arm frequently, to secure general relaxation, while continuing to hold the violin by means of shoulder support, is decidedly useful. Still more effective, because more exactly outlined, is the treatment for *local* cramped conditions; for instance, cramps of the ball of the thumb (left), or stiffening of the wrist (left), regarding which more will be said at the proper place. At all events, we are justified in demanding that, when such an adjective as "relaxed" is used, those parts of the arm to which it applies should be mentioned at the same time, as well as the occasions when that partial suspension of muscular tension has to take place. For even the most fanatical adherents of this nomenclature must admit that no movement is possible without the tension of certain muscles, and that the use of the catchword in question becomes a mere matter of empty phraseology unless we are simultaneously informed *where*, *when* and *in which way* the procedure of relaxation is to develop.

Intonation

(b) Intonation. The main purpose we have in view, as regards the collective activities of the left arm, is that of producing a certain number of tones, in a prescribed sequence, as well as at a prescribed rate of speed, with the number of vibrations peculiar to them in accordance with the laws of acoustics, that is to say, *purely*, or *in tune*. To this main end all mechanical procedures developed by the living organism of our left arm are subordinated.

Yet, for this reason, before we pass to the consideration of actual left-hand technique, we must, above all,

* As soon as he has accustomed himself to it the player will hardly notice the finger-guard. *César Thomson* played in public for years wearing a finger-guard of this kind on his index finger.

arrive at a clear understanding of the problem of *purity of intonation.*

The violin has only four strings, but on them we are able, nevertheless, to produce approximately 53 different notes in the semi-tone system. If we count tones which differ from each other in color as well as in pitch, we can obtain twice as many. To these must be added the harmonics, as well as the combinations of two or more notes, simultaneously sounded, which, in violin technique, we call double-stops or chords. We produce a note differing from the open string in consequence of a greater or lesser shortening of the string, by laying the finger on the string and, as it were, segregating one portion of it, and preventing it from vibrating. The finger, with regard to the open string, fullfils the same function as does the so-called nut (i.e., the little raised support on which the strings rest, at the uppermost part of the violin-neck). According to acoustic law, each tone has an exactly defined number of vibrations. When these are produced in the quantity prescribed, we feel and describe the resultant tone as being *true*, or "in tune," and in the contrary case, as being *false*, or "out of tune." Helmholtz's investigations seemed to prove that it is the so-called Cortian organ in the ear which carries out these astounding mathematical calculations during fractions of a second, although this has been denied by modern authorities. For the purpose we have in view it is immaterial whether we know exactly *where* the "calculation" of the sum total of a tone's vibrations is made, if only we know the fact itself. Hence, *playing in tune* would mean that we "take" the note in that place where the shortening of the string secures a certain number of vibrations mathematically determined in advance. Is this possible? In order to find the correct answer to this basic question let us consider two notes:

A String

5. 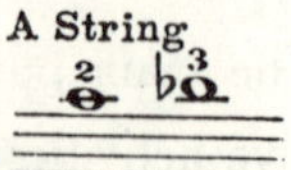

Impossibility of Perfect Intonation

The two notes differ one from the other by approximately 60 vibrations. The *spatial* distance from A^2 to $B\flat^2$, however, is no more than approximately nine millimeters (1): hence, the 60 vibrations are divided between nine millimeters, that is to say, there is one vibration to each 1/6 of a millimeter (2).

Therefore, granting that I have played the A in tune, in order to play the B♭ mathematically correct, I would have to place my third finger at so true a point as not to vary 1/6 of a millimeter, which would seem only possible with some implement which had a surface breadth of 1/6 of a millimeter, and not the finger, which is with some players 10 millimeters (3) broad at its tip. Even were I to assume, however, that some fortunate chance would make it possible for me to touch the exact spot at 1/6 of a millimeter it would be impossible to do so in a sequence of tones such as represented by the scale. Hence, much as we regret to do so, we must rob the term *purity of intonation* or *playing in tune* of its *gloriole. In the physical sense, "playing in tune" is an impossibility.*

Yet there are a number of violinists who create the impression of playing in tune. How are we to explain this apparent contradiction? By the simple fact that these violinists, though they do not strike the note exactly, do *correct* it during the fraction of a second, either by shift of position or by means of a *vibrato* which approximates the *true* note. All this, when the player is correspondingly skilful, takes place so rapidly that the listener feels as though the note had been *true* from the very beginning, whereas it has only *become* so after a tiny lapse of time. *Hence what we call "playing in tune" is no more than an extremely rapid, skilfully carried out improvement of the originally inexactly located pitch. When playing "out of tune," on the other hand, the tone, as long as it sounds, remains as false as it was at the moment of its production.*

The opinion is generally entertained that the cause of *impure* intonation, of playing "out of tune," must be sought in some manual lack of skill and should be, so to speak, conceived as an error of movement. In reality, however, the primary cause of this evil is an *aural*, not a *manual* deficiency. In order to realize this fact more clearly, we must try briefly to visualize the processes which take place in our inner consciousness while we are improving these false notes.

---

(1) Approximately 1/4 of an inch.

(2) A millimeter is 0.0394 of an inch.

(3) Approximately 3/8 of an inch.

spon- ility the r

Once we have set the string in motion, its vibrations reach our ear-drum, thence pass to the "counting apparatus" which calculates their oscillations, and finally come to the auditory sphere situated on the border of the cerebrum. The consciousness judges whether the tone is *true* or *false*. In the last-named case the pupil gifted with a keen sense of hearing experiences a most disagreeable sensation, which enforces a corrective movement of the finger. The more powerful the feeling of discomfort, the greater the need to secure the true pitch as quickly as possible. This change results in a different number of vibrations It is evident, therefore, that this correction is merely a *consequence* of an uncomfortable impression. Indifference brings about immobility, and boredom even stiffens the features. Only intensive feelings of pleasure or dissatisfaction release corresponding movements. *Hence, everything depends on making our sense of hearing so acute that an impure note makes the most disagreeable impression on us, and in this way automatically brings with it a corrective movement.*

Ear-training

It is due to these considerations that the practical *ear-training exercises*, which I have been using with unquestionable results with my pupils for years, have been developed. They consist (a *Rode* Caprice in an uncomplicated key is best used), in the pupil's sustaining each note and examining its purity (without *vibrato*, and if possible with the aid of the corresponding open string), until he is absolutely convinced that he has reached the correct pitch. After practising several hours a phenomenon which at first glance seems strange results, one which is apt to terrify the pupil unprepared for it: it seems to him that he is playing even more out of tune than when he began. Yet what has really happened? Owing to the contrast of the true and false notes the ear soon grows so sensitive that the outburst of despair on the pupil's part which has just been described seems quite natural.

After this attack of discouragement has been effectually combated by the teacher with an explanation of its actual cause, regular and intensively continued practice will soon (usually in a week's time) show a decided improvement; and furthermore the pupil, by this time, can judge the purity of his intonation so capably as to make the needed correction within a second's time, although the said correction is still distinctly audible. Yet I do not regard this first and most important period of intonation exercises as completed until the pupil instinctively corrects himself in a *Cantilena*, played with natural feeling, and not as study material. When he has reached this point, then he must be made to realize that the alteration of every false or impure note should be regarded as the foremost principle of his art, and that the improvement of his hearing attained by such arduous toil will be lost as soon as carelessness in the observance of intonation once more accustoms his auditory apparatus to inexact registration of the number of vibrations of the tones he plays. He must be imbued with the conviction that *slow practice* of technical difficulties, aside from many other advantages, above all, has *the* advantage that every individual note may be examined and improved. He must be made to realize that there is absolutely nothing *disgraceful* about placing the fingers inexactly on the strings, if only the note is so rapidly corrected that the listener is unconscious of the original, incorrect pitch. When the player, however, hears that his pitch is false, without endeavoring to improve it, then this sin of omission, as a rule, is the consequence of a fatal indifference, which will always prevent him from making progress. The violinist should never forget that a good sense of hearing is a valuable possession, and the most important prerequisite for higher artistry.*

---

* While a note is being corrected, the stroke of the bow should change as little as possible;

Bruch, G min. Cto, 1º Mov't.

for instance 6.

in order to test its purity of intonation, each note should be sustained on a *single* stroke of the bow, until the ear is satisfied. Played in the usual grotesquely unsettled manner, the tonal effect is approximately as follows:

7.

Incorrect

(See p. 159 for further information regarding practising intonation in chords)

Tonic (Grk tonikos, fr. tonos tension, tone) characterized by tonos 3: relating to or based on the first tone of a scale. n. 2: the first tone of a diatonic scale: keynote
enharmonic. scale employing 1/4 notes, notes written differently (Ab, G#) but [theoretically] sounding the same

As is known, the pitch of a note, in spite of an identical appellation, differs according to its harmonic affiliations. We know, for instance, that a note on the seventh step (leading note) must be played higher than when it merely appears as a third. Hence we would play the F sharp in  with the customary number of vibrations, while the same note in  would be played a few vibrations higher, since it is moving toward the tonic. The last mentioned F sharp-G is simply a half-tone, diminished by a certain number of vibrations.

Half-tones and Quarter-tones

In general, two great families of violinists who "play in tune" may be distinguished. There are the few who approximate *quarter*-tones in their playing; and the many whose auditory senses already are satisfied when they play in the *tempered* intonation of the piano, i.e., make no distinction between  and  though a difference by no means negligible exists between these two notes. In  the G flat is twelve vibrations lower than the F sharp in , hence in both cases the half-tones should be taken very closely. We might remark, in addition, that the F^2 and G^2 retain their physical pitch-level; while the G flat^2 and the F sharp^2 must be correspondingly lowered and raised.

enharmonic

Or, take I  and II 

In the case of I, the pitch-level of the C sharp is normal, and is determined in accordance with the perfect major third to be formed with the A without any reference to the D which follows. In the case of II, however, the C sharp is nothing more than the raised leading note, resolved on the D.*

Problems of Intonation

Every violinist is acquainted with the intonation problem in the following passage of *Brahms'* Violin Concerto:

8. 

It can be solved only by exaggerating the low pitch of the B flat and taking the leading note, G sharp, high.

The following case is a peculiar one:

9. 

If we play this example on the E-string, we find that E^2 represents the leading tone to be raised, and F^2 the fundamental tone. Since, however, we cannot raise the E, the only satisfactory solution (so far as the ear is concerned) is to play the F *too low*. If we keep this F, and continue playing,

10. 

we find that it is unmistakably too low in the minor sixth, and must be played higher. This unsatisfactory substitution of a lowered first degree for the raised seventh is the reason why the violinist instinctively plays Example 9 in the third position, where he actually can raise the seventh degree, while the first degree remains normal.

Hence it is evident that, while it is theoretically possible to determine the number of vibrations of each individual note, in actual practice we are obliged to rely solely upon our ear, and decide each case according to its own merits—an additional reason for guarding and cultivating this precious instrument of our art.

Combination-Tones

As to the so-called *combination-tones*,* discovered by *Tartini*, and already mentioned in his letters of instruction to *Sign. Lombardini*, I find it impossible to regard them as very important from a practical point of view. It is true, however, that a knowledge of their existence supplies an effective means of control for purity of double-stop intonation.** One should be in a position, however, to be able to judge as to the latter even without a more detailed examination of the combination tones. They offer no direct, but rather an indirect means of securing purity in interval-playing, and may be said to represent the substitution of a mechanical procedure for purely personal responsibility.

---

* The third, or lower tone produced by the simultaneous sounding of two tones differing in pitch.

** Souzay's "Etudes harmoniques" may be recommended as admirable practice material in this connection.

rrec- n of rong tes

We already have alluded to the fact that a certain space of time is required for pitch correction, its length depending on the auditory sensitiveness of the player and the corrective technique of the hand. At all events, the note to be corrected must be sustained approximately half a second, in order to be susceptible of improvement. The shorter the note in question, however, the more prominently the manual *moment of skill* comes to the fore. We no longer have enough time to carry out the complicated procedure just described, and we must endeavor to develop the skill needed to play a note when we take it for the first time, with *approximate* accuracy. It is true that our demands with regard to absolute purity of intonation diminish in degree as the tempo in which we play a succession of notes becomes more rapid. A good example is afforded by the contrast between slow and rapid scales or broken triads. While in the first instance our ear is most keenly sensitive to the inexactness of each individual note, and it is therefore supremely difficult to play a succession of notes in slow tempo in absolute pitch, it is comparatively easy to present a rapid scale to the entire satisfaction even of critical listeners, provided the first and the last note are perfectly in tune.

sic ve- nt of ft nd

In concluding this section, the teacher, first of all, should be seriously admonished that in elementary instruction the impossibility of playing in *absolute pitch*, as well as the imperative necessity of *pitch correction* should be made plain to the beginner, thus preventing the formation of entirely erroneous conceptions at the very start. For a long time I was at a loss to understand, why so many pupils were reluctant to correct a wrong note, even if shocked by its deviation from the right pitch and convinced of the necessity of its adjustment. At last I succeeded in explaining this contradictory fact. At the beginning of their studies they had been brought up by their teachers in the belief, that playing in perfect tune was possible, and consequently every wrong note was considered by the teacher as an unpardonable sin. Unable to satisfy him, they saw their only way out in trying to cheat the teacher by passing as quickly as possible over the wrong note. They retained this bad habit during the different stages of their violinistic education, until it became nearly impossible to uproot it.

(c) Basic Movements of the Left Hand. By this we mean the appropriate use of the individual parts of which the left arm is composed; while the types of note combination which may be produced by them are comprised in the conception known as the *general technique of the left hand*. The number of left-arm movements essential to violin-playing is a restricted one, the technical types capable of production, however, are numerous; and their combinations beyond computation. I have discussed the original or basic movements in detail in my *Urstudien*. In that specific work the aim I had in view was to reduce the time required for technical study to a minimum by confining myself to the thorough development of their purely anatomical factors. The consequent saving of labor, the release of a certain amount of time which could be more advantageously used for purely artistic purposes —these two things mainly have been responsible for the still growing popularity of the unpretentious little work, published in 1910 and explain its favor, in particular, with violinists who have but little time at their disposal. (In my own practical work as a teacher I have used it principally as a *diagnostic aid* to determine, in an unobjectionable manner, existing wants in the *bowing*. It is seldom that the movements of the right hand show so complex an inadequacy or distortion, that the division of the bow-stroke into its component parts by means of the basic movements will not bring to light the mechanical causes of the evil.) The fundamental thought of the *Urstudien*, one which also pervades the present work, is the recognition of the fact: *that the cure of any error never lies in doing away with its consequences but, first of all, must be sought in the avoidance of causes which, in most cases, are purely mechanical.*

Basic Studies Urstudien

Left hand technique, collectively, may be traced back to five basic movements (to be practised without the bow):

1. The *falling movement* of the four fingers:

11.

2. The *lateral* movements, as they are used in the chromatic scales and in stretches.*

---

*It is needless, and in the case of small hands even dangerous, to carry out *exactly* the stretches here recommended. It will suffice if the fingers lying motionless are in a position allowing the finger which is gliding to move freely.

"Mute" Exercises Without Bow

12.
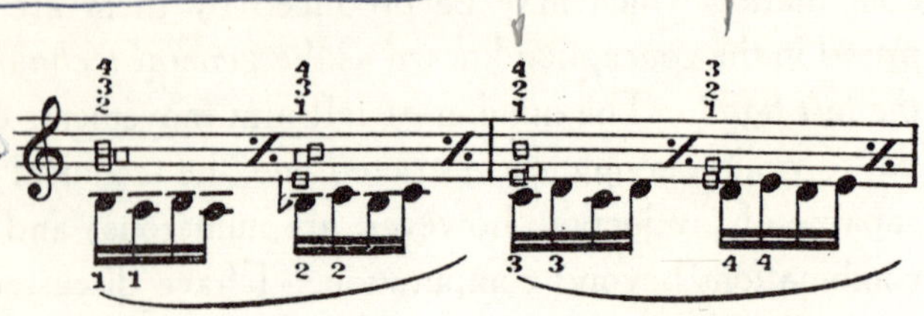

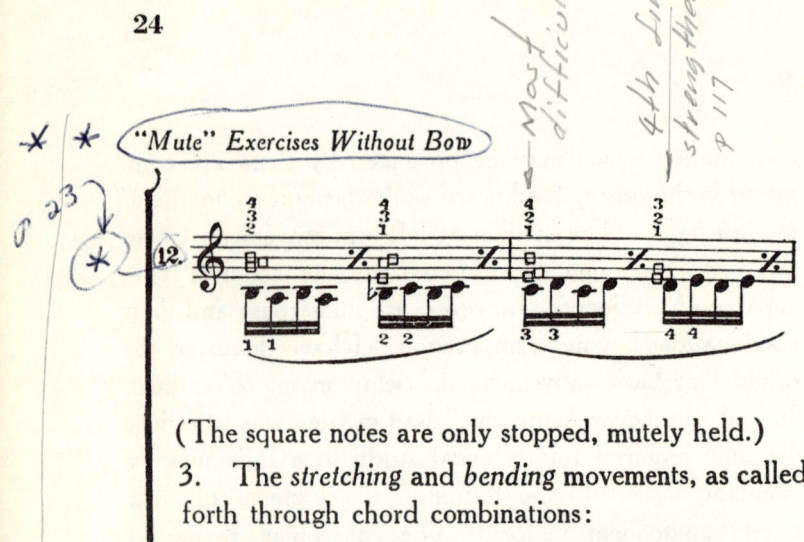

(The square notes are only stopped, mutely held.)

3. The *stretching* and *bending* movements, as called forth through chord combinations:

13.

4. The *thumb movement*, representing the moving back of the thumb from the third to the first position (See p. 27.)

5. The combined movements of the *hand and the elbow-joints*, which result when the player, his four fingers on the strings, moves from the first to the highest positions and back again (basic movement of the *change of position*).

The *utilization* of these basic movements, as well as that of the tonal *combinations* resulting from them, forms the collective technique of the left hand, and the subject of the considerations presented in this section. First of all, we must consider some of those movements more closely from a purely mechanical standpoint.

The *fingers* should fall on the strings only with the flexibility they have naturally acquired, and with an effort proportionate to their weight. (See p. 18). Exercise 11 may be made more difficult, and advantageously so, by chaining down those fingers which are unemployed.

14.

Stretching Exercises

Stretching exercises. Purity of intonation in one and the same position is largely dependent upon the first finger (resting on the strings) and the fourth being exactly a *perfect fourth* apart. On this account I am opposed to all exaggerated and systematic attempts at stretching, because the position of the fourth, natural to the hand, is in danger of becoming a *position of the fifth.* If, in apparent contradiction, I have recommended the preceding exercises (as, later on, I recommend the study of fingered octaves), it is with the premise that the exercises will be used only in small doses, and that stretches of more than a fifth will be avoided. Incidentally, the control of the technique of fingered octaves offers such important advantages with regard to musical expression and tone formation that the drawback of a temporarily extended finger-position is negligible in comparison. *Tenths,* too, should be practised with caution, in view of the excessive stretching which they demand.

To raise stretching exercises, however, to the dignity of the *one true principle of salvation* appears to me, to put it mildly, an absurdity. It is high time for us to abandon our unfruitful search for the philosophers' stone, and to realize that violin technique and, to an even greater extent, violin-playing as an art, represent the *sum total* of a large number of determinant factors. To pick out a single one among them is much the same as praising some particular variety of pills as a cure-all for any and every illness. Both procedures belong in the realm of *quackery.* Exaggerated stretching exercises, in addition, are dangerous because they may strain the sinews, and thus contain the germ of permanent professional disqualification. For the same reason I reject the *finger-gymnastic apparatuses* so frequently advertised in these days. They have the additional disadvantage that when using them the arm is never in the correct position called for in violin-playing.

Mute Exercises

The *mute exercises,* in reality, should be used only when exceptional circumstances make it desirable, *but never habitually* (as regular finger-technique exercises). They are in order when the warmth of the hand is to be developed (in the case of cold fingers, in unheated rooms) or when considerations of space and time do not permit of actual tone production (prohibition against playing in a hotel or in an artist's room too close to the concert-stage); that is to say, only in case of *need.* For we must not blind ourselves to the fact that these finger exercises are fundamentally deficient in two respects: there is no control with regard to purity of intonation, and tone production.* Hence they are only a substitute, and should only be used *occasionally*, when playing in the same position, when the intonation offers no special difficulties. (See p. 24.) My *Urstudien*, too, primarily aim at preserving those violinists, who have but little time at their disposal, from downfall; they do not pretend to crowd violin technique into a vest-pocket form. Nor is the employ of mute left hand basic exercises during elementary instruction advisable; for the latter's main task, before all, should consist in developing the beginner's hearing, together with his sense of duty, with the result that, following an irresistible inner compulsion, he should in a short time automatically correct and improve his intonation. (See p. 21.)

ange ring eft and)

d. Change of String (to the left). There are two reasons why a smooth change of string is so rarely noticeable. To begin with there is the trend toward those angular and expansive movements of the right arm which we discuss in detail on p. 61; and furthermore the necessity of the most exact co-ordination as regards time, of the left hand change of string, and the movements of the right arm. Let us consider the procedure involved in the latter case more closely:

Bruch, G min. Cto, 3º Mov't.

15. 

Between B^2 and G^2, the *right* arm must move from the E-string to the A-string, and the fourth finger of the *left* hand must take G^2. These two movements must occur *simultaneously*. When this is not the case, the notorious unequalized change of string results. Which is the guilty member in that case? Unquestionably it is the left hand, which is *unable* to carry out the movement it has to make as rapidly as the right arm, and hence arrives the fraction of a second too late, so that the empty string is audible for an infinitesimal length of time:

(the same)

16. 

In order to do away with this evil, therefore, we must accustom ourselves, while *practicing* (of course *not* while playing in public) to put down the finger which is to carry out the change of string a little *too soon* (the finger in question is indicated by a square note (□), in the following example).

(the same)

17. 

The resultant preparatory movement of the finger concerned, which falls into the class of *beneficial exaggerations*, is also retained in ordinary performance to a certain extent. It prevents the too tardy arrival of the finger; and by means of the simultaniety of the movements of both hands in point of time, procures a smooth change of string. The application of this very valuable fundamental rule presents the following picture when scales are played:

18. 

In broken triads and chords of the seventh in etudes.

Ševčik, School of Violin Technique, Book 3, Nº 7

19.  *etc.*

Kreutzer, Etude Nº 3

20. 

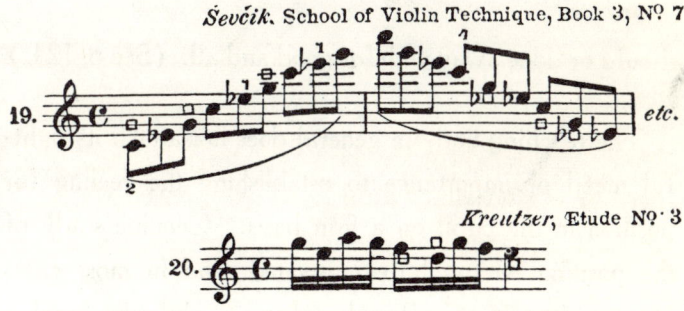

In addition, see p. 61, for the discussion of the same subject. (Change of string with the bow.)

Position

e. Positions and Change of Positions. Playing in the *higher positions* differs in mechanical respects from first position playing, inasmuch as the lower arm assumes a more vertical position, while from the 4-5 position on, the back of the hand gradually approaches a more and more

---

* The frequent playing on a "mute" violin, in such cases, has the disadvantage of making it almost impossible to judge the quality of the tone produced.

horizontal line, while the distance existing between the individual fingers diminishes in proportion; the thumb shoving itself, more or less, *under* the neck; the lower arm rolling outward, the upper arm turning inward in a marked manner; and, finally, the bow being obliged to approach the bridge the more closely as the shortening of the string brought about by the left hand increases*.

The chief difficulty which stands in the way of the beginner's control of the positions is the fact that the various notes in every new position must be taken, in part by various fingers, in part on different strings, a difficulty, however, which intelligent study will soon overcome.

Existing methods for *beginners* disagree as to whether the *second* or the *third* position should be taken up after the first. Without laying undue stress on this question, I would give the third position the preference over the second, if merely because it is less difficult. However, I consider the question of the equal importance of the second and fourth positions of much greater importance as well as that of the half-position, that step-child of the position family. The old humdrum, red-tape procedure, in the following form:

Correct

21. 

Incorrect

should be done away with for good and all. (See p. 121.)

The teaching body in general does not attach its rightful meed of importance to establishing the feeling for position in the pupil on a firm basis. Genuine study of the positions is too little cultivated, and in most cases *change* of position is already taken up while the pupil is still in that initial stage when, especially beginning with the fourth position, he is obliged to calculate before he can use the right finger. In this connection, the second book of *Sevčik's* "School of Violin Technique" is of the very greatest importance to every violinist, even the most advanced.

Shifting

Far greater difficulties are offered by the *transition* from one position to another, the so-called *change of position.* This forms the most arduous portion of the whole system of left hand technique. It represents the measurement of a fixed, exactly defined distance, in which, in the lower positions (until the fourth position is reached) the lower arm alone, and thenceforward the upper arm, hand and thumb are concerned, the fingers remaining more passive. The last-mentioned are, so to say, no more than the agents of the lower arm, which does not prevent their being held responsible for any failure to carry out the change of position. This is quite unfair, since insufficient or exaggerated bending of the arm, an incorrect thumb position, or a wrist stretched too far upward, or bent back and down too far, are the only guilty factors. In fact the role of the upper and lower arm and the hand consists in estimating the distance essential and covering it, while the finger confines itself to touching the string at the point indicated. Only when the distance has been incorrectly or inexactly estimated, may the finger change its position of its own accord—and undertake a *correction.* In the considerations which follow, however, in order to make them clearly understood, we shall retain the old, traditional forms of expression with regard to the sole responsibility of the finger, although the latter's relation to arm and hand is merely that of the executive to the legislative power.

The *descending* change of position also offers the experienced player far greater difficulties than the *ascending* one. This is due to the following cause: Pressure calls for counter-pressure if the body upon which it is exerted is to remain in the same place. The pressure of the fingers develops counter-pressure of the thumb. If, then, I pass from the third to the first position, my thumb gliding into it simultaneously with the other fingers, both, owing to their horizontal movement (gliding) are prevented from carrying out a vertical one (pressure), and the entire counter-pressure devolves upon the shoulder. Since the latter, however, is not parallel to the fingers which are in action, the effect is quite negatory. Hence we have the tendency on the part of untrained violinists to rest the lower part of the hand on the body of the violin during the transition from the third to the first position, in order to secure in such primitive fashion the counter-pressure which after all is such an absolute necessity. In addition, the player experiences a disagreeable sensation as though the retreating arm, so to say, were attempting to withdraw the violin from the clamp formed by the collar-bone, shoulder and arm. Hence the feeling of insecurity which accompanies the procedure. Thus we are compelled to divide the movement, to send the thumb into the first position in advance, while the finger still remains in the third position. During the gliding of the finger which immediately follows, the thumb, which has already reached its place, supplies the necessary counter-pressure without effort.

When changing from the third into a *higher* position, the thumb-support should also be prepared somewhat *in advance*, so that it does not coincide with the movement of the finger in progress, something which usually results in a failure to carry out the transition. The preparatory movement of the thumb opens the way needed by the arm to swing upward. The thrusting forward in advance of the thumb, when the hand rises from the first to the third position, however, is something I regard not only as altogether unnecessary, but also as unnatural, and unquestionably injurious, since the arm, moving on in the direction of the face, presses the instrument so close to the body that an additional point of support is created, which makes this compulsory movement of the thumb superfluous.

he role f the is- ance

Mathematical calculation of the right distance between the different positions as expressed in fractional parts of inches is obviously impossible. We must be content to arrive at a final establishment of the pitch by means of acute listening, and immediately subsequent, and as far as possible unobtrusive, correction. Our skill in striking the correct notes will consist in placing the fingers in the closest proximity to the one mathematically correct point, whence the correction, either by a movement forward or backward, or by means of an equalizing *vibrato*, may be carried out so rapidly and unobtrusively that the listener receives the impression of the right pitch from the start. *Hence, sureness in change of position depends on the agility with which the distance to be covered is exactly estimated by our muscular feeling in order to reach the point with so slight a deviation that the acting finger is able to make the correction in an effortless and unobtrusive manner.*

If we wish to understand clearly the process of carrying out a certain change of position, we must first of all be informed with regard to two points:

22.

How great is the distance which is to be covered in the preceding example? Which finger is called upon to traverse it? The answer is: the distance to be covered runs from B^1 to D^2, and must be covered by the first finger. If the first finger and, together with it the arm, is in the desired position, then the fourth finger need only take the G^2. Hence the fourth finger during the position change has remained passive; while the first finger has been active. We call the D between the B and the G *an intermediary or auxiliary note. It is the most important and helpful aid for establishing the exact distance to be covered and therefore of decisive significance for the systematic study of position changes.*

Intermediary Notes

In order, however, to nip in the bud any possible misunderstanding which might arise, we will at once mention that the use of *intermediary notes* is solely a technical *auxiliary means of study* for the development of the muscular instinct, which thereby is presented with an exactly defined and unmistakable task. When used in performance it must be regarded as one of the most objectionable of habits, by means of which any interpretation laying claim to the appellation "artistic" is rendered impossible. From the standpoint of *interpretation*, a change of position such as the following:

23. 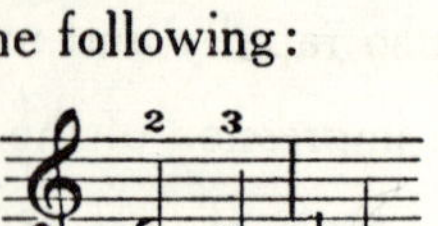

should reject the routine custom:

24. 

in favor of the following manner:

25. 

in its notation.

Wherever I have departed from this, and throughout this work, have fixed the intermediary note according to the position of the hand in the new position to be reached, I have done so in the interests of general comprehensibility, as well as with the assumption that the student would make the considerations already adduced his permanent possession. In sequence follow some examples on the G-string with (bracketed) intermediate notes:

26. 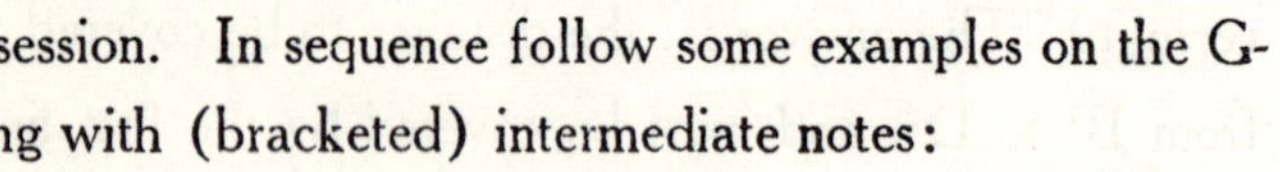

27. 

28. 

28a.  etc.

More detailed examination reveals the fundamental principle *that change from one position to another is in reality invariably carried out by the self-same finger*. The boundaries of the distance to be covered are established by one of the two notes to be played, as well as by the intermediary note. As has already been mentioned, the latter must not be heard in *performance;* while it may be of supreme importance, when *practising* change of position.

Glissando and Portamento

The gliding of the finger is expressed by the word *glissando* or *portamento;* both expressions commonly being regarded as synonymous. There are, however, two methods of gliding, differing radically one from the other:

Beethoven, Vln. Cto, 2o Mov't.

29. 

30. 

In Example 29, the movement of the same finger strives to express heightened emotion, and is *intentional;* in Example 30, it is *compulsory*, since otherwise it is impossible to reach the lower position. The first type of gliding, according to individual taste and feeling, may be carried out more slowly or more rapidly; the more unobtrusively, however, the second type of gliding occurs, the better. Hence, a fundamental difference exists between technical and emotional gliding, a difference which, unfortunately, is all too infrequently taken into account, and which should also be expressed in the terms used to establish it. I would propose, therefore, that the first, as a matter of principle, be known as a *glissando*, the second as a *portamento*.

In order to discuss the *glissando*, I must once more emphasize: The most exact determination of the point of departure as well as of the intermediary note is most urgently necessary in acquiring a sound change of position. In the following example the point of departure and point of arrival are pointed out by means of the intermediary note (♪):

31. 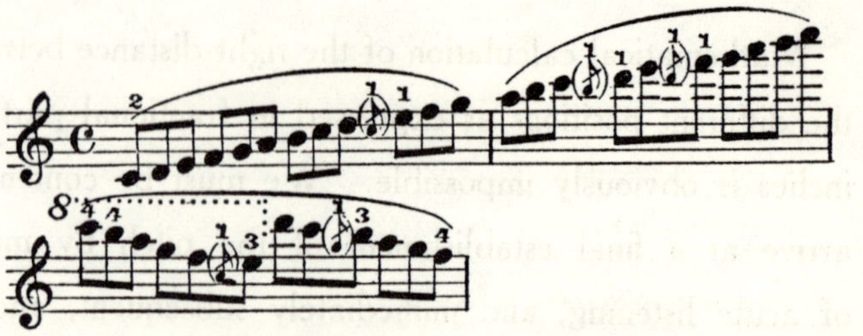

32. 

At times, in studies for change of position, the following intermediary notes are indicated:

Incorrect

33. 

Correct

33a. 

A simple comparison of these two examples will in itself at once reveal the incorrectness of the higher auxiliary note from a purely tonal standpoint; since, while the auxiliary note in Example 33a coincides with one of the three notes directly concerned in the change of position, that in Example 33 substitutes for it an altogether new fourth note, on occasion one foreign to the harmony.

ow or pid ange Posi- n

Should the *technical* change of position be carried out *rapidly* or *slowly?* This question has already been answered above. During practice it should be carried out slowly, with gliding, *not jumping* fingers; in performance as rapidly and unobtrusively as possible. (Only the technical *glissando* is in question here, and not the emotional *portamento*, born of the player's free will.) Slow *glissandi*, carried out for practice purposes, have the advantage that the exact distance is better impressed on the finger action through the medium of muscular instinct, and that it avoids the involuntary accents developed by a jerking progression; at the same time it is an excellent preparation for the *portamento*. To sum up one might say that:

nger- g in ange Posi- n

The *glissando* can be *practised* in the most useful way by *gliding* into the new position, making use of the intermediary note instead of *leaping* into it. In a purely musical performance, however, the *glissando* should be as unobtrusive as possible.* Hence we must endeavor to cover distances of the smallest possible length, that is to say, half-tones by preference. While referring to p. 130 in this connection, we will give a few examples here:

34. Major 

* During the process of gliding, incidentally, the pressure exerted by the finger in action should be noticeably diminished. When this is not done, there is danger, above all, of super-exciting the nerves, and the so-called "playing through" of the finger-tips lies near at hand. Furthermore, increased finger pressure during a *portamento* leads to a corresponding bow movement, resulting in the incorrect use of the < > discussed in detail on p. 34.

35. Minor 

For the same reason the *glissando* should be carried out, so far as possible, by the finger which guarantees that the shortest distance will be covered, *especially in rapid passages*, for instance:

Correct

36.

Incorrect

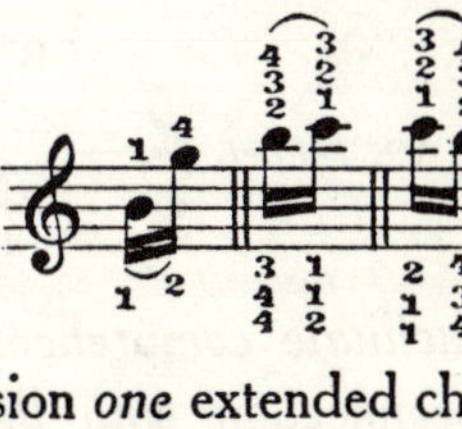

It is true that on occasion *one* extended change of position is preferable to two close-lying changes of position:

Correct

37.

Incorrect

Because of the danger of involuntary accents, we should allow the change of position to coincide, preferably, with the *strong beat* of the measure, since it is better able to carry an accent than the weak beat.

Correct

38.

Incorrect

Shifting in Double Stops

(In ascending passages, incidentally, there is least danger of hinderance because of the fact that the violin is thrust up against the chin.) The same principles apply to change of position in double-stopping. Some examples follow:

39. 

40. 

Expressive Portamento

With the consideration of the *portamento*, the *emotional* connection of two notes, we take up the most delicate question in the whole domain of violin pedagogics. Here we are confronted with a series of traditional prejudices which, it is true, are designedly ignored by concert players, but which, as in the case of "playing in tune," and other problems which will be considered later, have been, because of their great age, irradiated by the false nimbus of an incontrovertible dogma, one which may not be questioned lest the whole venerable structure of artistic violin-playing fall into ruin. Hence it is a question of investigating which of the two fingers concerned in the *portamento* should assume the task of gliding to the proper note:

B-and L-Portamento

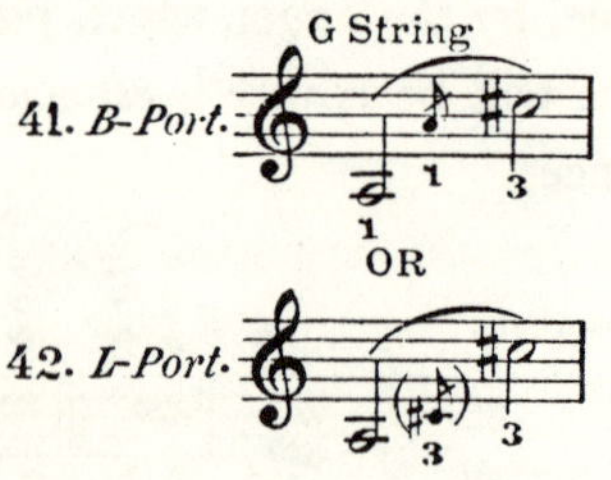
G String
41. B-Port.
1
1
3
OR
42. L-Port.
3
3

(*In order to facilitate comprehension, we will call the portamento in connection with the* **B***eginning note the B-portamento, and that carried out by the* **L***ast finger the L-Portamento.*)

When we consult the best-known violin methods with regard to this point, we are obliged to admit that all their authors, without exception, recognize the *B-portamento* as the only road to salvation, while the *L-portamento*, on the other hand, is excommunicated as a devilish invention of bad taste. This ostracism reminds us of a similiar occurence, when, nearly two centuries ago Leopold Mozart stigmatized the spiccato as an "indecent" bowing!

In this field, however, there exists an intimate interconnection between individual taste and technical execution, since the latter, in a way, is the logical sequence of the former, and is absolutely dependent upon it.

Although the problem of "Artistic Realization" is intended to form the second volume of this work, nevertheless we must--for the reasons already stated—give attention in this place to the *aesthetic* values of the *portamenti*, as also in the corresponding section of "Applied Technic."

The history of violin-playing if considered from the aesthetic angle teaches us that the changing taste of the times is quite as valid in this as in other fields of art. In the past century all the arts have undergone tremendous transformations, so that it seems no more than natural that musical interpretation is also influenced by contemporary feeling and adapts itself to it. Hence, if we have the most unquestioned right to accept certain purely technical principles as unchangeable (every movement corresponding to the natural functioning of the organs, every note of perfect purity and beauty, true to the required pitch, as well as rhythmically correct,) then the far-seeing pedagogue must either avoid setting up rigid *aesthetic* fundamental rules or must garb them in the modest mantle of his own personal opinion.

As regards the question of the *portamento*, in addition, a gulf which cannot be bridged yawns between theory and practice. It is a fact that among the great violinists of our day there is *not one* who does not more or less frequently use the *L-portamento.* A refusal to accept it, therefore, amounts to a condemnation of all modern violin-playing and its representatives, beginning with *Ysaye*, and it is questionable whether there are any who would go so far.

The intimate vocal connection between two notes should be the result of a heightened urge for *individual* expression; and hence our best violinists cling to unconditional freedom with regard to the kind of *portamento* they use. *Freedom*, however, is not synonymous with *license;* that is, the *portamento* should not be employed indifferently, but rather must have the closest interconnection with the musical content of the work which is to be performed. Every true artist should possess sufficient self-control to forego a beautifully sounding—and, oh, so seductive a *portamento!*—when it does not conform to the emotional content of a work. Here the teacher's influence should make itself felt. The pupil's *portamenti*, as a rule, afford valid grounds for estimating the musical cultural level of his teacher. The latter should make the structure and the emotional content of the work clear to the pupil, and in case a doubt regarding the *portamento* arises, should present it to the pupil as a matter of conscience whether he had really experienced the need of heightened expression at the place in question, or whether he had succumbed to the sensual tonal charm inherent in it; or, again, whether, perhaps, the *portamento* was due to the wish to reach another position in a comfortable way (i.e., a technical lack). In the case of every musically unfounded, and merely "beautiful"-sounding connection of distant intervals, it is the teacher's duty relentlessly to reveal the disguised "straining after effect." In practical teaching I usually stigmatize the kind of an audible portamento which is aestetically inexcusable but technically convenient as "bus-portamento"—the cheapest and most comfortable way, to move between positions by taking the "portamento-bus."

When the pupil's taste has thus been purified, he may then be allowed entire freedom in applying the *portamento* as he sees fit; and the teacher should rejoice whenever his pupil carries out a note-connection, not according to routine, but on his own initiative. For originality in the means employed, as a rule, is a happy augury for the collective originality of a personality, whose preservation and development, after all, is the final aim of all sane pedagogy.

The choice of the fingering is determined by the three following possibilities, and in this connection the question as to the use of the *B-* or the *L-portamento* may be for the moment disregarded.

Fingering in Expressive Portamento

I. From the lower to the higher-lying finger:

43. 

II. With the same finger:

44. 

III. From the higher to the lower-lying finger:

45. 

The first (I) is the customary fingering. The difference between the various kinds consists in the fact that the distance to be covered usually varies, something we may verify by observing the intermediate note:

46. 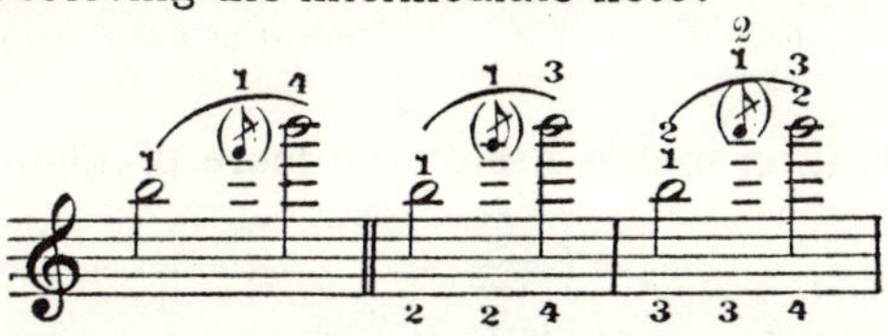

In No. II the intermediate notes drop out altogether. This is not the case in No. III:

47. 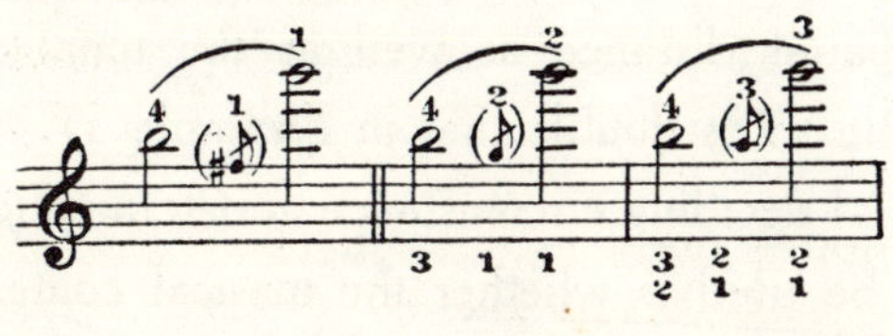

In order properly to understand the problem of the fingering to be used here, we must remember that it may be considered from varied points of view, namely: from the point of view of *finger technique*, from that of *tone*, or that of *music*. The nature of the purely technical *glissando*, carried out at a rapid tempo, is far less complex than that of the *portamento*. The execution of the former is determined by the unchangeable fundamental law which declares that the distance to be traversed must be covered as rapidly and unobtrusively as possible. In the *portamento*, on the other hand, above all, the motive of the necessity of the most rapid action disappears. In

48. 

we have time enough to take the upper F with any finger at all. Agility in reaching the sixth, seventh and eighth positions, instead of the fifth position, must be taken for granted at the very least, in a slow tempo, after thorough study of the positions. Though it cannot be denied that the change of position

49. 

from the first to the ninth position is technically more difficult than

50. 

that from the third to the seventh position, yet we have no right, in case we feel the need of a *long portamento*, to give the *shorter* one the preference, merely because it is technically easier to execute.

It is here and for the first time that we encounter a profound influencing of the means of expression through technical ability. It is already evident that without a perfected mechanism our means of expression never can attain to the full development of their inner treasures. The thorough control of change of position, therefore, together with purity of intonation and sound, is an indispensable prerequisite of higher artistry. From the lower levels, in which the interpreting artist is influenced by technical preoccupations, the violinist can only rise to higher spheres of achievement when his left hand has learned to move with complete freedom on the fingerboard. This may be attained by intensive study of the *glissando*, determined by the intermediary note, as it already has been considered in detail. Hence, as regards the type and execution of the *portamento*, motives which above all are musical, far less frequently sensually-tonal, and never technical, must be the determining factors. Correct execution of the *portamento*, furthermore, depends on our realizing that a *portamento* representing an imitation of the human voice approaches the latter the more closely in the same degree that the intermediary note is less audible. Every violinist may convince himself as to the truth of this contention by experiments with audible and inaudible intermediate notes. This principle offers us a firm point of support from which to approach the problem of the *B-* and *L-portamento* more closely. If in the following case,

Choice Between B- and L-Portamento

the *B-portamento* sounds incomparably better than the *L-portamento;* this is due only to the fact that in the *L-portamento* the intermediate note D is too noticeable. However when I take the upper A with the second finger, then the following method:

is unquestionably better than:

This, however, with the mental reservation that the intermediate note B, in the *L-portamento*, is not distinctly audible. In general, it might be said that the *L-portamento* is indicated only when the two executing fingers are immediate neighbors, as for instance, in:

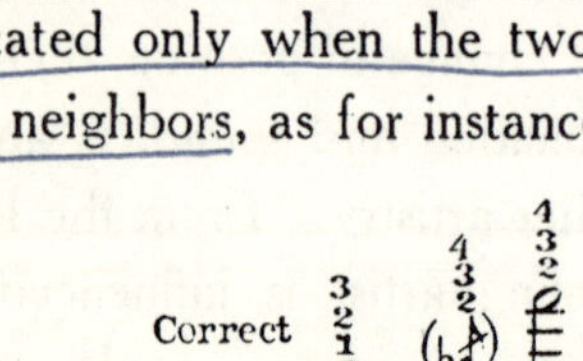

In case, however, an inactive finger lies between them, then the *B-portamento* should be used:

In this last instance the *L-portamento* would make an unpleasant impression:

Owing to its great intensity the *L-portamento* should be used only with care. No matter what the stand taken, however, from a purely technical point of view, it is essential for every modern violinist to control it. Attractive tonal effects, which flatter the senses, are only in order where the *portamento* is concerned, when they conform to the musical content.

When we examine the three manners of executing the *portamento* presented in detail on p. 31, from the practical standpoint, with regard to their tonal peculiarities, and their expressional possibilities, we are able to sum up our impressions in the declaration that the *penetrative power* of a *portamento* is in exact proportion to the length of the distance to be traversed.

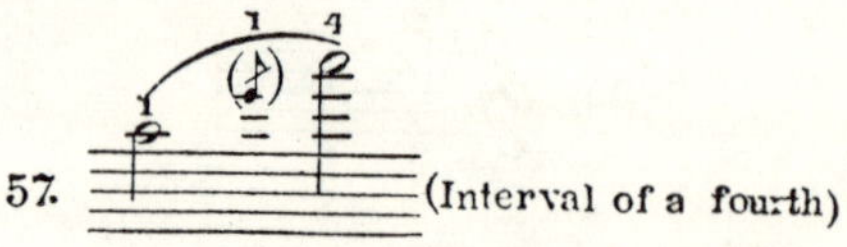

sounds less emphatic than:

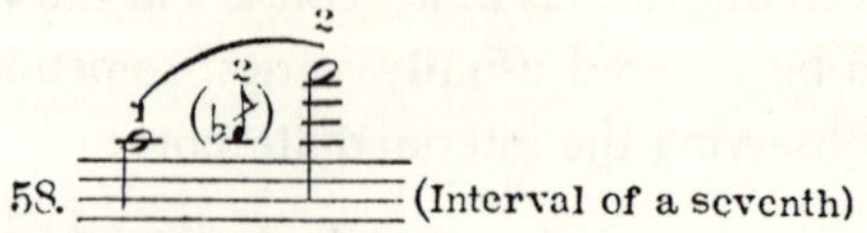

This sensation makes itself even more pregnantly felt in:

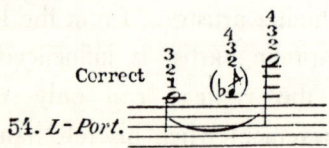

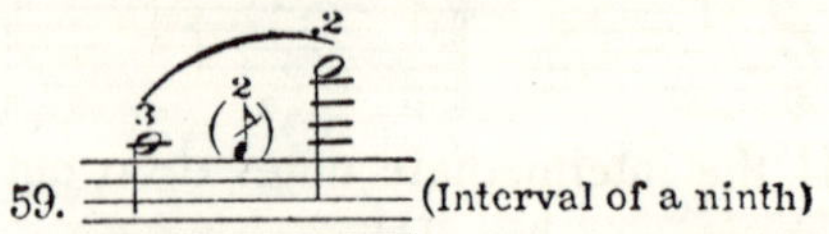

The spatial distance as well as the tonal intensity in Example 59 is double that in Example 57. Therefore, the initial deciding circumstance in determining the fingering to be used is whether the musical content calls for greater or lesser power of expression. Without anticipating our detailed treatment of this subject in the chapter on "Applied Technique," two examples may be presented in order to make what has been said more understandable:

60. 

Here the fourth finger (*B-port*) is better than the second (*L-port*), because too great an intensity is not in keeping with the restraint here demanded. On the other hand, in

61. 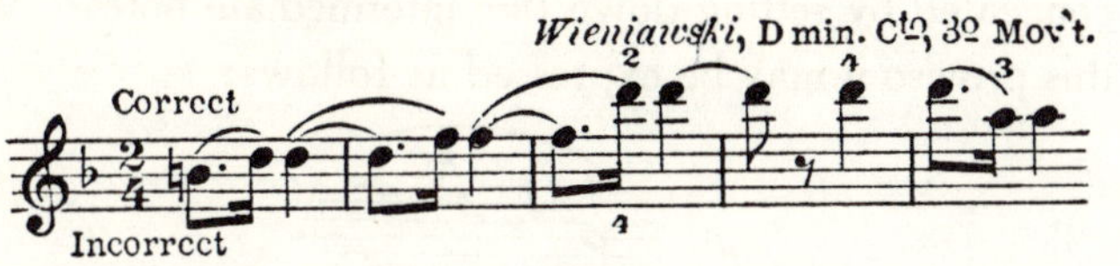

the sensual pathos peculiar to this theme demands the most *ardent portamento* possible. Hence, as regards the manner in which the *portamento* is to be carried out, its relation to the emotional content and mood to be expressed, must, in the final analysis, be the determining factor.

scend- g rta- nto

In the examples already given, principally *portamenti* and *glissandi* in an ascending line are those which have been considered. It goes without saying that descending changes of position are subject to the same laws as regards the intermediary notes. On the other hand while in the great majority of ascending movements both kinds of *portamento* may be used, a descending *L-portamento* must unhesitatingly be called an unaesthetic one:

62. 

63. 

64. 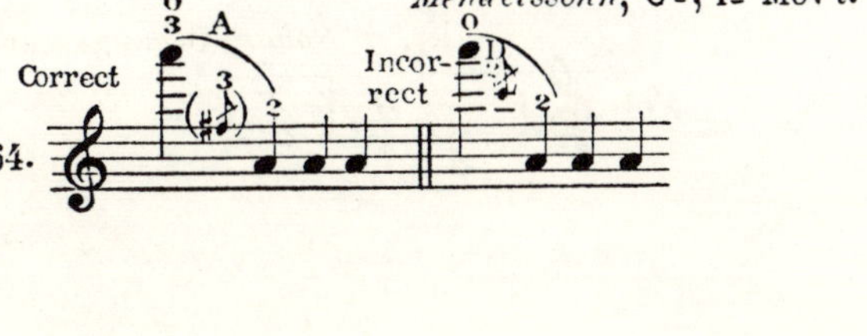

An incorrect type of *portamento* more rarely encountered, one which tonally makes a most disagreeable effect, consists in the altogether too audible, because involuntarily *stressed* addition of a parasitical note, distant approximately half a tone from the initial note:

65. 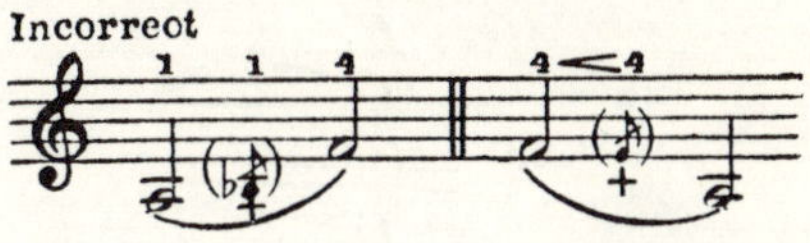

All these examples referred to two notes, united by means of a single stroke of the bow. Should these notes, however, be separated one from the other by two different bow-strokes in spite of being united by a *glissando*, the first question arising is, which of the two bow-strokes should carry out the *glissando*, for instance:

66. 

Grace-Notes in Portamento

In this case the great majority of violinists commit a musical error which may be expressed as follows:

67. 

This grace note is neither more nor less than the interpolation of a foreign note in the musical text, a procedure which is in glaring contradiction to the rules of musical ethics and hence must unconditionally be condemned.* The correct execution of this *portamento*, above all, depends on whether the *B-* or the *L-portamento* is used:

68. 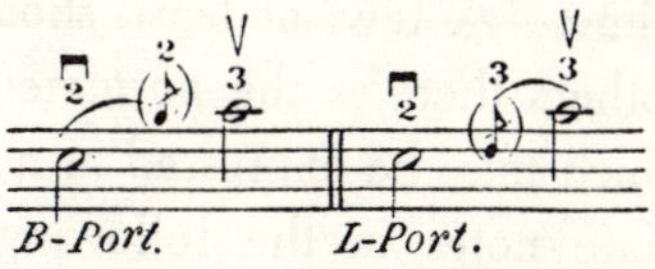

Thus, in the *B-portamento*, the intermediary note would fall on ⊓ and in the *L-portamento* on V. The intermediary notes, in these cases, however, should be even less audible than in *legato, hence the precedent notation should be regarded merely as a delimitation of the distance which is to be covered.*

* The unmusical nature of such a proceeding may clearly be seen were we to imagine a pianist indulging in such an unwarranted liberty.

Portamento and Shading

The nature of the subject here calls for an excursion into the field of bowing technique; for not alone the left hand, but the *bow* as well, is often responsible for a faulty *portamento*. The shading developed by the bow may be any one of four kinds:

69. 

Yet there is also a *pseudo-shading* or *nuance* preferably affected by violinists of certain schools, (in particular the German School between 1860 and 1920,) which may be approximately expressed in notation as follows:

70. 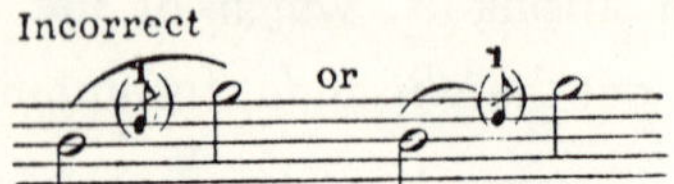

Apart from its particularly unpleasant tonal effect, which only habitual use can make endurable, it is also unmusical in the highest degree to lay greater stress on the connection *between* two notes than on the notes themselves. One can only shudder when thinking of the tonal effect which would result were this procedure to be applied in *singing*. This unfortunate mannerism cannot be cured until the player who employs it fully realizes its ugliness.

Fantasy Portamento

Aside from the three groups of *portamenti* presented on p. 31, as well as the two methods of execution, the B and the L, there remain a few "*fantasy portamenti*," which have been discovered and are employed by distinguished violinists as an expression of their own intensely individual mode of feeling. A few, at least, should be mentioned. Before all others there is the *portamento* discovered by *Thibaud*, which may be expressed in notation by the aid of intermediate notes in the following way, the intermediate note F sharp being played as close as possible to the G.

71. 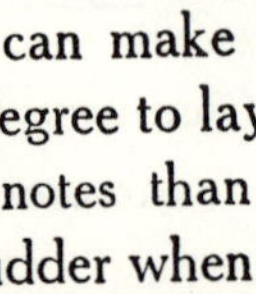

It has an inimitable charm with a somewhat perverse aftertaste; and in certain compositions of French origin, when *employed by the proper personality*, produces an extraordinarily suggestive effect. In general, however, the player is warned against using it, for it is often out of place, and the slightest awkwardness makes it sound as though the G had in first instance been taken too low, and had not been improved quickly enough. In the meantime (between the first and second editions of this work), this *portamento* has become, alas, the indispensable requisite of every jazz musician.

The most important "*fantasy-portamento*," however, and at the same time the only one which admits of a general practical application, represents a *combination of the B- and L-portamento.* It has the advantage that its intermediary notes are absolutely inaudible, something which otherwise is only the case in the *portamento* played with the identical finger. It is, therefore, difficult to express in notation, since its outstanding characteristic (the absolute inaudibility of the intermediate notes), is entirely concealed by setting down *two* intermediate notes. With this proviso it may be expressed as follows:

72. 

When correctly executed it is to be highly recommended, because it represents a medium between the renunciatory *B-portamento* and the sensual *L-portamento*, while, on the other hand, its capacity of modulation through alternate use by the two concurrent factors may be described as well-nigh illimitable. Even in the case of intervals of a *second* it is at times appropriate, especially when a *portamento* with the same finger seems too emotional or too commonplace. Less recommendable is a *portamento* toward the *open string*:

73. 

It is colored with a somewhat dubious coquetry and, when frequently used, produces an impression of the greatest vulgarity.

Quick Portamento

There are violinists who make it a rule to carry out every *portamento quickly*, by means of leaping change of position. Apart from the fact that they thus deprive themselves of one of the most important means of expression, in most cases, especially in slow *tempi*, they produce an *involuntary accent*. Only when an accent is prescribed at the place in question, as for example, in

74. 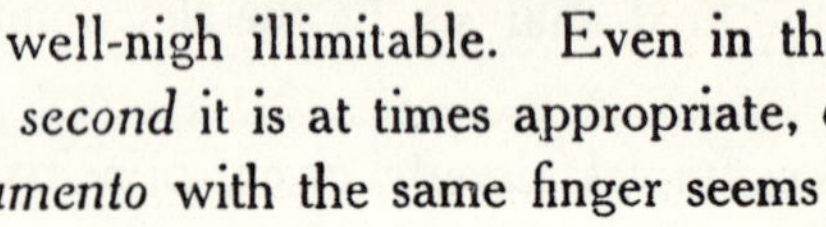

a brusque change of position is advisable, since it appreciably strengthens the bow accentuation. But in compositions of a rather lyrical mood a jerky slide seems certainly out of place; showing also that the player does not feel the inner urge of a soulful connection between the notes concerned. It is indubitable that technically well executed *portamenti* at the right place, *sparingly* applied, enrich the palate of interpretative art with new, wondrously exotic colors, but that their abuse eventually becomes unendurable. A *portamento is the more convincing the less frequently it is employed*. Two *portamenti* in immediate sequence always are unbeautiful. As far as possible, the *portamento* should coincide with the culminating point of a musical phrase. When too frequently used, or used in wrong places, it produces an effect of artificial pathos, insincerity and weariness. Indeed, it may even, when successively applied, call forth in the listener an insupportable physical disgust.

Hitherto, for the sake of systematic arrangement, the intermediary note in the *B*- and *L-portamento* has always been assigned to that position which corresponded to the place on the fingerboard of the *final note* itself. When making *practical* use of the intermediary note, however, and in order to facilitate the acquisition of definite change of position, a considerable alteration must take place. If, for example, we examine:

ter- ediary otes in igh osi- on

75.

the systematically fixed intermediate note will fall upon

Yet if we pay no attention to the rigid rule, and drop the first finger, after we have taken the E, upon that place on the string where it falls in a natural way, we shall find that the intermediary note thus secured, according to the individual conformation of the hand, wavers between G and G sharp.

76.

And now, in view of this fact, we must admit that in higher positions the intermediary note cannot be fixed in accordance with an inflexible schedule of rules, but that the natural position of the hand is its standard of fixation. (See p. 27.)

In conclusion, the fact should be mentioned that even the greatest proficiency in change of position is fruitless when the violin is not held firmly at critical places with increased strength by the chin, collar-bone and shoulder. The consequent unburdening of the left arm makes it possible for the latter to be devoted exclusively to the arduous task of estimating and measuring the necessary distances. The failure properly to play difficult passages, in which the main work is assigned to change of position, is frequently due to the disregard of this fundamental principle.

(f) The Vibrato. While the right arm has to solve sharply defined, mentally controllable tasks, namely—as will be shown—the free development of the string vibrations, as well as the rhythmic and dynamic shading of the tone-sequences, the duty of the left hand, besides the most exact verification of the tonal pitch, consists in an unconscious merging of the tone with psychic powers slumbering deep within our subconsciousness. The result makes itself heard in the so-called *vibrato*. This "vibrating" of the left hand cannot be indicated by unmistakable signs but, according to its character, animation and duration, must be left to the violinist's personality. That the player's individuality is most decidedly expressed in the *quality of tone* peculiar to him and to him alone, would be hard to deny. The contention, however, that the special character of tone quality is first of all determined by the *vibrato*, seems strange. Yet only for a moment. If two violinists, whose tonal qualities differ most widely, play the same sequence of notes on the same instrument behind a curtain, each using his own *vibrato*, each individual player may be easily and surely distinguished, while without participation of the left hand, that is to say, using open strings or natural harmonics, the identity of the player can only be determined by chance. The same would be the case, were they to attempt to perform a *cantilena* previously played in a natural manner, with entire elimination of the *vibrato*. ***Vibrato***

As a result of the lifeless tone quality thus developed, the two modes of rendition are desperately alike. Because of the vital importance of the vibrato the preliminary mechanical conditions of its production form one of the most important parts of mechanism in general; and its application in accordance with good taste one of the most difficult problems of violin-playing. In this field opinions will invariably conflict violently—for, when all is said and done no distinguished violinist cares for the vibrato of his colleagues. Yet it would be wearisome in the extreme were all violinists to "vibrate" in the same manner. "There is something even more agreeable than beauty, and that is change," a Frenchman once said.

Before I formulate my own opinion, it seems appropriate to cast some light on the vibrato from the standpoint of historical and biological development.

Origin of Vibrato

Undoubtedly the *human voice* represents the unattained model for the treatment of musical instruments, just as the *imitation* of the voice, on the basis of the tonal peculiarities common to every species of instrument represents the ideal every player has in mind. Now, in the case of the speaking voice, it already is evident that emotionally, in joy, pain, hatred or love, it is impregnated with a swinging, vibratory, uncertain intermixture, owing to the fact that we no longer completely control our vocal chords when under the influence of strong passions. Since such a condition of exaltation is relatively infrequent in the daily life of the normal human being, a permanently vibrating voice, the vocal chords otherwise being healthy, indicates a somewhat morbid condition of excitation. The same applies to the singing voice. The singing voice, too, should flow clearly and quietly; yet should be capable of an artistically modulated vibration to express emotion, even where the quieter inflections of feeling are concerned. Next to the singing voice—which has been their radiant example—come the string instruments. Our tone-production has the advantage of the singing voice in its superior mobility with regard to tempo and nuance, yet is inferior to it in penetrative quality. The union between our feelings and our larynx happens to be far more immediate than that between a psychic emotion and the instrument, which, in order to be merged, first of all demands the mediatory activity of the arms, one of which, in addition, must employ the bow as a lever. At the same time the violin has a right to be considered an indirect instrument of song, and when in possession of an adequate technique, we too, are able to produce tones which approach those of the human voice in expressiveness, and even exceed it with respect to the number of possible varieties of expression.

The vibrato of the human voice is transferred to the violin by means of a "trembling" on the part of the fingers determining the pitch. It presents itself acoustically as a deviation from the true pitch occurring at regular intervals, upward and downward. To the eye it appears as a series of broad and slow, or narrow and rapid oscillations of the hand. The broad oscillations naturally result in deviations of the original pitch far larger and carried out more slowly than the narrow ones, so that the conceptions: *broadly vibrating*, and *slow*, as well as: *quickly vibrating*, and *close*, are synonymous. For the sake of conciseness we will in future designate these two main types of vibrato as *slow* and *rapid* vibrato.

Mechanics of Vibrato

Three parts of the body—seldom independently, in most cases in conjunction—are mainly concerned in the production of the vibrato: *finger*, *hand* and *lower arm*. In addition, the lower arm may be active in a twofold manner: in the direction of the face (as during change of position), or with a slight twist in the elbow-joint. The oscillation of the *finger* alone, without the participation of the *hand*, can produce no more than an exceedingly rapid vibrato; while the *hand*, oscillating in the wrist-joint, is able to carry out decidedly broader movements. The oscillations of the *lower arm* in the elbow-joint, for their part, according to their kind, may be carried out more rapidly or more slowly. The *rapid* vibrato, in the main, is produced by vibrations of the finger or arm, the *slow* vibrato, in most cases, by vibrations of the hand.

If we seek to attain absolute transference of the emotional complex aroused in us by a composition as the final aim of our violinistic-artistic efforts, and regard the vibrato as one of its most important agents of conveyance, we cannot help but consider the possession of perfected mechanical means an absolutely *vital question* for the artistic human being.

Faulty Vibrato

A faulty *vibrato* will always remain an unbridgeable obstacle to the attainment of higher aims. And what has been done thus far to aid unfortunates whose career has been threatened by a deficiency in this connection? Practically nothing. The teaching body has been content to call the *vibrato* "natural" and "impossible to learn," confusing personal need with the mechanical prerequisites for its creation. How *does* the beginner commence to vibrate? Does it come to him suddenly, like a divine revelation? Not at all. The process is far more prosaic. He notices that his teacher is able to ennoble his tone by means of vibration and, after a time, either encouraged to do so by his teacher, or following some inner impulse, he is led to imitate him. *Hence every pupil originally has the kind of vibrato peculiar to the teacher under whose guidance he made his first attempts in that direction.* Should the general development of violin instruction result in making more thoroughly trained *teachers* available, then there will be no more pupils with a faulty vibrato. At present, however, we must seek means and ways to do away with the mechanical reasons of a *faulty vibrato* and smooth the road by following which the pupil will be able to find the kind of vibrato best suited to his own individual nature. For this purpose three kinds of faulty vibrato may be distinguished:

1. *The Over-Close* (*Finger*) *Vibrato.* This is developed by exaggeratedly quick and close oscillations of the fingers or arm, with stiffening of the wrist. The over-close vibrations produce a bleating sound.

2. *The Over-Broad* (*Wrist*) *Vibrato.* This is developed by exaggeratedly broad and slow oscillations of the hand in the wrist-joint, while eliminating the finger and lower-arm movements. The excessive deviations from the original tone produce the well-known "flickering" or "howling" tone, which makes so unpleasant an impression because the original tonal pitch is no longer distinguishable.

3. *The Over-Stiff* (*Lower Arm*) *Vibrato.* Though on occasion surprisingly good in tone, it is very injurious for the collective technique, since the stiffening of the wrist which attends it produces a heaviness of the left hand, making the attainment of a perfected change of position technique out of the question.* The two previous failings therefore, result in *audible* evils; while the third is followed by an unfavorable influence upon the collective technique of the left hand.

Correction of Faulty Finger-Vibrato

1. *Correction of the Exclusive Finger-Vibrato.* Here it is a question of securing the participation of the wrist, and thus giving the vibrations greater breadth. *Preparatory Exercise*: Mechanical flexing of the wrist by means of gymnastic exercises without the aid of the instrument. The hand should be raised and lowered at regular intervals. As soon as weariness develops the exercises should be stopped at once, and the arm dropped. *Main Exercise:* The division of the *vibrato* into individual movements. *Achille Rivarde*, a distinguished violinist and teacher living in England, recommends that the individual *vibrato* movements be studied in the following manner: the left lower arm is firmly rested against the body of the violin, and thus condemned to absolute immobility. The first finger is applied to the string very *flatly;* the hand carries out a forward movement with an inclination to the left, without the finger leaving the string. This brings about a merging of the finger and wrist movements, together with a slight roll of the lower arm in the elbow-joint. The movement may be carried out slowly or rapidly. (Ills. 15 and 16.) In this way the wrist is loosened, and the prerequisites for a broader vibrato with participation of the wrist-joint are created. *The Mode of Practice*: Without bow, four *vibrato* movements of the same finger in succession. *The Practice Time*: Five minutes, in the form of a scale in which all four fingers are used, at first played ten times daily, later on less frequently, as circumstances may determine. If, after a certain time, a noticeable flexibility of the wrist is evinced, then long, sustained notes may be attempted, still with the lower arm closely pressed against the body of the violin, and using a *vibrato* coming from the wrist.

The preceding exercises, however, should begin in the third or fourth positions, because resting the lower arm against the violin in these positions seems more natural.

Correction of Faulty Wrist-Vibrato

2. *Correction of the Exclusive Wrist-Vibrato.* The excessively developed hand movement must be diminished, and the *finger* itself drawn into more active participation. The movements, instead of being exclusively horizontal,

* In such cases the right wrist as well, through a form of sympathetic action, will be stiffened automatically at times.

should be pushed away more perpendicularly, into the fingerboard, so to speak, and in this way made closer and more rapid. I would suggest the following manner of procedure, one which has admirably proven itself in my teaching experience: A movement which propagates itself exclusively in a vertical direction, and may be approximated in notation as follows:

77. 

is carried out by the individual fingers. The preceding graphic presentation should have made this movement sufficiently comprehensible. The question is one of laying on the finger quite lightly, somewhat in the manner of taking a natural harmonic; this for its first movement; followed by a slight pressing down of the string as its second. These two movements, carried out one after the other in rapid succession, supply a disjointed *finger-vibrato*. In the case of too broad and unmixed a *wrist-vibrato* where it was a question of weakening the *wrist*-movement and favoring the *finger-action*, it is to be highly recommended.*

Furthermore, an exaggeratedly *hollow* position of the hand acts as a hindrance to the oscillations of the wrist, but will promote the oscillation of the fingers, while on the other hand this position may incite the violinist to play somewhat sharp and on the extreme edge of the finger-tip. In the case of many violinists the rapidity of their *vibrato* may be promoted indirectly by taking the by-way of influencing the bow. The *martelé* stroke at the point is admirably adapted to this end because, owing to its short duration, any excessively long *vibrati* are made impossible, and as the vibrating hand instinctively tries to adapt its speed to the short duration of the *martelé* stroke.

In addition, I often have observed that a correctly executed *portato* on one and the same note spurs on (if one may use the term) and carries along the left hand to a heightened vibratory activity. (See p. 73.)

In case the exercises of *finger-vibrato* are not efficient, we must try to obtain the participation of the lower-arm while vibrating, with the final object to secure a perfect amalgamation of wrist and arm movement and in consequence a considerably diminished action of the hitherto predominant wrist movement.

Up to date we know two exercises of this kind:

(*a*) Apply the finger to the string as flatly as possible. Push the lower arm forward through the elbow-joint, the wrist remaining absolutely stiff while the finger, which rests on the string follows the arm-movement by assuming a right-angle position. The same series of movements in reversed order back to the original position (Known since about 1920).

(b) Applying the arm movement of the "Bockstriller" (goat's trill, see p. 47) for the purpose of putting into action the lower arm. Trill movements in high positions with stiffened wrist *and finger*, the movement is produced exclusively through a rapidly shaking movement of the lower arm in the elbow joint.** Both exercises to be practised without the bow.

Correction of Faulty Arm-Vibrato

3. *Correction of the Exclusive Lower-Arm Vibrato.* In the case of too close a *vibrato* this is secured by using the *Rivarde* exercise; in the case of too broad a vibrato, by using my own exercise, already explained. After a time try to vibrate with the wrist in the third position, and then in the first position. When the object sought, the participation of the wrist-joint, has been attained, but the *vibrato* itself having become too slow, my vertical exercise should be used.

Although the substitution of an exclusive *wrist-vibrato* for an exclusive *arm-vibrato* is practically possible, it has, at least in my experience, nearly always proved to be a failure as to its sonorous results. The owner of a primary *arm-vibrato* must be satisfied with combining it with a certain amount of wrist-movement, till a mixture satisfactory from the tonal point of view is attained.

At times the cause of a certain stiffness of vibration lies in a cramped *pressure* of the *thumb* or the third *joint of the index finger* on the neck of the violin. *Vibrato exercises* with elision of the thumb, supporting the violin against a door or wall, often exert a beneficial and curative influence in such cases.

On occasion we also encounter an absolute *physical inability to vibrate.* In such cases the tone makes an icily cold impression, it lacks all quality and—in consequence of the missing vibratory correction—usually sounds out of tune. This fault should be treated in the following manner:

(*a*) Loosening of the wrist by means of the *Rivarde* exercises.

(*b*) Loosening the fingers by means of *my* exercise.

This kind of vibrato-impotence may also be caused by the exaggerated cultivation of slow finger-exercises, as well as by the neglect of rapid ones: lazy fingers produce a lazy *vibrato*. Dexterity exercises at the highest possible rate of speed are in order here.

Other Faulty Vibrati

The following variant of faulty vibrato often may be observed: the *ability* to vibrate is actually present, as well as the will to do so; yet *apparently* the player does not feel the *need* for a partial expression of his emotions

* Whether this exercise is not also adapted to the correction of too high raising of the fingers in general, and during the trill in particular, will be left for later investigations.

** This ingenious application of the "Bockstriller" for securing increased cooperation of the lower-arm while vibrating, has been discovered by my former pupil **Simon Goldberg.**

by the left hand. He *feels*, so to speak, only with his right arm, and is thus betrayed into exaggerated bow-pressure and a forced, lifeless manner of tone production. In such cases, first of all, the will to vibrate should be strengthened by concentrating it exclusively on the left hand. This may be brought about in the most natural manner by making the *eye* watch the left hand during the *cantilena* in question. For when the inner wish does not suffice to procure increased participation of the left hand, we find that external *visual observation* seemingly motivates an increased will-transferance, one which is capable of exerting a heightened influence on the left hand, and actually *compels* it to be more active. In such cases the pupil, during a period fluctuating between one and four weeks, according to the tenacity of his evil, should play nothing but *cantilena* of various kinds, in which his eye must remain in constant contact with the fingers of his left hand.

Incidentally, there are many violinists whose ability to vibrate is most intimately bound up with their general physical or psychical *disposition* and hence, so to say, presents a species of mood thermometer. *Cold fingers* also exert an unfavorable influence on vibratory activity, as well as temporary or permanent emotional coolness or restraint. Many violinists have formed the habit of not vibrating on a note until it already has been sounding for a time, using a *late-comer-vibrato*. It seems to me that this procedure is only valid when based on the melodic line of expression, that is, when a *heightening* of expression is to occur on the same note. This naturally does not imply that the vibrato should begin full blast on each and every note when it is carried out.

Occasionally, in the case of singers as well as violinists, we find a type of *vibrato* which, in itself technically unobjectionable, calls forth in the listener a certain, at first quite inexplicable discomfort, disturbing his enjoyment of an interpretation in other respects excellent or even admirable. On closer examination it will be noticed that the vibratory movement is not *equally* developed around the exact tonal pitch, but favors a certain specific direction so that the finger, in substance, vibrates upward or downward. It is true that such tones are more endurable than those in which the wrong number of oscillations remain permanently unchanged; yet their frequent occurrence is apt to lower the level of an artistic performance. Intonation exercises without vibrato should suffice to enable the player to overcome in time this very annoying fault.

A kind of *indirect* vibrato results when having to play a long note on an open string, we vibrate on a note situated an octave higher.

77½.

vibr.
Bruch, G min. Cto, 1º Mov't.

Perfect Vibrato

A *perfect vibrato* is produced by the combination of the finger, hand and arm movements. The extent to which each of these factors participate is an individual matter; yet all the joints must be loosened and prepared to take an active part at any moment. The resultant vibrato is not prominently noticeable, but is joined to the tone in an indissoluble union, and corresponding to it as its fragrance does to the flower; a vibrato which has a reflex action on the most intimate consciousness, just as it has been developed out of the latter. The opposite to this vibrato is one which produced mainly by an awkward, slow wrist-movement seems to have been "pasted on" the tone, and creates the impression that the two have nothing in common. During the past few years, together with the industrialization of musical activities, this banal manner has domesticated itself more especially in second-rate places of amusement, so that it might be appropriately designated the *café and "movie"* vibrato. In it the tone is squeezed together to form a syrupy mush which, consequent upon the uniform, continuous application of vibration lacks all contrast and more intimate expressional possibilities, and in a short space of time becomes unendurable. This type of vibrato, in nearly all cases, is too slow and broad, and in general a more rapid vibrato should be preferable to a slower one, because in the former the deviation from the original tone is much less, and this makes the tone sound firmer and steadier. The greatest objection to the employ of a slow, broad vibrato movement, however, is the fact that in the *high positions* it exceeds the interval of a whole tone or more. If in the lower positions, it is more endurable, its effect is absolutely catastrophal higher up, since the fundamental tone—the immovable pole in the passing flood of tonal appearances—owing to its half tone upward and downward oscillations, comparable to a ship on the high seas, becomes quite unrecognizable to the ear.

Continuous or Occasional Vibrato

With regard to the question whether vibration should be *continuous* or only *occasional*, the most strikingly contradictory differences of opinion exist. From a purely theoretic standpoint, the vibrato, as the means for securing a heightened urge for expression should only be employed when it is musically justifiable. Yet, if we consider the celebrated violinists of our day, it must be admitted that in nearly every case they employ an uninterrupted (though technically unobjectionable) vibrato, while the great violinists of the middle of the last century were opposed to uninterrupted vibration.

The Vibrato from Joachim till Kreisler

Joachim's medium of expression for instance, consisted of a very close and quick tremolo. The same holds good for *Thomson*. *Sarasate* started to use broader oscillations while *Ysaye's Vibrato*, which followed closely every mood of his admirable personality became the ideal goal of the generation around 1900. But it was *Kreisler* who forty years ago, driven by an irresistible inner urge, started a revolutionary change in this regard, by vibrating not only continuously in cantilenas like *Ysaye*, but even in technical passages. This fundamental metamorphosis has put his indelible stamp on contemporary Violin-playing, no matter whether one agrees with it, or not. In any case it seems to meet the demand of the average concert-goer of the present time to such an extent that our ears object already to the traditional gulf between the expressive theme and unexpressive neutral passages.

Vibrato During Passages

Now the question arises—which is the most efficient way to effect this change, both mentally and technically. In my teaching practice, the pupil has to concentrate for a certain amount of time nearly exclusively on playing comparatively easy studies (Kreutzer, Rode), in a Cantilena-like expressive way, which automatically brings about a slight shaking sufficient to remove the dryness inherent to "practice-tone." When in this way not only the technical habit of vibrating in passages has been taken, but also the mental need of it has been created, the cure may be considered as terminated.

But our first duty as teachers remains to teach the pupil the *mechanical* prerequisities for a correct vibrato; on this basis the latter will quite instinctively favor that type of vibrato which best corresponds to his temperamental or meditative, his impulse or sober-minded personality. We must convert him to the view that the vibrato should never be used as a matter of habit, but only as the consequence of a heightened need for expression, and that this need, for its part, should be grounded in the musical content of the composition to be presented and interpreted. The vibrato which from the artistic point of view may be termed ideal, is one *differentiated* in the highest possible degree, one which, owing to its perfected mechanism, is able to traverse a gamut of emotions progressing from the softest, well-nigh inaudible, to the most passionate, overwhelming oscillations.

Left-Hand Technique

(g) The Basic Forms of Left-Hand Technique. The possibilities of combination between the various notes at the disposal of musical creation are limitless. If, however, conformably to purely violinistic needs, we seek a firm kernel, the *raw material* which awaits development by the creative spirit, we may point out the following thirteen different primal forms:

1. Simple Diatonic Scales.
2. Disjointed Triads and Chords of the Seventh.
3. Disjointed Thirds.
4. Chromatic Scales.
5. Chromatic Scales in *Glissando.*
6. Thirds
7. Fingered Octaves.
8. Sixths.
9. Octaves (with 1st and 4th fingers).
10. Tenths.
11. Trills.
12. Harmonics.
13. Pizzicati.

Diatonic Scales

1. *Simple Diatonic Scales.*

(*a*) In one octave, in the first position:

78.

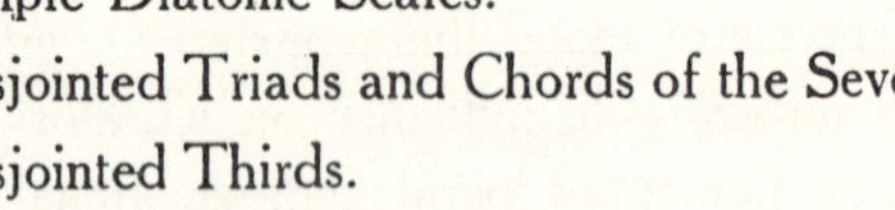

(In *ascending* with the fourth finger, using the open string when *descending*.) The procedure to secure smooth change of string discussed in detail on p. 25, is to be used here in the following manner (the square notes are "taken in advance," without being sounded).

79. 

(*b*) On one string:

80. 

The real distance between the two notes which limit the change of position should be determined by means of the intermediary note. (See p. 27.) In returning, the half-tones are exclusively used for position change, hence the difference in fingering between major and minor.

(*c*) In two octaves, on all four strings:

81. 

(*d*) On one string:

82. 

The two octave scale on one string (Example 82) is generally only playable when begun on one of the three lowest notes on each string, since the higher octave is uncommonly difficult in descending. (This is the reason why violinists who are preluding invariably play the two-octave E-major scale on the E-string upward, and never downward!)

(*e*) In three octaves:

83. 

84. 

(The fingering differs in major and in minor, according to the half-tones. See p. 130.)

(*f*) In four octaves:

85. 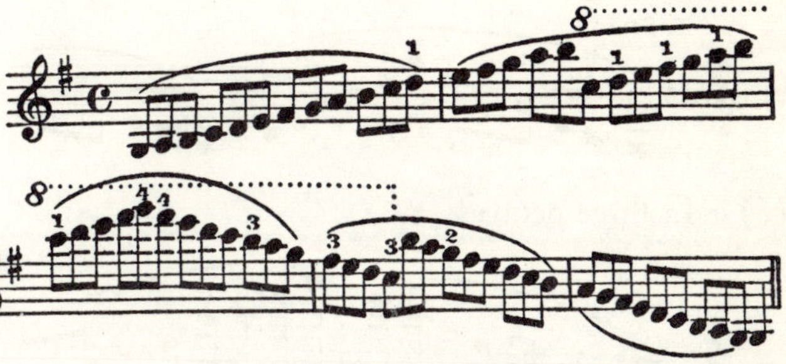

If we attempt to play the open string between two high notes on the E-string, it is not the open string which sounds, but the *octave*. This circumstance may be turned to account in very rapid virtuoso-like descending scales in the following manner:

86. 

In which case the open string is indicated by $\overset{0}{0}$.

2. *Broken Triads and Chords of the Seventh.*

Broken Triads

The best chord-sequence is unquestionably that given by *Sevčik* in his "School of Violin Technique," Book 3, Nos. 3 and 7. BI, 22 has in all keys!

(*a*) In one octave, in the first position:

87 

(*b*) On one string:

88  etc.

as on p131

In order to overcome the difficulty of change of position in this case, the first note of the new position, when practicing, should be sustained for a somewhat longer period of time, in order to test and improve it:

89 

(*c*) In two octaves, on all four strings:

90  etc.

(*d*) On one string:

91 

(*e*) In three octaves:

92 

(*f*) In four octaves:

93 

(Intermediary notes and change of string as in the case of the diatonic scales.)

Broken Thirds

3. *Broken Thirds.*

(*a*) In one octave, in the first position:

(*b*) On one string:

94 

(*c*) In two octaves, on all four strings:

(*d*) The same in three octaves:

95 

Chromatic Scales

4. *Chromatic Scales.*

(*a*) In one octave, in the first position:

(*b*) On one string:

96 

(*c*) In two octaves, on all four strings:

(*d*) In three octaves. (For fingering, see p. 134.)

5. The *chromatic scale in glissando* is a problem in itself. It represents a species of uninterrupted half-tone *glissando*, and like the *staccato* (see p. 69), results from a combination of two movements, a horizontal and a vertical one: the former produced by hand and arm, the latter by a tremulant, *vibrato*-like movement of the lower arm in the elbow-joint. This dual mechanism must function in a well-equalized manner. Neither of these movements should dominate at the other's expense. If the *glissando* predominates, the half-tones are wiped out; if the half-tone interruptions predominate, then the *glissando*-movement is not fluent enough. When investigating a faulty chromatic *glissando*, we must first of all determine which of the two is the guilty factor. The neglected movement should be strengthened, the exaggerated one weakened. (*Glissando* with neglect of the half-tones, or sharply accented half-tones with a neglected *glissando*.) In both cases I use the following exercise with success: The pupil first of all plays the chromatic scale in question as a simple *glissando*, without any interruption, perhaps a dozen times in succession. When he has made sure of the regular forward movement of the lower arm in this manner, a *vibrato*-like shaking movement of the hand, representing the regular vertical half-tone movement, is grafted on the *glissando;* which at first produces irregular, but after longer study exact chromatic *glissandi*. When this is of no avail, a forcing of the biceps may produce the desired result while carrying out an uninterrupted *glissando*. In any event, the greatest importance should be assigned to the *glissando movement*, since in ninety-nine out of a hundred cases insufficient participation of it is responsible for faulty execution; while at the same time the half-tone progressions are carried out too clumsily.

With regard to chromatic *glissandi* in double-stops the same principles apply.

Thir

6. *Thirds.*

(*a*) Scales in two octaves:

97 

(*b*) Chromatic scales:

98
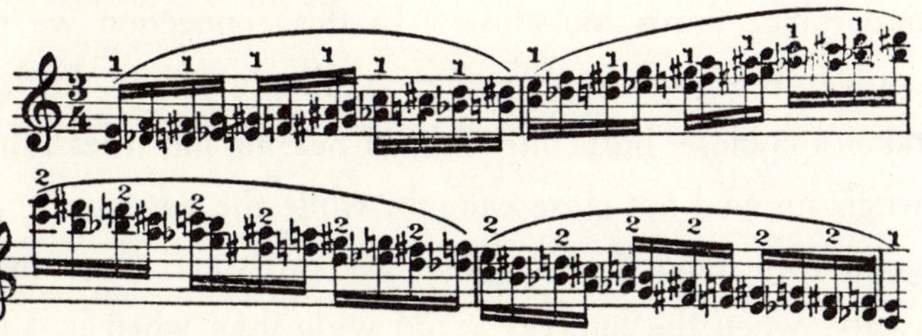

Here the change of position, so far as possible, should be made on the strong beat of the measure; that is, on the first and third, not the second and fourth notes, and the open strings should be taken into account in fingering. (See p. 135.)

[Fin]gered [Oc]taves

7. *Fingered Octaves.*

(*a*) Scales in two octaves:

99

(*b*) Chromatic scales (in actual practice they are always carried out in ordinary octaves):

100

(*c*) Broken Triads and Chords of the Seventh:

101

(With regard to fingering, see p. 139.)

The mechanism of fingered octaves as well as of thirds rests fundamentally on the activity of the self same fingers but at various distances and on different strings. Their manner of practice is the same and hence they may be considered together.

Practice of Fingered Octaves and Thirds

It is seldom that perfect successions of thirds are heard, and still more rare is it to hear clean scales in fingered octaves. The latter, in particular, are avoided with well-nigh holy awe. This is quite unnecessary, for when correctly studied it is possible for every violinist to master these two technical types equally well. The prerequisite for so doing consists in the realization and practical carrying out of the following fundamental principle: *The majority of technical problems are made up of various difficulties which must be separated one from the other, and be individually overcome.* The Problem of thirds and fingered octaves consists of four kinds of interwoven movement:

The *falling movement* and the *stretching movement* (in the case of the fingered octaves):

102

The *change of position*:

103

And the *change of string*:

104

Every violinist knows from his own personal experience that the reason for the failure to play scales of this kind is almost entirely due to faulty change of position and change of string. In three months' time, however, the whole problem may be overcome if a half hour be devoted to its study daily, along the following lines:

During the first month *technical exercises for falling* and stretching, *excluding* change of position and change of string, should be practiced:

105

106

During the second month: *Change of Position*:

107 

108 

During the third month: *Change of String*:

109 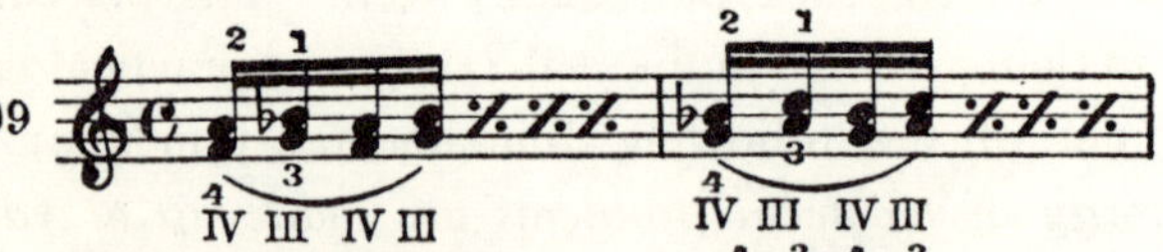

110 

Thereupon both kinds should be practised in the form as indicated in the scale system (see p. 108). The purity of the octave interval is easily determined, since even a poorly cultivated ear will at once recognize a false unison and sense its annoying effect.

Intonation of Thirds

As regards the vibratory relations of the two notes of the third to each other, there is hardly any field of virtuoso technique in which as many sins with regard to purity of intonation are committed especially in the following combinations: *Two major thirds side by side:*

111 

The lower note of the first third, as well as the upper note of the second third are in most cases not stopped close enough to one another. In playing these two notes,  the fingers should be pressed close together; only then will the simultaneous sounding of both thirds be satisfactory. In the *half-tone with the fourth finger*

112 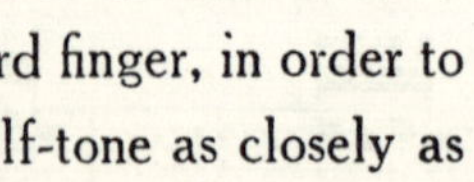

however, the latter usually is placed too high, which makes the upper notes of the third seem too low. Here only the raising of the third finger, in order to permit the fourth finger to take the half-tone as closely as at all possible, is of avail. But the most customary shortcoming, while playing thirds, consists in taking major thirds too far apart and minor thirds too close. In this connection we encounter the curious phenomenon, that a major third, if taken too close, hurts our sense of hearing much less, than when stopped not close enough, while the contrary holds good with minor thirds, which we can stand much more easily, when the interval is too wide than when it is too narrow. Therefore the teacher should always insist on very close major and rather wide minor thirds.

8. *Sixths.*

Sixths

(*a*) Scales in two octaves:

(The use of the same fingers in the higher positions is better than change of fingers.)

113 

(*b*) Chromatic scales:

114 

These are employed mainly with the avoidance of any change of string, unless the latter might chance to occur simultaneously with change of bow. The most advantageous fingering consists in the retention of the fingers used for the first sixth:

115 

At a very rapid tempo they are produced by means of the tremulant movement peculiar to all varieties of *glissando.*

9. *Octaves With the First and Fourth Fingers*

(*Simple Octaves*)

Octa[ves] with the F[irst and Fourth] Finge[rs]

(*a*) Scales in two octaves:

116 

With an *intermediary* note on the open string.

117 

118 

The higher the position in which an octave is played, the more closely the fingers approach one another, since the space between the first and the fourth finger diminishes, and in addition the fourth finger has smaller distances to cover than the first finger. In this connection the rôle of the two passive fingers, the second and third, is very important. They should neither be stretched upward nor sideways, nor pressed convulsively on the strings, but must be relaxed. It is through them that the distance from the first to the fourth finger is measured. They may be raised higher only when the octave-stops, growing increasingly closer in the higher positions, imperatively demand it. (With regard to the temporary substitution of the third or the fourth finger, see p. 118.)

(*b*) Chromatic Scales.

119 

(*c*) Broken Triads and Chords of the Seventh.

Use the same exercise recommended for the fingered octaves, Example 101. In *legato*, with the first-fourth fingers, it is especially difficult owing to the simultaneous change of position and string, which it is hardly possible to carry out without interruption. An excellent study.

nths

10. *Tenths.* Here the difficulties to be overcome consist in the excessive stretch (sixths instead of fourths), very tiring for small hands; in the distance between the first and fourth fingers, diminishing when ascending and, finally, in the difference in the forward movement of the two fingers (half- or whole-tone progression), according as the tenth to be taken is a major or minor one. Pure intonation in scales in tenths is very seldom heard, since the forced position of the hand and fingers which they necessitate prevents most violinists from studying them systematically. To this should be added the player's fear (in most cases unconscious) of straining the sinews which exaggerated stretching threatens to bring about. Furthermore, an abnormal stretching prevents a corrective *vibrato*, so that a tenth which is false to begin with, usually continues to remain untrue. The incidental use of tenths in many compositions of real musical value (for instance *Brahms'* Violin Concerto, 1st Movement), however, makes the control of even this branch of violin technique necessary.

The practical utilization of the technical formulas which we have just discussed, in the form of daily exercises, is presented in the "Scale System" (p. 109.)

Trill

11. *The Trill.* The trill represents the transformation of an originally slow, repeated, singly controllable *voluntary* movement into a most rapid, and with regard to its component factors, *involuntary* tremulant movement. It may be defined as a *benign* species of tremulant motion which finds its counterpart in the *staccato*, the *tremolo* (to the right), and the chromatic *glissandi.* From a purely theoretical standpoint every violinist in command of dependable and rapid technical ability should also possess a perfected trill.

In reality, however, *vicious* cramped conditions of certain parts of the hand very often prevent the development of that benign tremulant movement which is known as the trill. Their cure is often hindered by prejudices on the part of teachers, who also call an aptitude for the trill a "natural" gift, hence one which cannot be acquired. Although this is correct insofar that many violinists, especially Gipsy musicians, are possessors of a naturally good trill, yet it in no wise justifies the deduction that it is generally impossible to acquire or improve it. The most expedient manner in which to acquire a good trill is through the use of the three following preparatory exercises:

Kreutzer, Etude Nº 13

121 

122 

123 

In Example 121, the trilling finger is raised as high as possible, and drops back upon the string with the greatest possible elasticity. In Example 122, the finger is raised as little as possible. In the third exercise the trill is carried out in slow, regular beats and in the end as a quick trill exercise in its original form. The way prescribed will lead to the desired result in most cases. It is a different matter when vicious, cramp-like contraction of any portion of the hand interferes with the development of the trill.

Trill Hindrances

Various hindrances may exist, for instance:

1. Contraction of the *ball of the thumb*.
2. Stiffening of the *wrist*.
3. Stiffening of *fingers* not concerned in the production of the trill.
4. Convulsive pressure on the part of the *finger fixed to the spot*.
5. Too *high a raising* of the finger, with consequent retardation.
6. *Insufficient raising*, i. e., dropping of the finger, with resultant lack of elasticity.

As in the case of every illness, here too the diagnosis must be the decisive factor; yet since in this instance the physician who has the case in hand, that is to say the teacher, is hardly able to verify the *inner* processes of the hand, and at the most can only guess at them, he must proceed inversely by trying to find first the right remedy. Hence if the following measures are taken up in sequence, and an improvement in the trill occurs when they have been employed a week, the physiological cause of the evil will have been established beyond controversy and a combination of exercises should make a cure possible.

1. Trill study with *elimination of the thumb* (this prevents the cramped contraction of the ball of the thumb). The latter floats freely in the air, and the violin is supported by leaning it against a door or wall.

2. While trilling the *wrist-joint* is artificially loosened by being forced to carry out very slow *vibrato movements*. (To prevent stiffening of the wrist.) Many excellent violinists are compelled to have recourse to this movement even when performing in public, in order to prevent stiffening of the wrist.* In case this measure proves to be inefficient, we must apply a somewhat stronger remedy. This consists in grafting on the trill a permanent *wrist-vibrato* movement and to produce in this way a perfect mixture of both, similar to the mechanics, which many pianists are using, while playing trills. The problem consists in dividing both movements equally without either of them dominating. The most brilliant trills are sometimes produced in this way.

3. (*a*) While the second finger is trilling, the third and fourth fingers *swing* with it; they should not spread out, however, but should hang loosely. (To prevent stiff, immovable holding up of the fingers not taking part.)

(*b*) Exercises with the *first finger*, the other fingers swinging with it:

124 

4. (*a*) In imitation of *pianistic* trill-mechanics, the raising of the lower finger when the upper finger touches the string.

(*b*) The trill on the natural *harmonics* (both prevent cramped pressure of the fingers holding the lower note):

125 

5. Exercise 121. (To prevent raising too high.)

6. Exercise 122. (Prevents insufficient raising and want of elasticity in the finger.)

These exercises (giving a week to each exercise) should be tried out in succession. That which yields the best results should be used every day and supplemented by kindred exercises until a permanent improvement of the trill has been secured.

As general study material the trill studies contained in the *Kreutzer* Etudes would first enter into consideration. Then would come the *Sevčik* Preparatory Trill Studies (see p. 116). As a daily trill exercise the quite unjustly neglected *Kreutzer* Etude No. 38 deserves a special recommendation.

125ª 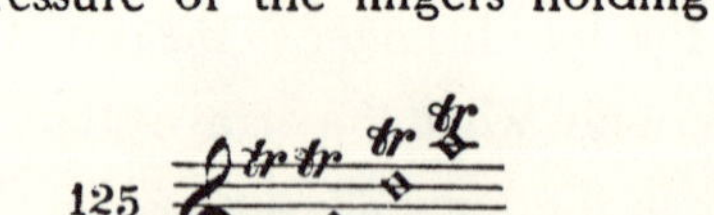

Owing to the holding down of certain fingers while trilling, this study is decidedly more taxing than its predecessors, to which it also is superior in invention.

Double-stop trills to be considered at this point are those in thirds, fingered octaves and sixths. The latter

* Leaning the wrist against the neck of the instrument may render good service under these conditions at times.

can occur at variable distances of seconds, thirds and fourths to each other:

126 

Why is it that a trill beginning unexpectedly with a maximum of rapidity awakens an uncomfortable feeling in the listener? It is difficult to find an explanation of this fact. We must content ourselves with determining that a trill which begins slowly and grows more rapid sounds better. Trills slow in themselves, in addition, will appear to be faster the more slowly they are begun and *vice versa.*

The crowding together of many trill-beats in the smallest possible space of time is known as the *inverted mordent* or short trill (brisé, Pralltriller). Aside from the hindrances already mentioned and their means of cure, which also may exert a favorable influence on the inverted mordent, the best possible *accentuation* by means of the *bow* plays a large part in its effective production. Here we have another positive fact difficult to explain, the fact that the rapidity of the trill movement during the inverted mordent is practically doubled by a sharp *bow-accentuation.* Many violinists who are able to execute a long trill only with the greatest difficulty can produce a perfect inverted mordent through this expedient.

Chains of Trills is the name given a series of interconnected trills, in most cases played without an after-beat. They are difficult and quickly tire the hand. They form good, yet not necessarily essential material for practice.

In the very high positions *thick fingers* find it impossible, especially in the case of half-tones, to produce a perfect trill. When this is the case, the player helps himself in the following manner: Forearm, wrist-joint and finger are stiffened. After the finger which is to trill has been brought to within about .039 inches from the string, the lower arm (from the elbow-joint) carries out a convulsive tremulant movement that, with every vibration of the prepared finger (which itself remains immovable) allows the latter to touch the string and, if regularly carried out, produces an extraordinarily quick, clean and well-sounding trill.*

A rarely used variant of the trill is its *combination* with the chromatic *glissando.* While the stopping finger glides, the uninterruptedly trilling finger marks the half- or quarter-tones. (*Sarasate*: Habanera.) The extremely complex question of trill afterbeats, since it is exclusively a matter of artistic form, will be discussed in the next volume of this work.

Harmonics (Natural)

12. *Harmonics.* Those notes which have been produced by *partial* vibration of the whole string are known as *natural* harmonics. When the place of the violin nut is taken by a finger firmly pressed upon the string, making it possible for us to divide the partial vibrations of the string as we please, the kind of harmonics thus produced are known as *artificial* harmonics. The *natural* harmonics are most frequently and at the same time most incorrectly used. In the days before *Sevčik* the fourth (next to the second) position was the most dreaded. They were avoided by leaving the hand in the third position and only bringing the finger into the fourth position, where it could reach the natural harmonic tone without effort or danger by stretching.

127 

At the same time not the slightest attention was paid to whether the note in question did not demand that heightened expressiveness which the natural harmonics never can supply. For their tone-color is characterized by that rigid lack of expression which the French, in the case of the singing voice, term *voix blanche* ("white voice"). It is empty, colorless and lifeless. (*Nikisch* forbade the use of harmonics and open strings in expressive passages even in *orchestral* playing.) Hence the employ of harmonics is permissible only in three instances: First, where the sense of the musical connection calls for a certain chaste reticence:

Mendelssohn, Vln. C^to^, 1º Mov't.

128 

or a playful, arabesque-like charm:

Pierné, Serenade

129 

Secondly, when the note in question is greatly exposed, in a slow tempo, and there is an especially dangerous possibility that when taken firmly it will not come out well or be missed entirely:

(Unprepared Entrance) *Smetana*, Str. Quart. 4º Mov't.

130 

* Known in German as *Bockstriller* ("Goat's-trill").

And, finally, in cases where only sureness and brilliancy and no other expression of any kind are in demand:

131 

Yet if the concluding E of Example No. 131 were to be held as a sustained note, it must be stopped firmly:

132 

One would think that the natural harmonics would hardly ever be missed on account of their larger circumference. Experience, however, proves the opposite to be the case, because the sliding finger, owing to a certain nervousness, usually does not reach the end of the distance which has to be covered.

133 
Dohnányi, Cto, 4o Mov't.

133a 
(the same)

In order to do away with this disadvantage it is sufficient to hold the harmonics a little longer while practicing them, which guarantees the reaching of the desired goal. The choice of the *B-* or *L-portamento* is also of importance, at times, in this connection. The following passage, so generally dreaded because it is so frequently and audibly missed:

134 
Wieniawski, D min. Cto, 3o Mov't.

may be more successfully played, in my experience, with a *B-portamento:*

135 

than with an *L-portamento.*

136 

The fact that a natural harmonic frequently will continue to sound even *after* the finger has already left its place, may be utilized in the following manner:

137 
Lalo, Sym. Espagnole

Here the long-sounding harmonic, A^2, allows us to make a cautious, *inaudible* portamento on the D^1.

Artificial Harmonics

Artificial Harmonics have only received their violinistic citizenship papers since *Paganini's* time, although they already were known before, and certain prominent violinists (*Lolly*) had used them. *Berlioz,* I believe, was the first who made use of them in the orchestra (*Romeo et Juliette, la fée Mab*). *Spohr* condemned them with harsh words in his violin method.

With regard to their aesthetic value it is possible to entertain different opinions; unquestionably, however, they represent an uncommonly charming component of self-sufficient violin technique, and hence should be controlled by every violinist whose skill makes any pretension to completeness. It is best to take them up when quite young, before turning to more dignified and serious tasks. At a more mature age, above all, one no longer can muster the necessary patience for work of this kind, which at the best is somewhat insipid. In Book 4 of *Sevčik's* "School of Violin Technique" exercises adequate to conquer this subject will be found. To succeed with simple and double harmonics, absolutely exact placing of the fingers with firm pressure of the upper, and a lighter one on the part of the lower finger, and rapid and pressureless bowing with the stick inclined, are necessary.

In no other branch of technique does one have to struggle harder against the malice of the object than in this. Sometimes the *vibrato* helps improve a faultily stopped harmonic, which has "not come out." The *double-harmonics* must be counted among the most unreliable customers of the fingerboard. Woe to him who relies upon them without having developed them by arduous hours of toil! He will produce a series of kaleidoscopically mixed cacophonies, inciting the risibility of the hearer to the same extent as would elementary exercises practised on a bassoon by a beginner.

Once the single or double harmonic has been taken at the right place it must be made to sound impeccably. Plenty of bow and little pressure represent the main means to this end, and in addition good, adequately rosined bow-hair is essential.

Sarasate, Zapateado

138 

Here as short as possible a stroke at the nut, pointing into the air, is in order, producing a whistle-like *staccato* effect.

Paganini, "Witches Dance"

139 

Here the descending scale should be played in the manner just described, at a *moderate tempo;* at a *rapid tempo*, however, with springing bow in the middle, and a simultaneous left-hand *glissando*. A *détaché* at the point or in the middle is out of place in such instances, since owing to the lack of pauses between the strokes the progressive movement of the left hand would become disagreeably noticeable.

zzicato ight- nd)

13. *Pizzicati.** Orchestral players, as a rule, have a better *pizzicato* than soloists. It is true that in late years composers such as *Schumann* (D Minor Sonata, 3d Movement), *Brahms* (C Minor Trio, 2d Movement), and *Debussy* (Scherzo from the String Quartet), have compelled the soloist to study the *pizzicato* more intensively; but in general it is neglected. Not only the index (or middle finger), but the right-hand thumb as well as upper arm (in the rolling movement in the shoulder-joint), are involved in the *pizzicato*. In rapid sequence the thumb leans against the edge of the fingerboard in order properly to support the index finger.

In the case of *single* tones in slow tempo the thumb, however, only supports itself against the fingerboard *before the pizzicato;* while after it has sounded the arm carries out a swinging movement like that made by a harpist. In the case of chords the thumb support appears seldom or not at all. Arm and hand carry out a far reaching movement beginning at a certain distance from the string and embracing the chords in its course. Such a movement not only produces well sounding vibrations, but also gives an impression of gracefulness. The *pizzicato* has to be carried out from left to right, and not upward from below, since here the string would touch the fingerboard, which, at once, would interrupt the vibrations; the upper arm, for its part, participates in the change of string by passing to the level of the string touched by means of a rolling movement in the shoulder-joint. With a stiff upper arm, for instance:

140 

would be difficult to execute.

Chords may be attacked with the index or the middle finger; while the index finger is better suited for single tones than is the middle finger.

The most favorable point of contact between string and finger is about 2.364 inches distant from the bridge; nearer the bridge the tone effect is too hard, and at the opposite point too weak. On occasion it is proper to carry out the *pizzicato* alternately with the index finger (*i*) and the middle finger (*m*).

141 

Pizzicato (Left-Hand)

Left-hand pizzicato has only a very limited right to existence. Above all, it is tonally not free from objection, since in most cases other notes, besides those meant to be heard, are sounded. In addition it sounds thin and ragged, since the finger in action can make no far-reaching movement. In the lower positions the string is prevented from sounding freely because it strikes the fingerboard after being plucked; while in the higher positions, excepting upon the E-string, it is quite impossible of execution.

* Although mainly produced by the fingers of the right hand, and hence belonging in the next section, (4. The Right Arm) I have included this among the "specialties" considered in this chapter.

Its study can only be expected during the boyhood years when pleasure is still derived from such flighty achievements. The fourth book of *Sevčik's* "Violin Technic" provides plentiful material of this kind together with exercises for inter-connection of simultaneously bowed notes, with all of which the youthful violinist may strain both his fingers and intelligence.

At first, until a callous has formed at the finger-tips, such exercises are very painful. The notes stopped by the fourth finger, it goes without saying, must be produced by the bow (more rarely by a right-hand *pizzicato*), and here it is of greatest importance that the latter itself produces a tone approximating a "pizzicato" tone by an elastic blow at the extreme point, while *avoiding any kind of a stroke*, so that the impression of an uninterrupted *pizzicato* is produced. When practising, the "pizzicato" movement should be carried out with great force, for in public performance the player habitually loses part of the finger power so very necessary in this technical type, owing to perspiration and nervousness, so that only weak uncertain sounds are audible. Hence the player must possess an over-abundance of finger-power, that even part of it still will suffice to develop a fair sound. As a jest I add the following combination of left- and right-hand *pizzicati*:

142 
Paganini; Caprice No 24 Var. IX
I Andante
II Presto

I. Left-hand pizzicato and bow-stroke mixed, in slow tempo.

II. After the Variation has been completed, it is repeated in *a tempo twice as fast*, in which the *right*-hand *pizzicato* is substituted for the bow.

4. The Right Arm

Right Arm

(a) Remarks in General. While fingers, hand and arm on the left side are mainly concerned in determining the tonal pitch and breathing life into the individual notes, the outstanding task of the right arm is to produce pure vibrations, as well as to determine the dynamic and agogic qualities of the notes, their *strength and duration*. Hence tone-production is essentially a result of bowing, and forms an indissoluble unit with it. Despite this fact, systematic reasons compel us to treat each subject separately. In this section the purely *mechanical* conditions under which the bow-stroke is carried out, as well as the so-called *varieties of bowing* are considered principally; while in the section following the *tonal* results of bowing, allowing for the participating left hand, will form the main subject of discussion. A sharply defined separation of both groups, incidentally, is impossible.

The terms which are used in this section are not intended to be scientifically correct but generally comprehensible. When, for instance, I speak of a vertical or horizontal movement of the wrist, the designation is incorrect from the anatomical point of view, since in the first place no joint of the body moves of its own volition, but a member of the body moves in or by means of it; and, secondly, numerous muscles and sinews of the hand, the lower and the upper arms, the shoulder and even the breast participate. Nevertheless, the term "wrist movement" is the one best calculated to give the reader an idea of the process to be described—a movement of the hand from above downward, or from left to right, or *vice-versa*, with immovable lower arm—in a way which cannot be misunderstood. A *generally comprehensible* technical idiom has the additional advantage that from the very start a portion of the student's receptiveness does not have to be devoted to the comprehension and retention of expressions hitherto unknown to him, and he is able to give his entire attention to what really matters, that is in the case of theoretical principles, content and demonstration, as well as their practical application.

The swaggering about with Latin words taken from anatomical works—something which has become customary in the case of so many publications of late years—

often merely serves very insufficiently to conceal paucity of content and inadequacy of demonstration.

The technique of *bowing* is more complex than the mechanism of the left arm, because in the case of the latter the finger is in direct contact with the string; while the right arm comes into contact with the string only through the medium of the bow-stick and bow-hair. The main task of bowing consists in making the strings vibrate regularly and uninterruptedly. (See p. 81.) To do this the bow is carried across the strings by the right arm at an angle of 90 degrees. In this process every portion of the right arm participates: that is to say, the fingers, the hand, the lower and upper arm. The *fingers* are the most important, because, as they alone touch the bow, the movements of the other parts of the arm are transferred to the bow-stick by them. Hence we first will consider the manner in which the bow should be held.

Position of Fingers

(b) How the Bow Should Be Held. We may distinguish among three methods of holding the bow:

1. *The older (German) manner.* The index finger presses upon the stick with its lower surface, on an approximate level with the knuckle *between the first and second joints;* whereby the remaining fingers are brought into the position thus determined, the thumb lying opposite the middle finger. All the fingers are pressed closely together, and the bow-hair is moderately tensed (Ill. 17 and 17a).

2. *The newer (Franco-Belgian) manner.* The index finger comes into contact with the stick *at the extreme end of its second joint,* which is hereby thrust further forward to a noticeable degree. There is an intervening space between index and middle fingers, with the thumb opposite to the middle finger; the bow-hair being at an excessive tension and the stick in an inclined position (Ill. 18 and 18a).

The newest (Russian) manner.* The index finger touches the stick at the *line separating the second from the third joint,* and in addition embraces it with its first and second joints.

There is a very small interval between the index and middle finger. *The index finger assumes the guidance of the bow,* and the little finger only touches it at its lower half while playing. The bow-hairs being slack, the stick held straight (Ill. 19 and 19a).

The Russian Way

I regard *the Russian way of holding the bow* as the most advantageous of these three types, without concealing the fact that my opinion as yet is not generally shared. In view of my experience, however, I believe that with this way of holding the bow the greatest tonal results are attainable with a minimum development of strength.

If we investigate the tone effects proper to the three types, we must first of all determine the influence of the various finger positions on the other parts of the arm and, above all, on the *lower arm.* We will consider the old school under *b-1*, the newer school under *b-2*, and the Russian school under *b-3*.

b-1. The lower arm is held horizontally, approximately as when playing the piano (Ill. 19b).

b-2. There is a slight outward turn of the lower arm in the elbow-joint (pronation), at an angle of some 25 degrees (Ill. 20).

b-3. There is a marked outward turn of some 45 degrees (Ill. 21).

What is the effect of these various positions of the lower arm upon the bowing?

b-1. Press the thumb (without the bow) strongly against the lower surface of the index finger, between the first and second joint (older school).

b-2. Laterally, against the end of the second joint (newer school).

b-3. Laterally, against the beginning of the third joint (Russian school).

When this has been done, it will be noticed that the *expenditure of force* is greatest in the first attempt, and slightest in the third. In general, too, when for instance, I wish to exert a strong pressure upon some fixed object, I shall always have a tendency to turn the lower arm in the elbow-joint as far outward as possible.

---

*I have chosen this designation for the reason that *Leopold Auer*, formerly active in Petrograd, seems to have been the first teacher who taught this manner of holding the bow. Thus far I have found it impossible to make sure whether other masters have taught according to the same principle. A tradition, however, is warrant for this statement that *Wieniawski* held his bow in this way.

Having established *by experience* that the Russian manner of holding the bow enables the most effortless manner of tone production, as well as combining with this the greatest stability on the part of the stick, I ascribe it less to the position of the index finger itself, than to the powerful outward rolling of the lower arm in the elbow-joint, whereby the pressure of the index finger on the stick takes place automatically in the most natural, that is, the most strength-saving manner. Furthermore, this position allows the first and second joints of the index finger, so to speak, to take possession of the stick, control it and compel it to do its will, instead—as in the case of the Franco-Belgian school—of dropping them as a useless appendage.

The supremacy I claim for the Russian manner of holding the bow is in no wise weakened by calling attention to the numerous outstanding violinists of other schools; the only valid standard of measurement of comparison would be that afforded by the teaching results covered by a *large* circle of variously gifted *pupils*.

With regard to the practical acquisition of the Russian manner of holding the bow, we must draw a sharp distinction between the *beginner*, who as yet knows no other manner, and the more or less advanced violinist, who is trying to exchange the bow-position hitherto used by him for the Russian, the man who is trying to "resaddle." According to my own experience and that of the teachers associated with me, the *beginner* finds the Russian position altogether unstrained and quickly accustoms himself to it. It is noticeable that using it, even at the very start, he does not "scratch"; but is able at once to produce a comparatively perfect and healthy tone. The further development of his bowing technique, with suitable instructive guidance will be entirely normal, and characterized by an astonishingly natural and gradually perfected tone.

But the process of "resaddling" is not quite so smooth a one. As a teacher I recommend the following course of procedure:

I. After an exhaustive theoretical explanation, the manner of holding the bow is changed insofar that the *index finger* rests on the stick between the third and the second joint, embracing the stick with the two remaining joints. The *thumb* rests between index and middle fingers, the bow-hair is rather slack; the *stick* held not slantingly, (edgewise) but above the bow-hair. Then I have the pupil play with the whole bow, and even let him play some *cantilena* known to him, in order first of all to accustom him to the proportions of pressure, turning and equilibrium which still are entirely new to him.

II. Hereby the following difficulties reveal themselves occasionally: In the upper half, in the *détaché*, the point of contact between bow and string shifts in an unmotivated, desultory manner—the bow "*flickers*," the wrist is *stiffened* at the *nut*, the player is hindered in every way. To do away with the upper impediment: The reason of the "flickering" in the case of the *détaché* at the point is always that either the index finger participates too slightly in the guidance of the bow, and the other fingers too much, or that the first finger touches the stick too far above its second joint. Hence the index finger must be imbued with the feeling of its unconditional necessity as a guide. For this purpose I have the pupil play détaché exercises one hour every day, three days in succession, from the middle to the point of the bow, while the *index finger* is required to guide the bow by itself with the other fingers hovering in the air. In this way an especially marked outward turn of the lower arm is brought about automatically.

If these exercises do not suffice to imbue the index finger with the feeling of its absolute leadership, mute pressure exercises (see p. 85) are also in order. To do away with stiffness at the nut, I have the pupil play numerously repeated notes *prestissimo* at the nut without pressure of the first finger.

143
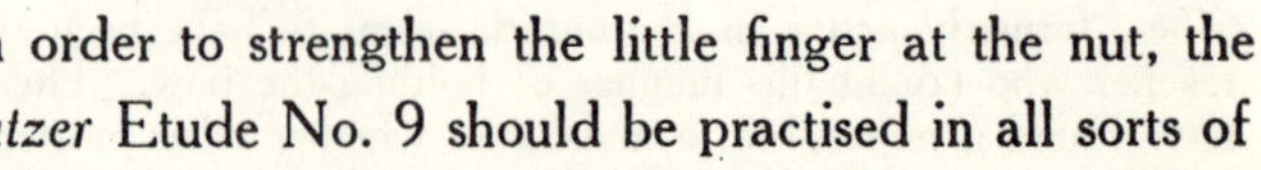

In order to strengthen the little finger at the nut, the *Kreutzer* Etude No. 9 should be practised in all sorts of variants (see p. 54). One should soon feel completely at home at the nut, even though the player accustomed to exaggerated wrist movements should erroneously feel himself hindered at the beginning. It too much weight is put at the nut by the first finger, nut-exercises with temporarily lifted first finger will be useful. The "*flickering*" at the point usually lasts longer, and is often very difficult to overcome. Here the only remedy is to practise the *détaché* with the index finger alone, in taking care not to pass over the border line between the second and the third joint, and this must be continued until the evil is obviated, which will be the case in a longer or shorter period of time.

Is the slack tension of the bow really indispensable, while playing in the Russian way? Which of the two kinds of tension is to be preferred in general?

In my opinion it seems impossible to fix an infallible rule in this regard, for the reason that here a purely individual predilection is often decisive. Personally, I leave it as a rule to the pupil himself to decide the way, which he prefers. When he has made his choice, the only thing I want him to do is to hold the bow *straight* in loose tightening and *inclined* in strong tension.

(Thumb Right)

The *thumb* calls for special consideration. It is most appropriately rested, half against the edge of the nut, half against the stick. To all appearances it lies opposite the middle finger; yet this opposition is only apparent, for if we raise the nail-joints of the first and second fingers we will find that the thumb, in reality, lies *between* them. Its task is to offer a counterpart to the pressure exerted upon the stick by the fingers; that is to say it presses upward while the fingers press downward; and the power of this upward counter pressure corresponds to that of the downward pressure. The pressure of the thumb, therefore, must accommodate itself to the pressure coming from above. In a natural, non-artificial bowing the thumb quite unconsciously assumes a slightly stretched position at the point and a slightly curved position at the nut, and passes from one to the other quite naturally during the stroke. The thumb position at a certain *distance* from the nut, or *vice versa*, in its indentation, influences bow technique in an unfavorable manner, as has been proven by experience. In the first instance the thumb has no hold, and the tone is quantitatively insufficient; in the second the bowing is clumsy and the tone produced, crude.

This brings us to *distribution of weight* of the bow. It is extremely unequal. Let us confine ourselves, experimentally, to holding the bow loosely in the fingers, without in any way influencing it by pressure. If we do this we shall find that when resting on the string it is too *heavy* at the *nut*, i.e., prevents the string vibrations, and too *light* at the *point*, i.e., unable to set the strings vibrating; and that only in the middle will it produce tone through its own weight. Hence, the bow must be pressed down upon the strings at the *point*, and at the *nut* it must be slightly raised. The pressure at the point is produced by the *index finger*, the raising of the entire bow at the nut by the *little finger*. The first is paired with pronation (turning outward), the second with supination (inward turning); yet by no means to the degree accepted as correct by *Steinhausen*.* I even claim that during the finger pressure we must carry out the rolling of the lower arm quite *subconsciously*. *Steinhausen's* theory of the necessity of a *conscious* supination at the nut is quite untenable, and can only be explained as the result of inadequate practical experience. But on the other hand it is certainly just as bad to maintain supination at the point as to carry on pronation at the frog. In the latter case the fourth finger does not touch the stick at the frog—a serious warning-signal for the teacher. It is a deficiency, which in the long run and at an advanced age may prove fatal for the bowing technique as a whole.

1st and 4th Fingers

It is the index finger, therefore, which in the main acts in a *tone-producing* way, and the little finger in a *tone-preventing* manner. The pressure of the *index finger* according to the kind of finger position, occurs at various points, as already has been described above (see p. 51). The habit common to many violinists, of *stretching* the *index finger* when playing at the nut, is very injurious in my opinion, because in that case this finger voluntarily abandons its leadership while remaining at the lower half of the bow, and the control of the tone production is left to the other fingers, the tone growing noticeably less expressive toward the nut. The index finger should never give up its right to lead, but toward the nut, should allow its influence to be neutralized, so to speak, by the pressure of the little finger.

---

* *Steinhausen*, "Physiology of Bowing on the String Instruments," 1903.

The most important prerequisite for a suitable use of the *little finger* is contact with the stick by means of its *extreme* end (Ill. 22). When it is applied flatly, its ability to move is eliminated from the start, and the finger-stroke (see p. 58) cannot possibly be carried out (Ill. 23). The old school was accustomed to keep it on the bow during the *entire* stroke, on account of the position of the first finger and insufficient pronation at the point, the newer raises it at the point, while the Russian school, in consequence of the powerful turning of the lower arm, only allows it to touch the stick in the direction of the nut. Indispensable as is the activity of the little finger at the nut, it is just as unnecessary and injurious when playing at the *point* and holding the bow in the modern way; because here it weakens the very necessary pressure of the index finger. Only when it is also a question of *raising* the bow at the point, that is to say in the case of "thrown" strokes, or in purposely expressionless accompanied figures, such as so often occur in chamber music, is its participation at the upper half of the bow useful and even necessary. The continuous employ of the little finger by the older school is explained by its manner of holding the bow. The majority of contemporary violinists, however, already have turned their backs upon it, so that it has been regarded as overcome, and before long merely will possess an historical value. The newer Franco-Belgian, as well as the Russian manner of holding the bow already control the field absolutely and incontestably, and it is between them that the battle for supremacy will henceforward have to be waged.

The *third or ring finger* plays a subordinate part, and is passive rather than active. The index finger supplies the pressure, the little finger, supported by its neighbor, the ring finger, attends to the raising.

Middle Finger

The part of the middle finger requires a more detailed explanation.

Jean Pierre *Maurin* (1822-1894) pupil of Baillot and Habeneck, was a teacher at the Paris Conservatory, who adhered to the rather queer principle, that the secret of a perfect bowing-technic lay in the leadership of a kind of ring formed by the middle finger and the thumb, around which the first and the fourth finger became active each in its turn at the point and frog, assisted by adequate pronation and supination. This seductive theory was adopted by Maurin's best pupil, Lucien *Capet* (1873-1924), who used it as the leading principle in his "Art of Bowing." I consider it as erroneous and misleading, if it were only for the reason that even in daily life we do not grasp or handle any object with our middle finger, except when we do not want to soil our hands. But there are still many other considerations from a purely violinistic point of view which prove this assertion to be a mistake: in the first place the necessary leadership of the first finger in bowing and the ineffectiveness of a pressure on the bow by the middle finger. The partisans of this principle are easily found out by the thin quality of their tone as well as by its lack of efficient possibilities of shading. The popularity of this theory during a certain period may be held responsible for a temporary decline of the French school of violin playing since the beginning of this century.

The exact moment of activity on the part of all the fingers, and especially on that of the index finger, is revealed by the fact that the sources of their strength dwell not in themselves, but in the part of the arm situated higher up, in the lower arm, upper arm and muscles of the back. The transfer of strength occurs most naturally when the elbow part lies *above* rather than *below* the level of the fingers. Stiff and independent pressure of the fingers is absolutely wrong.

Bowing

(c) Bowing. The bow-stroke is produced as the result of the following movements of the individual parts of the right arm:*

1. A vertical movement of the upper arm in the shoulder-joint.
2. A horizontal movement of the upper arm in the shoulder-joint.
3. A rolling movement of the lower arm in the elbow-joint.
4. A horizontal movement of the lower arm in the elbow-joint.
5. Wrist movement.
6. Finger-stroke.

Steinhausen was the first theoretician who recognized that the sources of strength were situated in the upper and lower arm, and who assigned a merely mediatory role to the hitherto immoderately over-estimated wrist and to the fingers. His opinion has proven to be the right one, not alone because of its compelling logic, but above all, owing to its confirmation by actual experiment.

---

*Flesch, "Urstudien." (Basic Studies.)

1. *The Vertical Movement of the Upper Arm in the Shoulder Joint* makes its appearance principally during the change of string at the upper half of the bow.

144 

As a rule the upper arm should be on the plane of that string which the bow happens to touch at the moment. The old school preached the low-held upper arm, and even pressure of the upper arm against the body (Ills. 24 and 25). It would be carrying coals to Newcastle to explain either of the two illustrations just given. We will content ourselves with mentioning that the voluntary raising of the *lower* arm which must take place in consequence of holding the *upper* arm low while playing on the G- and D-strings, and whose line then approaches the vertical, is destructive under any circumstances, since in no matter what connection, any effective pressure of the hand when the upper arm is held too low is possible. (A person in the habit of using his hand in this way, or merely shaking hands, with the upper arm pressed to the body, would impress one as being a moron). Only in case a very *rapid* change of string at the *point* is desirable should a movement of the *wrist* be substituted for the movement of the shoulder-joint, which at a certain speed appears too clumsy (see p. 56). The opposite counterpart is the upper arm held too high, marked by an elbow sticking out sharply in the air (Ill. 26). This position, it is true, is ungraceful and impracticable, yet not injurious to tone production, if only the upper arm may move freely in the shoulder-joint; it then might be said to function from an artificially elevated point. Experience teaches that such violinists at times may even possess extraordinary tonal qualities (*Thibaud*). Hence when it seems impossible for a pupil to play with his upper arm in a normal position, the teacher must resign himself to this, on condition that with every change of string at the point, the upper arm also carries out the corresponding movement. At all events the exaggerated *high* position of the upper arm with simultaneous regular functioning of the shoulder-joint has never prevented anyone from becoming a great violinist—provided that he possessed the other qualities needed.

The following exercise compels the raising and dropping of the upper arm in the shoulder-joint. (It is exceedingly beneficial for violinists who have been playing with too low an upper arm.)

145. 

This exercise should be carried out at the extreme point, almost without drawing the bow. The bow remains almost on the same spot, the entire arm is stiffened, and turns in the shoulder-joint. Furthermore:

146. 

A *pause* is made after every note, during which the upper arm, with stiff lower arm and stiff wrist, carries out the change of string through the shoulder-joint alone. (*Marsick*).

2. *Horizontal Movement of the Upper Arm in the Shoulder-Joint.* By means of this movement the bowstroke is produced at the lower third of the bow. Here the two contrary tendencies of the high or low position of the upper arm conflict sharply. The *détaché* at the lower third of the bow also calls for participation of the shoulder-joint in a vertical direction, up to a certain point. Two illustrations will make the difference between the two ways plainly evident (Ills. 27 and 28), the *rectangular* and the *straight*, both conditioned by the lower or higher position of the upper arm. I must confess myself an uncompromising adherent of the latter mode, the only one securing the free development of the entire strength of the arm, something demonstrable in the most unmistakable manner by comparison of the tonal results of both categories in public performance. Here, too, everything formerly was tried in order to substitute for this movement another, produced by the lower arm and an immoderately *advanced* hand, at a right angle to it. It seems as though in the eighteenth century some evil sorcerer had banned the upper arm with a curse destined to endure until the seventh generation: "Thou shalt not function!"

Only in case of a very *rapid détaché* at the nut is the movement just discussed (because of its too troublesome execution) to be supplanted by a wrist movement.

3. *The Rolling Movement of the Lower Arm in the Elbow-Joint.* Since with the change of string at the *nut* the lifting movement of the upper arm in the shoulder-joint, especially at a rapid tempo, seems awkward, a *rolling movement of the lower* arm in the elbow-joint is substituted for it, resembling that made when someone opens a locked door with a key. The upper arm, meanwhile, does not remain entirely passive, but accompanies the movement with a tiny roll in the shoulder-joint.

We now understand that the slow change of string is carried out partly by the upper arm (at the point), partly by the lower arm at the nut and, furthermore, that the two movements meet in the middle of the bow, and melt into one another. Frequently and very incorrectly, since both are anatomically quite different actions, the rolling movement of the lower arm is confused with the wrist movement. The exercise:

147. 

can be produced at the nut only by means of rolling movements of the lower arm. And the contrary,

148. 

is possible only with shoulder or wrist. A combination of both types of bowing:

149. 

does not as yet signify that both movements are merged; but merely a frictionless passing from one to the other, from the loose wrist movement at the point to the rolling elbow movement with strong finger pressure, at the nut. *Kreutzer's* Etude No. 9 supplies an ideal exercise, when studied in diverse variants, for securing a perfected technique of string change at the nut.

4. *Horizontal Movement of the Lower Arm in the Elbow-Joint.* This movement corresponds to the generally used *détaché* from middle to point. The hand should not form a right-angle to the lower arm in the middle, but a straight line with it; while the wrist at the point should not lie lower than the hand itself. If the détaché is to be played very *rapidly*, the movement of the *wrist* is substituted entirely or in part for the vertical lower arm movement.

5. *The Wrist and Its Functions.* The wrist movements should be employed only in the following cases:

(*a*) As a substitute for the vertical *upper arm movement* at the nut (*détaché*) when it appears to be too clumsy in a rapid tempo.

(*b*) For the same reasons, as a substitute for the horizontal *lower arm movement* (short quick *détaché*, between point and middle, springing bow and *tremolo*).

(*c*) As a substitute for the *vertical movement* of the *upper arm* in rapid change of string at the upper half.

(*d*) In *change of bow*, especially at the nut. The points a, b, c, call for no further elucidation. Before we pass to a consideration of *change of bow*, however, I must make clear the *horizontal* wrist movement. This is best explained by laying the palm of the hand on the table and—with stiff lower arm—moving it from right to left and *vice versa*. Nature has not intended any voluntary employ of such a movement or she would have provided the *hand* with a socket as it did for the elbow- or shoulder-joint. The movement is one of which we make no use in life. Even in writing the hand only moves *seemingly* in a horizontal, but in reality in a vertical direction. How is it, nevertheless, that in spite of this up to recent times, especially in the case of the older German school, it was used in quick, small *détaché* as well as for change of bow, to the entire neglect of the vertical movement? The key to the solution of the problem must be sought in the finger and arm position of this school. Compare the three manners of holding the bow described on p. 51, and at the same time try to produce with each type an extremely rapid, small *détaché*, respectively a springing stroke with the wrist.

We will find that first of all, with the old manner of holding the bow, the attempt at a downward movement from above will fail, because in this position the raising and lowering of the hand is able to produce a *change of string*, it is true, but not a horizontal bow-stroke on one and the same string. And such a stroke is then alone possible in consequence of a forced, artificial *horizontal* movement of the wrist. Secondly, it is evident that when holding the bow in the manner of the Russian school, *as a result of the outward turning of the lower arm*, the intended horizontal stroke may be produced by an originally vertical movement in an entirely natural and effortless way.

The main value of the two newer types of lower arm position lies in the very circumstance that owing to the outward swinging of the lower arm, they permit of a natural functioning of the wrist in a *vertical* direction on the same string. Fortunately, since in the past few years the young generation has turned away from the old manner of holding the bow, the *horizontal* wrist movement may also be expected finally to disappear with it from the scene of action, and together with the upper arm pressed close to the body, soon astonish as a survival of a vanished age. One never should forget that wrist movements in *every* form have the right to appear only in the case of a *rapid tempo*, as a substitute for the much clumsier elbow- and shoulder-joint movements. The cultivation of the wrist movement as a fad, or its elevation to the highest factor in bow technique, according to the teachings of the older generations, must be declared a fatal error.

In the case of the *vertical* wrist movement the damage done is confined principally to loss of time. Woe to the pupils, however, who are forced to over-train the *horizontal* wrist movement! At least three-fourths of all arm troubles may be traced back to this cause, and many a promising career has been ruined thereby.

6. The *Fingerstroke* will be considered in connection with change of bow. (See p. 58.)

In bowing, furthermore, the *direction of the stroke* must be considered. It is clear that the bow when moved should remain parallel to the bridge along its entire length, and must cut the string at a right angle. For in this way only will regular vibrations, free from accompanying noises, be produced. Deviating from this rule we find that the bow is at times drawn:

1. At the nut, in the direction toward the face.
2. At the nut, in the direction toward the fingerboard.
3. At the point, away from the body.
4. At the point, toward the body.
5. Alternately toward the body and away from it (in the form of horizontal waves).

1. This is mechanically wrong, since the hand is brought into rectangular relation with the lower arm, whereby the latter automatically lowers itself.

2. Acoustically wrong; as the right angle between bow and string is missing, the latter no longer vibrates freely.

3. Acoustically dubious, since the bow is automatically crowded toward the bridge, resulting in a pressed and, in the *piano*, an inappropriate tone color at the point.

4. Entirely wrong, since the bow slides off upon the fingerboard, whereby the tone breaks in case the pressure is unrelieved, or, if not, the bad habit of a constant > in ⊓ is taken.

5. Erroneous, since the rectangular line needed for purity of vibration is permanently broken. (This manner is mainly employed by violinists who are afflicted with nervous tremors, and endeavor to do away with the trouble in this way.)

Correction. All five types may be improved by means of *beneficial exaggeration.* By this term I mean the temporary supplanting of an erroneous movement by one quite as incorrect, but its opposite. Accordingly, 1 is improved by means of 2; 3 by means of 4 and *vice-versa.* The horizontal, wave-like movement (at times involuntarily), should be used only as a preventive measure against trembling of the bow, and will disappear of its own accord when its cause has been removed. (See p. 88.)

The position of the bow-stick in its relation to the bow-hair may assume any one of three positions: *straight*, inclined toward the *fingerboard*, or inclined toward the *bridge*.

In the straight position of the stick the entire breadth of the bow-hair is applied to make the string vibrate, while in the *inclined* position only part of the hair touches the string. The *Franco-Belgian* manner of holding the bow conditions the position inclining toward the fingerboard (edgewise), with the hair tensely strung; that of the *Russian school* in the *forte*, the straight, weakly strung bow. *Inclined to the bridge* the stick is used only exceptionally, in the case of certain springing strokes in the middle, as well as during the down-bow *staccato*.

The close connection between the *position of the stick*, *tension of the hair*, and the *bow pressure* may be noted in the fact that slack tension makes bow pressure in an oblique position out of the question, since otherwise the wood would touch the string in a *forte*, and produce a disagreeable accompanying noise; while strong tension the straight position brings with it the danger of too strong a bow pressure in consequence of insufficient possibilities of controlling the elasticity of the stick. On the other hand, the edgewise holding of the bow-stick in the *piano*, even with the weakly tensed bow of the Russian school (as already mentioned on p. 53) is an absolute necessity, because string contact with a lesser number of hairs in itself produces a weaker tone.

Change of Bow

(d) Change of Bow. As an introduction to the theory of change of bow, we must discuss the manner in which the *hand is held* and the *finger-stroke*. The hand may be held at the nut in three ways. We distinguish:

1. The rectangular position of the hand (Ill. 27).
2. The sloping position of the hand (Ill. 29).
3. Straight-line position of the hand (Ill. 28).

1. The *rectangular* position of the hand should be repudiated, since this curvature represents a forced position, automatically causes the lower arm to drop and because the hand loses at least half its freedom of movement in the wrist-joint.

2. The *sloping* position should be repudiated because the index finger absolutely loses its influence on the stick, the latter resting mainly *upon* the fingers (instead of the opposite being the case), and the production of tone is reduced to the low level of a colorless *piano*.

3. The *straight-line* position of the hand is the only right one, because the index finger is invariably able to make felt its influence on the stick, while the hand possesses the greatest possible radius of movement in the wrist-joint. (See also p. 55.)

In the *middle* and at the *point* there are also three different positions of the hand.

1. With the wrist *rounded* upwards and the hand hanging down (Ill. 30).
2. With the wrist *dropping* downward and the hand raised (Ill. 31).
3. With hand and lower arm in a *straight* line (Ill. 32).

1. This is wrong, because the pressure of the index finger no longer can be exerted in a vertical but only in an oblique direction against the bridge, which has an unfavorable effect on tone production.

2. This is wrong because the index finger has to produce the necessary pressure by itself, without being supported by the lower and the upper arm, and therefore grows cramped and stiff.

3. This is correct because the evils instanced in the case of 1 and 2 are avoided.

Finger-stroke

The *Finger-Stroke*. It is difficult to determine when the necessity of also making the finger-joints flexible first began to be recognized; at all events, like so many excellent things, this innovation came from Belgium.*

Even though the use of the wrist may be conceded, to some extent, only as an occasional substitute for elbow- and shoulder-joint, the finger-stroke, on the other hand, should never be independently used, since it hardly contributes in any way towards tone production.**

Its importance, above all, rests upon its connection with the vertical wrist movement, whereby *a most unobtrusive change of bow* is secured. These finger-joint exercises, the importance of which I cannot stress enough, are easy to learn even at a more advanced age, when one realizes that in the case of this movement it is a question of stretching (Ill. 33) and curving (Ill. 34) the five fingers, which should produce a small *martelé* stroke without aid of the wrist.

---

* The author was initiated into the mysteries of the finger-stroke during his student years at the Paris Conservatoire, in 1892, by a Dutch violinist.

** For the sake of completeness a habit common to many violinists of the German school, that of carrying out independent finger movements while playing a whole bow at the point, should be mentioned. The effect of this entirely purposeless, senseless and energy-consuming distortion of the fingers on tone and bowing technique is fatal.

The pupil must first of all be able to carry out these exercises perfectly without the bow; then take up the following five exercises (a new one each succeeding day). 1. Stretching and curving the fingers with the bow in hand, the bow being held horizontally, yet with the hair turned *upward*, so that the stick rests on the second or third joint of the index finger; 2. the same exercise, with the bow held *vertically*.

3. The same exercise with a *horizontal* bow, the hair turned downward. The purpose of this gradation is gradually to accustom the little finger to the difficult role assigned it in these movements. During the first week it always will glide from the stick; yet the student must not grow discouraged, since the muscles grow so strong in a comparatively short space of time that the evil mentioned disappears by itself. It goes without saying that the little finger must rest on the bow with its *extreme* end, since otherwise it will have no freedom of movement on the bow-stick.

4. Finger-stroke, *martelé*, on the open string in the middle of the bow.

5. Finger-stroke, *martelé*, on the open string at the nut.

Not until the violinist is able to produce a tonally beautiful finger-stroke at the nut without aid of the wrist may he lay claim to the possession of flexible finger-joints, and will be capable of a perfect, inaudible *change of bow*.

All, from the beginner to the finished artist, admit that before a new stroke is begun a peculiar process takes place in the change of bow, the bow-stroke just ending being prolonged a very little bit, before the arm commences the new stroke. It seems as though there exists some physical necessity which prevents us from changing the bow-stroke before we have added a small portion to the one coming to an end. The law underlying this procedure is the following one: A body moving in a certain given direction has a tendency to continue in it even when compelled to interrupt the motion or to continue it in another direction. In a moving trolley-car a person standing maintains his equilibrium as long as the car is in motion, yet bends forward when it stops. When the car once more begins to move, the passenger who is standing inclines backward, that is to say, invariably in the direction which has just been left. It is impossible for a runner to come to an immediate stop when called upon to halt, he is obliged to take a few more forward steps. The arm moving downward or upward is subject to the same law. In our considerations we will term this movement the *stroke-continuation*.

Stroke-continuation

The difficulties involved in change of bow present themselves principally at the *nut*, since at this point the dead weight of the bow is so great that, if not diminished by lifting, the pressure exerted by the stick annuls the vibrations of the string and produces the variety of secondary sounds generally summed up in the term "scratching." To prevent this remains the chief problem (one seldom solved) of nut technique.

The task is one which, naturally, is made decidedly more difficult by reason of the technical problems which the change of bow in itself develops. At the point or in the middle, it is true, the same necessity of stroke-continuation exists, yet its disturbing influence at these points is greatly diminished in consequence of the far slighter dead weight of the bow. As a matter of fact, for a hundred violinists with faulty change of bow at the nut, hardly one with the same defect at the point will be found. Hence we will concern ourselves with this procedure in its most important connection, its relation to the nut.

The fact that even the beginner produces the stroke-continuation, for all he does so with a violent slinging-like movement of the upper arm and a noticeable jerk, may be regarded, perhaps, as evidence that it was also done in the old days, when the art of violin-playing was still in its infancy. For just as the development of the human embryo symbolizes the gradations which the lower species of animal life traversed in the course of their evolution into higher forms, so, from the stages of development of the individual violin-player, we may deduce those of the entire species.

Thus the beginner produces the stroke-continuation by prolonging the bow-stroke through a horizontal movement of the *upper arm* in the shoulder-joint, with the result that, at the end of the stroke, a jerking accent which anyone who has ever had anything to do with beginners will remember, is developed. One cannot be mistaken in taking for granted that in the initial stages of violin-playing this species of bow-change was generally prevalent, unless the violinist preferred to make no use at all of the lower third of his bow, a supposition which is very probable. (At the end of the nineteenth century, old violinists still were to be found in Paris who made no use of the nut section as a matter of principle. In 1890 I saw with my own eyes old *Dancla* accompany the Paganini Concerto on his violin by holding his bow three inches above the nut! In old prints, too, we never see violinists playing at the nut.) Great individual talents may have regarded the periodically returning jerk preventing every attempt for a smooth and even *Cantilena*, and abandoning shading to chance, as so annoying that they asked themselves whether this movement could not, perhaps, be carried out by *part* of the arm instead of by the whole arm. The lower arm did not enter into consideration, since it was not employed at the nut in a horizontal direction. There remained, first of all, the *wrist*. Here we have the origin of the wrist movement in its relation to the change of string. We see that here, too, it may be regarded only as a necessary *substitute* for another, too clumsy movement. At this stage, therefore, the stroke-continuation was achieved by a slight pushing forward of the hand in the wrist-joint, with the legitimate object of carrying out the change of bow in the least noticeable and audible fashion. Yet soon, in this field also, the object and its means of attainment were confused. The development of as flexible as possible a wrist-joint (without regard for the joints of the individual fingers) was regarded as the main object; the actual end in view, however, the *inaudibility* of the stroke-continuation, was neglected. The tonally inadequate results secured by this procedure, as well as the constantly increasing hand evils appearing in its train, gave rise to the question whether it would not be possible, at least, to substitute for the movements of the wrist a still smaller, inconspicuous partial movement of the fingers. This was the origin of the idea of the *finger-stroke*. Towards the end of the nineteenth century many violinists used this movement for the production of the stroke-continuation *exclusively*. Yet they, too, suffered shipwreck, for the final object: the entire inaudibility of the change of bowing. Yet, but a *single* forward step lay between this and the solution of the problem. Soon not alone one but many at one and the same time—(for the truth, so to speak, was floating in the air)—recognized that a *combined movement of wrist-joint and fingers* was the *only* one capable of producing an absolutely frictionless, inaudible stroke-continuation. The practical results obtained by this method prove that the problem of change of bow may be regarded as having been solved once and for all, and that to-day it is possible for every violinist to carry out the change of bow without any accompanying noises if he possesses the technique of a correct *vertical* wrist and finger movement, and is able to merge the two into a unified whole. *The most practical kind of bow change at the nut, therefore, consists in producing the stroke-continuation by means of a combined movement of the wrist and fingers.* In order to attain this end, the following procedure should be observed:

1. *Mastering the finger-stroke* (without participation of the wrist-joint). (See p. 58.)

2. *Wrist-joint exercises* in the form of very rapid repeated notes at the nut, without participation of the upper arm (if the fingers have been rendered flexible by means of the preceding exercise, they will begin to take part automatically in the wrist movement) should be practiced:

150. 

3. Slow *détaché* exercises at the nut. The eye should test the movement, the ear the effect; the change of bow should gradually become inaudible.

Hence the *faulty kinds of change of bow* which actually occur may be summed up as follows: *Fault Chan of Bo*

1. Change of bow by means of the *upper arm* (it occurs only in the case of beginners, or in that of violinists of the earliest elementary grade).

2. *Horizontal* movement of the wrist-joint.

Correction: Change of finger position by means of a slight outward turning of the lower arm (Franco-Belgian or Russian school), and acquisition of the finger-stroke as well as of the vertical wrist-joint movement on one and the same string. The combination of both.

3. *Vertical* wrist movement with stiff fingers.

Correction: Learning the finger-stroke, and merging both movements.

4. Correct, yet too far-reaching movements of the wrist (slinging).

Correction: A détaché at the outer extreme of the nut, with an entirely *stiff* wrist, and also *Kreutzer's* Etude No. 9, at the nut, in rapid tempo.

5. Through means of exclusive finger-stroke.

Correction: Amalgamation of the finger stroke and the vertical movement of the wrist-joint.

The fact that before all, the least audible stroke-continuation must be secured cannot be sufficiently stressed. For this purpose the necessary movement should be as slight and inconspicuous as possible. An over-extended flinging about of the hand or finger is the very thing producing that jerk which is to be avoided at all costs. *Good change of bow is inaudible and well-nigh invisible.*

(e) Change of String (to the right.) (See also p. 25 regarding *Change of String by Means of the Left Hand.*) The transition from one string to the other by means of the right arm takes place in the following manner:

1. *In slow tempo* between middle and point, by rolling the upper arm in the shoulder-joint; from the middle to the nut by combination of the same movement with a rolling of the lower arm in the elbow-joint. The upper arm should be adapted to the position of the two lower strings, since, contrariwise, the wrist will lie higher than the lower arm.

2. *In rapid tempo* at the upper half, by means of a vertical movement of the wrist; toward the nut by means of a clean-cut rolling of the lower arm in the elbow-joint.

It is incorrect to carry out the *slow* change of string with the wrist, because in this case the wrist comes to lie either higher or lower than the fingers, whereby the principle—so important for tone-production—of the straightness which should be developed by hand and lower arm would be impaired.

The *tempo* prescribed, therefore, is the determinant factor for the correct execution of change of string.

In a markedly rapid or slow tempo, therefore, the manner of execution may be fixed beyond a doubt, but not in such cases as:

Kreutzer, Etude Nº 26

151.

where a *rapid tempo* is combined with a comparatively *slow* change of string. Here the three movements (of the upper arm, lower arm and wrist) which enter into consideration, interact to such a degree that the transition from one to another is no longer distinguishable. However, should the mechanical factors, as a consequence of too great complexity of procedure, escape our observation, it is the tonal result which remains decisive. When the change of string *sounds* uneven, unequal and falsely accented, although to all appearances carried out correctly from the mechanical standpoint, we may, guided by our sense of tone, subconsciously transform the faulty movements into well-sounding, i.e., correctly executed ones. Yet before we have recourse in this case, to this empiric method, and abandon our principle of considering first of all the cause and not the result, we must make sure that not alone the movement itself but the manner of execution is correct. Example 151, for instance, may be carried out in two ways. Either the bow measures the distance between the A- and D-strings as narrowly as possible, corresponding approximately to the following graphic line:

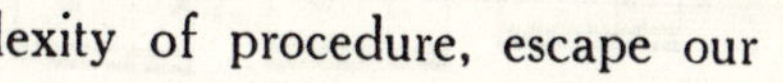

or so broadly that it approaches the G- and E-strings, which would look approximately as follows:

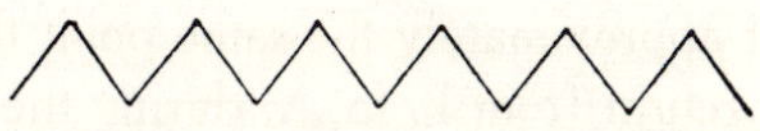

The *difference* between the distances which the bow and arm have to cover in the two instances is very great. It is evident that the angular manner is the wrong, and the wavy, the practical one.

In every change of string, whether in rapid or slow tempo, one should try, no matter at which point of the bow it may be, to avoid movements unnecessarily broad, and carry out the necessary turns so that they are hardly visible. In Example 151, try to let the bow move in a well-nigh straight line. Preliminary exercise:

Kreutzer, Etude No. 26

152. 

In the case of regular, unaltered change of string, in the *détaché*, as in:

Bach, E-major Partita

153. 

Sonata #6

or

Viotti, 22º Cto, 1º Mov't.

154. 

the *détaché* movement (horizontal lower arm movement in the elbow-joint) must be reduced so much that in Example 153 the bowing seems to be produced entirely by a rolling movement of the upper arm in the shoulder-joint, with all other parts of the arm remaining immobile while in Example 154 a slight vertical wrist-movement is added. Both strokes have to be played at the middle instead of the point, where the change of string requires a much larger radius.

Vertical movement of upper arm p 55

but at middle

Change of String in ⊓ and V

The relations between the *change of string* on the one hand and, on the other, the *up-bow* (V) and the *down-bow* (⊓) are among the technical problems treated in the most careless fashion. The following explanations may serve to cast a clearer light on their mechanical interconnection:

155. 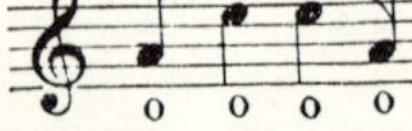

If we look carefully at this example we shall find that the bow during the ⊓ touches the E-string about half an inch lower. Hence, with a slight expenditure of bow it touches E at approximately the same point that it did the A. On the return from E to A, during the V , the bow once more touches the A-string half an inch higher (see p. 13). In both cases, therefore, a *gain of space* must be recorded.

156. 

In the V , on the other hand, it *loses* half an inch each time, and a *loss of space* takes place.

157. 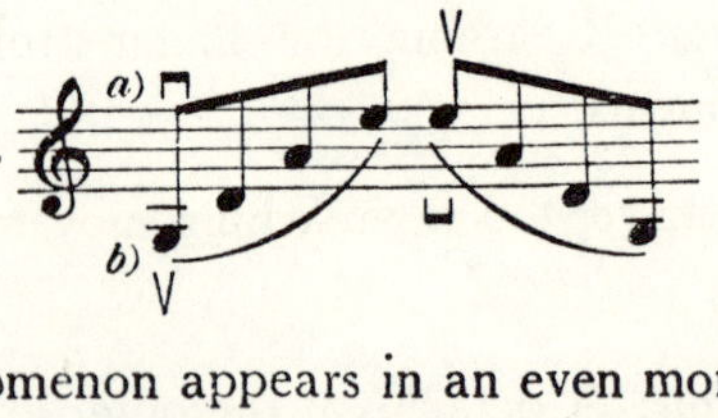

Here this phenomenon appears in an even more emphatic manner: in *a* we have a *gain* of space, in *b* a *loss* of space amounting to approximately 1½ inches. Hence the change of string should be carried out, as far as possible, with an ⊓ in the *ascending* line, and with a V in the *descending* one. When both directions change in a single bow-stroke, the majority determine its rising or falling character, and in consequence the direction of the stroke.

The problem differs when the most rapid expenditure is prescribed, as in quick, brilliant passages:

158. 

Rode Concerto #7 p4

Here the ⊓ would make too clumsy an impression, apart from the fact that even in this typical violin passage the involuntary *crescendo* which accompanies it peremptorily calls for the V .

The change of string appears in the most perfected manner in *arpeggiated chords*:

159. 

It is possible to distinguish seven types of this family: those detached, springing or thrown on separate strokes; the tied, the mixed strokes, and those springing or thrown on a *single* bowing. The last are considered on p. 79, whereas we will here consider the peculiarities of the other types, since they fall into the category of changes of string rather than of varieties of stroke.

N1404

if bow is moved only vertically & not horizontally

Arpeggios (broken chords)

Sevcik, Violin, Pt 1, 29
Bow, " , 28
Violin " 3, p6-16 (Flesch I, 44 "best")
Bow " 2, pp 27-29
Violin " 2, p10-11; 40-41

What distinguishes the execution of arpeggios in general from bowings with only incidental change of string is the coincidence of the horizontal movement of the lower arm with the lifting or raising movement of the upper arm, as well as the steadiness and regularity of the latter movement. Experience has taught us that the following rules apply in the proper performance of every kind of arpeggio:

1. The use of a minimum of bow.

2. Seeing to it that the lifting movement takes place as regularly as possible without interruption.

3. Seeing to it that in detached arpeggios the movements of the lower and upper arm coincide exactly.

4. In legato, choosing the ⊓ for ascending arpeggios; and the V when the arpeggios descend, with the proviso that a rapid tempo and a resultant more rapid arm movement are desired.

However, if the arpeggios are to produce more of a singing effect, while being executed in a more moderate tempo, as in:

160. 
Moderato
Dohnányi. Vln. Cto, 1º Mov't.

then the opposite type of bowing, in consequence of the greatly prolonged bow-stroke, is indicated.

The combination of different bowings with *arpeggios*, in my opinion, supplies the best material for right arm practice. Owing to the seemingly endless number of their variants, they offer us an inexhaustible source of bow-technique problems, whose conquest should be difficult enough to satisfy even the "finished" violinist. (See *Sevčik*, "School of Bow Technique," Books V and VI.)

For the sake of completeness we must also consider a type of bow-stroke closely connected with the technique of double-stopping and change of string; one which might be called *intermittent change of string*.

161. 
Bach, Partita in A-min. 3º Mov't.

The movement of the bow should be as wavy as possible, not angular. By means of this type of stroke the phrases of the theme and the rhythmical groups of the accompaniment are synchronized, making an uncommonly charming effect.

Division of Bow

(f) The Division of the Bow. Before we pass on to the different kinds of bowing we must take up more intensively the question of the sectional division of the bow in actual playing.

The classic division is as follows: point, middle, nut. Actually, however, we differentiate eight different sections of the bow, as follows: the extreme point, the middle, the extreme nut; the greater point, the greater middle, the greater nut; from the middle to the point, from the middle to the nut. When considering these separate divisions we must, above all, draw a sharp line of partition between their use for study and for purely artistic purposes. The well-known violin passage in *Brahms*' Piano Quartet, for instance:

162. 
Brahms, Piano Quart. Op. 25. 1º Mov't.

when played at the *nut*, represents an *exercise* which, although very difficult, is admirably calculated to improve the nut technique. If thus played, however, in performance, it would not only sound far less beautiful, even were the player's technique perfect, than when played at the point; but above all it would mean an unnecessary strain without tonal benefit. In principle, *every* kind of bow-stroke is practicable at *every* part of the bow; in practice, however, there is but a *single*, narrowly circumscribed division of the bow within the limits of which each bow-stroke appears natural. Hence, when in the following consideration we assign an appropriate bow-stroke to each individual part of the bow, our choice has been made with regard to the greatest technical ease and the best tonal result. The following is a grouping of the various parts of the bow, and the bowings best suited to them:

1. *At the Extreme Point*: Rapid *tremolo*, small *martelé*:

2. *At the Middle*: All springing or thrown types of bowing:

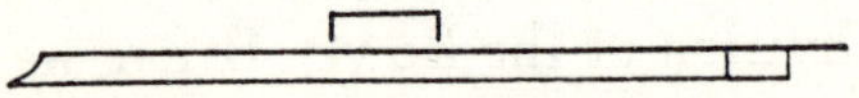

3. *At the Extreme Nut*: Rapid détaché on the G-string; a "standing" *staccato* (see p. 78):

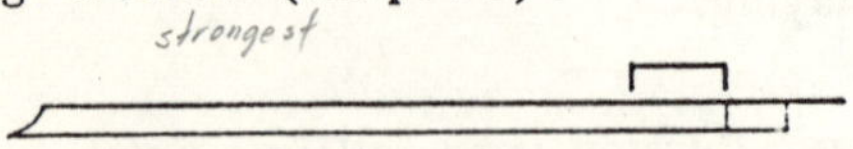

4. *The Greater Point*: All types of bowing combined with *détaché* and *martelé*, *martelé staccato*, and quick change of string:

5. *Greater Middle*: Flying *staccato*, change of string in the *détaché* with intermediate unused strings:

6. *Greater Nut*: Slow *détaché* on the G-string. Double stops in the *détaché*, with or without breaks. The *détaché or the* bowing types combined with it, which in view of the phrasing or the division of the bow cannot be executed at the upper third. Short notes, separated from each other by raising of the bow, short chords:

7. *Upper Half*: Broad *détaché* and *martelé*, as well as mixed bowings, long *staccati* and rapid change of string in legato.

8. *Lower Half*: Broad *chords*, a slow, flying *staccato*:

The sectional division of the bow is important not only in view of the right choice of the point best adapted for the type of bow-stroke prescribed on each occasion, but even more, perhaps, with regard to the appropriate declamation of the musical phrase, and to avoid contradictory accents, for instance:

163. 
Rode, Etude № 5
Correct
Nut
6
Incorrect
U.H.

If in this instance I play the five notes at the beginning, at the point *technically* most appropriate, that is, between middle and point, I should have to try to reach the nut at C sharp, whereby a totally inappropriate accent would fall on this note. In order to avoid this I must play the five notes at the extreme nut.

The close interconnection between the division of the bow and phrasing will be considered in detail later. We will turn at present to the four great families of *bowing types*: The *long*, the *short*, the *thrown* and *springing* and, finally, the *mixed strokes*.

(g) Long Bowings. Their characteristic feature does not consist, as one might believe when hearing the technical denomination, in a larger stroke, but in the absence of a break between two strokes (see p. 68). Within this group three strokes may be differentiated: **Long Bowi**

1. The "*spun*" note (*son filé*).

2. The *legato* stroke.

3. The *détaché stroke*.

1. The "*spun*" note (*son filé*). This is the name we give a note sustained by a single stroke of the bow long enough to receive a singing character. Its duration varies between 1 and 15 seconds. When it is *less* than a second it passes over into the *détaché*, but from 15 seconds upwards it is used less in playing than for purposes of study. The "spun" note, more than any other type of bowing, is dependent upon the collaboration of the left hand, through addition of a correct and colorful vibrato. **Spun tone**

The least audible change of bow, as well as evenness of stroke (save when a prescribed shading calls for the opposite), are the prerequisites of its perfect execution. The whole length of the bow should be employed as a matter of principle. The use of no more than a portion of the bow and, in particular, the avoidance of the lowest quarter, is fraught with serious disadvantages such as: diminution in the strength and carrying power of the tone (since the shortened length of stroke demands a stronger pressure for the sake of balance), as well as lack of swing (because the technical prerequisite of impetus depends in particular upon the use of the lowest quarter of the bow). An old French catchword, which despite its seemingly primitive form conceals a profound truth, says: *De l'archet, de l'archet et encore de l'archet!* (Much bow, more bow and still more bow!) It is unnecessary to say more in this connection, since we will return to the question in the section dealing with the production of tone.

2. *The Legato-Stroke*, in common with the "spun" stroke, is characterized by a greater or lesser sustaining of the bow-stroke, but differs from the latter inasmuch as here it is not a single *note*, but a succession of notes, uninterrupted by pauses, which have to be produced. Besides, here the bow does not, as in the case of the nuanceless "spun" tone, remain on a place determined by bow pressure, length of stroke and height of position, but on account of an occasional change of position must fluctuate between finger-board and bridge (see p. 92). The possible number of notes to be slurred varies between two, and, approximately, a hundred. Since in the main they have to be taken on different strings there is added to the difficulty of bow change and the uniformity of the stroke already mentioned in the case of the "spun" tone, the problem of securing the most inconspicuous change of string (see p. 61). In view of these explanations, however, it must be clear to everyone that correct change of string is secured only when the movements of the shoulder, lower arm or wrist essential to that end are no larger than necessary for the passing from one string to another, that the movements themselves are to be carried out in wavy and not angular fashion, and, finally, that up-bow and down-bow are taken according to the falling or rising change of string.

While the uniformity of the "spun" tone must be controlled mainly by muscular instinct and the eye, it is possible to test the correct division of the bow during the *legato* by means of the number of the notes to be played. This problem is given the most thorough consideration in the *Capet* "School of Bowing Technique." Now, although it surely cannot be denied that an exact division of the bow during a *legato* to be played uniformly is very important, on the other hand, we cannot disregard the fact that shadings require an *unequal* division of the bow.

Beethoven, Vln. Cto, 1º Mov't.

164. 

This is an example of a stroke which theoretically should be divided into 16 equal parts. Contrariwise in:

Mendelssohn, Cto, 3º Mov't.

165. 

the correct execution of the < and > is tied up with the following bow-division:

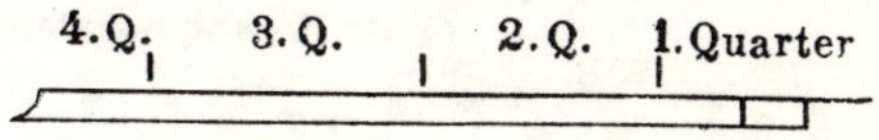
4.Q.
3.Q.
2.Q.
1.Quarter

greater the length " " Volume, pressure remaining same. How about speed?

An equal division of the bow would require increased bow pressure at the detriment of tone quality. The same holds good in:

Saint-Saëns, 3º Cto, 1º Mov't.

166. 

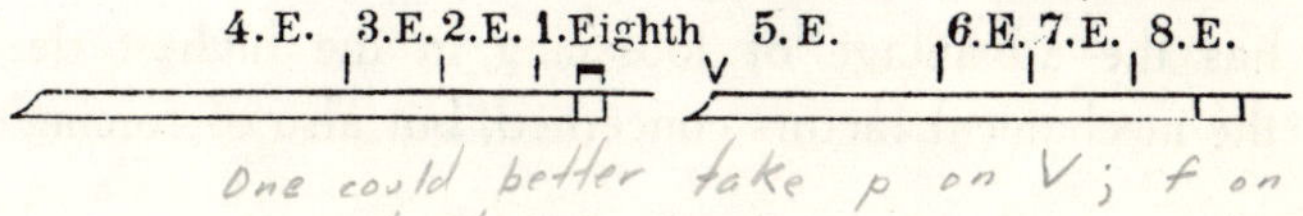
4.E.
3.E.
2.E.
1.Eighth
5.E.
6.E.
7.E.
8.E.

One could better take p on V; f on ⊓, opposite to Flesch here!

Partial disregard of the close connection between shading and bow-division impairs the value of *Capet's* work, so important in other respects.

Détaché

3. *The Détaché.* This most important fundamental stroke, in contrast to the *legato*, is characterized by the fact that, contrary to the legato, the various notes are separated one from the other through change of bow; however, the separation must take place only by means of a pause, *unavoidably* consequent upon the change of bow, yet hardly noticeable in point of time, and not by means of a longer or shorter (*consciously carried out*) stopping of the bow. We distinguish between:

(*a*) The *détaché* with the whole bow.

(*b*) The large, broad *détaché*.

(*c*) The short, small *détaché*.

(*a*) *The Détaché with the Whole Bow.* This bow-stroke stands midway between the *détaché* and the "spun" tone. Its inclusion in one or the other group depends solely upon its duration. The type of bow-stroke in the following example:

167. 
Pugnani-Kreisler, Prelude and Allegro
W.B.

is to be found almost exactly on the boundary line between both. At a rather slower tempo, for instance:

168. 
Saint-Saëns, 3º Cto, 1º Mov't.
W.B.

it already passes over into the rapid, "spun" tone. Similarly in:

169. 
César Franck, Sonata, 4º Mov't.
W.B.

Its use is indicated in slow *détaché* passages, to be played with great impulsion. The mechanical process, by means of which the expressive form of the "impulsion" is carried over to the bow, is a certain *accentuation* of the beginning of the stroke, caused by an extended *bow-expenditure.* This stroke belongs to those types which are unjustly neglected in teaching. Played in a rapid tempo, it not alone has the advantage of loosening in the highest degree the mechanical factors concerned, but also of forcing the player whom nature has afflicted with a lazy, dragging form of stroke at least to possess himself of the *external* indications of temperament, whereby in many cases the psychic qualities slumbering within him are awakened and developed. Its daily study, carried on in the manner indicated as follows by *M. P. Marsick*, *at the most rapid tempo possible*, is able to work wonders in the case of pupils *lacking temperament*:

170. 
Presto
W.B.
sf sf segue

Broad Détac

(*b*) *The Great, Broad Détaché.* Hereby a type of stroke is meant which calls for the use of at least half the bow, and is only possible of execution in slow time. A *détaché* carried out in rapid tempo with half the bow may easily lead to "sawing."

171. 
Allegro
Beethoven, Cto, 1º Mov't.
½ B. Point
½ B. M.

Correct execution, whereas again, in:

172. 
Vieuxtemps, A min. Cto, 2º Mov't.
Adagio
W.B. ½ B.
W.B.

the upper half of the bow in its whole extent is indicated. If necessary the *détaché* should be carried out at every part of the bow; on the other hand it is suitable only at certain parts in consequence of the duration and power of the tone, as well as of the peculiarity of the string. By "suitable" in this connection we think primarily of the purely musical requisites, and only secondarily of the easiest mode of execution. Practice and interpretative objects should never be confused. From a purely technical standpoint we favor the *upper half* of the bow, especially on the higher strings, because the pressure we exert in that case demands less exertion than the requisite raising of the bow at the lower half. It is not so on the G-string. The power of the pressure to be exerted is doubled here; nay, tripled in consequence of the harder consistency of the G-string. On the other hand, it is then needless to diminish the bow pressure at the nut by means of lifting the bow; on the contrary, it is just here that the bow causes the string to sound through its individual weight. This is the reason why the *détaché* on the G-string is produced with least effort at the *lower* half of the bow. For *practice purposes* it is advisable to proceed inversely. The *détaché* should be practiced on the higher strings with the lower half, and on the lower string with the upper half. Professional orchestra players are easily recognizable by their habit of using too much bow in détaché, by "sawing." We must lay the blame for it on the conductors who, in most cases, judge the amount of enthusiasm and devotion of the performers by the size of their détaché!

nall étaché

(c) The *Small Détaché* (or merely *détaché*) represents the most important and most widely used of all types of bowing. Its complete control is an absolute prerequisite to a good bow technique. It is playable with least effort just above the middle, with the greatest effort at either end of the bow. The methods of teaching hitherto in vogue have committed two great errors in this connection. On the one hand, the pupil is always encouraged to execute this bow-stroke in exercises and compositions, at the extreme point; while on the other, he is hardly ever told to study it at the nut for practice purposes. Both are fundamentally wrong principles, for on the one hand, from a purely musical point of view the détaché appears with the greatest perfection toward the middle of the bow, approximately:

while on the other, the proof of a good general bow technique cannot be held to be valid unless it is possible to produce the détaché in a tonally beautiful manner, at *any* part of the bow. Even in elementary instruction the pupil should be encouraged to *practice* all détaché strokes at the three principal parts of the bow (point, middle, nut); while in a composition to be played he should execute them between the middle and the point as a matter of principle. The forced, arduously produced détaché at the point would then disappear together with the peculiar shrinking fear of the extreme nut, innate in most violinists.

The frequently occurring woody, scratching or whistling accompanying noises during its execution often are due to the fact that the bow has been brought too near the bridge. The more rapid the détaché, the more closely the bow must approach the fingerboard if the strings are to be set vibrating faultlessly. (See p. 81.)

The détaché at a normal rate of speed at the nut is produced by almost horizontal upper arm movement at the nut, and by horizontal lower arm movement in the middle and at the point. In a more rapid tempo, however, these movements prove too circumstantial and awkward and a vertical wrist movement is substituted. It is *wrong* to produce the détaché, when *slowly* played, solely by means of a wrist movement. In dubious cases, the decision rests always on the speed required: slow tempi—heavy parts of arm, quick tempi—light parts. On the other hand, the wrist always should be flexible and ready to carry out the change of bow with participation of the finger-joints. Too far-reaching a movement, so-called "tossing" or "flinging about," is absolutely to be rejected, since it makes the change of bow all the more audible and hence defeats its purpose entirely (see p. 61).

When the détaché is uninterruptedly used for a longer period of time at a rapid tempo, an annoying hindrance the exact source of which is difficult to define is frequently noticed in the right arm. This distressing feeling is usually felt in the biceps. At times it may become so painful that it is necessary to stop playing for the moment. The physiological cause of the evil undoubtedly is a faulty, cramp-like tension instead of relaxation of certain groups of muscles, a phenomenon which, in most cases, already is evinced in the first years of study, especially when too great demands are made upon the pupil's powers of bow technique while his right arm still is inadequately trained. My experience has been that it is hardly possible *absolutely* to cure this evil, although it is quite possible of amelioration by means of détaché exercises gradually increasing in speed. The mere will to "relax," unfortunately, does not suffice; and "encouragement" on the teacher's part remains without result. Hence pieces of the type of *Paganini's "Perpetuum mobile"* cannot be included in the repertoire of such a violinist.

French Détaché

The transition to the short strokes is formed by the so-called *French* détaché. It differs from the generally accepted German ones by reason of a slight "break" between the individual notes. It might be expressed in notation as follows:

173. 

The French détaché has the advantage over the German with regard to its greater impulsion, as well as in its increased carrying power of tone; but the disadvantage of inferior possibilities of expression. It might be termed an elegant type of stroke, yet one wanting in any sharply defined character. Still used exclusively in the *Baillot* School of the first half of the nineteenth century, it now and for some time has been regarded as antiquated and unfitting for the interpretation of modern works, even in France.*

* It still is preferred by Gipsy musicians of the present day, hence may be used successfully in compositions of a marked Magyar type, for instance:

174. 
Dohnányi, Cto, 1º Mov't. (Gipsy variation)

Tremolo

It may sound paradoxical to include the *tremolo* among the "long" strokes, yet on closer investigation we find that when the fundamental difference between long and short strokes does not lie in their time of duration, but in the existence or non-existence of a markedly noticeable pause between the individual notes, the *tremolo* belongs to the pauseless, that is, the long strokes.

175. 

It is represented by as rapid as possible a succession of small détaché strokes, produced by a pure, tremulant wrist-movement (as a substitute for the far too extensive movement of the lower arm), preferably at the extreme point. In practice it is employed almost exclusively in the orchestra, far less frequently in chamber music, and almost never in solo playing. It may be produced with least effort by using the *Russian* manner of holding the bow at the extreme point, the stick turned toward the bridge, and raising all the fingers with the exception of the index finger.

Short Bowings

(h) Short Bowings.

1. The *Martelé*.
2. The *Martelé-Staccato*.

The short strokes usually are believed to depend mainly on their degree of shortness and their accentuation. The performance of a détaché which is both short and accented, however, will prove the untenability of this idea, and the pupil will come to realize that the difference between long and short strokes does not rest on their duration of time, but above all in the continuity or interruption of the various strokes. The experimental proof of the fact that the so-called long and short strokes do not depend on their duration of time is easily demonstrated:

(M. 𝅗𝅥 = 120)

176. "Long" Stroke

Duration of a bar: 1 second; each note, 1/16 of a second.

(𝅗𝅥 = 30)

177. "Short" Stroke 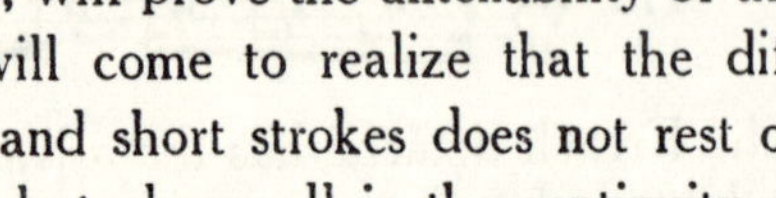

Duration of a bar: 4 seconds; each note, 1/4 of a second.

The *accentuation*, too, is a mark shared by both families of strokes, although it occurs less frequently in the case of the détaché. *If, however, I interpolate a pause between the individual détaché strokes, the character of a short stroke is at once created, no matter how long the duration of time may be.*

It is less the accentuation itself than the manner of its execution which supplies an additional characteristic. An *accent* may be produced in two ways: through pressure or through use of longer bowing. If the requisite stronger pressure coincides with the stroke itself, the perfected vibration of the string is prevented while the pressure lasts, and the tone is forced and perfunctory. On the other hand, a very strong pressure during the *pause* which precedes or follows a note is quite possible—if stopped when the stroke begins, and which merely seems strong enough to produce a hardly noticeable accompanying noise-like accent (almost like the slight noise produced by the consonants b, p, k; g) while the string, during the actual process of bowing, is not prevented from vibrating clearly and freely.

Hence, in using the term "short strokes" we mean *above all* a stroke separated from the preceding and the following one by a plainly noticeable pause. The interruption is used to exert a strong pressure on the string by means of the bow-stick, a pressure which coincides with the beginning of the stroke, and thus produces a kind of secondary noise which I call the *pressure accent;* while the pause between the two notes utilized for the purpose of producing this mute pressure should be called the *pressure pause.*

The mechanics of this kind of stroke, usually carried out between the middle and the point, consist of the combination of an almost horizontal movement of the lower arm (during the stroke) with a slight inward and outward (supination and pronation) turning of the lower arm, before and after the pressure pause in the elbow-joint.

Martelé We call this stroke the *martelé* ("hammered" stroke). It is, especially with regard to bow technique (less for purposes of interpretation), as important as the détaché. It is best practiced in the following manner:

Upper Third of the Bow
Pr. Pr. Pr. Pr.

178. Pr.=Pressure Accent

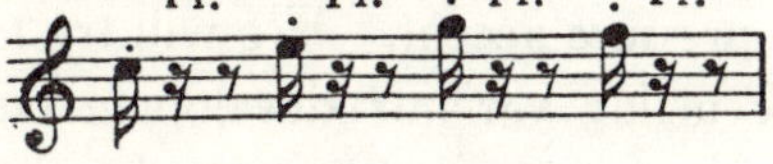

This manner of practise may appear pedantic at first glance; but it offers the student an opportunity to acquire a stroke which is flexible, sonorous and, so to speak, represents the tonal equivalent of human energy. Besides it forms the irremissible prerequisite for the study of the (*martelé*)-*staccato.*

Staccato 2. The (*Martelé*)-*Staccato.* Many teachers claim that the *staccato* is the key to a good technique of the bow. Practical experience proves this contention to be false. Neither *Joachim* nor *Sarasate* were masters of a normal staccato. On the other hand, we often will find mediocre violinists who, though their bow technique in other respects may be found wanting, possess an admirable *staccato.* Hence its importance with regard to technique as a whole should not be exaggerated. It signifies neither more nor less than a welcome, yet nowise necessary requisite of violinistic ability. In order to understand the origin of the staccato one must realize that the martelé stroke presupposes a comparatively slow tempo, at any rate one not above the tempo given in the following example:

M.M. (♩ = 66)
179. (Extreme limit of Possibility of execution in the Martelé)

If the tempo called for is more rapid, and its execution with a springing or thrown bow *not* admissible, then the martelé strokes *must* necessarily be crowded together on *one bow-stroke.* The violin-staccato owes its creation to this necessity.

Here, too, as in the case of so many other technical peculiarities in violin-playing, we must make a sharp distinction between studying and performing. In no single branch of violin technique does so deep a gulf yawn between theory and practice, between study and execution, as in this. While in the first instance it is possible to conceive of definite, fundamental principles, based on the anatomical peculiarities of the arm, in practice the abnormal frequently becomes the rule. If for any reason the violinist fails to produce a staccato according to rule, he attempts to gain his end by breaking one of those rules which are not adapted to his needs, and often does so with success. In fact the most extravagant hand and arm distortions in the case of many players, are absolutely necessary in order to produce the staccato peculiar to them. In any discussion, therefore, which pretends to be at all exhaustive, in addition to the fixed rules, the most usual *exceptions* leading to the same end must also be considered.

The mechanism of the *martelé* differs from that of the *martelé-staccato* inasmuch as in the former every horizontal movement of the lower arm corresponds to one single pressure accent; while in the violin staccato as many pressure accents fall on *one* horizontal movement of the lower arm as there are notes to be played. Both varieties of stroke may be pictorially presented as follows:

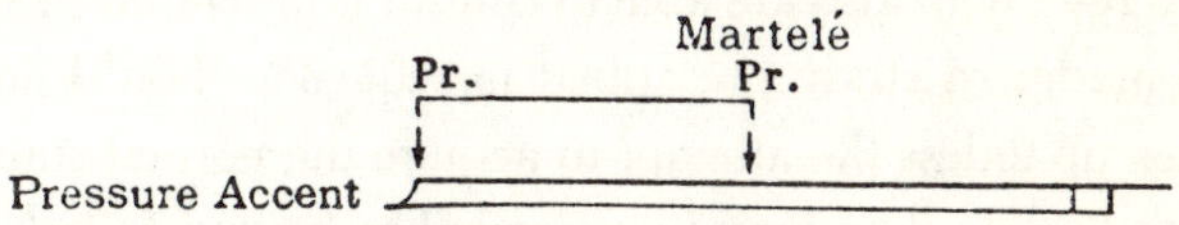

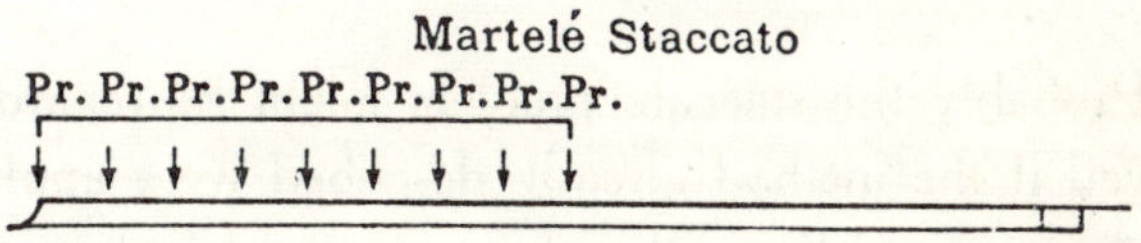

While in accordance herewith the stroke and pressure are carried out in ordinary martelé separately, the difficulty in the staccato rests in the very fact that in it the pressure accents have to occur *during* the horizontal movement of the arm; and that the amalgamation of both movements has to be secured. Only in such case may we count upon a correct staccato. When, however, one movement is stressed more than the other, numerous deformations develop, which, in spite of arduous study, scorn all improvement so long as the mechanical causes of the tonal defects are not removed.

Since the staccato is merely a succession of martelé movements in a *single* bow-stroke, it stands to reason that first of all one should try to conquer it in the same way one would go about overcoming the ordinary *martelé*, that is, by the separation of stroke and pressure pauses:

Kreutzer, Et. Nº 4

180. 

In the case of beginners this procedure invariably leads to the end desired. With its aid, it is possible to execute the *staccato* correctly from the beginning, at first slowly, and with increasing agility, more rapidly. Stroke and pressure stand in the same relation to each other, and the notes should be sharply separated without making them scratchy. The stroke movement, in this case, it is true, is interrupted in the beginning by the pressure accent; but as the rate of speed gradually increases, a *tremulant movement*, interspersed with a certain number of pressure accents, seemingly uninterrupted, and grafted upon a *détaché*, develops. I regard this kind of staccato study as the most suitable, since by its means control of all the possible degrees of staccato rapidity is most quickly attained. No doubt there are many violinists who possess a brilliant staccato, but very few, who also are able to control it in tempo. Hence the modes of study prescribed in sequence should not be taken up unless the attempt to acquire the normal staccato already described may be regarded as having failed.

Faulty Staccati

Probably the staccato problem might be regarded as solved if the method already described were applied to all beginners. Since this, however, seldom happens, it depends in most cases on the chance of personal talent as well as on the imitative ability of the individual, whether or no the end in view is gained. To tell the truth, approximately three-quarters of the professional violinists, including artists of the very first rank, have an insufficient staccato. Hence the capable teacher should not only be able to solve the comparatively simple problem of teaching the *beginner* a correct staccato, but above all, should have the faculty of curing faulty staccati of every type; should be able to undertake *staccato correction*.

In spite of the apparently extraordinary diversity between the faulty *staccati*, they belong to one or the other of *two* great families which share a disproportion between stroke and pressure accent, between horizontal and vertical movement.

1. Too rapid stroke, too slight pressure accent, or,
2. Too little stroke movement and too strongly marked a pressure accent. We will try to fix the most frequently occurring variants developing out of these fundamental errors, and indicate means for their cure.

1. (*a*) The stroke from the point to the middle is made so *quickly* that only very few pressure pauses can be applied. Part of the staccato has to be transferred to the lower half of the bow, the field most unfavorable for it, and the staccato fails.

Correction: Confinement to the upper quarter of the bow, with the imaginary object of remaining so far as possible on the same spot: Hereby the stroke movement is shortened to the smallest possible extent (the beneficial exaggeration already mentioned on various other occasions):

181. 

(*b*) The notes are not separated sharply enough one from the other; the effect of the staccato is weak and powerless.

Correction: Exercises with increased pressure accents and prolonged pressure pauses with the smallest possible expenditure of bow:

182. 

(*c*) The *staccato* is not emphasized sharply enough at the point, and only gains in sharper emphasis in its further development toward the middle of the bow.

Correction: Before the beginning of the staccato, to be played rather quickly, a long pause with a somewhat exaggerated pressure at the extreme point should be made, which may even lend the first note a somewhat scratchy incidental flavor. The remaining notes should be played without any specially noticeable pressure pause:

183. 

(*d*) After beginning correctly, the player, toward the *middle*, loses command of the bow, which carries out exaggerated, high *springing* movements, causing the notes to turn to noises.

Correction: The *avoidance* of the middle, and the crowding together of as many tones as possible in the upper third.

2. (*a*) The bow does not move forward quickly enough, and at times even remains on the same spot, causing the staccato to fail completely, in spite of correct pressure movement.

Correction: Staccato exercises with as few notes as possible, and the greatest possible expenditure of bow:

184. 

(*b*) The pressure pauses are too strongly emphasized; the staccato turns *scratchy*.

Correction: The staccato to begin with should be practiced in broad *portato strokes* (see p. 73), until the evil in question disappears.

185. 

These six principal types of faulty staccato strokes, at times appear in conjunction. One should then try to segregate the individual errors and master them separately.

There might be mentioned, furthermore, the incorrect observance of the pressure pauses through *dropping* and *raising* of the hand in the wrist-joint, instead of by rolling of the lower arm.

Correction: One should try to immobilize and, so to speak, stiffen the hand in the wrist-joint by means of continuing pressure of the index finger, whereby the wrist movement will be automatically prevented. In consequence the staccato at first will sound somewhat scratchy, an evil which must be prevented by subsequent relaxation of the hand pressure.

At times *psychic* reasons make it impossible to improve a faulty staccato, in spite of the most exact knowledge of what causes it. When, for instance, a violinist has made a failure of his staccati for many years, his dread of this type of stroke, as well as the conviction of his own incompetence will be so strong that the best technical prerequisites will be nullified thereby. In that case all he can do is to cut the Gordian knot and alter and renew his manner of playing staccato fundamentally. Here, above all, it is the *staccato in the down bow* (*upper half of the bow*) which is in question. It should be practiced like the ordinary *staccato*, but with the very material difference that the bow-stick must be held *in the inverse direction*, i.e., *toward the bridge*.

Staccato in Down Bow

Even if this attempt fail, all hope need not be abandoned, for above all else there still remains to be considered the fantastic *staccato in the down bow, in the lower half* of the bow.

Manner of Execution: The bow position is normal, the stick inclining toward the fingerboard.

Further, there is the *flying staccato* in the middle of the bow (see p. 77). In the case of staccati, which mock every regular mode of treatment, the *raising of the right shoulder* may be tried. It brings about a certain stiffening, and hence is appropriate in the case of exaggerated wrist movements, or a preponderance of the horizontal stroke. Nor should we forget to mention the greater or lesser *pressure* of the individual fingers on the bow-stick, or the *raising* of all the *fingers*, with the exception of the index finger. If all this is of no avail there still remains a type of staccato, one which bids defiance to all rules of logic in the most insubordinate, savage and brutal fashion, yet which, when rightly understood and conceived, may be brilliantly effective. This is the *stiff staccato*. *Manner of execution*: With total stiffening of the upper arm, and accompanying convulsive contraction of all the participating groups of muscles, the violinist *at times* may be able to make the whole arm carry out an extraordinarily rapid and equalized trembling, in conjunction with a forward movement of the lower arm, whereby an extremely rapid, contracted and well-sounding staccato is produced. Every teacher will remember more or less frequently recurring cases of pupils who, after having tormented themselves for years with all sorts of exercises without the least success, became the happy possessors of a magnificent stiff *staccato* overnight.

Its only disadvantage lies in the fact that it cannot be carried out in slow tempo; hence, for example, it is inapplicable in *Spohr's* works. Notwithstanding, every violinist who has vainly exhausted all other curative means should try this ultima ratio.

Manner of Practice: Absolute stiffening of the entire arm, cramped contraction of the hand and arm muscles, and, above all, exclusion of every independent wrist movement:

186. 

It should be executed as fast as possible, with a slow, *convulsively tremulant* forward movement. Should one succeed in producing a number of staccato notes plainly separated one from the other, although they may be uncontrolled, one must endeavor to unite them with a rapid finger movement of the left hand.

187. 

The degree of rapidity is determined by the bow, the fingers adjusting themselves to it.

A very frequent yet seldom recognized cause of failure is faulty coincidence of movement between right and left hand. In such cases the violinist regards the movements of the right hand as primary, those of the other as secondary, i.e., his left hand tries to adapt itself to the *staccato* movement. *A reversal of this fundamental principle often leads to surprisingly good results.* First of all the staccati have to be studied legato, and afterwards while playing a regular staccato one has to acquire the feeling that the fingers of the left hand determine the tempo, and that the bow should confine itself to following them.

In the staccato the *gain or loss of space* in change of string plays an even more important part, perhaps, than in the legato, since the success of the staccato often depends on the greatest possible utilization of the *upper* half of the bow. *Ascending* passages, therefore, are easier to execute in the ⊓ , and *descending* ones in the V . One of the most important prerequisites for learning the staccato in the ⊓ is the preferential use of the *middle* third of the bow, where in contrast to the V *staccato*, the capacity for down-bow staccato is chiefly located. Hence, in the ⊓ we must try to obtain the greatest possible amount of bowing space, and use this space sparingly, as one would conserve the breath to complete a sentence. Since in the V we can play with the whole bow, but in the ⊓ only half the bow, a thorough utilization of the middle is necessary.

In the case of all these types and variants the arm frequently is twisted into the most fantastic contortions: one or more fingers are raised; there is exaggerated lifting, dropping or shifting of the hand, elbow or shoulder; and the latter may be drawn up. There is turning of the stick, wavy arm movements, all this singly or combined, a genuine witches' sabbath of anatomical ugliness. And, nevertheless, "the end justifies the means." If they lead us to the attainment of the object in view, they should be welcome to us all, teachers or pupils, as one of Mother Nature's inexplicable means of help.

The so-called "*Viotti* stroke" is a variant of the *staccato*:

188. 

This is a repeated *staccato*, divided in two, the speed possibilities of which lies between a moderate *staccato* and a customary *martelé;* characteristic of this stroke, above all, is the robust *accentuation* of the second note forming the strong beat of the bar, secured by a strong expenditure of bow, as well as the *pauseless* joining of the accented note to the short note following it.

189. 

When practiced in this manner, the *Viotti* stroke may be conquered by anyone, irrespective of their greater or lesser talent for the staccato; in cases of extreme need it may even be used as a substitute for a staccato which does not call for too great a speed.

rtato

The *Wavy Stroke* (*ondulé, portato*) is an extraordinarily important variant of the staccato. It stands exactly midway between *legato* and genuine *staccato;* the various notes are separated one from the other by a hardly noticeable pause, the elastic pressure does not take place *during* the pause, but on the individual note itself. It is expressed in notation as follows:

190. 

or, if the separation is to be more marked:

191. 

With regard to its relation to tone production it will be discussed in greater detail on p. 85.

own ing- kes

(i) Thrown Strokes and Springing Strokes. Hereby we mean short strokes, separated one from the other by pauses, during which the bow (in contrast to the *martelé*) *leaves* the string in order to drop straight back upon it.

The *springing* and *thrown* types differ one from the other in point of origin as well as in regard to their tonal effect. The frequent confusion of the two explains the lack of tonal beauty they usually show. Yet not alone the bowing types themselves, but the names given them as well, are so often exchanged with each other that it unquestionably seems necessary to call attention to their difference in some external way as well. Hence, instead of the indefinite general terms *spiccato* or *sautillé* hitherto used, we shall employ the unmistakable terms: springing and thrown strokes.

In the thrown stroke the *player is active*, the *bow passive; I* throw the bow. In the springing stroke the player is *passive*, only watching over what the bow does; the *bow* is *active*, since, in consequence of its elasticity in the region of its balancing point, it *must* spring of itself, when not held down on the string by force. The type of stroke to be chosen depends on the tempo: in a *slow* tempo the bow must be *thrown*, in a *rapid* one it *springs* of itself:

Spring Bow

(♩ = 120)

192. 

Thrown Bow

(♩ = 60)

193. 

Example 192 only can be produced in the middle, Example 193 at any part of the bow.

1. *Springing Strokes.* When we try to produce a small *détaché* in the middle of the bow at its balancing point, we find that this is possible only when we exert a correspondingly strong *pressure* on the bow by means of the index finger. If we are satisfied, on the other hand, to allow the index finger to rest *loosely* on the stick, then it will start to leave the string after each stroke, that is, to leap up and down in an elastic manner. This type we call the *springing stroke*. Hence it is no more than a small *détaché*, carried out at the narrowly limited point where the bow-stick, remaining balanced, springs independently (as before explained). The inclination of the bow to yield to quivering, involuntary movements in the middle, so disturbing in a *legato* or in sustained notes, forms the mechanical prerequisites of a correct springing bow. **Springing Strokes**

The *part of the bow* best suited for it varies, however, according to the collective weight of the bow and its division of weight; hence it differs in the case of every bow, and must first be determined exactly by the player. In the same way *speed, dynamics, the use of high* or *low strings*, as well as polyphony exert an unmistakable influence in the choice of the most appropriate part of the bow.

194. *Tempo*

(♩ = 60)
Paganini, Perpetuum mobile.
Idem (♩ = 90)
Idem (♩ = 140)

195. *Degree of Power.*

Saint-Saëns, Rondo Capr.
f
p

196. *High or Low Strings*

197. *Double and Triple Stop Chords*

Vieuxtemps, E maj. Cto, 3º Mov't.
Vieuxtemps, Ballade and Polonaise

The *excess of weight* called for in slow tempo, in the *forte* on the G-string or in double-stops is automatically secured by the shifting of the point of attack toward the *nut*, while the diminished pressure in rapid tempo, in the *piano*, on the upper strings as well as in the case of one-voiced passages, is secured by approaching the ***upper half***.

The *position* of the bow-stick in relation to **the** hair plays a notable part in producing a successful springing bow-stroke. The stick should *never incline* toward the fingerboard, but must be held over the bow-hair in a vertical line. The fact is that the independent vibrations of the stick are well-nigh totally cancelled when it is held obliquely; while they appear undiminished when the stick is held straight. Only when, for some reason or other, one wishes to produce a *détaché* entirely free from springing in the *middle*, is the oblique position appropriate.

Should the springing bow be produced by the movement of the *lower arm* or of the *wrist?* In order to answer this important question correctly we must bear in mind that wrist movements in every form should only be applied when the use of more heavy parts of the arm in quick tempi seems clumsy and circumstantial.

198.

(♩ = 60)

In this tempo the shoulder movement still rules, with quite negligible participation of the wrist; at ♩=90 the wrist already predominates, and at ♩=120 it is exclusively active.

The involuntary springing of the bow is facilitated by *raising the little finger*. When the bow moves in the *lower half*, the fourth finger must remain on the bow-stick (in this case it quite naturally is inclined to rest upon the stick); yet if it remains lying on the stick when a higher part of the bow is used, disadvantageous mechanical hindrances occur. The pressure of the fourth finger automatically calls forth an inward turn of the lower arm and, in consequence, an inclination to lift the bow from the string. Hence this procedure should be used purposely only with the *thrown*, never with the *springing* bow. When this principle is ignored, both types are mingled and a stiff, scratchy middle type, betwixt and between the springing and the thrown stroke, lavishly provided with accompanying noises due to excessive raising and lowering of the arm, results; one which, perhaps, may dazzle *optically*, but which is *acoustically* repulsive. Only when the bow itself, because poorly made, or because inadequately haired, shows no tendency to "spring," the elasticity of the stick should be heightened artificially by opposition of the little finger.

Manner of Practice:

199 

(*a*) The swiftest and smallest *détaché* possible in the middle. The bow is pressed firmly to the string at the point of dead weight, and thus *prevented* from springing.

(*b*) The same exercise with diminished pressure—the bow commences to spring of its *own volition*. *The player should strive only to secure the effect of a small, rapid détaché, he must regard the springing as quite incidental.* It is an error to think that the excellence of the springing bow-stroke depends on the highest possible *leaps* of the bow; the exact contrary is the case. The *shorter* the space of time for which the stick leaves the string between the various notes, and the *less elevated* the height from which it drops back upon the string, the better sounding and freer from accompanying noises the stroke will become, while its possibilities of speed will be well-nigh illimitable.

Springing staccati. In this category fall all those springing bow-strokes in which several notes are crowded together on a single stroke. To these, in the first instance, belongs the "*drum stroke*." It is thus that we define two or more springing strokes carried out as rapidly as possible on a single bow in the middle, the effect resembling a drum roll:

200 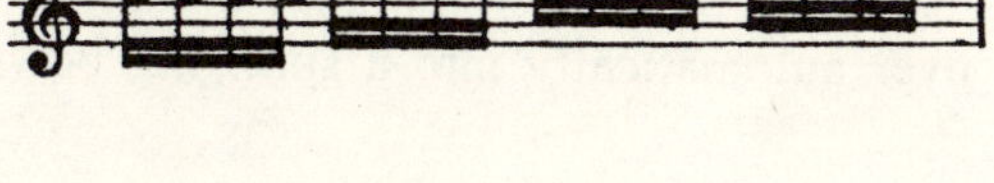

In the first half of the last century it was a much-used constituent of a virtuoso bowing technique, one sure of success; for instance, in *Prume* ("La Mélancolie") or *Léonard* ("Variation on the Austrian Imperial Hymn"). In our own day, however, it is used only for study purposes, and rightly so, for its purely acoustic effect hardly differs from that of the springing bow. Nevertheless, its control is part of a perfected bowing technique.

Here, too, as in the springing bow, the proper activity of the stick produces a raising and dropping of the bow, only that in accordance with the principle of as slight as possible an expenditure of bow, the length of the strokes increases in exact proportion to the number of notes to be played. Only at the start, the bow, in order to make the attack, is thrown on the string from a slight elevation, and then is supposed to carry on itself by means of its own activity. The "drum stroke," as well as the springing arpeggios (which will be considered later), therefore form a connection between thrown and springing strokes. It no longer is enough to hold the stick straight toward the end of the stroke, it must even be *inclined edgewise toward the bridge*. The player should only have in mind a long *détaché* stroke in the middle, but his intention is prevented by the involuntary springing of the stick. First, an irregular, wild "drum stroke" develops, whose taming must be the object of his study. Above all, the fastest possible tempo is taken for granted. In a slow tempo the stroke ceases to be a "drum stroke," and turns into a pure *thrown staccato* stroke (see p. 77). *Manner of Practice*:

201. I 

With pressure, the stick inclined toward the bridge.

202. II 

Without pressure, stick inclined toward bridge, control of the bowing, the fastest possible tempo. Similarly with three or four notes.

203. 

Wieniawski, Ecole moderne, No 1

204. 

Paganini, Caprice No 5

205. 

Saltati

Indirectly, the long *saltati* also belong to this family:

206. 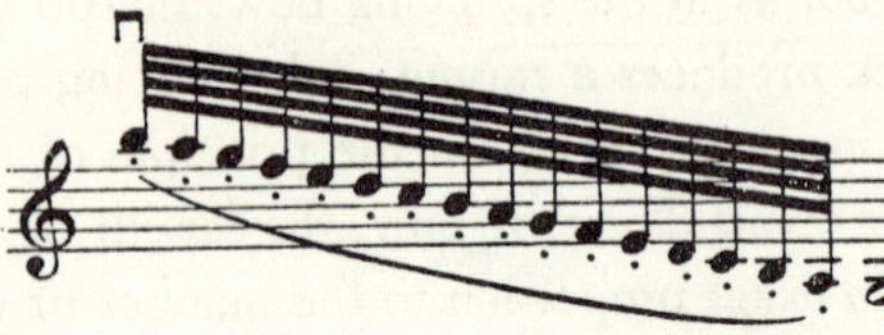

207. 

208. 

8
Wieniawski, "Faust"- Fantasia

(Finger-glissando)

Manner of Performance: Length of stroke is in proportion to the number and speed of notes, upper third or quarter of the bow. The bow is thrown on the string at the beginning only. The stick straight at first, later inclined toward the bridge. Since the involuntary action of the upper half of the bow is slight, the springing attack must be produced by a *throwing up* of the bow from a certain height, followed by the automatic continuation of the springing when the stick is inclined toward the bridge. Now comes the question of securing coincidence between the right and left hands, something not difficult in view of the slight degree of exactness demanded by this type of bowing.

Springing Arpeggios

Springing arpeggios is the name we usually give to broken chords which, covering a range of from two to four strings, are each played with a springing bow stroke.

209. 

Manner of Practice: One should begin with a perfect *legato*

210. 

as a preliminary exercise. The chief requisite is the determination of the balancing point of the bow. The stick is held in a straight position, slightly inclined toward the bridge. *As little bow as possible,* in a very rapid tempo. Change of string is secured by means of exclusively rolling movements of the shoulder-joint. The line formed by hand or forearm remains unalterably straight; the wrist, in particular, must not move of its own volition. The part of the bow best suited to this type of bowing should be determined by experiment. The connection between change of string moving upward and the down-bow, as well as between the up-bow and descending change of string (see p. 62) is especially noticeable here. As a matter of fact, the springing arpeggio with reversed stroke is practically impossible of execution. The most frequent causes of the failure of this bowing, or the insufficiently sharp division of its individual components, lie in the insufficient bridgeward tendency of the stick, too great an expenditure of bow, and too *intentional* throwing of the bow.

Thrown Strokes

2. The *Thrown Strokes.* These are much more numerous than the springing strokes, because the latter are bound down to the middle of the bow as the only point of involuntary action (rebounding); while the former may be produced at practically any part of the bow—adequate technical facility being presupposed.

All combinations arranged under the head of *springing bowings* at once pass into the class of *thrown bowings* the moment the tempo demanded becomes so slow that the note groups can no longer be produced by a collective movement, each note necessitating a consciously intended raising of the bow for itself.

Since this is most conveniently done by means of the *little finger,* its remaining on the stick, in contrast to the springing strokes forms a most necessary prerequisite. The "flying" *staccato* is the only exception, because no rules for it may be set up, and because at a high rate of speed it passes over automatically into a springing bowing.

see p 75, col A too

The *Thrown Stroke*, if merely because of the frequency of its appearance, forms one of the most important components of bowing technique; nor is the orchestral player the least concerned in its absolute control. It is used on every occasion where the tempo indicated by the composer is too slow for the springing bow. It can be executed as well in the middle as at the nut or point, although more difficult of execution in the last instances. In a *piano* the middle is best used.

Bach, Son. G-min. 2º Mov't

1

211. 

In the *forte*, the lower third of the bow:

Mozart, Son. E-min. 1º Mov't.

212. 

In the *pp* at the point (when the greatest possible shortness is desired):

Beethoven, F-maj. Son. 3º Mov't.

213. 

At times it is played very shortly, as in:

Beethoven, Son. A-maj. Op. 12, Nº 2

214. 

or, between short and long, in which case it is indicated with this sign ⁃̣ :

Beethoven, Romanza F-maj.

215. 

Frequently, for the sake of a correct division of the bow, and a musically correct accentuation, two or more notes are played on one bow, as in Example 216, and the bowing, for this reason, need not assume the character of a flying staccato. It might be more correctly defined as a thrown staccato:

Mozart, D-maj. Ctº, 3º Mov't.

216. 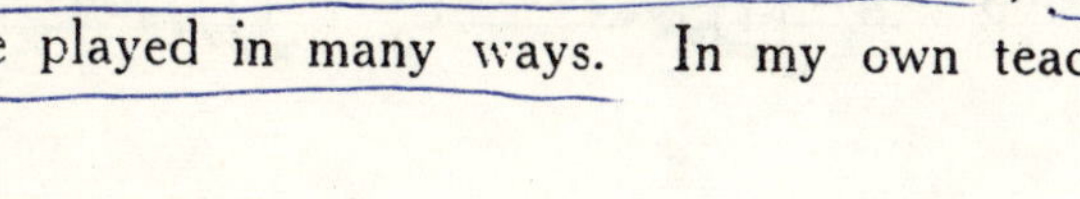

To this category, too, belongs the main bowing in the third movement of the *Mendelssohn* Violin Concerto, which may be played in many ways. In my own teaching practice I first try to find out which part of the bow seems most suitable for the individual bowing technique of the pupil, to be followed by an investigation of his preference to spend more or less bow during the slow flying staccato or to remain even on the same spot.

In this broad field, incidentally, the most varied combinations are possible:

Dvořák, Dumky Trio, 2º Mov't.

217. 

The choice of giving the preference to the middle or the lower half (the point comes into consideration only in quite rare instances) should be determined by the *musical* character of the passage in question. The following general lines of procedure might be laid down:

Nut	half short *forte* massive	*Middle*	short *piano* gracefully	*Point*	quite short *pp*

(Thrown)
Flying Staccato

The Flying Staccato practically represents a combination of the martelé staccato with the "thrown" or "springing" staccato bowing, inasmuch as a number of short notes are produced by a single bow-stroke, while the bow leaves the string after each note. From the standpoint of mechanics, it differs from the ordinary staccato owing to the fact that the *raising* and *dropping* of the bow is substituted for *bow pressure*. From the musical point of view it is less essential than the martelé-staccato since there is no adequate substitute for the latter, while the springing or thrown bowing may quite adequately take the place of the flying staccato. It is more important as an auxiliary for those violinists who, for some one reason or other, cannot master the martelé-staccato. Executed in a virtuoso manner it may produce a charming effect:

use in case (4) p 75

Vieuxtemps, Fantasie-Caprice

218. 

Saint-Saëns, Havanaise

219. 

It is used almost exclusively in the middle, although I know of some rare examples of charming flying staccato at the extreme point. In order to include the greatest possible number of notes, many violinists slow up the forward movement of the lower arm by means of a wave-

NB: ∴ use martelé-staccato when you have staccato marking, instead of flying staccato shaped horizontal movement of the arm, quite successfully. Its control may be hampered by similar mechanical hindrances, as in the case of the *martelé-staccato.* The curative means are approximately the same, as long as the raising and dropping movements take the place of the pressure movement.

"Standing" Staccato

The "*Standing*" *Staccato.* I use this somewhat strange-sounding expression to designate a succession of rather slow "thrown" bowings, produced with one bow-stroke, by the wrist, in such a way that arm or hand return tonelessly to the point of departure after each note; hence, to all appearances, there is no expenditure of bow at all:

220 

Its use is indicated in the case of a longer succession of notes at not too rapid a tempo, for instance:

221. *Mendelssohn,* Cto, 3o Mov't.

It may be executed on every part of the bow, yet the weaker staccati are indicated at the upper part, and the stronger staccati at the lower part of the bow; the effect is especially charming at the nut. The command of the "standing" staccato, which should not be lacking in perfected technique, is attainable without effort by everyone by means of short exercises, which, however, should be spread over a longer period of time. In combination with regular change of string, as in:

Kreutzer, Etude No 7

221 a 

it must be classed as one of the most difficult exercises from a tonal point of view. A counterpart of the short *up-bows* are the short *down-bows,* calculated to combine sharp accentuation with sharp division. They are applied principally at such places where it is necessary to give the pauses between the individual notes the greatest emphasis. The necessary wrist movement must be combined with an upward movement during each break, the bow seemingly falling down on each note.

Wieniawski, Polonaise A-maj.

222. 

Saint-Saens, B-min. Cto, 3o Mov't.

223. 

In using it one should take care that the little silver ring at the nut does not produce any noises.

Arpeggios

The *thrown arpeggios,* too, owe their existence solely to the need of a comparatively slow tempo:

Paganini, Caprice No 1

224. 

Up to ♩=60 thrown arpeggios, in a more rapid tempo springing arpeggios, are used in the above case. The essential difference between the two types lies in the way the little finger is held: during the thrown arpeggios it rests on the stick, while in the springing arpeggios it is raised. Turning the bow edgewise, toward the bridge, as well as a rolling movement of the shoulder-joint corresponding to the change of string will generally suffice to carry out this bowing successfully. Control of the many variants of springing or thrown strokes depends principally on a proper knowledge as to which of the two groups they belong. Not until then can we be clear as to how they should be executed, or as to the tonal effect they will produce. The slower the note succession, the higher the bow is raised, the swifter it is, the closer the latter remains to the string. In both types first consideration should be given to the most finished tonal effect, free from all accompanying noises.

Mixed Stroke

(j) Mixed Strokes. The number of possible combinations between the bowings hitherto discussed is practically illimitable. The best-known selection, comprising 4,000 variants, is that contained in *Sevčik's* "School of Bow Technique" (see p. 115.) We shall have to confine ourselves here to the general consideration of those combinations of the individual groups which, as the types most used, call for considerations of a special character.

Spun Tones+Détaché.

Beethoven, Trio Op. 70 No 2, 1o Mov't

225. 

One of the most important bowing combinations.

Here the *détaché* is always appropriate at that place where the bow happens to be after completion of the "spun" stroke. There never should be any audible difference between the tone quality of the *détaché* at the upper or the lower half.

Spun Tones+Staccato.

Kreutzer, Etude No. 4

226. 

A very violinistic combination, since the serenity of the preceding "spun" note allows thorough preparation of the *staccato.* The difficulty of combining the staccato and the "spun" note in the same stroke of the bow may be overcome easily by means of the following type of exercise:

227.

Legato+Détaché. Under this head come, first of all, the innumerable combinations of both types between point and nut; a few outstanding examples follow:

Beethoven, Cto, 1o Mov't.

228. 

Vieuxtemps, A-min. Cto

229. 

Mendelssohn, Cto, 1o Mov't.

230. 

Here a correct division of the bow offers the only possibility of avoiding an accentuation contrary to sense and meaning. Furthermore, there is the deliberate false accent, the so-called *Paganini stroke*:

231. 

Legato+Thrown Staccato. The practice of this combination is unquestionably the best means of accustoming one's self to a correct division of the bow, and the avoidance of false accents:

Separated thrown strokes are not possible here if only because of the faulty (shortened) legato which would follow.

232. 

A single thrown bow is not possible here, if only because of the incorrect stroke which it would develop.

At a very rapid tempo the thrown *staccato* then turns into a springing *staccato*:

Beethoven, Kreutzer Son. 2o Mov't.*

233. 

Legato Arpeggios+Thrown or Springing Stroke:

234. 

Whole Bow Détaché+Martelé+Thrown Bow:

235. 

In order to avoid the inequality in bowing developed by the change from thrown bow at the nut and *martelé* at the point, this type of stroke usually is turned into a combination of détaché and thrown *staccato* in the middle third of the bow:

236. 

Martelé+Small Détaché:

Beethoven, Kreutzer Son. 3o Mov't.

237. 

From the standpoint of *agogics* the quarter-note, in this instance, is the longer, the eighth note the shorter. In reality, however, we play the quarter-note as quite a short martelé, with a concluding pause; and the eighth-note faster, without a subsequent pause, closely connected with the immediately succeeding quarter-note. This pearl among bowing varieties seldom radiates in all its spotless clarity. Why? Because most players convulsively strain themselves to emphasize the quarter-note, as the accented beat of the measure, in accordance with the manner of

* By which it should not be inferred that I consider this virtuoso bowing as the correct one.

its notation, whereby the quarter-note itself becomes too long, the pause too short, and the eighth-note too clumsy. The solution of this problem is astonishingly simple: the *accent* is transferred *to the* ⌉, on the eighth-note, supported by the most powerful pressure accent possible, during the pause. This "unmusical" accent only defies the law of musical phrasing in appearance, in reality it is not audible. The audible accent, now as before, rests on the strong beat of the measure:

238. Notation as given 

239. Manner of Practice Pr. Pressure Pause 
Pr.

At the *nut* this combination is far more rarely employed, and then only when the bowing sequence is reversed. Here it is only appropriate in a slow tempo and in the *forte*, and besides (in contrast to the delicate character of this bowing at the point), it sounds massive and heavy. When this bowing combination is carried out in *the same bow*:

240. 

the accentuation of the weak beat of the measure no longer is necessary, since the division of the bow allows for the value of the notes; the pressure accent, too, may be appreciably weaker during the pause. When playing with the *whole bow*, the pressure accent falls away altogether at the nut, and a *raising* of the bow is substituted for it, in order to avoid the scratchy accompanying noise otherwise produced.

Détaché+Martelé:

241. 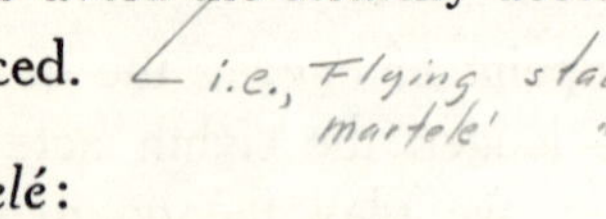
(♩=36)
Pt.

An excellent exercise, seldom applied in actual practice.

Détaché (Middle)+Springing Bow:

242. 
(♩=120)
f
p

A well-sounding combination to produce echo effects.

Detache + Thrown Staccato:

Schubert, Trio, B♭ maj. 4º Mov't.

243. 

This passage may be played in either of two ways. (*a*) Without a pause between the quarter-note and the first eighth-note; (*b*) with a pause; the bow in *a* springs less than in *b*, where it once more is thrown on the string; *a* is more suitable for rapid tempi, *b* for slow tempi.

Springing Bow+Thrown Bow+Thrown Staccato:

Beethoven, Trio, G maj. 4º Mov't.

244. 

A tricky bowing! The transition from involuntary springing into voluntary throwing without shifting of the rhythm, demands a very considerable command of the bow.

Saltato+Thrown Staccato+Legato (a rare combination)

Bazzini, Ronde des Lutins

245. 

Within the framework of these and many other bowing types, move the countless bowing possibilities, whose sum total could be verified only by abstruse computations. As a curiosity we shall mention a bowing combination here, introduced by *Thibaud* exclusively for practice purposes, by means of which a decided strengthening of the fingers of the right hand is secured.

246. 
Nut
Point
Nut
Point
Nut
Point

It represents a union of the shortest *martelé* stroke with a very powerful pressure accent at the nut and point, in the *inverted* stroke. The bow must pass over the distance between nut and point in the air, as rapidly as possible, which can be done only when the bow is held in an iron grasp.

5. Tone Production

Acoustic rob- ems

(a) Remarks in General. While the left hand determines the *number* of the vibrations to be produced, it is the task of the right hand to set the strings themselves *vibrating*. The *sound* or *tone* is the result of a certain number of *regular* vibrations; when they are irregular, *noise* results. According to generally established experience and acoustic laws, sounds do not differ absolutely from noises, but noises are mingled with most notes, and most noises comprise definite tonal pitches. Violinists call the noises which accompany the notes *accompanying* noises, and endeavor so far as possible to avoid them in tone production. This, it is true, is not entirely possible on the violin, since even the noises created by the bow-hair rubbing the strings never can be obviated entirely. When they are weak, i.e., when they do not interfere with the vibrations of the strings, they are only audible in closest proximity. When the contrary is the case, however, if, for instance, they degenerate into "*scratching*" in consequence of too strong a pressure, they must be numbered among the most disturbing factors in tone production, which to do away with is one of the main objects of the following considerations.

echan- al ob- ms

The string is made to vibrate in the following manner: the bow-hairs are provided with tiny hooklets which, originally smooth, are rendered sharp and uneven by means of rosin-dust. When carried over the strings in this condition, they in a manner of speech "tear" at the strings and set them vibrating. In order to secure uninterrupted contact between bow-hair and strings, a certain *pressure* must be exerted on the bow-stick at its upper part by means of the index finger of the right hand. This pressure must not be so strong that the string is prevented from vibrating, nor yet so weak that it can only be set vibrating imperfectly. In either case scratchy or whistling accompanying noises result. At the lower part of the bow, however, not only the pressure of the first finger is more or less suspended, but through a counter pressure of the fourth finger the weight of the bow is in some way neutralized. Hence, a *healthy* tone, first of all, depends on the correct *quantitative administration* of the pressure to be used, the strength of which varies to a considerable degree in accordance with the prescribed *shading*, *duration of stroke*, the character of the respective *portion of the bow* which is active, and, finally, the number of strings which are to vibrate. In all these cases the *point of contact* between bow-hair and string is subjected to constant change. Hence the production of a good tone is the result first, of a correct administration of pressure, determined by shading, length of stroke, portion of bow used, length of strings and number of strings; secondly, of the correct point of contact between bow and string. In the choice of this *point of contact* the above-mentioned factors are determinative in the finding of this exact point of contact (something which takes place intuitively in advanced bowing technique) in which lies the secret of good tone production.*

Point of Contact

(b) Point of Contact Between Bow and String. The point of contact between bow-hair and string is subject to constant change. It is dependent upon the *duration* of the *bow-stroke*, the *strength* of the *bow-pressure*, and the *position* to which the left hand is shifted. The student will do well to work through the following examples, not only in the manner prescribed, but also in the opposite, faulty manner, in order, as it were, to prove them by contraries.

1. *Duration of Stroke.*

(*a*) Long, "spun" bow stroke, point of contact in the *neighborhood of the bridge*:

247. 

(*Proof by contraries*: at the fingerboard; result=a break in the tone.)

(*b*) Short stroke with the whole bow: *in the vicinity of the fingerboard*:

248. 

(*Proof by contraries*: at the bridge=hoarse scratching.)

---

* *J. Hellmesberger, Sr.*, was accustomed to advise his pupils always to play as near the bridge as possible; while *Sarasate* usually led his bow a considerable distance away from the bridge, hence with a very slight pressure, securing an equalized but indifferently pleasing tone. Incidentally, exaggerated raising of the violin aids the bow in approaching the bridge automatically.

2. *Tonal Power* (*forte* and *piano*)

(*a*) *f, in the vicinity of the bridge*:

249. 

(*Proof by contraries*: at the fingerboard=a break in the tone.)

(*b*) *p, in the vicinity of the fingerboard*:

(*Proof by contraries*: at the bridge=hoarse scratching.)

3. *Height of Position*

(*a*) Lower positions, *between bridge and fingerboard*:

250. 

(*Proof by contraries*: at the bridge or fingerboard=whistling.)

(*b*) Upper positions, *at the bridge*:

251. 

(*Proof by contraries*: at the fingerboard=a break in the tone.)

To sum up:

(*a*) *Long stroke* / *forte* / *High positions* } *in the vicinity of the bridge*

(*b*) *Short stroke* / *piano* / *Low positions* } *in the vicinity of the fingerboard*

Although, on the basis of the attempts which every violinist may undertake on his own account, the fundamental correctness of this rule is placed beyond question; yet its inflexible application in actual practice is impossible, if only for the reason that the individual types soon become too mixed with each other, or nullify each other so that a middle road must be sought in order to equalize the contradictory influences; for instance:

Beethoven, Cto, 2º Mov't.

252. 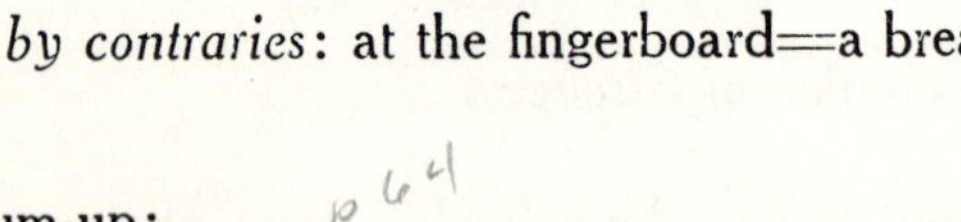

Long stroke=Bridge
p =Fingerboard } Middle

253. 

Short stroke =Fingerboard
f =Bridge
High position=Bridge } Middle-Bridge

In general, the purity of the tone is tested by the player's ear; yet the *eye*, too, may assist in watching the point of contact. Especially in the case of very *high*, sustained notes it is absolutely necessary not to take one's eyes from the bow, to be sure of its remaining in the vicinity of the bridge, on the one hand, and on the other, to prevent its gliding *over* the bridge (the soloist's nightmare). In the case of all other sound combinations which are difficult to materialize, eye-proof as well does excellent service; and for this reason alone, the *lying position* of the head during the performance of tonally difficult passages should be absolutely repudiated (see p. 16).

Taking for granted that the bow is used with the proper pressure, one may boldly affirm that the technical cause of most of the impurely vibrating notes accompanied by secondary noises, lies in an incorrectly selected point of contact between bow and string.

Contrary to the thoughtless opinions of many teachers, who demand that the bow remain in one and the same region, the unhindered *freedom of movement* on the part of the bow between bridge and fingerboard therefore, must be insisted upon as the fundamental law for a purity of vibrations which does justice to all bowing combinations, as well as to all degrees of power and pitch. The fluctuation of the bow appears especially in the case of sustained shaded tones:

254. 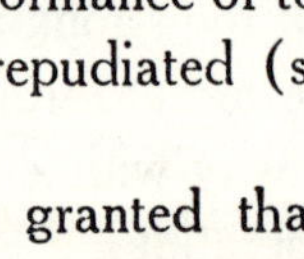

× = Middle
×× = Bridge

255. 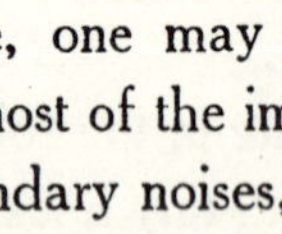

× = Bridge
×× = Bridge-Middle

256. 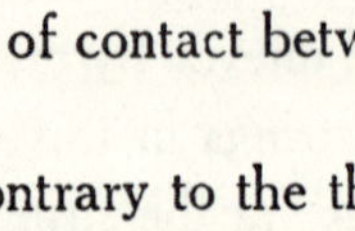

× = Fingerboard-Middle
×× = Bridge-Middle
××× = Fingerboard-Middle

A special difficulty is presented by the choice of points of contact in the *double-stops* and *chords*, a problem closely connected with the mechanics and aesthetics of polyphonic playing, and which must be considered in connection with them.

Since the bow pressure stands in exact relation to the number of the strings across which the bow is to be drawn, double-stops would call for a two-fold increased, and chords for a three- or four-fold increased pressure, especially in view of the convex curve of the bridge. Here the point of contact is determined before all by duration of stroke, height of pitch and nuance; yet with a decided tendency to approach to the bridge, which is easily explicable in view of the fact that the string offers the strongest resistance near its end.

More complex is the relation between the *double-stops* and the *positions*, when the latter are different on the various strings:

Sarasate, La Muñiera

257. 

Here it is a question of finding an equalizing point of contact conformable to the exigencies of the widely differing length of the two strings, a golden middle way. The frequent *breaking of the tone* in double-stops is due mainly to the fact that the player does not take into account the need of approaching the bridge owing to the necessary double bow pressure, and that in the case of positions lying far apart (octaves, tenths) he, as a rule, neglects adapting the various points of contact to each other.

Chords

The inability of most violinists to produce unarpeggiated *chords* in a tonally beautiful manner has resulted in the violin losing reputation, more or less, as a polyphonic instrument. Instead, however, of taking hold of the evil at its root, and striving for a general improvement of bowing technique with regard to chord playing, some have tried to make the form of the modern bow responsible, and to recommend a return to the old form of bow for polyphonic playing. First of all, it is impossible, in view of the failure of testimony by witnesses, to gain an idea of the supposedly better tonal achievements in chord playing by seventeenth and eighteenth century violinists. Hence, I believe that, given a good bow technique, it is quite possible to make three individual notes (when the time duration is not too long) sound simultaneously, namely, at the fingerboard; while the necessary "breaking" of four-note chords may take place in a manner hardly making an arpeggiating effect on the listener's ear. The tonal difficulties in the execution of three-note chords depends on the following circumstance: *Simultaneous* attack of three strings, theoretically, calls for three-fold pressure in corresponding proximity to the bridge. In practice, however, the string position grows the higher (rounder) the more it nears the bridge, while it becomes flatter again in the vicinity of the fingerboard. The point of contact in three-note, non-arpeggiated chords, therefore, would lie in the flatter fingerboard neighborhood, while the requisite increased pressure would afterward make an approach to the bridge necessary:

Not to be arpeggiated

258. 

To be arpeggiated

259. 

It sounds like a truism to declare that we must take for granted that simultaneous sounding of the three strings will result from *simultaneous* contact on the part of the bowhair, and yet in disregard of this self-evident supposition must be sought the customary unjustifiable arpeggiating. The pupil must first of all convince his *eye* that the hair touches the three strings simultaneously. This, in view of the apposition of curved string position and straight hair direction can only be secured, it is true, by the exertion of a certain bow pressure. This follows in form of a pressure accent, i.e., a pressure pause, preceding the attack (see p. 68). Since *four-voice chords* have to be arpeggiated in the proportions of 3:2 or 3:1, they are subject to the same law with regard to the points of contact as are the three-note chords.

Breaking of Chords

We now come to the necessary *chord-breaks*. The word "chord" in itself presupposes the *simultaneous* sounding of several notes.

While the non-observance of this fundamental rule in piano playing rightly stamps a pianist as inferior, not only the majority of violinists, but their listeners as well have grown used to regarding the *arpeggiating* of chords as a matter of course; and, at the most, as an unavoidable evil. That, given a correct bowing technique, it is unnecessary to arpeggiate three-note chords when the tempo is not too slow, already has been explained. At a slow tempo, it is true, arpeggiating cannot well be avoided.

There are five possible ways in which a *three-note chord* may be broken:

260. 

Here No. 5 in Example 260 represents the only correct way of arpeggiating, since the chord is divided into two double-stops, and hence has more of a chordal character than in the other examples. The only exception are those instances in which the melodic line calls for the stressing, i.e., the continued sounding of a certain note.

The ways in which a *four-note chord* may be broken are as follows:

261. 

It will be clear at once that of these ten ways the *last* represents the correct manner of division: 3:2. Exceptions to this rule should be made only in view of certain thematic demands, as well as in the *piano*, where the chords *must* be arpeggiated.

Beethoven, Sonata, A min. 3º Mov't.

262. 

The breaking of the tone in the case of chord strokes is often due to the following causes:

263. 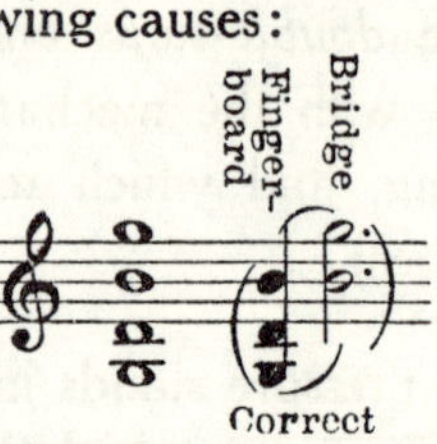

In this chord we begin with the *simultaneous* attack of three strings. The point of contact here lies in the vicinity of the fingerboard, because the beginning of the stroke is somewhat rapid (quick stroke *near the fingerboard*), and furthermore, because the simultaneous grasping of three strings presupposes a less rounded string position. No sooner has the stroke been made, however, than the bow must leave the low strings, and set the two upper strings vibrating. Here, on the other hand, it is a question of a *long-bowed double-stop*, hence one near the bridge. Thus, as we see, a *change* of *point of contact* must follow in sustained chords, during the stroke. If this is neglected, and the three-note chord is begun in the vicinity of the bridge, scratchy accompanying noises will result; while the tone will break when the double-stop forming the second part of the chord is played near the fingerboard.

Defects of Tone Production

(c) Defects of Tone Production. These make themselves felt acoustically in the provenience of plainly audible secondary noises, due to the following mechanical causes:

1. Too *strong* a bow-pressure on the lower half of bow (scratching).
2. Too *slight* a pressure on the upper half of bow.
3. Wrong selection of *point of contact* between bow and string (secondary noises of every kind).
4. As a result of unsatisfactory accessories.
5. Owing to *inexact limitation* of the string-lengths, due to too slight pressure of the applied fingers of the left hand. This last-named hindrance may be disregarded, since it should only be observed, in beginners. (Yet I have noticed some cases of too slight finger pressure even in advanced players due to the thoughtless advice of their teachers to play "relaxed"!) The lines of direction, too, to be observed in the selection of the point of contact already have been discussed in detail (*b. Point of Contact Between Bow and String,* page 81). On the other hand, in connection with the principal mechanical

causes of defective tone production, we must treat one of its most unpleasant and mysterious developments, separately: the *trembling of the right arm* or *bow* in sustained notes.

xag-rated ow ressure

1. *Exaggerated Bow Pressure* mainly on lower part of bow (Scratchy Tone). The natural pressure of the bow, uninfluenced by the player, and produced by the bow's dead weight, varies during the duration of the stroke. If the player should confine himself merely to guiding the bow, the vibrations of the string will be prevented by the bow's own natural weight, in the lower half, causing a crushed tone. Contrariwise, at the point: the uninfluenced bow will find it impossible to set the strings vibrating, since its dead weight alone will not suffice to do so. The player's principal preoccupation, consists of diminishing the bow pressure in the lower half by raising and strengthening it in the upper half by pressing down (the adjustment between the two movements, as well as the transition from one to the other, taking place in the middle of the bow). The danger of too strong a pressure, therefore, is decidedly greater below than above, and is most strongly in evidence during the change of bow at the nut (see p. 59). In any case the bow pressure is dependent on the manner in which the bow is held; in the main it is carried out by the index finger, and only slightly by the middle finger. The little finger (and in a far lesser degree the ring finger) attends to the raising. It is quite clear, therefore, that powerfully exaggerated, vibration-diminishing pressure must, in the main, result from too strong a participation of the index finger, and too slight a participation of the little finger. The daily use of exercises calculated to strengthen the ring and the little fingers —whereby the pressure of the index finger is, so to speak, held in check—should cause the elimination of the scratchy tone. I recommend the following *Exercises*:

Rapidly repeated notes at the extreme nut in *pianissimo*, with as little bow as possible, executed with the greatest velocity.

264. 

265. 

266. 

267. 

2. *Insufficient Bow-Pressure* mainly on upper part of bow (hoarse, whistling tone). This develops owing to lack of realization of the fact that it is the task of the index finger to press the bow so strongly upon the string that the latter is set vibrating regularly. Since at the lower half the dead weight of the bow alone is not only sufficient, but must even be weakened by the pressure of the little finger, the participation of the index finger is principally important in the upper half. The index finger must be accustomed to its tone-producing mission. The following *series of exercises* are recommended for that purpose. **Insufficient Bow Pressure**

(*a*) *Mute Pressure Exercises.* After the bow has been laid on the string at the middle, it is pressed down upon the string by means of the second or third joint of the index finger (according to the school of finger-position), and the pressure relaxed again when a second has passed (eight repetitions).*

(*b*) *Martelé-Exercise*, from the middle to the point, with pressure pause (see p. 68).

(c) *Portato Stroke* (see p. 73). While *a* and *b* are to be regarded merely as preliminary studies, the *portato*-stroke should be considered the principal exercise, as in itself it is able to give the bow that precious quality of elastic adherence to the string which the French school, in its untranslatable fashion, terms *l'archet à la corde.* Every legato may be turned into a *portato* exercise. The stroke must possess a soft, singing character, without pressure pause. The elastic pressure is made upon the note itself, and not as in the staccato *between* the notes.**

268. 

*Not to be exaggerated!

**Regarding the unjustified use of portato instead of legato in performance see p. 97.

Defects in Tone Color

3. *Defects in Tone Color.* If we now proceed from the *cause* of faulty mechanics to its *effect*, in the form of insufficient tonal results, we find that the following tonal insufficiencies occur most frequently:

(*a*) *The Scratchy Détaché. Effect*: Scratchy accompanying noises, as in *ponticello* playing.

Cause: Point of contact too near the bridge.*

Correction: Transference of point of contact in the direction of the fingerboard.

(*b*) *The Indistinct Détaché. Effect*: Indeterminate, hoarse accompanying noises.

Cause: Insufficient bow-pressure.

Correction: Mute pressure exercises.

(*c*) *Breaking of the Tone in Double-Stops*—too near the fingerboard. The pressing down of two strings demands a redoubled pressure, to which the string can best offer the necessary resistance in the neighborhood of its terminal end at the bridge.

(*d*) *Breaking of the Tone in the Case of High, "Spun" Tones*—not near enough to the bridge.

Rode goes over this!

269.  (not harmonic)

This note, for instance, can only sound pure when the bow is shoved up so close to the bridge that the latter at times is touched by its hairs.

(*e*) *The Colorless, Flat Tone Formation.* With this term ("flat tone") we understand in general a quality of tone which is unpleasantly noticeable because of a certain lack of body, though a definite breaking or failing of the sound cannot be verified. The technical cause of this widely prevalent fault lies in the player's tendency to choose a point of contact somewhat too near the fingerboard, and to exert the pressure at a point so far removed from the bridge that the string no longer possesses the necessary power of resistance to bear up against it. *Spun tones* or *legato exercises*, played *pp*, and in the *immediate neighborhood of the bridge*, used as daily exercises will usually root out this fault.

---

*Especially noticeable in violoncello-playing!

(*f*) *Breaking of the Tone* in consequence of the sliding off of the bow at the point upon the fingerboard with undiminished pressure. When, on the other hand, the pressure at the point is diminished, a *diminuendo* occurs regularly which may easily degenerate into a mannerism. The sliding off of the bow may only occur in consequence of an *intentional* diminution of the tone power. When it occurs involuntarily, on the other hand, it is the result of technical shortcomings, for instance:

(*a*) Drawing the bow to the back instead of straight.

Correction: *Détaché* exercises (middle to point) in the opposite direction, away from the body.

(*b*) *Holding the Violin too Low.*

Correction: Temporary exaggeration of an elevated position of the violin.

One of the reasons for the frequent occurrence of all these tonal faults lies in the fact that we all share a tendency to ascribe the failure of a note to sound, less to ourselves, than to some unlucky *chance* or the treachery of the instrument.

Even players accustomed to strive for perfected *intonation* are in the habit of passing over *accompanying noises* produced by the bow without making a single move toward bettering them; this proves that an ear may react ever so sensitively to the *number* of *vibrations*, and yet in spite of the fact may not be keenly sensitive to impeccability of *quality in tone*. It is a question, therefore, of developing the ear into as delicately responsive an instrument as possible in this respect as well. This is most surely attained when the player accustoms himself to improve not merely the false note, but also those accompanied by disturbing noises, letting his eyes determine the presumably wrong points of contact between bow and string, and trying to find (along the lines already laid down) the narrowly bounded point of contact peculiar to each note, and dependent upon its power, duration and pitch.**

**A special treatise dealing with the rules of the point of contact in a more extensive way has been published by myself under the title "*Problems of Tone Production in Violin Playing*" (Carl Fischer, New York).

fec- rials e Ma-

4. Among the faulty tonal results due to defective material, the tendency of the strings to whistle in too damp or too dry temperature has to be mentioned first. It is true that the reign of the gut string, one of the most sensitive barometers, is over for ever, but how violinists have suffered in the past under its unbearable domination! With the predominance of steel strings, we are now almost independent of weather-conditions and there remains only a slight disposition of the metal E to whistle when change of strings on the open string in legato-playing takes place. This may be prevented by using as a rule the fourth finger on the A instead of the open E, or by drawing the bow near the bridge in such critical instances. Furthermore, strings have to be cleaned carefully with a silk cloth to prevent the forming of a rosin-crust.

As a consequence of too low a bridge or too oblique a position of the violin-neck, and the consequent excessively high fingerboard position, the strings, too, may touch the fingerboard when a powerful stroke is used, whereby *rattling* or *buzzing* accompanying noises are produced. We have, in particular, the frequent rattling of the G-string, to which players so easily accustom themselves, and which produces a most disturbing effect on the listener. These varieties of secondary noises may be avoided with ease by means of a correctly placed violin-neck, a sufficiently high bridge, as well as a regularly rounded fingerboard, provided the player does not expect the violin to give him more in point of tone than it has to give.

The unintentional *simultaneous touching of two strings* may also be most annoying. Here the *bridge* is mainly to blame, unless it is so curved that the player can exert strong pressure on the middle strings without the bow touching their neighbors. When the bridge is cut too flat it is almost impossible to touch the A or D strings clearly when too near the fingerboard.

The degree to which the bridge should be rounded is determined by the individual strength and elasticity of the bow pressure, which differs in the case of every violinist. I myself prefer the bridge cut in the French style, because even when playing near the fingerboard it still permits of a certain pressure on the string, something impossible in the case of a flat bridge. It is well known that *Ole Bull* played on a bridge almost completely flat, in order to make possible the simultaneous sounding of a four-note chord. That in such cases a *forte* on single notes on the middle strings becomes impossible, is evident.

When the bridge inclines too far *forward*, the high notes are apt not to respond ("speak"). A bridge provided with expertly cut feet should either form a right angle with the belly, or incline a little backward. In general a bridge which leans forward is responsible for a deterioration of tone quality, as well as scratchy accompanying noises in the case of high notes. The bridge may incline forward for three reasons: The feet may have been so cut that they automatically compel a forward inclination of the bridge; or the wood used for the bridge may not be quite dry and may bend, in which case only the upper part of the bridge will incline forward; or, finally, when the player does not occasionally correct the forward inclination of the bridge due to drawing up the strings, by making it return to its original position whenever he winds up a new string. This operation should be carried out with the greatest care, if the bridge is not to be completely tipped over. The best thing to do is to have some experienced violin-maker show one the trick of doing it, simple enough in itself, during which the violin is held securely between the knees.

Bow-stick

The *bow-stick*, in its character of a tool principally necessary for the production of tone, must comply with the following requirements: appropriate weight, equalized division of weight, stability in the middle, a straight-linear direction, sufficient elasticity, bow-hair which as yet has not been used up, equalized and correctly proportioned rubbing with rosin. When the bow is too light too much strength is needed to press it down at the point; while too heavy a bow is awkward to handle at the nut. When the stick trembles in the middle, a wavering tone results at that point. Too weak a stick disadvantageously affects the springing and thrown strokes; while on the other hand, the softness of tone production as a whole suffers from too great hardness and inelasticity of the stick.

Bow-hair which has been used too long, no longer takes up the rosin-dust (it no longer "grasps" the strings), and the tone gives out in *forte*. When rosin is too lavishly used, the strings are "torn" too sharply, they scratch; when too little rosin is used the hooklets of the bow-hair glide over the strings without finding enough resistance; it whistles (see p. 13).

When the bow-stick bends in the direction of the finger-board, or when the hair has been torn gradually, *touching the string* with the *wood* of the bow-stick can hardly be avoided. We know that this evil is least to be feared when the bow is held straight, since in that case the stick lies *directly* over the hair, and hence is never in a position to touch the strings. When the bow is held slantwise the cause of undesirable contact must be sought either in too slight a bow-tension or too strong a pressure. In the first case the evil may easily be remedied by increased tension. In the second, the pupil's attention must first of all be called to the accompanying noise mentioned, for in most cases; he has already grown so used to this "scraping" that he no longer notices it. Once this has been done, the stick must either be held less slantingly, or the pressure be diminished. The manner in which the bow is held, however, here exerts too great an influence to permit of the setting up of general rules. Under all circumstances contact between wood and string must be avoided.

Trembling (Shaking) With the Bow

We now approach a phenomenon in which the violinistic world has always taken the greatest interest: *the habitual, involuntary trembling of the right arm*, and, together with it, of the bow. First of all, we will exclude in advance the lack of stability in the stick due to faulty division of its weight, demonstrated in the middle by independent vibrations, which the player is hardly able to prevent: in the case of a really good bow, neither too heavy at the nut nor too light at the point, the independent vibrations of the stick in the middle are reduced to a hardly visible, sensible and audible minimum. We will here concern ourselves only with the curious, involuntary movements of the arm which prevent a steadiness of tone, and which are generally defined by the word "*trembling*." In the case of a violinist afflicted with this mysterious malady, we first must ask ourselves the question: Is the trembling due to mechanical or psychic causes, in other words, is it caused by hindrances of body or of mind? Hence we will undertake a thorough examination of the hand, in accordance with the primal movements determined in the *Basic Studies*,* and endeavor to do away with whatever mechanical hindrances we may encounter by means of corresponding exercises, keeping the wrist and the finger-stroke especially in mind.

Mechanical Causes

It is also important to find out whether the fingers hold the bow with too uniformly tense a grip, which in itself would suffice to call forth the unhappy condition mentioned. An effective curative means in this case is the pressing down of the stick with an increased outward *turning of the lower arm* in the elbow-joint, whereby the sources of strength are transferred from hand and fingers to the upper and lower arm. Many violinists also succeed in preventing trembling of the hand by means of a *wave-like vertical or horizontal movement* of the arm in a vertical or horizontal direction. Under normal conditions, these wave-like movements, it is true, must be rejected as a waste of strength (at the most the *vertical* movement, in the case of very long sustained strokes, may be appropriate and effective in making them slower). When, however, they are able to exert a favorable influence on the trembling, one need not hesitate to use them, since it already is a sign of progress when a lesser takes the place of a greater evil. Since the vibrations peculiar to the bow-stick, so little desired in this instance (in contrast to those desired for the springing bowings) appear principally with a straight position, and much less frequently with a slanting position of the bow-stick, the question obtrudes itself whether placing the bow *on edge* may not be regarded as one of the first curative means to which recourse should be had. It is true that the bow would have to be far more tensely screwed than the specific character of the Russian manner of using the bow permits, so that the latter would have to be abandoned altogether which, on occasion, might mean a severe sacrifice.

**Carl Flesch Basic Studies* (*Urstudien*) Carl Fischer, N. Y.

When the visible, mechanical hindrances, so far as the teacher is able to tell, have been overcome and no improvement is evinced, our endeavors must be transferred to the *psychic* field.

It is well known that the incitants to disease first attack the place of least resistance in an organism. Similarly *stage fright* makes itself evident, first of all, at the weakest point of the technique as a whole. In consequence, the violinist may play out of tune (because either his hearing or his change of position is uncertain); his runs may be indistinct (because his finger power is inadequate); and so forth. The same applies in the psychic field. When the pupil possesses only a limited amount of temperament and sensitiveness, he loses both completely when he becomes frightened. If, on the contrary, he inclines to extravagance, he will "plunge" with the greatest detriment to technical smoothness and a musically refined interpretation. Hence, should a fear of public performance continue to evince itself, in spite of the elimination of visible defects in bowing technique, we cannot help but conclude that the bowing as a whole is not as yet sure enough, and another attempt should be made to raise the bowing and tone producing technique of the pupil to a higher level by means of appropriate exercises. Since the involuntary vibrations of the stick in the middle, in themselves call forth a trembling of the bow, which is most marked when the stick is held vertically, the patient should be admonished, should there be danger of trembling, immediately to hold the stick edgewise, that is, slantingly. In addition, he must first of all change the bow *more frequently*, and avoid long-sustained notes—for psychical reasons—in order that the idea that he *must* tremble will not obsess him to an even greater degree. At times too rapid, nervous and uninterrupted *vibrating* of the left hand may automatically transfer this excessive excitation to the right hand. In such case exercises in the form of an occasional complete elimination of the *vibrato* during practice may have a beneficial effect.

The situation is quite different when the trembling is produced by *neurasthenia* or some organically conditioned *nervous disorder*. In such cases the physician must intervene.

Psychic Causes

He must also do so when the coercive conception of trembling cannot be dispelled by our curative measures. By the term *coercive conception* or *fixed idea*, we mean a conception which appears again and again against a person's will. And the fear that the bow will tremble may become a coercive idea of this kind. In general, two varieties of violinists are afflicted with chronic trembling: younger violinists, who began as "infant prodigies," and violinists advanced in age, in whom the trembling is merely a normal indication of senility. Those in the second class have no place in our investigations. But it is positive so far as the *child* playing in public is concerned, that, until it reaches the age of puberty, i.e., up to about the thirteenth year, it plays quite unconsciously and in the main by impulse. It does not give much thought to the difficulties of every kind to be overcome, and enjoys the applause of the multitude as it would some manifestation of fairyland. In the crises of puberty the child first becomes *conscious* of its achievement, its difficulties and faults, and makes the acquaintance of the slinking, invisible enemy of artistic perfection, *fear*. Its technique becomes uncertain, its ability to concentrate develops gaps, and some day, when especially ill-disposed to appear on the concert platform, the right hand, and with it the bow, begins to tremble. The impression made by this hitherto unknown defect is a crushing one. The player dreads its return, it is constantly in his thoughts, and the mere thought in itself is enough to bring about the return of the evil. Now the coercive conception is fixed, appearance in public and trembling are indissolubly united, the one brings the other in its train. Since apparently it is unavoidable, the player seeks to disguise it by drawing the bow as rapidly as possible across the dangerous spot in the middle, by constantly changing the stroke, and subordinating his interpretation as a whole to his efforts to avoid the trembling. Thus his performance takes on an unnatural character, and no longer makes a convincing effect. *Piano* sections as well as quiet cantilenas are now forbidden him, the thought of his fatality paralyzes his technique, dries up the well-spring of his receptivity, and makes him the unhappiest of creatures.

The teacher is only helpless with regard to this complex if he confines himself purely to mechanical measures; he must therefore transfer his efforts to the realm of psychic influence; must, so to speak, change his profession and become a psychologist and nerve specialist. He should insist upon raising the general physical condition, abstinence from stimulants and the avoidance of excesses; above all, he should never reproach the pupil with his defect, but present it as a negligible one, pointing out that it usually disappears by itself in the course of time. The pupil should be encouraged in every way, and his self-confidence should be raised. The teacher must show himself a *friend*, helpful with good advice, rather than a *judge* sitting in judgment.

Cure of Shaking

But apart from this purely psychical influence I believe I have succeeded in discovering an undoubtedly efficient way of checking the gradual violinistic deterioration occasioned by the fixed idea of shaking.

Let us follow the different stages through which my thinking faculties had to pass before reaching the final conclusion.

The mental *expectation* of shaking preceeds always the actual shaking itself. The mind concentrates on the bowing, the eye watches anxiously its different parts, fatalistically awaiting the much dreaded catastrophe. It seems impossible to persuade the player *not* to think of the fact of shaking; but what about if we found a way to force him to concentrate on *something else*—for instance on the movements of the left hand—on the Vibrato? This procedure would produce indirectly a kind of natural diversion, which could never be obtained through purely verbal persuasion. The only way to prevent the mind from thinking of a certain subject consists in leading it in a different direction, by concentrating on a *different* subject. The results of this method have proven its rightness. If a "shaking" violinist feels the approach of its complex and looks instantly at his left hand, concentrating on the Vibrato, the tendency to shake will disappear immediately. This remedy, the use of which does not require any special exercises, may be strongly recommended to all sufferers of this Violinistic Cancer.

Dynamics

(d) Dynamics. It is the gradation of tone power, *dynamics*, which in conjunction with tone color, conjures forth those illimitable tonal possibilities which raise the violin to the rank of the greatest interpreter of homophony.*

We differentiate among five points of junction in the endless chain of dynamic possibilities, as follows: 1, the *strong* (*f*); 2, the *weak* (*p*); 3, the swelling (*crescendo* $<$) and the diminishing (*decrescendo* $>$); and 4, the *accentuated* ($>$ or *sf*) tone.

Forte

1. *The Strong Tone.* The violinist's mode of expression when judging tone production is well-nigh exclusively dominated by the adjectives "great" and "beautiful," or by their opposites. Acoustically a beautiful tone means sounds free from accompanying noises, with as many and as well graded over-tones as possible. The term "large" or "big" tone calls for the following explanation. It is not enough for a tone to sound powerful nearby; before all, it must be clearly and distinctly audible at a certain distance; it must be a *carrying* tone. We distinguish between the nearby and the distant effect of a sound. Good Italian instruments usually sound weak in a room and resonant in a hall. Furthermore, individual tone production may at times call forth an impression of power in a small room and weakness in a large one. In a room of 13 cubic yards even the thinnest tone will seem gigantic.

* The theory of rhythm, since it is most closely connected with artistic performance as a whole, will be considered in detail in the second volume of this work.

Hence the test of largeness or "bigness" of tone is not its power in a small room, but its carrying capacity in a large one. Besides the purity of the vibrations, their breadth has a determining effect on the carrying capacity of the tone. The vibrations, however, gain in breadth the less friction there is between bow and string. Now this same degree of tonal power may, *apparently*, be produced in two ways:

With *little bow* and *strong pressure* in the vicinity of the bridge.

With *much bow* and *weak pressure* further away from the bridge. Which is really the more powerful, that is, which carries the furthest? The strings themselves supply an answer. An examination of their vibratory breadth shows us that when the greater length of bow is used they vibrate with double the breadth produced by the lesser length, and this conclusion is absolutely justified by the result obtained. The teaching gospel of the large bow stroke is the kernel of the Franco-Belgian as well as the Russian school of violinists and, in general, is surely one of the most valid and recognized of principles. That on occasion a firmly limned, self-determined personality unconsciously may give the preference to a mode of playing opposed to the laws generally observed (*Kreisler*), does not alter the fact. Such external examples, however, usually are too closely bound up with the inner need of expression, the personal means are so necessarily the consequence of an individual receptivity, that the mere *imitation* of their technical peculiarity without, so to say, its having been compelled by the inner impulse, bear the stamp of insincerity, and even of artistic falsification. In general, increased pressure at the expense of diminished bow expenditure in the *forte* is to be rejected. The only exceptions which might be made in this case are: an undeniable inner compulsion and the unreliability of the material used (an instrument which does not respond easily, unresponsive or whistling strings, worn-out bow-hair). In the following examples an increased expenditure of bow, one which touches the extreme limit possible, is indicated:

Beethoven, Romanza, F maj.

270. 

Bruch, Cto, G min. 1º Mov't.

271. 

Lalo, Cto, F min. 2º Mov't.

272. 

Mozart, Cto, A maj. 1º Mov't.

273 

Ernst, Cto, F♯ min.

274. 

Long-drawn Bowings

When a *forte* is to be produced, its execution had best begin with the *down-bow*, since there the necessary pressure is automatically furnished by the weight of the bow, and does not, as in the case of the up-bow, first have to be produced by an increased exertion of strength. One of the noblest privileges of a good bowing technique is the ability to play sustained movements with a *long-drawn bow*, rather than being forced to change the bow frequently.

Beethoven, Quartet Op. 127. Cavatina

275. 

How much more expressively the noble grandeur of this *cantilena* is developed in this case by means of a *single* bow-stroke, rather than by dividing the second from the third quarter!

Bach, Cto, E maj. Adagio

276. 

In this case, however, a change of stroke in the second measure is decidedly advisable, since otherwise, in view of the extremely slow tempo (♪=about 48) here indicated, the tonal beauty is seriously threatened. Violinists who take the greatest pride in giving the individual bow-stroke its longest possible lease of life, irrespective of whether the result obtained is tonally beyond objection, in my opinion, place sporting interest before artistic seriousness.

Bach, Partita G min. Siciliana

277. 

The counterpart of this type of player is the violinist whose "big tone" is only possible as the result of an all too frequent change of bow. When the bow is otherwise quietly led, the art of executing long-sustained notes in *forte* without effort is not so difficult to acquire, if one will practice long-drawn notes in *f* for a while, gradually increasing their time of duration until the extreme limit has been reached. The longer the bow-stroke lasts, the nearer the point of contact, which remains unchanged, lies to the bridge. We should not forget to mention the artificial strengthening of a tone by purposely making the octave sound with it, as for instance:

apparently one does not bow the octave; it just sounds or vibrates sympathetically!

mute stopping — *Bach-Wilhelmj*, Aria

276a. 

"Reprendre l'archet"

It would be proper to call attention here to the widespread habit of once more bowing back a bit in a manner more or less audible ("*reprendre l'archet*") when there is danger of the initial bow stroke not sufficing as to bow length. When the pause which thereby results is musically justifiable and remains inaudible, no objection need be made. Yet, instead of:

Bach, Partita G min. Siciliana

#1

277. 

one often hears:

278. 

Hereby not only foreign notes are interpolated, but the rhythm of the Siciliana as well is completely destroyed. This procedure can be justified only when its breathless and oppressive moment corresponds to the character of the passage to be interpreted, for instance:

Adagio — *Dvořak,* F min. Trio, 2º Mov't.

279. 

(Take back the bow)

In a rapid and powerful legato the point of contact is subject to continuous change, mainly determined by the length of the stroke and of the strings (height of position). It is most plainly evident where a decided difference in position demands an adjustment of the two points of contact which it is difficult to determine:

Paganini, Caprice Nº 12

280. 

In the following instance the case is different:

(in the 2º Position) — *Rode,* Caprice Nº 3

281. 

The point of contact, in consequence of the equalized length of stroke as well as of the position, which remains the same, is subject to but few changes.

Double Stops in f

Double-stops in themselves already call for a doubled pressure, which must be decidedly increased in a *forte.* The well-known exercise:

Dont, Op. 35, Nº 16

282. 

must invariably be played at the *nut,* since the coincidence of double-stops, *forte* and increased pressure at the *point* demand three times as great an exertion of strength as at the nut, whereby the weight of the bow, greater in itself, already assumes part of the pressure.

In *legato,* on the other hand, in comparison to the single notes, only double the power is needed, and all other proportions with regard to length of stroke, height of position and change of string remain the same.

Chords in Forte

In the case of *three- and four-voice chords* the pressure to be applied in the *forte* would only be increased in direct proportion to the number of strings, were it possible to continue sounding more than two strings simultaneously. Since in the case of three strings this is only possible for a short space of time, and is altogether impossible in that of four strings, the tripled string pressure may, perhaps, occur with rapid strokes; but calls for consideration in slow bowings only at the beginning when a simultaneous attack is made on all three strings.

All in all, in producing a "big" tone it is a question of measuring pressure and bow expenditure with the aid of an equalized bow mechanism, and of bearing in mind the correct point of contact (dependent on length of stroke and height of position) so exactly that a *maximum breadth of vibration* is attained.

Soft Tone (p)

2. *The Soft Tone* (*p*). As a result of a lesser breadth of vibration, the listener receives the impression of a softer tone. It is secured by means of diminished bow pressure, diminished bow expenditure and

proximity to the fingerboard. *Diminished bow expenditure* is a comfortable, yet in general an inferior means of securing a lesser degree of tone power, because the carrying power of the tone is noticeably diminished thereby. It should be used only in exceptional cases:

283. 
Schubert, Rondo brillante
p
extreme point

Here the use of the entire upper half of the bow would cause an unmusical accent on the eight-note. Furthermore:

284. 
upper half
Beethoven, Quart. Op. 95, 3º Mov't.

Here the use of the whole bow is synonymous with an unnecessary increase of difficulty in effecting a change of string at the nut, as well as increased danger of failure of the string to respond. In *chamber music*, too, as well as in *orchestral playing*, in the case of subordinate accompanying formulas, where the main question is not the production of the best possible tonal effect, but seeing that the attention of the auditors is not distracted from the leading voice, diminished bow-expenditure to secure a *piano* is to be recommended.

The *diminished pressure* is the most natural way of producing a soft tone. When only part of the entire bow length is used, the *upper* half, in consequence of its diminished natural weight, should be preferred to the lower one. Individual soft notes or the beginning of a sequence of such notes would most appropriately be produced in the *up-bow* (because of the greater lightness of the bow) and at the point. The *piano* with the *lower* half of the bow, produced by diminution of the weight, is one of the most difficult tasks in bowing technique, and whenever possible is avoided in practice. For study purposes, however, it is one of the most useful bowing and tone exercises, by means of which a frictionless coordination between the upper and lower halves of the bow, especially difficult in a *piano*, may be secured. A *piano* on the fingerboard presupposes the greatest possible expenditure of bow:

285. 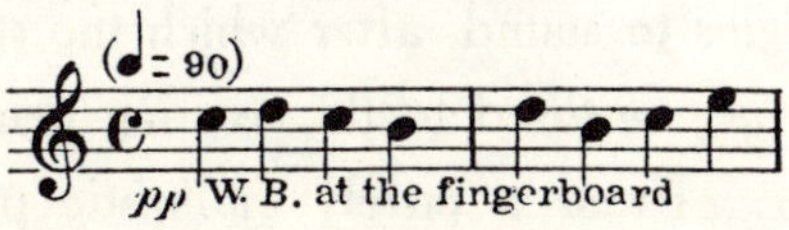
(♩= 90)
pp W. B. at the fingerboard

On the other hand, this exercise in the following tempo, ♩ =30, played with the whole bow on the fingerboard, would lack tonal substance. In the above tempo the point of contact is in the middle of the playing surface, while hardly any pressure is exercised.

Change of Positions in p

Diminished pressure which is not produced by raising the bow, but resulting automatically when the player inclines the *upper part of the body* (and with it the bow) more or less *to the right*, whereby the bow pressure is suspended to a certain degree, still calls for mention. This manner of holding the body is in most cases unconsciously used; yet it does not seem out of place to call the pupil's attention to its great advantages in a passage like the following, where the necessary sureness and delicacy develop automatically:

286. 
Mozart, D-maj. Cto, 3º Mov't.
A

287. 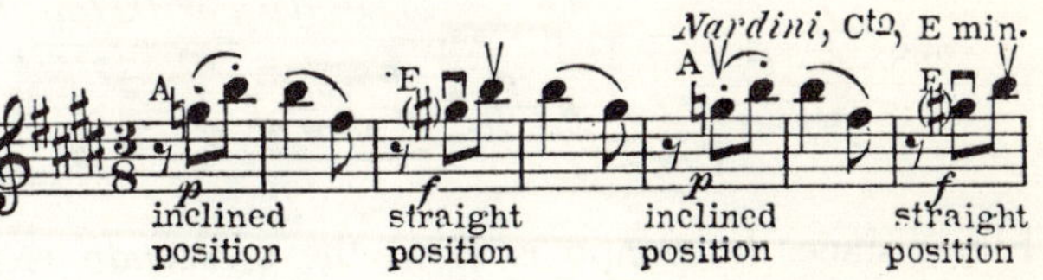
Nardini, Cto, E min.
A
E
A
E
p
f
p
f
inclined position
straight position
inclined position
straight position

Shoulder Pedal

Akin to this is what I call the "*shoulder pedal.*" If, while playing, we raise the right shoulder unnaturally high (see Ill. 35), a strange dampening of the tone results, whereby it takes on a similar color to that produced by the use of the soft pedal on the piano. I will content myself with establishing this easily proved fact, and will leave to the professional anatomist and physiologist the discovery of its causes. I realize that by calling attention to this automatic means of dampening I am putting a dangerous *toy* into the hands of many violinists. Hence I warn my colleagues not to be induced to make continual use of this means in order to secure a soft tone production minus effort. The tonal disadvantages would be the same as those developed by constant use of the piano soft pedal; at first, a pleasurable sensation, little by little indifference on the listener's part in consequence of the absence of strong, healthy tone colors. To this must be added the unnatural drawing up of the shoulder, soon causing intense fatigue; abuse in using this position may degenerate into **chronic** arm trouble. *Occasionally* employed (for instance, in the case of prescribed echo effects), it supplies an entirely effortless mode of producing a *piano*, one which borders on the miraculous. Without wishing to anticipate further investigations about this mysterious process, I must declare on the basis of my personal investigations that the pedagogic and *conscious* utilization of the shoulder pedal seems impossible; and I incline to the opinion that this movement belongs among those which might be termed "subconscious movements," and which consciously used, exert a paralysing effect on immediacy of expression.

Crescendo and Decrescendo

3. *The Swelling and Dying Away of the Tone* (*crescendo and decrescendo*). The *crescendo* may be produced in either of two ways: by means of a gradually increasing expenditure of bow, or by means of a gradually increased bow pressure.

Bach-Wilhelmj, Aria

288.

Here, since the tempo is slow, the *crescendo* is mainly produced by increase of pressure, to secure which in the up-bow the bow-weight of the lower half in itself is enough.

Vieuxtemps, Cto, A min.

289.

Here the *crescendo* is produced by means of *unequal bow division*:

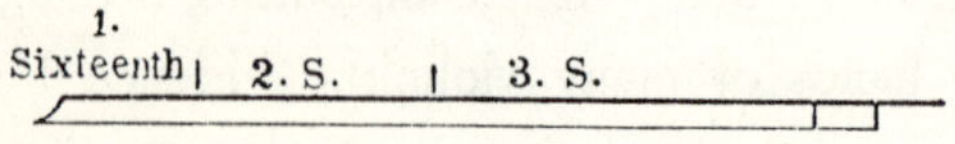
1.
Sixteenth
2. S.
3. S.

With regard to the manner of producing the *crescendo*, the length of stroke as well as the choice of the ⊓ or the V determine it before all else: in the ⊓ increased bow-expenditure; in the V increased pressure.

The choice of the *down-bow* or the *up-bow* is of great importance here, because the down-bow always indicates a natural *decrescendo* and the up-bow a natural *crescendo*. Hence, in *performance*, the player should adapt himself to this condition; while when *studying* the very difficulties of the down-bow *crescendo* as well as the up-bow *decrescendo* will tempt him at times. The swelling of the tone is supported by *raising* the violin. In certain cases this is advantageous if only for the reason that the raising of the instrument accompanying the increase in power of the tone represents a logical and visually satisfying movement and, so to speak, makes the *crescendo* visible. Employed as a matter of *principle*, however, it is less commendable, since it induces the bow to remain passive.

Inversely, the decrescendo always is produced by *diminution* of pressure, or by a gradually *diminished* expenditure of bow, in which case, as in that of the *crescendo*, the duration of stroke as well as the V or ⊓ decide.

The *lowering* of the violin to produce a diminuendo injures tone production as well as the whole manner of playing. Besides, it does not look well, and hence should be repudiated unconditionally. Nor should we omit to mention the incorrect execution of the *crescendo* and *decrescendo* (as well as *ritard.* and *accel.*) directly brought about by inexact estimation of the note-picture; one can only increase in power when beginning softly, and decrease when beginning powerfully. In order to become slower I must first play relatively fast; in order to increase in speed I must have played relatively slowly.

< means, first of all, *piano, afterward crescendo.*

> means, first of all, *forte, then decrescendo.*

(*ritard.* means beginning relatively fast and gradually growing slower; *accel.* the opposite). Most players at < think principally of the *forte*, at > before all else, of the *piano*. They already slow up before the entrance of the *ritard.*, and begin to storm onward as soon as they catch sight of the *accelerando* sign.

Accents

4. *The Accents.* By the term *accent* we understand the emphasizing or strengthening of an individual note when it *begins* to sound, after which the strength of the note is at once restored to the existing general plane of tone power. From a purely violinistic point of view,

as well as with respect to the tonal effect and the manner of production, we may distinguish between three kinds of accent:

(*a*) Accent *after change of bow*, yet *without* preceding pause:

Beethoven, Quartet, Op. 18, Nº 4, 1º Mov't.

290. 

(*b*) Accent *after change of bow*, but *with* preceding pause, i.e., as *an initial accent*:

291. 

(*c*) Accent *in the midst* of a *legato*:

Beethoven, Quartet Op. 59, Nº 1, 1º Mov't.

292. 

The accentuation is always produced by means of heightened pressure or increased expenditure of bow; the latter in such case has a more violent character than in the *crescendo* or *decrescendo*. Example 290 requires increased bow expenditure, since heightened pressure (at the nut), would easily cause danger of *forcing*. In Example 291, on the other hand, the accent is best produced by means of a combination of mute *pressure accent* and accelerated bowing. In Example 292, again, the right mixture of acceleration and pressure is called for, which must be in proportion to the general level of tonal strength prescribed, inasmuch as here an accent in the *piano* would be produced merely by acceleration, and in the *forte* by acceleration *and* strengthening.

Judgment as to the more or less appropriate manner of carrying out an accent is passed, first of all, on the basis of the *tonal* results which are achieved thereby. In spite of the violent movement, we must try to secure *pure* string vibrations, and not a tone interspersed with accompanying noises. Only in the case of an accent following a pressure pause is a species of accompanying noise of the shortest possible duration admissible and even necessary; as in the case of the *martelé* stroke, the study of which at the same time carries with it control of this accent. We also often call this type of beginning accent an *attack*. The application of the attack after a preceding pressure pause, the violinistic symbol of energy, is a characteristic peculiar to the Franco-Belgian school. Its tonally unobjectionable execution may even be considered a criterion of good bowing. Its application in accents is best shown by the following example:

Brahms, Ctº, 1º Mov't

293. 

Here only those chords marked with a > are produced by an *attack* after a very short pressure pause.

Accents in V

Accents in the Up-Bow indicate a waste of strength, and should be avoided whenever possible in actual *performance;* in *exercises*, however, they are of practical service. An exception in this connection is the accentuation in certain bowings combined with change of string, in which the accent makes the best effect in the V, for instance:

Wieniawski, Scherzo-Tarantelle

294. 

or

Mendelssohn, Ctº, 1º Mov't

295. 

In both cases the accent can only be produced with corresponding distinctness when studied in a slow tempo at the extreme point, even with *raising* and *flinging down* of the bow. The *left hand*, too in its way, may assist in strengthening the > brought about by the bow, by means of violent change of position, as well as of excessively strong setting of the finger in question:

Ernst, Airs hongrois

296. 
G String

Saint-Saëns, Cto, B min. 3º Mov't.

297. 

Accents in p

Accents in *piano* demand a corresponding diminution of pressure or of bow expenditure while favoring the vicinity of the fingerboard, and absolutely eliminating the attack. The danger of accompanying noises of every kind is decidedly greatest at the beginning of the attack. This brings us to a consideration of accentuation in the negative sense, that is, *the avoidance of undesirable accents.*

Attacks

While the accented attack actually is characterized by a tiny accompanying noise, the *unaccented attack (start)* must be absolutely impeccable. Here we might mention the old debatable point whether, at the beginning of a stroke, the bow-hair should touch the strings the fraction of a second *before*, or whether the bow should begin its movement in the air and, so to speak, *take along* the string on its way. In connection with our reflections it is possible, perhaps, to develop guiding lines through aid of which a decision regarding the best method of attack may be arrived at as demanded by individual cases. These reflections are:

1. That method of attack is best which produces no manner of accompanying noises.

2. When a phrase begins on the up-bow the preceding contact between string and bow (even in *piano*) is desirable.

3. At the *nut* an absolutely faultless attack in *piano* is easier *without* a preceding contact. Here the "taking along" of the string after a tiny soundless stroke in the air seems most advisable.

4. In no case should the bow drop down upon the string from above (the "attack" of the orchestral player, see p. 97).

Dynamic Fault

(e) Dynamic Faults. Among these must be counted first of all:

(*a*) Unjustified, habitual *increasing and diminishing* in the course of a single bow-stroke.

298. Notation: 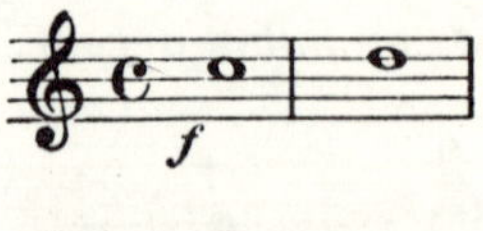
f

299. Faulty Execution: 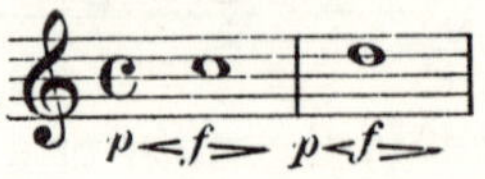
p<f> p<f>

a mannerism which, though in the long run unendurable to the listener, is very widespread, and which excludes any more delicate shading. It produces its most unpleasant effect in the *portamento* (see p. 34).

300. Notation: 
1
4
f

301. Faulty Execution: 

Correction: The avoidance of the increase by means of decisive, very exaggerated *crescendo* and *decrescendo* exercises:

302. 
ff> p ff> p

and the reverse:

303. 
p<ff p<ff

In addition, bow-strokes with a sharp opening attack and an exaggeratedly rapid initial speed:

304. 
sf sf sf sf

(b) Unjustified, habitual portato.

This is in evidence especially in the slow *legato*. For all that it may incidentally be so useful as an exercise, it is quite as objectionable and insupportable to the listener when used as a means of expression. A performance good in itself may be completely distorted by this intolerable habit:

Wrong *Beethoven*, Cto, 1º Mov't.

305. 

Correction: Demonstration of the fault by means of comparison between *legato* and *portato*. When the pupil can make an absolute distinction, he may at first take up simple, slow legato exercises, for instance:

Rode, Etude Nº 12

306. 

and practice the absolutely uninterrupted connection of the various notes with the keenest concentration of his auditory sense, until he has acquired a correct *legato* for all time.

(c) Unjustified, Initial Accent. Another tonal bad habit is illustrated in the following example:

307. 

This accent, produced by increased bow pressure, and spreading into a *diminuendo* which returns regularly after every change of bow, though it produces the effect of a certain spirited bow-stroke, quickly tires in the course of time, especially when the composition to be interpreted has a quiet, contemplative character. This habit is unfortunately in great favor with the younger generation of violinists!

Correction: Long sustained bow-strokes in 4/4 or 3/4 measure, while observing a mathematically exact division of the bow into four or three quarters.

(d) The Unbuoyant Stroke. The contrast to the preceding is the habit of beginning every bow-stroke carefully and slowly, in order only gradually to attain the degree of tonal strength prescribed, resulting in a pronouncedly unbuoyant and untemperamental stroke.

308 

Correction: Stroke exercises with an exaggeratedly great expenditure of bow at the beginning of every stroke.

Orchestral Attack

(e) The Orchestral Attack. We now come to one of the most usual abuses, the faulty *forte* attack out of the air, known as "hacking." Instead of vigorously taking hold of the note to be accentuated by means of a pressure accent preceding the beginning of the stroke (see p. 95) the player, presumably through ignorance of the bowing technique needed in this instance, as well as fearing scratchy accompanying noises, throws the bow down upon the string at a certain distance from *above*, whereby a pseudo-accentuation results, which produces a rude instead of an energetic impression. The accompanying noise hereby produced results from contact of the string and silver bow-ring, together with the effect of the vertical bow-drop. This type of attack is mainly used in the *orchestra*, and there (probably as a result of its multiplication) does not produce a too disturbing effect. In *solo playing*, however, it indicates a low level of bow culture, and in itself suffices to place the soloist in an inferior class*

(f) Tonal Studies. The question now arises: is it possible to cultivate and perfect tone production as a special branch, on the basis of systematic study, as is the case with the technique of the left and right hands? The question

* Rapid sequential down-bows, mainly on the G-string, form an exception, when there is not enough time to place the bow on the string (see p. 78).

309. 

must be answered in the affirmative, since in reality *every* note we produce should vibrate, and hence in itself presents a tone problem to be solved, a *tonal exercise.* Every bowing exercise is at the same time a tonal exercise. It is quite conceivable, on the other hand, that the necessary tone-producing factors, such as length of stroke, tonal power and position height (all in correct proportion to the point of contact), when separately taken in hand, so to speak, for the cultivation of tonal purity, offer the material for actual tone exercises. The especially difficult conditions for tone production which may arise are demonstrated by the *tone exercise in the high positions* (see Example 257). The higher the position, the more closely the point of contact between bow and string approaches the bridge. Yet what takes place when we play a scale on one string and at the same time play the nearest open string?

Bag-pipe Exercise

310.

It is then—as has already been proved (p. 83)—a question of uniting the demands of two string-lengths widely separated from each other. Hence it is useful to carry out tone exercises of the following type from time to time:

311.

312.

313.

314.

315.

One always should choose a key which contains in its triad the open string to be played, since otherwise, owing to its harshness, the simultaneous sounding will affect the ear of the player (or the involuntary listener) in too disagreeable and tiring a manner.

In addition, the *portato*, already mentioned so often, supplies a tone exercise of outstanding importance. In consequence of the increased pressure activity here developed, the point of contact between string and bow should approach nearer to the bridge than to the fingerboard. It should not be practiced without *vibrato*.

In the same way the *varied accentuation of longer bowings* offers desirable results in the study of shading, for instance:

316.

(With Vibrato)

"Spun" Notes

Further "*spun*" *notes* (*sons filé*) in every degree of strength, are among the oldest, best-known, most popular and also most appropriate of tone and bow exercises. They call for great regularity and evenness in tonal expression, as well as in the leading of the bow, and adhesion to the right point of contact without wavering hither and thither. In the case of the so-called *mute* "*spun*" notes, the bow should only touch the string, without resting on it, and the tone must become a mere breath. The duration of the "spun" notes varies between 6 and 24 seconds in the *forte*, and 12 and 60 seconds in *pianissimo*. The exercise should be as brief as possible, lasting at the most 15 minutes, since (apart from the left hand *pizzicati*) it may be regarded as the most tiresome item in the whole field of violin technique. In spite of its great usefulness, especially to the violinist as yet in the earlier grades, it is far from being a cure-all for every kind of bow fault, as many claim. In fact, I have often noticed that the exclusive practice of "spun" notes lends the bow-stroke a certain indolence, in spite of its great evenness.

In order to avoid this evil, it is practical to mingle *rapid accentuated whole-bow* strokes with the "spun" notes when practicing them.

Their simplicity and usefulness, however, in any case give them a place of honor in the arsenal of bowing and tonal exercises.

Finally, the practice of *buoyant, weakly accented whole-bow strokes* may be useful, especially for individuals who are wanting in sensibility, and emotionally indolent. From the mechanical standpoint they are the consequence of an increased initial rapidity of the bow-stroke,

317. 

in which three-quarters of the entire length of the bow already is expended on the first eighth of each quarter-note, without the application of increased pressure, however. Control of this stroke, as has already been mentioned, is not merely able to stimulate the inner impulse, but may even actually produce it by means of reflex action. Its uninterrupted use, however, is a bad habit, considering the great number of musical works, which demand rather a steadily quiet expression than an impulsive one.

(g) Tone Colors. What distinguishes the violin from all other instruments is the fact that owing to the manifold nature of its tone colors, it bears within itself a multiplicity of voice registers and musical instruments. The *E-string* possesses the fresh keenness of the dramatic as also the charming lightness of the coloratura soprano; while the *A-string* approaches the mezzo-soprano in its tonal coloring. Does not the *D* suggest a well-nourished contralto voice, and cannot the *G-string* measure itself with the heroic or the lyric tenor, without being limited to the high C in its urge for expansion? In the wonderful *polyphony* of the *Bach* fugues does not our instrument resemble the organ? And in respect to its artificial harmonics is it not possible for us to challenge even the feathered songsters? Its mysterious charm, however, rests in its possibility of giving one and the same note, even when not transferring it to another string, three different tone colors, whose origin is due only to change of the point of contact between bow and string. It is possible for us to give a note the tone color of a *flute*, when we play it near the fingerboard. When taken close to the bridge the tone assumes the warm, incisive character of the *oboe;* while on the parts lying in the middle a *clarinet*-like timbre may be secured.

Beethoven, Trio, Op. 97 3rd Mov't.

318. The *Flute* timbre 

Beethoven, Cto, 2nd Mov't.

319. The *Clarinet* timbre 

Beethoven, Cto, 2nd Mov't.

320 The *Oboe* timbre 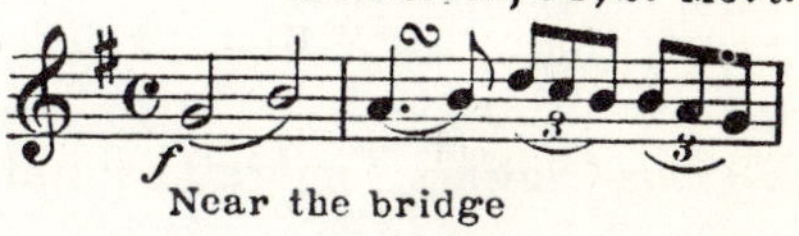

Those who defend the theory of a fixed point of contact, therefore, voluntarily resign the noblest part of those auxiliary means of vivifying and changing the tone colors which dwell in the instrument itself.

Very few violinists understand how to *mix* the colors of their palette in such a manner that the musical character of the phrase to be played not alone is made clear, but the differentiation of its individual components by means of suitable tone color mixtures also is attained, with the result that the listener is not exhausted by a uniformly grey tone-production.

It is true that the application of the various tone colors must not be carried out in arbitrary fashion, merely for the purpose of pleasing. Their use can be justified only when the artistic purposes of the composer are thereby thrown into the lime-light and the listener is made more clearly conscious of them. The *admixture of tone colors* always and invariably should be the consequence of a powerful inner need on the part of the interpreter, called forth by the individual content of the tone poem. Hence, to be exact, it cannot be taught.

We often meet violinists, however, who have a marked urge for expression by means of strongly differentiated tone colors: yet who are unacquainted with the corresponding auxiliary means of its finest shades. In such cases practice of the bowing technique combinations already known to us, the correct execution of which will bring with it a definite tonal color, is especially to be recommended (regarding Fingering and Tone Colors, see p. 146).

1. *The Flute Timbre* (veiled tone), at the fingerboard, the most rapid whole-bow *détaché* possible, *pp*, in the lower positions:

Kreutzer, Et. N? 5

321. 

2. *The Clarinet Timbre* (natural normal tone), between fingerboard and bridge; more sustained notes, *mf*:

322. 

3. *The Oboe Timbre* (pressed tone), near the bridge, "spun" notes (see p. 64) or *legati* with as many notes as possible to one bow, both *ff*:

323. 

324. 

Ponticello The *sul ponticello* indicated by many composers to secure a mood of mystery should be rejected from a purely tonal standpoint, since its object is to produce a scratchy, impure vibratory picture mingled with distinctly audible, irregular over-tones. So long as it is prescribed for purely selfish virtuoso motives (as in the 3d Variation of the "Moses" Fantasy on the G-string, where *Paganini* has indicated that it be used), no objection can be made to its use, since the production of an exotically fantastic mixture of tone and noise is actually intended. In Example 325, however,

Schumann, Trio, D min. 1? Mov't.

325. 

the mysterious, far distant tonal effect is more apt to be secured when the player avails himself of the *neighborhood of the fingerboard* (*sulla tastiera*), dispensing with the unpleasantly scratchy addition which clings to the *piano* at the bridge. If it did not sound a little too heretical in speaking of such a genius as *Schumann*, one would have to take some misunderstanding for granted in this last instance. When applied at the composer's request in the orchestra, playing at the bridge comes nearer making the desired effect, just as other violinistic peculiarities, unendurable in solo playing, turn into advantages as *collective* means of expression (the slow vibrato, the "hacked" accent).

An effect well-nigh unknown, yet uncommonly charming, may at times be secured in order to produce a marked *impression of distance*, by a seemingly exaggerated use of the fingerboard section:

Bach, Chaconne

326. 

The tonal picture thus produced, one absolutely dematerialized, involuntarily reminds the listener of the echo-effects of an organ.

Expression in Tone (h) Tone as a Means of Expression. Hitherto we have confined our observations to the production of vibrations faultless in the highest degree, that is, vibrations lacking secondary noises. Important as this is, it is yet no more than a preliminary, although an absolutely necessary one, to the sequence of technical factors aiming to further ideal violin-playing. Not until one has completely mastered it does one approach the final object of all music-making, the production of tone as a *means of expression*.

Looking backward, we might say that each degree of the dynamic and agogic step-ladder has a kind of tone-presentation which may be called its *best.* Yet how about giving the tone a soul? How about *expression?* Are our most intimate feelings also transferred to the string by mechanical means? Unquestionably, the answer is *yes.* Can this transfer be taught? Unquestionably the answer is *no.* The movements of both hands to be considered for this purpose are so entirely beyond control, that it is impossible to record them. With the complete possession of all technical means the violinist finds and combines the movements expressing what he feels, as unconsciously as the actor does his facial expressions and gestures. It would be a pity, probably, were this not the case, for the mere attempt to influence such an unmeasurable and already well-nigh spiritualized complex of movements would unquestionably destroy the immediacy of every kind of expression.

Far more favorable are our prospects of comprehension when we confine ourselves to investigations regarding the general nature of the *tone quality* favorable to the transfer of expression. Here, too, it is possible for us to say that there are two (coarse-grained, it is true) visible types of movements to be considered with reference to the transfer of expression. For the *right* hand it is the *pressure of the index finger*, for the *left* hand the *vibrato.*

Within the small surface of the index-finger joint which presses on the stick, are compressed, so to speak, all the movements carried out by the different parts of the arm. As already mentioned (see p. 53) I regard the index finger, by virtue of its quality as a leader, as well as chief mediant between the bow and the strength-dispensing parts of the arm, as that factor which takes the most prominent part in tone production, with regard to purity of vibration and also to the degree of tonal power.

If the right hand is responsible for the purity of the vibrations as well as the quantitative administration of the tone, the *vibrato* acts in a determining way upon the actual tonal *quality.* A *vibrato* which is not due to some bad habit, but is carried out with perfect mechanical freedom, is the most exhaustive expression of the subconscious psychic impulses of each personality (see p. 35).

The *right* arm attends to the dynamic differentiation, the *left* hand proportions the psychic fluid, the combination of *both* hands the agogic (tempo) nuances. The fundamental difference between the duties of both arms is only this, that the dynamic and agogic nuances owe their origin, in the main, to a conscious expression of the will; while the vibrato represents the most delicate expression of our general psychic constitution, of our congenital temperament. I can, it is true, turn a pupil's slow vibrato into a rapid one, when it is the result of mechanical insufficiency. Never, however, would I be able, nor should I attempt, to substitute a rapid for a slow vibrato if the latter represents the perfected expression of his personality. Hence, from the mechanical standpoint, the vibrato is capable of being changed, but only when a corresponding inner transformation takes place in the individual can it be changed psychically.

The Expressive Proportion of Both Arms

We must now consider a remarkable fact. Experience proves that with regard to tonal expression there exist two groups of violinists, sharply separated one from the other. Those of one group have a beautiful tone as part of their *technical* possessions. They command it at all times, whether in the mood or not, whether they play with or without expression. It always is at their disposal. We will call it the *tone beautiful in itself.*

Those of the second category do not find things so easy. They first have to achieve their personal tone quality by steeping the tone in feeling, by giving it a soul. When played without inward participation, or in a wrong psychic mood, or under wrong physical conditions, this kind of tone makes a dry and cold impression; it needs *feeling* to give it life and blood. In order to distinguish it from the tone beautiful in itself, we will term it the *inspired tone.* During the last half century *Ysaye* was the most perfect representative of the tone beautiful, while *Joachim* possessed the inspired tone in its most ideal form.

Tone Beautiful in Itself

The question which type should be preferred is a difficult one to answer. Without doubt the possessor of the *tone beautiful in itself* finds things much easier than the other. It is hardly necessary for him to practice before a concert; even while preluding he already controls his seductive tone expression (in most cases with even greater sureness than his finger technique). This surely is an advantage. Yet such a violinist easily falls into a certain emotional indolence and into routine; since why exert one's self, why *feel,* when apparently the mere *appearance* of an inward activity of this sort is enough to produce the illusion of emotion? Finally he often turns into a violinist who surprises and captivates during the first ten minutes by the beauty of his tone, only to bore his listeners quite as intensively after a little time.

Inspired Tone

The artist of the *inspired tone* is placed in a more difficult position. When he takes up his instrument his tone lacks all charm at the start, only with increasing sensibility, awakened by the composition itself, does his tone grow warmer, and in favorable cases attain an apex of intensity. The ideal condition is that of possession of the tone beautiful in itself, when the owner does not content himself with the self-understood, purely sensuous effect of his tone, but also strives to express the psychic values peculiar to the composition. One might take for granted that two manners of playing so fundamentally different from each other in effect would also show visible signs of difference in the *way* they were *produced.* In fact, a certain *inflexibility* of the *vibrato,* in connection with a tonal expression otherwise good, on the part of the right arm, is the hall-mark of the inspired tone, while *vice versa,* in the beautiful tone, a certain *monotony,* and even clumsiness of *bowing* contrasts with the always vivid *vibrato.* In order to understand the mechanical causes which are operative in this case the following explanation is in order: when the collective expression of both arms is expressed by the numeral 1, then, according to rule, the right as well as the left arm should take over 1/2, that is, half of the collective performance.

In that case a good vibrato should be accompanied by a bowing *dynamically* just as expressive. When the vibrato is insufficient, representing, let us say, 1/4 instead of 1/2, then the remaining 3/4 would have to be supplied by the right hand; in which case the latter would have to exert an excessively strong pressure on the strings. Inversely with an excessive vibrato equaling 3/4 of the collective emotion to be transmitted, only 1/4 would remain for the right hand. Hence a weak, insufficient, monotonous, dynamic status would result.*

The following experiment seems to confirm this theory. When we play a sustained tone with absolute *elimination of the vibrato* (left-0), we will find that it is not difficult to force the tone with the bow to such an exent that only a scratchy noise will be audible (right-1). If we begin to *vibrate,* the pressure exertion is noticeably more difficult, and well-nigh impossible in the case of the most powerful *vibrato.* (The bow, of course, must be led in the vicinity of the bridge.)

Besides the ideal violinist, whose emotion flows in equal proportion (1/2:1/2) from his soul into his arms, we have therefore the cold type of violinist with slight vibratory capacity, and a tendency to force the tone (1/4 left, 3/4 right), as well as the excessively vibrating, effeminate violinist (3/4 left, 1/4 right), who has at his command no more than a small tone incapable of modulation. It is of the greatest importance for all, even for the apparently finished violinist, to know exactly to which of the two groups he belongs, or to which he is nearest akin. In the case of insufficient *vibrato* and a forced tone, the vibrato should be favored (vibrato studies), and the bow pressure should be diminished by *piano* exercises. In the opposite case, shading exercises should be practised, while neglecting and even totally eliminating the *vibrato.* In any case, the balance of both arms in connection with the transfer of emotion is one of the main objects for which every violinist who wishes to attain the maximum of expressive capability should strive.

---

* In this connection I would call attention to the similarity between this theory and that in Weininger's *Geschlecht und Character* ("Sex and Character") regarding the changing equations of masculinity and femininity in the individual.

Defects Connected With Tone

Inexact Intonation (especially half-tones which are too wide), or an intonation continuously too high or too low may seriously impair expression. The more exact the number of vibrations, the more the tone carries and is effective, and the better the instrument itself sounds. The average person instinctively experiences discomfort when listening to a violinist who plays falsely with a beautiful tone, finding it inexplicable in most cases; while an initiate with good hearing soon discovers the cause of his discomfort.

Too Pointed Fingers, also, with too slight or narrow a cushion of fat, often are responsible for a colorless tone. The creation of little artificial fat cushions by a flat laying on of the fingers is the only means at our disposal against this physical lack (see p. 18).*

There remains to be mentioned the diminution of the volume of tone by artificial *elimination* of part of the instrument, for instance:

1. A missing *chin-rest*, whereby part of the lower left violin cheek is prevented from taking part in the vibration.

2. The protection of the chin by a *cloth*, which at the same time covers part of the lower half of the violin, and makes it incapable of vibrating.

3. The covering of the right upper rib with *leather*, in order to prevent the perspiration generated from affecting the wood, whereby the upper rib is prevented from taking part in the vibration. All these and similar artificial hindrances must be repudiated as inadmissible. Mechanically a dampening combined with a certain effeminacy of tone is produced by means of the *sordino*, which may be made of wood, bone or metal. Wood, as experience teaches, sounds the best; the so-called "Tone-wolf," a *sordino* weighted with a lead filling, weakens the tone to a still greater extent and makes it possible to play in rooms otherwise not adapted for it. In this category falls the so-called *mute violin*, an instrument in skeletonized form. In general, the dampening effect must be accounted one of the cheapest of the violinist's art, and hence is used by violinists of high artistic standing only when prescribed by the composer. The customary muted *practicing* should be repudiated, since the artificial tone production deceives the ear, gives it a false impression, and makes the tone appear more beautiful than it really is. One should use mutes which are built as *low* as possible, in order not to interfere with bowing at the nut.

* A good violin hand is never externally beautiful, since its finger-tips are always too broad.

The technique of tone production represents the noblest portion of the collective technique of violin playing. Pure tone is the most valid interpreter of emotion.

Yet it should never cease to be only a *means*—although the most distinguished—to the end of the most perfect "after-creation" possible. The violinist whose ideal consists only in the production of the most beautiful sounds possible, is not yet entitled to call himself an artist. In his case the art-work serves only as a foil for sound, because with him the means has become an end.

Herewith we have reached the end of our considerations regarding the production of tone and, at the same time, that of the first, fundamental part—Technique in General—of our whole work. General technique is surely no more than the "craftsman" part of our art, yet only to those who can exercise their craft in the most perfect manner is it given to recreate an art-work. First of all, in order to climb Jacob's ladder, one must have learned how to climb!

II. Applied Technique

Applied Technique

The term "Applied Technic," as I interpret it, means the application of "Technic in General" to conquer the difficulties which occur in *musical compositions*. What the two classifications have in common is the means necessary for their control—*practice*. The difference consists in the relative simplicity of *general* technical formulas, in contrast to the illimitable possibilities developed as soon as a creative spirit makes use of them in order to write a *tone-poem*. Put in a rather prosaic way, technique in *general* might be compared to raw materials, *applied* technique to finished goods.

---

1. General Remarks as to Practising

Practising (General Remarks)

Let us first of all deal with "*practising*," that is, the road which leads from "*inability*" to perform a succession of notes to "*ability*" to do so. Psychologically, we must look at this in the following manner: when we play a succession of notes, hitherto unknown to us, for the first time, the sight of each individual note conveys a definite impression of the pitch and duration of the sound; and this impression calls forth an exactly circumscribed movement of the fingers, arm or hand. When the same sequence of notes has been played a number of times in direct succession, the originally motived and executed movements, so to speak, are gathered up into a mechanized movement-complex, which in the course of time no longer depends upon the note-picture for its external suggestion, but is memorized, and allows the chain of movement to roll along *automatically*. Hence we may distinguish the following three stages on the road from "*inability*" to "*ability to do*."

1. The *conscious* performance of separate movements suggested by the note-picture: the *not knowing*—and *not being able to do*—stage.

2. The grouping of the individual movements in complexes, mechanical execution as a result of an impulse given by the *sight of printed music*: *knowing, without knowing by heart*.

3. The sight of the printed music becomes superfluous, execution takes place *automatically*, solely as the consequence of an inner impulsion: *knowing — playing by heart*.*

---

* The fact that many need the printed music for their otherwise finished artistic performance (*Raoul Pugno*, etc.) is above all due to morbid fears, and in no way alters the case that as a usual thing, *knowing* is synonymous with *knowing* by heart. If we always play chamber-music from music the reason, aside from practical considerations, is one connected with the idea of avoiding the least appearance of selfish virtuoso aims. Yet even here it is an open question whether this branch of artistic activity would not gain greatly as regards control of material as well as directness of expression, if those taking part in it did not stick so closely to their music. But the quartet which "plays by heart" is something reserved for the future (written in 1920).

The road leading from inability to execute a succession of notes to the knowledge and ability to do so, therefore, corresponds to the change of conscious into subconscious movements. If, in spite of this, we begin to *think* about a run while playing it, in most cases a technical blunder, an occurrence only too familiar to every concertizing violinist, will result. The more subconscious the movements required in playing, the surer is the player's technique. In the case of such movements, however, the perfect execution of which depend largely upon chance (as, for instance, in the case of extended *leaps* on the piano, long-sustained high notes on the violin, conditioning a leading of the bow near the bridge), conscious checking up with the eye is necessary. In the same way mechanical activity of movement does not attain its end when the structure of a composition is such that a theme or figure is repeated several times with various modulatory or rhythmical *changes*, the variety of which in each case demands that the change be fixed in the player's consciousness in the form of a clear memory picture (see p. 169).

When we consider that the performance of a work such as *Beethoven's* Violin Concerto calls for several thousand such movements on the part of both hands, it is easy to understand why such a gigantic task must be facilitated so far as possible in its component parts. *Saving of strength*, the avoidance of every sort of *waste of energy*, an *expenditure of power* conscious of its aim, are indispensable prerequisites to this end. Every unnecessarily difficult or generally superfluous movement which does not directly serve the purpose of tone-production should be eschewed. The movements which are practically the most useful appear in the form of the best (i.e., those representing the greatest saving of energy) fingerings and bowings. To discover these is one of the main objects of study.*

* In this connection we often have to struggle against an inner opposition, of which we ourselves are not conscious. The fact is that there are fingerings and bowings which, though we may feel they are illogical or out of date, are closely connected in our recollections with the achievements of some artist enthusiastically adored in youthful days, and from which, during the remainder of our life, reverence prevents us from freeing ourselves. Reasons of this kind often are responsible for the retention of quite notoriously primitive fingerings or bowings, representing some interpreter's individual legacy.

The fact that, in order to incorporate, mentally and technically, some definite succession of notes we must *repeat* it more or less frequently, has induced the great majority of violinists to draw the erroneous conclusion that purposeful *practising*, and the incessant repetition of the passage in question, until one is "able to play it," are identical. It is a fatal error. Practice is not merely a necessity, it is also an evil—*a necessary evil*. The frequent repetition of a passage, in fact, has nothing whatever to do with the music itself. And every violinist knows from his own experience that the long continued practicing of technical difficulties renders him incapable of taking real pleasure in making music. Hence every concertizing artist instinctively avoids mechanical exercises immediately before a concert, since he has a presentiment that in such case technical improvement can be secured only at the expense of his psychic mood. And habitual, thoughtless and endless repetition invariably destroys a player's capacity for musical feeling, and at the same time robs him of that which makes the artist—his *personality*. Moreover, in repeating a passage, we must be careful not to rehearse eventual defects. We must therefore first of all make sure that the series of movements which constitute the run are correct in every way.

Practising by Repeating

As a rule, we should endeavor to find a certain hygiene of practice, one which, in spite of a fixed number of unavoidably necessary mechanical exercises, allows us to preserve unspoiled our musical sentiment and our joy in music itself.

Hygiene in Practice

As shown in the above, three principal points are to be considered:

1. The discovery of the most appropriate movements in the form of energy-saving *fingerings* and *bowings*.

2. The transformation of the original *conscious* movements into *unconscious* ones.

3. The ideal execution of these principals without injury to the artist's collective personality.

Whoever sets himself a goal of attainment and keeps it in view is opposed by inimical powers—inner and external ones—which endeavor to prevent his success. In our profession *exaggeration* in every form is especially apt to change sane and healthy principles into their opposites.

Excessive extension of practice-time, undue favoring of individual technical groups, a preference for studies which are dry—unmusical—all these errors originate in the belief that gaining dexterity in any degree depends first of all on certain allotments of time, which if utilized in rapid succession with as little interruption as possible, will hasten the end desired. In reality the exact contrary takes place, and just as when supplying the stomach with bodily nutriment, the latter is able to do its duty only when it receives food in *small* quantities we, too, cannot *mentally* digest too large portions. (See p. 165.) It is certainly better to practise the *staccato* ten minutes a day, eighteen days in succession, than to practise it an hour a day for three days.*

As a rule every technical item should be practised frequently, yet always in small doses. *Non multum sed multa.*

In general, we must be thoroughly convinced that it is due only to *practical, useful reasons* and never (owing to a certain perversion of our aesthetic sensibilities) for our *enjoyment* that we practice technical exercises. I do not mean to imply hereby that we are to regard practice as a disagreeable duty, of which we must rid ourselves as soon as possible. The final conquest of some technical problem which at first appeared unsurmountable will even call forth a certain pleasurable sensation in us, a feeling which, nevertheless, is not comparable to the satisfaction resulting from the understanding and reproducing of a purely musical idea. On the other hand it is extremely injurious to the general artistic development of the individual to believe that conscientious practicing will enable him to comply with the greater part of his artistic responsibilities. One should never cultivate practice as a *sport*, but simply keep in mind that its justification lies in the fact that it is just this toilsome road which makes it possible to establish the prerequisites necessary for higher artistic activities.

Divisi of Tir in Pra tice

In the closest possible connection herewith is the question of the *division of time*, as well as of the *practice material* to be mastered. Hence, *what* is one to practice, and *how* is the time at one's disposal to be divided? We will begin with answering the first question. We have three aims in view:

a. The acquiring of the greatest possible amount of *technique in general.*

b. The correct employment of this possession in the study of a musical composition.

c. The finished *reproduction* of the composition on the basis of the technical facility attained.

Should one of these factors be unduly emphasized, three possibilities are developed:

Wron Divisi of Time

a. Too Exclusive Devotion to Technique in General. The violinist devotes three-quarters of his practice-time to typical technical formulas, scales, etc., and finds he has little time left for the study of repertoire pieces or for performing.

b. Giving Preference to Applied Technique in form of an almost exclusive cultivation of the technical components of *repertoire* pieces. The neglect of general technical formulas in the course of time brings with it a letdown in the player's general technique. In addition the

* After a performance of the *Paganini* Caprices No. 23 (first part) and No. 17 (second part), which I have united under the title "Octave Study," I have sometimes been compelled to listen to the remark made by colleagues in a slightly sarcastic tone of voice: "You must have devoted an infinite amount of toil and trouble in obtaining your fingered octave technique." Yet I must confess that I owe this very portion of my technical possessions to a certain *disinclination* to work. When a student at the Paris Conservatoire at the beginning of the nineties, during the last century, I happened to live in a room insufficiently heated, so that as a rule I was obliged to practice finger-exercises half an hour before I came into full command of my powers. I thought about ways and means for improvement, and by chance happened to discover that I secured the same result in only five or ten minutes when playing fingered octaves, something which meant a great saving of time. As a consequence I played fingered octaves daily, for four or five years, though never longer than five or ten minutes at a time.

repertoire piece itself, owing to the exclusive attention devoted to the necessary technical studies required for its interpretation, is reduced to the rank of a practice piece, the musical meaning of the work is entirely lost in the course of time, and we are no longer able to feel and express it with that immediacy and freshness which is an essential prerequisite for its transfer to the auditor's emotional receptivity. The technical level of ability demanded for the reproduction of a work should *already* have been attained by means of *general* technical studies.

c. *Performing as a Main Preoccupation.* From a purely human point of view this is the most pardonable sin. In the long run, however, it inevitably leads to amateurishness, since not only do the player's general technical resources diminish, but such purely pleasure-giving, uncritical playing is followed by neglect of the technical side, whereby performance in concert style always will depend more or less upon chance. Hence, as the leading principle of all serviceable practice, daily attention must be paid to *all three of the factors mentioned*.

Yet should this also be carried out with regard to time, in a similar way? Should the player, for example, in a practice-time amounting to three hours, devote an hour to each group? The answer to this question is closely connected with the age and ability of the individual, and the immediate requirements of the repertoire. When one is a boy, for example, one does not object to occupying one's self with technical specialties of a lower order; while ten years later every true artist should have developed a strong inner objection to busying himself with problems of skill on this lower plane. Similarly, the continued practicing of mechanical problems which one already controls completely is an absurdity, whereas the very tracing and doing away with technical weaknesses is one of the most delightful tasks of practice activity. The necessity of bringing a composition to that point of perfection essential for concert performance within a *fixed space of time*, again, demands intensive study of its technical peculiarities, or the study of a composition musically complex compels paying diligent attention to its purely *musical qualities*.

Therefore, if we are to set up a schedule of time-division for practice, we must take for granted a violinist whom we may conceive to be proportionably well trained, normally gifted, and confronted with artistic tasks of an average kind.

Right Division of Time

The most advantageous *division of practice-time* appears to me to be the following (taking for granted a daily practice-time of four hours):

1. One hour of general technique (system of scales, with bowing exercises (see p. 109), other studies) favoring especially the weak spots in one's technique.

2. An hour and a half of applied technique (the technical study of the repertoire).

3. An hour and a half of absolute music (performance in concert style of works previously studied only from a technical standpoint, if possible with piano accompaniment, and the playing of chamber music).

This last study division, half work, half pleasure, so frequently neglected, is also most important from a technical point of view, because in it, still hidden *technical weaknesses* are openly exposed, and supply excellent practice material for the following day's work. Hence, if I regard the use of an important portion of the available practice-time for performing for pleasure's sake, as unconditionally necessary, the *amount* of time allotted to general and applied technique, on the other hand, as already has been mentioned, will have to be subjected to frequent change.

The most difficult and time-consuming study section will always be that devoted to applied technique, that is, the technical control of a *piece intended for performance*. Immediately following it comes that given to the *musical* contents of a work, which is rather a matter of mind and soul, than a technical one. Last of all comes the cultivation of general technique, which, if we take for granted a thoroughly equalized training, should be considered as the mere keeping intact of existing technical resources.

The sequence in which we advance, however, will at once give *precedence* to *general technical exercises* for the reason that their monotony demands that mental and bodily freshness which is at its height at the *beginning* of the day's work. Then follows applied technique and then—*finis coronat opus*—the player plunges into the musical art-work.

Daily Exercises (Scale-System)

2. Practice of General Technique

(a) Daily Exercises (system of scales) Since in the first part of this work, the most practical way of studying general technical formulas has been discussed in detail, we will now attempt to establish how these formulas may be used most advantageously as daily exercises. *

The difficulty consists in combining the greatest possible completeness with the least loss of time. This demand is generally sinned against so that either a small expenditure of time is confined to a few individual technical groups, or greater detail is combined with greater time-expenditure, so that neither the necessary leisure nor the necessary freshness of spirit are available for tasks of a higher nature. Let us first consider the technical requirements of both hands or arms.

The Left Hand. Most violinists think they have done their duty when they play the diatonic scales in succession once every day, through three octaves. They forget, however, that there are at least some twenty-five other technical formulas which may lay claim to the same right. These are:

A. *In the Compass of One Octave and on One String*:

1. Diatonic scales
2. Broken triads and chords of the seventh
3. Broken thirds
4. Chromatic scales

B. *In Three Octaves*:

5. Diatonic scales
6. Broken triads and chords of the seventh
7. Broken thirds
8. Chromatic scales

C. *Thirds in Double-Stops*:

9. Diatonic scales
10. Chromatic scales
11. Scales in intervals of a third

D. *Sixths*:

12. Diatonic scales
13. Chromatic scales
14. Scales in intervals of a third

E. *Simple Octaves*:

15. Diatonic scales
16. Chromatic scales
17. Scales in thirds
18. Broken triads

F. *Fingered Octaves*:

19. Diatonic scales
20. Chromatic scales
21. Scales in thirds
22. Broken triads

G. *Tenths*:

23. Diatonic scales

To these should be added *trills*, *harmonics*, and *pizzicati*-exercises for the left hand, of which the last two should be practiced only in case of need. It will be quite apparent that the cultivation of this collective complex in shorter periods of time is impossible when using methods of practice *generally current*. Hence the solution of this problem is nothing less than a matter of life and death for the violinistic development of the individual.

Right Arm. If we are to determine the exercises needed for daily practice by the right arm, we must do so on the basis of the *forms* of movement,* but *not* on that of their infinite possibilities of combination.**

If we take this line we encounter the following original forms:

1. *Détaché, lower half*
2. *Détaché, upper half*
3. *Change of string, lower half*
4. *Change of string, upper half*
5. *Swift, small bow-strokes, nut, middle, point*

To these should be added, in the guise of occasional exercises, the leading types of *mixed bowings*, as well as the *martelé*, *staccato*, *springing* and *thrown* bow.

If, so far as the left hand is concerned, the available practice material already is enormous, that of the right arm is still more extensive. The normal practice-time of three or four hours, with one technical specialty to follow upon the other, would be entirely consumed in the practice of general technical formulas. Yet I believe that it is possible for me to indicate a better method. I have assembled a sequence of general technical formulas for the left hand, which I call the *system of scales*. It may be practiced in the key of the repertoire piece which the violinist is playing at the time.

* My Basic Studies (Urstudien) do not here come into consideration as daily studies, since they have been conceived only as emergency studies for violinists whose study-time is extremely limited.

**Flesch, Basic Studies* (*Urstudien*) (Carl Fischer).

***Sevčik*, 4000 *Bowing Exercises.*

NB: 1) Sevcik op8, p2, starts on same note for all keys, shifting
p22 ditto, 3 oct. scales
2) Try taking diatonic scales 1st to get used to fingering A-G, p108

SEE p 130 on the principles for fingering these scales!

The System of Scales

Sevcik III, 3: arpeggios on one string

Sequence of the broken triads according to Sevčik

N1404

N1404

* These sequence-progressions within the compass of an octave, used for the double-stops, were already known to violinists of the French school at the beginning of the nineteenth century. This excellent tradition was handed on to **me by** *Eugene Sauzay, Baillot's* son-in-law and pupil.

G and D Strings
A and E Strings
D and A Strings
A and E Strings

A
E
G and D Strings
D
D
D
D
A

In order, however, not to draw unduly on one's practice time in training the *right arm* separately, it is possible to combine its basic movements with the system of scales in such a manner that the most divergent types of bowing may be grafted, so to speak, upon the system of scales. The possibilities hereby developed, naturally, are very numerous and, according to individual needs, may be extended *ad infinitum.* I will give only a few examples of the combination of bow-strokes with the system of scales.

328.

The system of scales, moreover, may be used for *tone studies* of every kind. For instance:

1. Forte, near the bridge, many notes to a bow-stroke.

2. Piano, at the fingerboard, 1-4 notes to every bow-stroke.

3. Crescendi.

4. Decrescendi.

5. Combination of Nos. 3 and 4.

6. With different accents.

7. With the portato-stroke (see p. 73).

8. spun notes & vibrato

Furthermore, the system of scales may be placed at the disposal of individual weaknesses of bowing technique. If, for example, the bowing  causes the violinist difficulties, let him employ it in the system of scales; after a time the existing difficulties will have been overcome without his having had to devote a single moment to its *exclusive* study. In addition, the system of scales may be used for *applied technique.* If, for instance, I wish to play *Beethoven's* Violin Concerto and the well-known passage:

329.

offers difficulties, nothing prevents my combining this bowing either completely or partially with the system of scales until I can absolutely control it. (Further details will be given in this connection in the section dealing with the self-invented etudes. See p. 163.)

General Rules for Studying Scale System

My experience has taught me that this procedure, in spite of (or, perhaps, in direct consequence of) its relative simplicity, will almost work wonders especially if, hitherto, only incomplete study material has been used. Yet, in its practical development, attention should be paid to the following points:

1. The exercise may be played either *slowly* or *rapidly.* In the first case it is more a study in *intonation,* in the second one in *agility.*

2. At first it should be studied only at a *slow* tempo, with the most meticulous correction of every wrong note. To this end every note *following* a change of position must be held somewhat *longer.*

330.

3. The *tempo,* as the practice-sequence becomes more familiar to the player, may be somewhat accelerated.

4. The *key* should be changed every day.

5. The scale should not be *repeated,* since otherwise the greatest advantage the system offers, that of *saving time,* is lost.

6. After a *month's* time it should be played twice daily, slowly and rapidly.

7. Its *time of duration,* taking for granted the necessary technical ability, should be from twelve to twenty minutes in a *slow* tempo, and from seven to twelve minutes in a *rapid* one.

When played twice daily, from twenty to thirty minutes are devoted to a thorough training and review of the general technical material, in which the problem of combining the greatest possible completeness with the greatest saving of time, at first apparently unsurmountable, may be regarded as having been solved.

It is left to individual discretion to determine whether a scale in trills as well as in harmonics should be added.

The system of scales takes for granted a thorough knowledge of the entire technical material. But what if this knowledge does not exist in the case of those less advanced? In such case the use of the system as a *whole* is not advisable as yet. When, however, the violinist's general technique is on so high a plane that the difficulties contained in the system of scales may be overcome, then his adoption and regular practice of the latter means nothing less than a *life insurance* against the diminution of his technical assets.*

Etude Material

b. Etude Material. Etudes (also frequently known as Caprices or Studies) enter into the realm of applied technique to the degree that the acquisition of general technique is contained in them and developed into independent compositions. On the other hand, they usually lack the quality inherent in a composition born of a purely musical impulse. They are not adapted for public performance and, in most cases, are intended mainly to increase the player's technical equipment.**

Hence, in the first instance, they come within the domain of general technique. Among the study works of the older Italian period, at best only the *Locatelli* Caprices are applicable to our purposes, and these especially from the standpoint of bow-technique, though the oddity of their finger technique and their poverty of thematic invention makes them seem like curiosities to us. Our interest is enlisted, first of all, by the Caprices of *Kreutzer* and *Rode*, which will probably supply for all time the most solid foundation of violinistic ability. Far less valuable, at the present day, seem to be those Etudes written at the same period by *Gavinies, Fiorillo* and *Rovelli* (the last with exaggerated attempts at stretching). Among the Germans, *Benda, Mayseder* and others hardly tell us anything that is new. *Spohr*, on the other hand, in his sterling Violin Method, lays a sure foundation for the technique peculiar to his compositions. The appearance of *Paganini's* Twenty-four Caprices blazed new trails in the writing of etudes. They are the most valuable work in this field. *Chopin, Liszt, Schumann* and *Brahms* have not disdained to transcribe them for the piano. Their wealth of invention, their charm of theme, their perfection of form reveal *Paganini's* talent as a composer to us in all its magnitude—as well as his lack of artistic conscientiousness; for in most cases he misused the gifts which nature had bestowed on him for the fabrication of works meant to serve his purely selfish virtuoso purposes. The triumphs of the *haute école* of fingerboard and bow, a practically unlimited technique as regards double-stopping and position-change, as well as the latest virtuoso conquests (artificial *harmonics, pizzicati* with the left hand, *tremolo* with the left hand) are exemplified in the works of such followers as *Prume, Ernst, Sivori* and others. Beside them the more serious studies in the French style by *Beriot, Alard, Dancla, Vieuxtemps* and *Wieniawski*, find a place.

In the seventies of the nineteenth century the Viennese violin teacher, *Dont*, published a series of studies, which may worthily be placed beside those of *Kreutzer* and *Rode*. He was the first teacher who endeavored to free the science of fingering from the fetters of old routine, and direct it into new paths. At the beginning of the eighties a School of Violin Technique from the pen of a hitherto unknown violin teacher, *Ottokar Sevčik*, appeared, followed by a School of Bowing Technique, and a series of preparatory studies, under the collective title: "Preparatory School of Violin Technique." The extraordinary importance of these works, which caused a revolution in the domain of practice material, will be considered shortly in due detail. Among the etudes more or less consciously influenced by *Sevčik*, and written in the course of the past thirty years, first of all those by *Schradieck* and *Sauret*, as well as those of *Petri, Hubay, Sitt, Spiering* and *Auer* should be mentioned. During the last decade, unfortunately, there has been a cessation of production in this field, although the technical, so-called unviolinistic problems introduced with *Brahm's* Violin Concerto and intensified by the latest violin compositions, urgently call for an extension of available study material.

The choice which the teacher makes among the study works at his disposal depends in many cases on his personal taste, but the sequence in which the pupil takes them up should depend, rather, upon the pupil's technical qualifications.***

*When I compiled the scale system in 1920 I thought it sufficient to write a pattern in C minor and to leave it to the students themselves to transpose it in the different keys. But I found out very soon that the majority of them were too indolent to follow my advice, and that they were satisfied to play the whole in C major over and over again. I decided, therefore, in 1927 to publish a separate supplement transposing the original compilation in all keys (*Flesch, Scale System*, Carl Fischer).

**The musical compositions which *Chopin, Schumann, Paganini* and others have published under the title of Etudes are naturally not included in this category.

***A selection of studies by various masters which I have collected has been published in three volumes by Wilhelm Hansen (Copenhagen). Yet, owing to questions of copyright, various very important composers (*Sauret, Hubay*, etc.) could not be included.

Hence our attempt to indicate a choice may be altered and supplemented from both points of view; furthermore the difficulties found within the same study work differ so greatly at times that other etudes have to be interpolated between their individual sections to lead from one to the other. This is the case, in particular, in *Kreutzer's* collection of Forty Etudes, in which it seems advisable to interpolate *Fiorillo* and *Rode* before the double-stop etudes are taken in hand. The following list of etudes should be judged and supplemented in accordance with the point of view just explained:

Kreutzer, 40 Etudes
Fiorillo, 36 Etudes
Rode, 24 Etudes
Sauzay, Etudes Harmoniques
Vieuxtemps, 6 Etudes
Dont, Op. 35
Wieniawski, Etudes-Caprices
Schradieck, 24 Etudes
Wieniawski, Ecole Moderne
Sauret, 18 Etudes
Paganini, 24 Caprices
Ernst, 6 Etudes

Sevcik, Bowing Technique and Finger Technique, 1 and 2.
Preparatory Studies for Change of Position.
Finger Technique, 3 and 4.
System of Scales (Flesch).

Violinists whose trend is principally in the direction of virtuosity should also go through Hoffman's *Schule der Flageolett-Technik* (Technique of Harmonics). The many special works for trills, thirds, octaves, etc., as well as the collection of etudes already mentioned, may also prove useful in case of need.

včik

To return to *Sevčik*, it should be pointed out, first of all, that in his case our considerations are limited to his theoretical works. The peculiarity of the method which he has discovered and so inexorably developed to its ultimate consequences, lies in its intentional elimination (which approaches absolute neglect) of the musical content in favor of technical considerations. *Kreutzer's*, *Rode's* or *Dont's* etudes are, after all, musical compositions, whereas *Sevčik* not only does not even attempt to tell us anything of a musical nature, but tries to develop the technical problem with absolute disregard of form and musical content. When, for example, a teacher formerly wished to have a pupil practice special studies for change of position, he had at his disposal, in addition to the established broken triad and seventh chord formulas, approximately the following list of studies: *Kreutzer*, No. 11; *Rode*, Nos. 6, 9; *Dont*, Op. 35, Nos. 3, 17, 20; *Spohr*, Nos. 47, 50, in which, owing to musical reasons, only the customary combinations were treated.

If we compare with this the material heaped up in *Sevčik's* Preparatory Studies for Change of Position, as well as in the third book of his Violin Technique, which treats of change of position nearly in all its logically possible forms, the purely technical advantage of his procedure is easily grasped. The same applies when we oppose to the three studies in thirds: *Kreutzer's* No. 31, *Rode's* No. 23 and *Dont's* No. 8, the three studies in thirds, Nos. 6-8 in the fourth book of *Sevčik's* School of Violin Technique. With the three last-mentioned studies far greater results will be secured in the same practice period than with the good old melodious studies; while at the same time it cannot be denied that it is far less fatiguing to study the former, because of their purely musical content, than the chains of tonal figures, intentionally dry, which are the hall-mark of the *Sevčik* studies. It is in the greater mental fatigue thus developed in the player that the danger of the *Sevčik* studies lies. Yet are the unquestionable major advantages of a technical nature which they offer to be sacrificed for this reason? Would it not be possible to find some way of using them which makes the most of their advantages, and reduces their disadvantages to a minimum? I do not hesitate to answer this question with an emphatic *affirmative*.

The *Sevčik* studies, as a whole, may most appropriately be compared to a *medicine* which, according to the size of its doses, kills or cures. Three or four hours daily devoted uninterruptedly to the *Sevčik* studies in the long run deadens the receptive capacity and causes a loss of artistic personality; whereas an interrupted study period of an hour at the most, is not at all dangerous. Hence, for left hand cultivation in accordance with *Sevčik* studies, we would advance the fundamental rule that the practice time should not exceed half an hour, while the daily task for the right arm should be restricted to ten exercises from the School of Bowing Technique. With regard to the Preparatory Studies, no more than a *single* trill-study should be practiced any one day, nor more than six preparatory studies for change of position. In view of my own personal and teaching experience in this field I am convinced that the good or evil consequences resulting from use of the *Sevčik* studies depend, first of all, on the *quantity* of the dose. Like all other left hand studies, his may be used in two different ways: slowly, as *intonation studies;* rapidly, as *studies for agility*. One should not be allowed to pass to the second kind until the sense of hearing has grown so keen that the least little deviation is registered with lightning-like rapidity and at once corrected. After a thorough knowledge of the different positions has been secured by the use of the *first two* books of the School of Violin Technique, one should try to discover, above all, in the third and fourth books, those exercises which later may be applied to my system of scales. This latter should become a permanent institution (with the simultaneous use of *Sevčik's* School of Bowing, the mingling of the scale system and bow-strokes, naturally, is dropped). Not until then should the remaining exercises be taken up.

Sevčik School of Bowing

It is my custom to give my pupils the following instructions with regard to the study of the *Sevčik* School of Bowing:

1. Begin with exercises 5 and 29 and continue to progress in a parallel order.

2. Take up *five* varieties *daily* of these two exercises, hence *ten* in all.

3. Do not for a moment believe that the *exceeding* of this apparently small number will result in greater or more rapid progress—the damage done by the exhaustion developed through increased practice will be greater than the advantage of a more rapidly acquired bowing technique.

4. Under *no circumstances* should the exercise be repeated. Every day ten *new* variants should be taken up in their turn.

5. The variants marked *M** (nut, middle, point) should *not* be repeated three times; but a third only of each exercise played with the portion of the bow indicated.

6. In order to avoid the annoyance of turning pages, the fundamental exercise should be *copied*.

7. The practicing of the ten exercises should in no case take up more than *twenty* to *twenty-five minutes*.

8. When the daily ten have been practiced, the last of the variants played should be *marked*, so that on the following day the student will know exactly where to begin.

9. It is not sufficient to carry out the exercises with the bowings prescribed—equal attention should be paid to *purity of intonation* and *beauty of tone*.

10. Their study should be made as *comfortable* and *pleasant* as the dry nature of the material permits so that the player will feel no inward compulsion to drop them.

11. It is advisable to provide the *exceptionally* difficult variants with a mark of some kind; the sum total of the exercises thus marked will furnish a valuable *collection* of difficult bowing exercises for later use.

12. When the entire study material has been covered, to do which in the manner indicated will take fifteen months, one should once more turn to collections of etudes in which equal attention has been paid to bowing and finger exercises.—The *preparatory trill studies* should be used with great caution, since they are among the mentally most tiring forms of exercises comprised in the literature of the violin. On the other hand, I am a confirmed believer in the *preparatory change of position* studies, which represents the simplest and the best that *Sevčik* has published. They may be of the greatest service, as well to those whose technique is in process of development as for the mature artist who in the course of time suffers from a periodically returning insecurity with regard to his change of position technique. The *Forty Springing Bow Variants* may do good service in case of special needs, though in general they do not rise to the level of the other *Sevčik* study works. (His *School for Beginners*, since it does not lie within the scope of this book, has not been considered.)

All in all, I regard the *Sevčik* study works as the most important and time-saving means for obtaining a modern violin technique, provided that they are used in the right way. If the *Bowing Exercises* in particular arouse the keen opposition of many teachers it is due, in my opinion, to the fact that those concerned are themselves not quite clear as to the manner in which they should be studied. In most cases enormous quantities of this material, so hard to assimilate, are taken in, and it is no wonder that digestive difficulties develop and the patient refuses musical nourishment. When intelligently used the *Sevčik* exercises not alone have *never* done any harm but, on the contrary, owing to their voluntary restriction to the mechanism of movement, have furnished the securest foundation imaginable for the acquisition of a perfect technique with the greatest saving of time. To them, above all, the raising of the general technical level in the last decade is due; in most cases violinists who have used them with unsatisfactory results may blame themselves. The effect of any remedy does not rest alone on its intrinsic value, but above all in the manner in which it is applied.*

In connection with the establishment of daily exercises of a general technical nature, we have often pointed out that apart from those forms which are valid for all violinists—such as scales of every kind—other exercises, applicable to purely individual weaknesses, often must be taken into consideration. In so far as they refer to difficulties found in pieces intended for performance, examples are given (see p. 159) of the manner in which they should be conquered. One definite hindrance of a general kind still calls for special discussion, since it is capable of influencing one's collective technique unfavorably and, in addition, tends to assume an epidemic character among violinists in general—I allude to that organic weakness of the *fourth* finger, which is produced by the latter's lessened use.

'eak- ess ' 4th inger

When the fourth finger is naturally weak, it may be strengthened by suitable exercises, beginning with elementary instruction. It is different in the case of very advanced violinists who prefer the *third* finger to the *fourth* with the result that the latter has far less opportunity for action than is usually the case. During the past twenty years some of our best violinists, whom the rising generation regards as radiant models, have discovered that the substitution of the third finger for the fourth, especially in the case of notes long sustained in the higher positions, offers extraordinary tonal advantages. This preferring of the third to the fourth finger eventually becomes a habit; the fourth finger continues to lose strength; and when the time comes that the player is accidentally compelled by the note-sequence to use the fourth finger for a sustained note in a high position, its vibratory capacity seems constrained, pressure becomes an exertion, and the finger may even give out altogether. It is evident that notable tonal advantages are counteracted by noticeable technical disadvantages. Should one give up the former, and in doing so risk a less perfect presentation of the art work? No true artist would ever agree to this. He will rather attempt to do away with the technical disadvantages by means of concentrated study and special exercises. The more the fourth finger is neglected and weakened because of the foregoing reasons, the more the violinist must give it his attention from a purely technical standpoint. The following series of daily exercises are intended to serve to this end. (Also see p. 129.)

12 Exercises for Strengthening 4th Finger

*On the other hand, I condemn unconditionally the preparatory exercises for different violin concertos published by *Sevčik* during the last years of his life. I consider them most dangerous with regard to the development of the *musical* components of a personality.

XIII see Musical Example 12

VIII 

IX 

X 

XI 

XII 

3. Practice of Applied Technic

a. Fingering in General. The word "fingering," as we understand it, means the choice of those fingers by means of which a certain series of notes is played. It is true that only four fingers need be taken into account—yet when we remember that they are able to climb on half-tones and on four strings from the nut to the end of the fingerboard, we realize how many possible fingerings the violinist has at his disposal. Their harnessing into "positions" does not help us much, for it must be admitted that the division of the fingerboard into these so-called positions (hand-positions) is an auxiliary the practical value of which is open to question. No matter how valuable the feeling for position may be in estimating distances (Comp. p. 26), it cannot be exhaustively established by means of the customary differentiations.

Conventionality of Position

332. 

Where, actually, *is* the hand in this case, in the second or third position?

333. 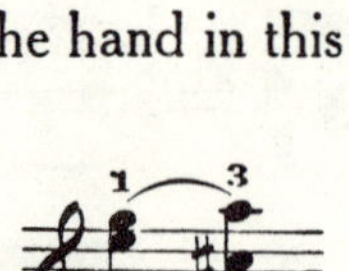

Here, in the third E^2-G^2, the first finger is in the second, the fourth in the first position. And the entire hand? It is certain that in the beginner's case the indication of the position is necessary as an easily comprehended aid in securing a certain amount of familiarity with interval proportions on the fingerboard. The advanced violinist, however, justly endeavors to free himself as soon as possible from the concept of a hand-position indicated by a number, a concept entirely foreign to the performances of modern violin-players. The true position of the hand often contradicts the position number assigned to it. Enharmonic changes, simultaneous use of various positions in double-stops, stretches and, above all, the intervals which steadily diminish when ascending—in short, all the differences between real and imaginary proportions—to all these it is due that the traditional measurements are valid only as an auxiliary in elementary study, and never as a standard of measurement in the case of positions of the hand to which more complex tasks are assigned. In spite of this I have retained the traditional indications of the positions in the following illustrations, for reasons of general comprehensibility, since at present there is no other way in which more exactly to define the position hand and fingers are to take on the fingerboard.

The "Best" Fingering

Are there firmly established fundamental principles according to which we may determine the most favorable succession of the fingers—the *correct* fingering? Not at all. There are none, so long as we subordinate choice of fingers to our own personal taste, and to the advantages and shortcomings of our technical dexterity.* From that moment on, however, when we grasp the fact that fingering is best which represents the *least exertion of strength*, we have gained a tower-height, from the altitude of which it is possible for us to consider the value of a fingering *objectively*, uninfluenced by the player's violinistic peculiarities. However, the *fingering objectively* the best, that is to say, the best in a general sense, by no means need be the *subjective* best one, that is, the one most suitable for a certain player. For instance:

334. 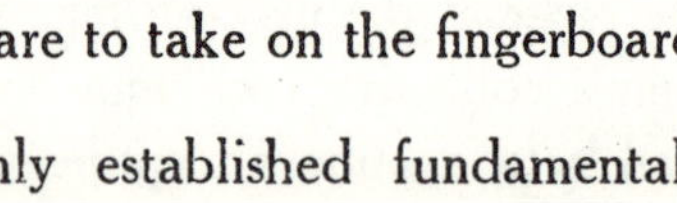

* The same holds good in publishing a new edition of a classical work: purely personal fingerings or bowings must be avoided, those fit for the average violinist preferred—with the mental reservation, that appropriate changes, motivated by personal reasons, may be permitted.

In the case of a weak fourth finger the upper fingering will unquestionably be the best, in spite of the fact that the lower fingering seems to be more correct objectively.

Beethoven, Vln. Cto, 1º Movt.

335.

With broad and fleshy finger-tips the half-tone A^3-G^3 sharp, hard to play exactly in tune, must be taken with the second and third fingers, since in this high position we are able to press the third finger closer against the second by means of a lateral or oblique inclination than we could with the far shorter and more awkward fourth finger. Furthermore:

336. 

Of what value, in this case, is the knowledge that the lower fingering, in consequence of a *single* change of position, is essentially more simple than the upper one, when the violinist in question commands only an insufficiently grounded ability in position-change, and feels uncertain in the second and fourth positions?

In spite of these limitations, however, it is impossible for serious pedagogical research to advance beyond a compromise, one which might be formulated in the following terms: After the best, that is, the least strength-commanding manner of fingering has been established, it may be adapted to the personal and technical peculiarities of the player, and changed in accordance with them. It is true that even in such cases a struggle at times develops between the *musical* conscience and the necessity of an impeccable *technical* performance.

Beethoven, Kreutzer Sonata 1º Movt.

337. 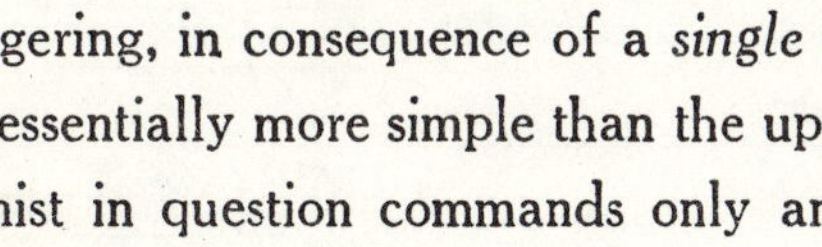

Here the melodic line in measure two is as follows:

338. 

the generally used fingering:

339. 

and the consequent incorrect tone-color mixture changes it to:

340. 

Only a fingering *without* change of string, between

341. 

will sound thematically right here, thus:

342. 

though it is extraordinarily daring, and may only be risked on the basis of uncommon sureness in change of position. Many a noble intention is wrecked on the insufficiency of existent means—in art as in life!

In the succeeding explanations an attempt will be made, first of all, not only to establish the *objectively* correct fingering, but also to present those moments which seem to justify a change. This object, however, can only be carried out if one important limitation is observed: disregard of technical insufficiencies which are a result of inadequate training. Insufficient technique in the positions and changes of position, above all, cannot be taken into account. Whoever does not, in advance, feel confident and at home in any part of the fingerboard will be unable to make use of the best theoretical advice.

Fingering in Technique

b. Fingering as a Technical Means: The following consideration may serve as our point of departure: So long as the fingers move in the *same position*, and at a normal distance one from the other, none but the natural fingering, ordinarily, comes into question—each finger preferably places itself upon that portion of the string above which it may chance to be at the moment; though, of course, it is doubtful which intervals in the form of half-tones and whole-tones between the individual fingers, most closely approximate to their conformation. In general the opinion seems to have established itself that the half-tone between the second and third fingers, expressed in the scale of D-major:

343. 

combined with the whole tones between the first and second, as well as the third and fourth fingers, represent the most natural relation between them. I agree, with the reservation that it merely shows us which scales must first be studied (G-major, D-major and A-major). It is far more difficult to determine whether the *fourth finger* or the open string should be preferred in *runs*. Current views in this respect have undergone a change since the popularity of the steel E-string has so greatly increased. Until a short time ago the following considerations were influential: 1. In general the open strings, because of their brighter tone-color as well as for reasons of convenience, were preferred to the fourth finger. 2. In particular, however, a choice was arrived at from the standpoint of making the change of string coincide as nearly as possible with the strong beat of the measure:

4th Finger or Open String

Francoeur-Kreisler, Rigaudon

344. 

(the same)

345. 

Beethoven, Son. Op. 30, No 3, 3º Mov't.

346. 

3. Change of string for the sake of a single note was avoided:

Correct

347. 

Incorrect

All these considerations, when a steel E-string is used, are thrust into the background by the fact that the open string, when it unexpectedly enters in tied, *ascending* change of string, very often whistles. In such cases we are compelled to substitute the fourth finger for the open E-string, though in general we still follow the traditional rules in the case of the three other strings.

Mendelssohn, Cto, 3º Mov't.

348. 

Beethoven, Cto, 1º Mov't.

349. 

Bruch, Cto, G min. 1º Mov't.

350. 

The retention, so far as at all possible, of the natural distance between the first and fourth fingers is extremely important. Certainty of intonation in the same position depends to a certain degree on the fact that the fingers, especially in the lower positions, only cover a certain part of the string, i.e., a fourth (Comp. p. 24):

351. 

On the other hand, in:

it turns into a diminished or perfect fifth-position: we have *stretched* the fourth finger. Similarly in:

352. 

where we are obliged to bend the first finger back.

Stretching

Stretching. Unquestionably stretching in general owes its origin to a certain leaning toward convenience, insomuch as by its means the change of position so justly dreaded by the great majority is *avoided*—yet only at the cost of a confusion of the proportionate relations of the fingers among themselves, which is dangerous to tonal purity. Even in this case, however, it is difficult to lay down fixed rules. For instance, is it possible to play:

353. 

at a rapid tempo on the same string without stretching the fourth finger? Surely not.

On the other hand, in:

354. 

the change of position on G will be far more advantageous than "stretching" the C. Similarly, in the case of downward stretches, in:

355. 

no other possibility exists, while in the following example:

356. 

the half-position is to be used. Hence, in order to avoid stretching, one is obliged, in most cases, to change position. Which of the two possibilities to prefer is something that can only be determined case by case. At any rate, stretching should mainly develop between the first and second, and the third and fourth fingers, much less, however, between the second and third fingers, since the anatomical structure of the hand forbids the latter.

I frankly confess that in this connection I am at a loss, since I have a decided prejudice against stretching.* Wherever I can, I avoid changing the fourth-setting (interval of a fourth) of my fingers, so valuable for correct intonation, and infinitely prefer a change of position. Incidentally, I make a sharp distinction between low and high positions:

357. 

would hardly be possible.

358. 

would be decidedly easier, while in:

359. 

the hand assumes quite a natural position, since here the interval of the sixth is hardly greater than that of the fourth in the first position. Stretches in high positions are more imaginary (following the printed music) than real.

The stretching back of the first finger into the half-position, and its consequent gliding forward into the first position is a survival of the "good old days," when the half-position and, as well, the second and fourth positions were timidly eschewed.

Some examples in point follow:

Bach, Sonata, E min. 2º Mov't. (*David*, High School)

360. 

Bruch, Cto, G min. 3º Mov't.

361. 

Mendelssohn, Cto, 3º Mov't.

362. 

Dohnányi, Cto, 4º Mov't.

363. 

Beethoven, Cto, 1º Mov't.

364. 

Joachim, Variations Nº 3.

365. 

Händel, Sonata D maj. 3º Mov't.

366. 

Reger, Op.42 Nº 1.

367. 

368. 

* Were my attention here called to the fact that the fingered octaves I have so often used, in themselves call for a stretch in the form of a fifth- (instead of a fourth-) position of the hand, and that in addition I have included stretching exercises in my "Basic Studies" (Urstudien), I would reply that the great technical and tonal advantages of the fingered octaves make the disadvantages of stretches of a half-tone or whole tone appear quite negligible, and that the stretching exercises in the "Basic Studies" (Urstudien) merely represent a somewhat violent, purely *gymnastic* attempt to loosen the hand (where time is wanting for regular exercises).

There are, however, exceptional cases, in which even a violinist trained in the modern sense of the word prefers to thrust back the finger instead of moving the whole hand into the new position:

Wieniawski, Légende

369. 

Here it would be taking too great a risk to move freely from the harmonic tone into the second position. Hence the lesser evil should be chosen, unless one prefers to play the entire theme on the D-string.

Even greater is the advantage when the finger is stretched back as in the following example:

Paganini-Kreisler, Caprice Nº XX

370. 

Between F[1] sharp and E[1] the hand must under no circumstances leave the second position.

We also, in many cases, are obliged to choose between the second and third positions:

Beethoven, Romance G maj.

371. 
Correct
Incorrect

Brahms-Joachim, Hung. Dance Nº 9

372. 
Correct
Incorrect

Spohr, Cto, D min. 1º Movt.

373. 
Correct
Incorrect

In Example 374, on the other hand, a gliding back into the second position on C sharp can be avoided only at the expense of sureness of intonation.

Brahms-Joachim, Hung. Dance Nº 1

374. 
(daring)

375. 
Correct
Incorrect

(The exceptions which occur, notably in the case of fingered octaves, are discussed in the section devoted to the latter.) It is strange to note how dulled the ear of many violinists seems to be with regard to this kind of blurred half-tone *glissando* in rapid passages.

In a sequence of notes like the following:

376. 
Correct
Incorrect

it is impossible to hear the A sharp and the B distinctly, since the *glissando* lying between, though carried out ever so rapidly, claims the greater portion of time allotted these two notes. Such runs sound indistinct and blurred.

The stretching backward or forward, incidentally, may also be determined by the circumstance that the hand , i.e., the arm, may be obliged to move upward or downward afterwards. In this connection I would call attention to a decidedly instructive personal experience: In the *Chopin* Nocturne, Op. 27, No. 2, transcribed by *Wilhelmj,* I first used the following fingering, at the beginning of the main theme:

Chopin-Wilhelmj, Nocturne Op. 27 Nº 2

377. 
D

Here, in the transition from the second to the fourth position (└─┘), I noticed an insecurity which at first defied explanation, and which showed itself in too low a sounding of the B. Closer examination disclosed the reason: it was due to the fact that the *lower* position of the thumb in the second position, absolutely essential in preparing the upward movement, could only be carried out in a most insecure manner, so that in the fifth position—which owing to the substitution of the third for the fourth finger could partly be regarded as the sixth position—the whole hand lay a little too low. This evil was entirely done away with by the use of the third instead of the second position, because in the third position I could shove the thumb beneath the neck with the greatest ease, and even temporarily rest the arm against the upper part of the violin-body, and the hand thus reached the position necessary for the upward movement in a secure manner:

378. 
D

whereby the sureness which at first had been missing at once began to return. This is a typical case, which once again proves what fundamental importance—an importance by no means properly appreciated in practice—attaches to the movement of the *thumb* in change of position.

So long as the stretching of the hand does not exceed the interval of a fifth, and is used only incidentally, it cannot do much harm.

Only in the lower positions does this imply a tension between the fingers, a tension which, unless it is absolutely necessary, should be avoided all the more when the hand has to cover sixth- or even seventh-intervals:

379. 

Here the *change of string* involves far less effort, even in the higher positions.

The most important advantage of these stretches consists in the avoidance of unnecessary change of position (*glissandi*), or change of string.

Brahms, Trio, Op. 8, 3º Mov't.

380. 

Dont, Op. 35 Nº 1.

381. 

Dont, Op. 35 Nº 5

382. 

Reger, Op. 42 Nº 1

383. 

384. 

Ernst, Cto F♯ min.

385. 

386. 

387. 

Corelli-Léonard, La Folia

388. 

Lalo, Symph Espagnole, 5º Mov't.

389. 

390. 

Hence stretches are only permissable when the change of position which otherwise must be carried out produces a musically or technically disturbing effect. When this is not the case, the stretch should be absolutely avoided:

Dont, Op. 35 Nº 7.

391. 

+ Change of position instead of a stretch

Dont, Op. 35 Nº 5.

392. 

+ Change position

Dont, Op. 35, Nº 11.

393. 

The fingers which take the chord in Example 393 must not leave the string, since dropping them again endangers the intonation.

394. 

It is better to break the chord  than to strain one's sinews.

In the *Kreisler* Cadenza to "The Devil's Trill," a stretch will be found which may be avoided if inconvenient.

395. 

Far more difficult is the well-known passage, combined with a double-trill, in the *Paganini* Caprice, No. 3:

And what can be said of violinists who take the greatest pride in being able to produce this stretch?

As a gymnastic feat it falls decidedly short of a somersault, and in public performance this stretch has not been used even by the player who cultivates virtuosity alone. The time and toil devoted to it, if applied to exercises in the normal position of the hand, would surely bear far better results.

Frequently a stretch appears necessary, but upon closer examination seems entirely superfluous:

see p132

Correct

396. 

Incorrect

Beethoven, Vln. Cto, 3o Mov't.

397. 

A-C, with the first and second fingers, in Example 396, hardly means a stretch, whereas C-E or even C-F with the third and fourth fingers, represents one of the most exhausting of stretches. Broken *minor* triads as well as chords of the sixth, therefore, always should be taken in the lower positions with the following fingering, 1-2-4, avoiding the third finger.

Kreutzer, Etüde No 12.

Correct

398. 

Incorrect

In the following example:

Brahms, Cto 1o Mov't.

399. 

Ysaye avoided the tenth, B-D, by playing the D³ as a harmonic:

(the same)

400. 

while I, for my part, substitute change of position for this unnecessary stretch:

(the same)

401. 

One of the most disagreeable stretches—since it makes absolutely impossible perfect surety of intonation—is the following:

Chausson, Poëme

402. 

Without stretching

In order to weaken the *glissando* produced by change of position I play the two tied sixteenth-notes with a light *portato*-stroke.

Compressing the Fingers

In a contrary sense, yet quite as disadvantageous, is the effect of an excessive *pressing together of the fingers*,* which particularly in high positions and with thick fingers may become exceedingly uncomfortable.

404. 

Here the third finger, between the A and the C, as well as the second and third, between the C and the D sharp, do not know what to do with their superfluous selves. If the third finger retains its usual position, although terribly compressed between the second and fourth fingers, the C of the fourth finger becomes too high. All that it can do is to project itself pointedly into the air at an angle of 45 degrees. In high positions a normal fourth-interval position of the fingers is almost impossible, and a fifth-interval may be advantageously substituted for it:

405. 

In this case, as in general, the following fundamental rule should be observed: In order to establish the correct fingering the *actual distance* on the fingerboard between the notes to be taken is determinative—and *not the intervals represented in print.* To make this clearer in detail, see the following example:

406.  is taken by the first and second fingers.

 Here the player will endeavor instinctively to use the first and third fingers, although the distance remains the same. If, then, we come to

407. 

the third finger is indicated for the D flat, but not in the case of

** (See page 125)

408. 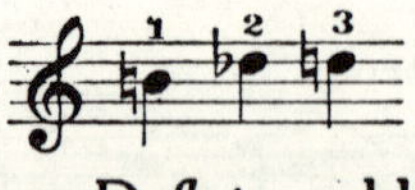

Here the third finger on D *flat* would mean an unnatural and unnecessary crowding together of the fingers.

* The following example, however, may be adduced to show an exception to the rule:

Tschaikowsky, Cto, Cadence

403. 

The open A-string, with G¹ and G sharp¹, permits of an exaggerated thrusting forward of the second finger which, from F¹ on, moves forward comfortably in half-tone progression without leaving the string and hence makes it unnecessary to use the fourth finger on G sharp¹.

One of the cases occuring most frequently, especially in broken diminished chords of the seventh as well as in melodic minor scales, is the substitution of the fingering used for the minor third for that of the augmented second:

410. 

411. 
Bruch, Ctº G min. 1º Mov't.

the same with major thirds:

412. 
(the same)

Enharmonic Changes

Yet, especially where harmonically complicated note-sequences are concerned, we are in a position to simplify noticeably the movements of the left hand, if we utilize *enharmonic changes* in the fingering. Some examples follow:

413. 
Dvořák, Mazurka, Op. 49

414. 
Brahms, Trio, Op. 8, 4º Mov't.

415. 
Dvořák, Trio, Op. 65, 2º Mov't.

416. 
Brahms, Sonata, Op. 78, 2º Mov't.

417. 
Brahms, Ctº, 2º Mov't.

418. 
Korngold, Suite, Op. 11, Nº 1
Sul G
p
espress.
rit.
a tempo

** (See music example 408). The objection that the mode of writing indicated is an unnatural one and not used practically is not valid—in modern music even more pronounced cross-relations may be observed, for instance:

409. 
Arthur Schnabel, Sonata for Vln. Solo

419. 
(the same)
etc.
Glazounow, Ctº

420. 

Here, too, belong the enharmonic change between the lowered third or second and the raised second or first positions.

421. 
Bruch, Ctº, G min. 2º Mov't.

As a rule one hears this passage played sharp, because the player thinks that he is in the second and then in the sixth position, while in reality the hand more correctly may be said to be in the first and in the fifth position. One must change this passage enharmonically as follows:

422. 
(the same)

The enharmonic change, above all, should be applied during change of string:

423. 

In these cases it is a necessity, since the use of the same finger, especially in *legato*, would cause a gap to develop, and the open string would become audible. Similarly:

424. 

425. 
Dont, Op. 35 Nº 2

426. 
(the same)

Fingers Remaining on String

There are teachers who put forward as a principle that the fingers should remain lying on the strings as much as possible. In my opinion this principle only holds good when unnecessary movements are thus avoided, for instance:

427. 
Mendelssohn, Ctº, 1º Mov't

but not when the compulsion it implies causes greater exertion than does the repeated raising and lowering. Furthermore, it must be remembered that the unnecessary resting of the unoccupied fingers on the strings lames the vibratory capacity of the entire hand in slow movements in a manner injurious to vitality of expression.

Simultaneous Placing of Fingers

On the other hand, we should place the fingers on the strings *simultaneously*, not only in arpeggiated three- and four-note chords, but also in two-note intervals divided between two strings:

Pugnani-Kreisler, Allegro

428. 

(The four-cornered note-signs indicate the finger which is to be placed on the string in anticipation.)

Beethoven, Cto, 1º Mov't.

429. 

Joachim, Hung. Cto, 1º Mov't. (also in public performance)

430. 

Brahms, Cto, 2º Mov't. (practice only)

431. 

Here, too, should be considered the holding down of certain fingers for study purposes (see *Sevčik*, I, No. 20), as well as the anticipated dropping of the finger which I recommend to secure smooth change of string (see p. 25).

If, however, demand for as frequent as possible a retention on the string of the unoccupied fingers is modified to the extent that a finger should not *immediately* be raised from the string once it had fulfilled its purpose of pressing down the string at a given point, then it is one with which every practical violinist may comply. Especially in the case of arpeggiated chords the fingers which take the lower notes should remain on the strings just as long as the resonance of the notes endures—the *echoing*-tone, though it is one in most cases not consciously heard by the listener, is none the less a necessary factor of the real tone.* Similarly, before a change of string, the finger which is to leave the note should remain for a fraction of a second longer—but no longer than that!

* The degree to which rules, correct enough in themselves, are and may be ignored by extraordinarily gifted individuals is proven by the example of *Mischa Elman*, who takes the two notes of the octaves at the beginning of the *Beethoven* Violin Concerto with technical and tonal perfection, not *simultaneously*, but in *succession*, not putting down the fourth finger until the moment when he needs it, and immediately raising the first finger as soon as he has used it. Thus he secures, above all, greater freedom in the fourth-finger *vibrato*.

Fingering in Shifting

If we now turn our attention to the interconnection between the fingering and the *change of position* we once more encounter the principle of the least expenditure of strength. This least strenuous form of movement expresses itself in the change of position in the greatest possible diminution of the distances to be covered.

If we take as an example: 

we find that we obtain the following medial space, measured from the intermediary note to the end one, which may be expressed, approximately, as follows (the first figure represents the finger used for B, the second the fingering for F sharp):

4/4=7 cm.	4/3= 9 cm.	4/2=11 cm.	4/1=14 cm.
3/3=7 cm.	3/1=11 cm.	3/2= 9 cm.	3/4= 5 cm.
2/2=7 cm.	2/1= 9 cm.	2/3= 5 cm.	2/4= 3 cm.
1/1=7 cm.	1/2= 5 cm.	1/3= 3 cm.	1/4= 2 cm.

As a matter of fact in accordance herewith 1/4, from the fourth to the fifth position, will represent the least expenditure of strength in the shape of the smallest possible distance to be covered.

It would be erroneous to take for granted, however, that this is the only principle which dominates the change of position. It stands for only *one* side of it, the purely *mechanical* one. Hence it must be reckoned with, above all, in *rapid, purely technical* change of position, where it is a question of either playing no *glissandi* at all or only the shortest and least obtrusive ones. In the case of change of position in *slow* tempos, expressed in the form of *portamenti* which will emphasize the emotional expression, on the other hand, the tonal and aesthetic element steps into the foreground, while the technical element, the striving for lack of effort, no longer enters into consideration.

Natural Harmonics and Their Misuse

Hence the effortless, yet tonally unfounded application of the natural harmonics should be discarded as a general rule. (As already mentioned on p. 47).

Mendelssohn, Vln. Cto, 2º Mov't.

Correct

432. 

Incorrect

(the same) 1º Mov't.

Correct

433. 

Incorrect

Spohr, Cto, D min. 2º Mov't.

Correct

434. 

Incorrect

On the other hand the use of a harmonic of short duration may at times make it possible to dispense with an otherwise unavoidable and disagreeably noticeable change of position.

Beethoven, Cto, 1º Mov't.

435. 

Bruch, Cto, G min. 3º Mov't.

436. 

Saint-Saëns, Cto, B min. 1º Mov't.

437. 

Lalo, Symp. Espagnole, 4º Mov't.

438. 

The same holds good in the case of more rapid, not expressive, notes:

Beethoven, Cto, 3º Mov't.

439. 

Brahms, Trio, Op. 8 (New Ed.) 1º Mov't.

440. 

Mendelssohn, Cto, 2º Mov't.

441. 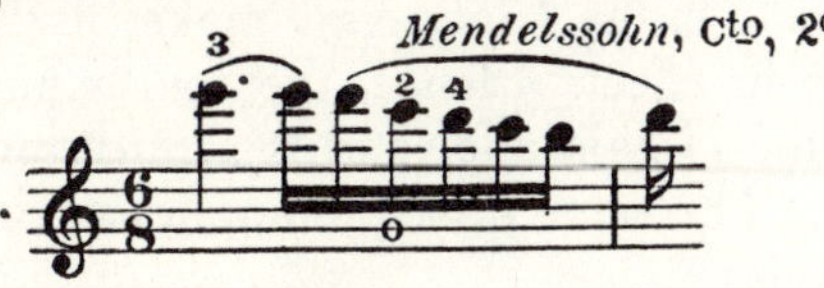

Saint-Saëns, Rondo Capriccioso

442. 

Suk, Op. 17, Nº 1

443. 

Reger, Op. 42 Nº 1, 1º Mov't.

444. 

Lalo, Symp. Espagnole, 5º Mov't.

445. 

Furthermore, to facilitate intonation:

Reger, Op. 42, 2º Mov't.

446. 

Reger, Op. 42, 3º Mov't.

447. 

In graceful expressional formulas:

Mozart, D maj. 3º Mov't.

448. 

When remaining in the same position, however, taking the harmonics, aside from the tonal disadvantages involved, should be avoided because the point of application in the case of the harmonics lies decidedly lower than that of the same, firmly taken notes. The alternative playing of both kinds of notes in the same position is therefore identical with intentional misleading of the muscular instinct, which is reflected by the highest degree of insecurity. Hence the following:

should be absolutely eschewed, while:

though easier, nevertheless is decidedly risky. In those cases—rare enough—where *portamenti* occur between two natural harmonics, care should be taken that during change of position the gliding finger presses the string down *firmly*, as otherwise whistling accompanying noises, caused through undesirable overtones will become audible.

Beethoven, Cto, 1º Mov't.

449. 

Aside from these rare exceptions, the manner in which the older school in particular has abused the indiscriminate choice of natural harmonics must be absolutely condemned. For, seeing that the tone color of the natural harmonics differs fundamentally from that of notes taken in the usual way (in consequence of the entire absence of overtones), we must first of all ask what right, from an aesthetic standpoint, has an acoustically foreign body of the sort to make a sudden appearance in the tonal organism? It is always deficient technique in change of position or muscular laziness which makes the effortless "reaching up" to the note in question, and this enforced change into a harmonic appear easier than the raising of lower arm or hand into a higher position.

Let us now return to the relations between the fingering and the change of position. In agreement with the prin-

Shifting on Half-Tones

ciple of least possible distance we will, first of all, prefer to carry out the change of position in scale-like sequence on the *half-tones* rather than on the whole tones.

450. 

451. 
Vieuxtemps, Cto, A min.

452. 
Saint-Saëns, Rondo Capriccioso

In very high positions the half-tones, when taken by different fingers, are not close enough, hence (principally in *cantilena* movements) use of the same finger should be preferred:

453. 
Brahms, Cto, 1º Mov't.

At times it will be possible for us to play them quite inaudibly, by thrusting the hand forward or backward (crawling into positions):

454. 
Mendelssohn, Cto, 1º Mov't.

455. 
Dvořák, Trio Op. 65, 1º Mov't.

456. 
Dont, Op. 35 Nº 2

Shifting on Strong Beats

We will also, when we have a choice between carrying out the change of position in the weak or strong beat of the measure, naturally give the *strong beat* the preference, because of the unavoidable, even though slight accent, which otherwise results (see p. 29):

457. 
Saint-Saëns, Rondo Capriccioso
(the same)

458. 

459. 
Paganini, Cto, D maj.

460. 
Ernst, Cto, F# min.

Leaps

The rapid covering of greater distances in change of position (leaps), is always accompanied by a decided risk. Here the right way is not to choose the most logical fingering but the one best adapted to the player's individuality, the most *convenient* one:

461. 
Saint-Saëns, Cto, B min. 1º Mov't.

B- or L-glissando

In Example 461 the third finger on D is the surest because it permits of a *B-* as well as an *L-glissando,* which last, if the intermediary note C sharp be used, guarantees the greatest measure of security by eliminating the danger of slipping off while the fourth finger with D as its intermediary note in the *L-glissando* makes itself unpleasantly noticeable in effect. Hence, the fourth finger should be used for the *B-glissando,* and the third finger for the *L-glissando.* The same principle applies in similar cases, as for example:

462. 
Brahms, Trio, B maj. 1º Mov't.
(B.gl.)
(L.gl.)

463. 
Ernst, Airs Hongrois
(B.gl.)
(L.gl.)

464. 
Dvořák, Trio, F min. 4º Mov't
(B.gl.)
(L.gl.)

Personally, in all these cases I prefer the third finger with an *L-glissando* which, however, ought to be inaudible.

The choice of fingering often depends upon whether one prefers to change the string or the position:

465. 
Brahms, Cto, 1º Mov't

In Example 465 I prefer to remain on the E-string, because its clearer tone-quality is better suited to the character of the phrase.

466. 
Correct
Sinding, Cto, A maj. 3º Mov't
Incorrect

In Example 466 change of position makes it possible to avoid too abrupt change of strings.

467. 
Brahms, Cto.
Correct
Incorrect

No further proofs are needed to show that in Example 467 the avoidance of the change of position on the E- and the remaining upon the A-string, although very convenient, is tonally quite out of the question.

468. 
Brahms, Cto, 1º Mov't.

In Example 468, on the other hand, the ascent at +, in the fifth position, is only possible for those who possess very narrow finger-tips, and when the strings are absolutely in tune, since otherwise the minor sixth may become nearly a major sixth.

The place of the fourth finger in the high positions, especially in the case of *cantilene*, may be taken by the third finger without endangering correctness of intonation. It is only in appearance that the use of the third finger conditions the use of a higher position. In reality, hand and arm, owing to the shortness of the fourth finger, are compelled to make a far more vigorous inward turn, while the thumb also can far more easily retain its point of support at the end of the neck when the longer third finger is substituted for the shorter fourth finger.

(In this connection also compare with what has been said on p. 117.)

469. 
Brahms, Cto, 1º Mov't.

470. 
Mendelssohn, Cto, 2º Mov't.

The stretch of a fourth between the second and third fingers suggested in Example 470, with exclusion of the fourth finger—which in this high position does not possess the strength to give the C^4 the fulness and roundness called for—is more natural and more easily carried out than the visual appearance of the note-picture would lead one to believe. One of the most unpleasant accompanimental phenomena of a preferential use of the third in place of the fourth finger, however, is the resultant large interval between the acting fingers, which in themselves present the temptation to make a musically unjustified *portamenti*.

471. 
Brahms, Cto, 2º Mov't.

The stretch, F^3-D^4, with the first and fourth fingers, is effortless. If the player, however, feels that the tonal character of the D (taken by the fourth finger) is too thin, he may only make use of the third, when the latter's tensional ability is sufficient to enable it to cover the stretch F-D without a portamento, since otherwise he would be compelled to make two *portamenti*, one after the other. Hence, an extended finger-reach as well as a highly developed change of position technique form absolutely essential prerequisites for the tonal advantages, indisputably great, accruing from a preferential use of the third finger in long sustained tones capable of large expressional possibilities. We will conclude with some typical example of special fingering problems.

Simultaneous Use of Two Positions

The simultaneous use of two positions:

472. 
Brahms, Cto, 2º Mov't.

473. 
Brahms, Cto, 1º Mov't.

474. 
Reger, Op. 42 Nº 1

475. 
(the same)

476. 
(the same)

477. 
(the same)

478. 
(the same)

Change of finger on one note:

479. 
(the same)

480. 
(the same)

Needless change of position:

481. 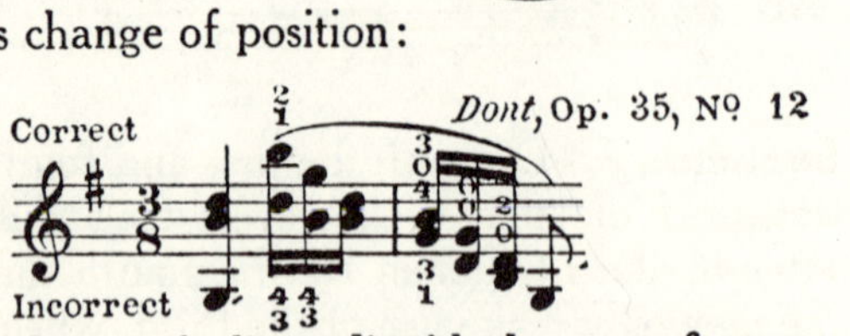
Correct
Incorrect
Dont, Op. 35, № 12

The avoidance of *glissandi* with the same finger:

482. 
Correct
Incorrect
Dont, Op. 35, № 3

483. 
Correct
Incorrect
Dont, Op. 35, № 4

Fingering in Scales

Fingering of Scales, etc. Let us now consider fingering in its connection with the established and generally used technical formulas. The fingering to be employed in rapid diatonic scales is subject, first of all, to the law of the least exertion of strength. Hence, the change of position should be preferably carried out by adjacent fingers, and on half-tones. Let us take the major scale in compass of an octave, on one string, for example:

484. 
a)
b)
G String

Here, when ascending, we have the choice between *a*: 3-1 (a half-tone, yet not the next finger); or, *b*: 2-1 twice (the next finger, yet involving a double change of position on two whole tones). Both modes have their advantages and disadvantages.

In spite of the fact that apparently 3-1 should be preferred, I, for my part, have decided in favor of the double 2-1, since the 3-1 is not applicable in the minor scale because of the whole tone, and as a result an unnecessary difference in fingering develops between the ascending minor and major scales, one better avoided for the sake of simplicity. In the *descending* major scale, however, where the two changes of position necessary are carried out in half-tones, the fingering noted above unquestionably offers the most effortless way of carrying out the change of position here needed.

In the melodic *minor* scale the half-tones have changed their place of occurrence:

485. 

In *ascending* we will be able the more easily to retain the same fingering used in the major scale because the half-tone D-E flat, if anything, has made it more advantageous. This is not the case while *descending*, where, by means of the fingering above noted, we are able to do justice to all demands—half-tones and adjacent fingers—necessary to an ideal finger-sequence. The fingerings for the diatonic scales through three octaves may be established in accordance with the same principles:

486. 

487. 

Fixed or Different Fingering in Scales

I am not in favor of the method which recommends practicing scales with *various* fingerings. Violin-playing in itself already is so difficult an art that the action it demands should be simplified so far as possible, and by no means (unless there be musical reasons) made more difficult. If we are accustomed to one certain fingering (which we consider the best) for the major or minor type-scale, it is possible for us, for instance, when reading at sight (following the visualization of the collective note-groups of a scale, and the subsequent lightninglike finger-reaction) to carry out the necessary partial movements in the form of a movement-complex with the utmost smoothness. This is not the case when we are accustomed to playing scales in all sorts of possible finger-combinations. When called upon to play unexpectedly, and not prepared by previous practice, difficulties invariably will develop, and express themselves in stoppages or even more serious mishaps, because the fingers are not, as in the first instance, able to carry out the movement-complex automatically but, so to speak, must first inquire in the central office of the brain which of the various fingerings at their disposal they really should use—something which, in view of the short time available, diminishes the qualities of the performance or even makes it impossible.*

In a broken triad, such as:

488. 

the fingering characterized by the first finger on the first note is the best, since change of string then takes place between two strings only.

489. 

In Example 489 as well, carried out upon one and the same string, no doubt is possible as to which fingering is the best. This is not so in:

490. 

Here, owing to the fact that the player remains in the fifth position, the stretch G-C, by means of the third and fourth fingers, is absolutely necessary if one wishes to remain on the G-string, which, however, in view of the risk involved is not compulsory.

491. 

The second finger on the first note C, in this case, is to be preferred to the first finger, because the change of string

492. 

in consequence of the simultaneous anticipatory taking of the G and C, proceeds more smoothly than in the third position, and furthermore because

493. 

may be carried out with less friction in the second than in the third position, since in the latter case the change of string takes place because of a single note—the C—which calls forth a violent movement of arm or hand, disturbing the equality of the figure.

494. 

Broken triads through two octaves are in most cases played on one string only when *ascending*, since most of the fingers when *descending* are to be placed without preparation, in which event exact intonation is a practical impossibility. Fingering 1 with the employ of the harmonic tone is better than Fingering 2 (unnatural tension); both, however, are very daring. In

495. 

it is true, the above fingering cannot be avoided, because of the absence of the harmonic; yet because of the higher position of the major third, A-C sharp, and the lesser distance it may be carried out with greater ease. Furthermore:

496. 
Paganini, Moses Fantasia

497. 
Ernst, Cto, F# min.

498. 

Fingering 1, in Example 498, represents the most rational mode of carrying the broken triad through three octaves. Fingering 2 is fairly good; Fingering 3 is poor.

In high positions the third finger may occasionally take the place of the fourth to advantage, for instance:

499. 
Wieniawski,
Capr. No 4

A humorist was in the habit of greatly embarrassing artists who, when preluding, played a broken triad through three octaves with the extremest "*brio*," by saying, quite dryly: "And now backwards, please!" In fact, isolated broken triads in descending are among the most difficult of technical tasks, for example:

500. 
Vieuxtemps, Cto, D. min.
Cadence

---

* The scale fingering recommended on p. 117 for the strengthening of the fourth finger is one which I regard purely as a gymnastic exercise.

The reason for this hindrance is simply the fact that in:

501. 

we can allow the first and third fingers in view of the return, to remain on the string, while in:

502. 

we must apply the two fingers without preparation of any kind. If we wait to do this until the moment when we need them, we will come too late, and either failure or choppiness and lack of clarity in the change of position will result. If, however, we place the two fingers on the string *before* we attack the upper E:

503. 

the passage will *never* fail. The same holds good of broken triads carried through four octaves:

504. 

In the interest of correct intonation:

505.  with 4, 2, 1

506.  with 4, 3, 1

should be taken as indicated. (See p. 124.)

Runs in Seventh Chords

In arpeggiated *chords of the dominant seventh*, the following fingerings seem the most desirable.

507. 

508. 

Here I prefer the slight tension to the whole-tone *glissando* B^3 to A $flat^3$.

In *diminished chords of the seventh*, stretching is more advantageous than *glissandi*, especially in high positions.

Correct

509. 

Incorrect

Similarly in:

Brahms, Sonata D min. 3º Mov't.

510. 

In the case of certain kinds of figured seventh-chords the *glissandi* cannot be avoided:

Vieuxtemps, Cto E maj. 1º Mov't. (Cadence)

511. 

We might add that in the case of broken triads and dominant or diminished seventh-chords, the rule always should be observed that their initial rate of speed be noticeably less than the tempo of the concluding notes. In the first place a passage seems more brilliant and effective in proportion as it increases in rapidity; and secondly, the quiet beginning in the first position ensures an equally calm preparation of the thumb movement. This is the reason why passages such as those which follow:

Saint-Saëns, Rondo Cap.

512. 

are always apt to be played more successfully when commenced at a somewhat slower tempo.

Fingering in Broken Thirds

A special fingering problem in connection with change of position is due to *broken thirds*. They are one of the figures most frequently used in violin literature. The composers of the seventeenth and eighteenth centuries, in most cases, seem to have intended them for two strings. In this form they already demand a certain amount of technical proficiency in change of string which (as we may note especially in the case of the *Locatelli* Caprices) seems to have been a specialty of the great eighteenth-century violinists. On the other hand, *Beethoven*, in the well-known figure in thirds which marks the entrance of the solo violin in his Violin Concerto, unquestionably meant them to played on one string. On the contrary, as regards the execution of the following passages:

Beethoven, Cto, 1º Mov't.

513. 
G and D
D and A
A and E

I always have been of the opinion that when played upon two strings it sounds not only far more expressive, but it also supports the theme in the orchestra.

With regard to the fingering of broken thirds on *one* string the following questions suggest themselves:*

1. Is it preferable to play them constantly on the same string, or may change of string occur now and again?

Beethoven, Cto, 1o Mov't.

514. 

The difference between the two kinds consists therein, that with *a* the tone-color of the broken thirds remains the same, although requiring a more frequent change of position; while with *b*, on the other hand, change of string takes the place of change of position, which substitution in turn endangers the responsiveness of the newly attacked string in figures such as the following:

515. 

It is very important that figures such as these should sound as equalized as possible, a result which cannot be achieved through mixture of both kinds of fingering. I am therefore in favor of separating them in a clean-cut and logically developed manner.

2. Should the change of *position* be taken *between* the two notes forming the third, or should it be carried out between the thirds as a group?

516. 

The answer to this question depends mainly upon the kind of *bowing* indicated. In *a* the thirds are separated one from the other by change of bow and a minimal pause (a "drawing off"), which allows the player to produce the usually critical change of position  inaudibly, even though he has to make it leap-wise; something which is impossible at *b*, in a *legato* succession of thirds, where the pause disappears. Hence, here, no matter to what degree it offend against the principle of avoiding more extended *glissandi* in *legato*-playing, I must employ this fingering, unless I prefer to play the thirds on two strings. The interesting and aesthetically valuable fingering-combinations which can result from a habit of logical thought are shown in the following example:

Customary fingering

Mendelssohn, Cto, 3o Mov't.

517. 

In this short passage we may count upon one backward *stretch* of the first finger; furthermore *three glissandi* covering a *third*, and one even covering a *fourth*. No wonder that this sequence sounds indistinct and blurred even in the case of the greatest virtuosos, in consequence of the extremely rapid tempo. At:

518. 
etc.

one hears, not the tones themselves, but only the connecting *glissandi*. As though by a miracle these evils are removed by the fingering which follows:

519. 
A

When descending, thirds are more difficult because of the greater complexity of every retrograde movement:

520. 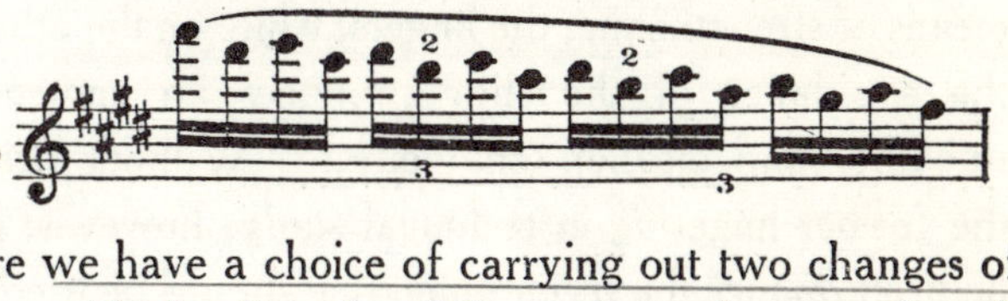

Here we have a choice of carrying out two changes of position, with the fingering 2-3, or three changes of position with the fingering 2-2. Both alternatives have their advantages and disadvantages, and are approximately of the same value. Finally, we might give an example of leaping change of position in *legato*, which may not do for every one, yet when well executed avoids the customary *glissandi* and sounds very even.

Glazounow, Cto

521. 
instead of 2 4 1 2 2 1

---

*The following rules do not affect the *broken* thirds on *two* strings, since in their case the same laws of fingering apply as for the thirds sounded *simultaneously*.

Chromatic Scales

Our art embraces certain musically objectionable peculiarities, insufferable to unspoiled ears, for which the nature of the instrument is blamed, as a rule; while it is rather the thoughtlessness with which our teaching flounders along, year after year, which is more truly to blame. I am alluding above all, in this case, to the *glissandi* which are seemingly inseparable from *chromatic scales* on our instrument. (See p. 42.)

522.

Violinist's ears, as a rule, have been so dulled that they no longer are able to notice the ugliness of these fourteen half-tone *glissandi*, and even musicians who do not play the violin have become so used to them as to accept them as unavoidable. Yet how easy it is to avoid them by means of the following fingering:

523.

Unquestionably the fingering with half-tone *glissandi* in chromatic scales represents one of the most effective means of strengthening the fingers, while on the other hand the avoidance of the slide produces an immeasurably smoother and cleaner tonal effect. Without neglecting the former fingering in technical *study*, however, in public *performance* the second fingering should be used almost exclusively. In the case of older violinists the habits of decades will usually prevent its adoption, even though they may be convinced of the correctness of the measure proposed. Yet all the more should the younger generation, as yet unaffected by "traditions," at once acquaint itself with this technical innovation—inconvenient, it is true, but unconditionally logical. With this reservation we may turn to the fingerings thus far customary for chromatic scales.

The half-tone *glissandi* may be produced on a string instrument by the uninterrupted *glissando* of *one* finger, the use of several fingers without *glissando* or by a *combination* of both types.

524.

The finger indicated at *c* is mainly used for practice purposes when it is a question of strengthening some particular finger. In the high positions, however (especially in the case of thick fingers), when the exact taking of whole series of half-tones becomes impossible, the chromatic *glissandi* offer the only alternative. They already have been considered in detail on p. 42.

b. The use of several fingers without *glissandi* has already been discussed above.

a. The proper mixture of the use of various fingers and *glissandi* by the same finger supplies the most usual manner of performance:

525.

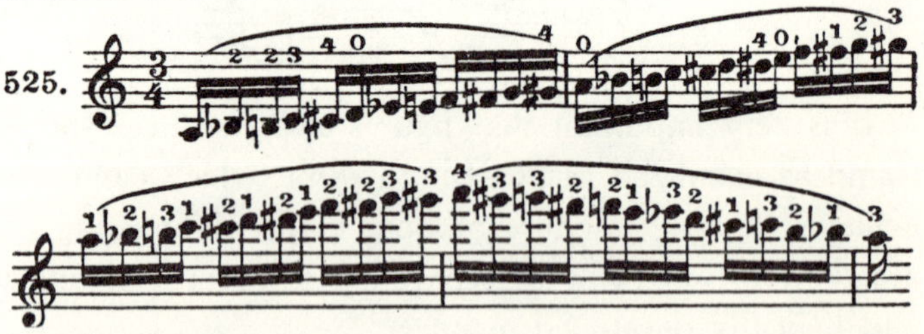

The number of possible combinations is extremely large, their choice a matter of personal preference. The smoothest, clearest and least interrupted succession of the half-tones is the sole criterion of the best fingering to be used.

Chromatic scales in the *high positions*, without change of position, are especially difficult and hence admirably adapted for *practice purposes*.

526.

A pressure not too tense, the rapid progression of the gliding finger, the correct admixture of gliding and stopping and, finally, change of position, preferably between neighboring fingers, assure an advantageous tonal effect in chromatic scales.

The following principles rule in the case of the fingerings to be used for *double-stops in thirds*:

1. Change of position should always take place on the strong beat of the measure:

527. 

These two examples show that the most rational fingering often is a consequence of the *rhythmic* nature of the tone sequence to be played, because the accents which cannot be prevented in change of position must coincide with the strong beat of the measure. Furthermore:

528. 

529. 

Here change of position must take place during the *pause* which is conditioned by the bowing used.

2. Taking advantage of the open strings when descending forms an exception to the rule of using the strong beat for changing position.

Paganini, Cto, D maj

530. 

The collaboration of the open string in the following example:

531. 

calls for only a simple change of position, as in:

532. 

in place of the double change of position, as in:

533. 

3. The open string must not be used when *ascending*:

534. 

because the use of the second or third position for a *single* double-stop, in consequence of the all too brief amount of time at one's disposal, provokes too brusque an upward and downward movement of the lower arm and disturbs the *regularity* of the lower arm movements (one of the chief requisites for smooth scale-playing at a rapid tempo).

4. The use of the open string as the fundamental note of the third, as in:

535. 

for *sustained* movements, that is to say in a slow tempo, should be avoided whenever possible, because in the first instance the leading of the voices becomes wrong:

536. 

and furthermore, a foreign element enters the tonal organism by means of the open string:

Chopin-Wilhelmj, Nocturne, Op. 27 No 2

537. 

5. *Glissandi* with the same fingers should be avoided so far as possible in a rapid tempo, because an audible change of position in quick runs is a decided tonal disadvantage.

6. For the sake of a regular hand movement as well as of correct intonation, I regard the following fingering as the best in ascending and descending scales:

538. 

In it the principles already presented find their application.

The taking of the third by two adjacent fingers (3-4, 2-3, 1-2) may be termed an *irregular fingering*, in which the use of the fingering 2-3 offers the greatest advantages, tonally and technically:

Paganini, Cto, D maj.

539. 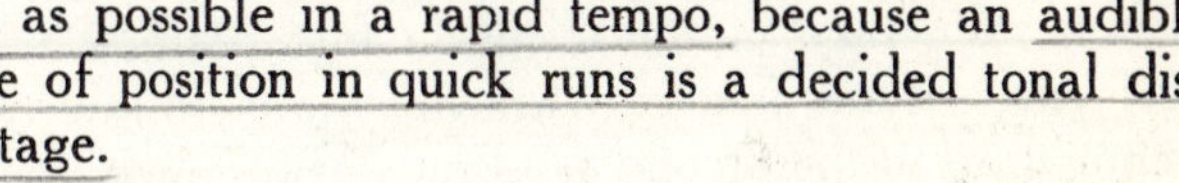

Sarasate, Spanish Dances No. 8

540. 

Beschirsky, Cad. to Cto *by Paganini*

541. 

Joachim, Hung. Cto, 1o Mov't.

542. 

Kreisler, Caprice Viennois

543. 

544. 

Apart from the fact that these thirds, when taken by the second and fourth fingers, are far more uncertain, hand and arm (because the fourth finger is so short) are obliged to move forward and also bend inward considerably. Any one who has once accustomed himself to this simplified fingering will prize it as one of the most agreeable and convenient conquests made by more recent research. We take major thirds in first position with the first and second fingers when they are followed by a minor third in the second position, for instance:

Dont, Op. 35, No. 12

545. 

or when they form part of a chord:

Bach, Partita B min. Bourrée

546. 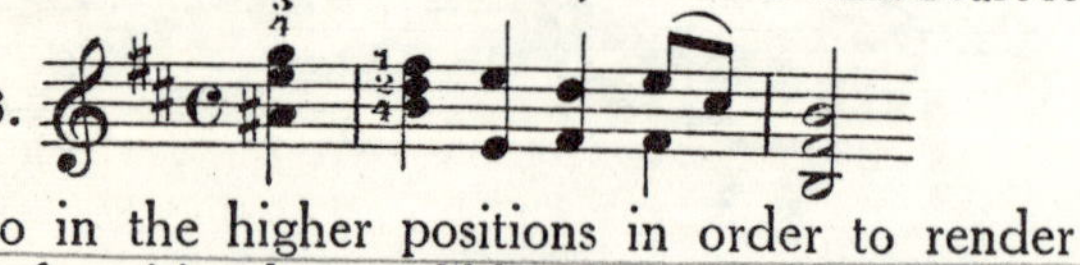

and also in the higher positions in order to render the change of position less audible: *Bruch,* Cto, D min. 3o Mov't.

547. 

The third and fourth fingers should be used only exceptionally in the first position, in the *détaché* and in slow tempo with *major* thirds, when for some reason it does not seem worth while changing position:

548. 

This fingering, owing to the diminished tone-producing capacity of the fourth finger, does not appeal to me, personally.

With regard to the fingering of *minor* thirds in the *high positions* on the E- and A-strings, it might be added that here the danger of the finger gliding off from the fingerboard is especially marked, because (particularly in the case of the short fourth finger), the second finger must be applied too obliquely.

Paganini, Cto D maj.

549. 

Here I have lessened the difficulty by trying to place the second finger on the string as flatly as possible, and to touch the A-string as a control. In *major* thirds in high positions the use of the second and third fingers instead of the second and fourth fingers still offers the greatest protection against slipping off.

Chromatic Scales in Thirds. These may be produced either by means of a regularly continued fingering or by *glissandi.*

550. 

In consequence of the necessary change of position taking place after every second double-stop, the changing fingering, especially when descending, is extremely difficult. It is greatly facilitated when the change of bow coincides with the change of string.

Saint-Saëns, Havanaise

551. 

In chromatic *glissandi in thirds* the first and third fingers are preferred. *Successions of fourths* occur so seldom in the literature of the violin that mere mention of their possibility of existence should suffice. Yet it is necessary, in view of their presumably more frequent use in the future, to call attention to the similarity between the manner in which they and the sixths are played. Four

Their study in connection with other intervals is important if only because among the double-stops they are hardest to play in perfect tune.

The fingering of *fifths* is determined principally by the breadth of the finger**tips, i.e., the fingers** which have the Fifth broadest ends are the best to use. *Successions* of fifths do not as yet occur very frequently in violin compositions. In high positions where the distance between the strings increases in breadth the inconvenience of taking the fifths is avoided by arpeggiating and changing the bow, especially in the case of a chord, for instance:

Tschaikowsky, Cto (Cadence)

552. 

To be played: 553. 

The natural harmonics are used by preference, for instance:

Brahms, Cto 3º Mov't.

554. 

Dohnányi, Cto 4º Mov't.

555. 

Broken fifths in slow tempo, however, between which a change of bow takes place, should never be played with the same finger, for instance:

556. 
Correct
Incorrect

In general, the more or less frequent use of fifths is a fair indication of the composer's familiarity with the peculiarities of the instrument.

Still more important for us is the fingering in combinations of fifths with other intervals:

Brahms, Trio C min. 3º Mov't.

557. 
dim.

In order to take the fifth, C-G, without lifting the third finger from the C, the nail-joint of the third finger would have to be tipped over. That this is a questionable practice, owing to the difficulty of securing perfect intonation of the fifth, will be readily understood. In addition a *vibrato* in this position is out of the question. The use of the following fingering obviates both evils:

558. 
(the same)

The A is prepared by the first finger and glides smoothly and skilfully into the third position.

Similarly

Chausson, Poème

559. 

Hence, at +, we do not take  but 

whereby a double shifting  as well as  is avoided.

The same holds good for other interval-combinations, such as:

Reger, Op. 42 Nº 1

560. 

In 561.  the fifth is already prepared during the preceding fourth.

Reger, Op. 24 Nº 1

562. 

Dohnányi, Cto, 1º Mov't.

563. 

In Examples 562 and 563 the fifth must be taken by two different fingers. How important, incidentally, the preparatory fifth-stop may be, even where other intervals are concerned, is shown by the following example:

Sinding, Cto, A maj.

564. 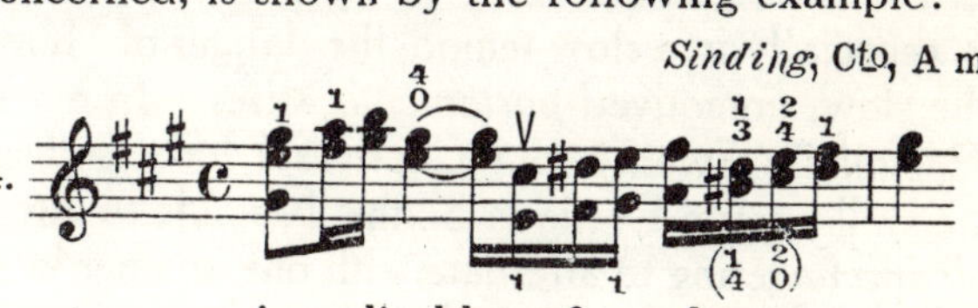

Here a stoppage, inexplicable at first, always occurs with:  until, upon closer examination it turns out that it is a consequence of the moving over (with insufficient rapidity) of the first finger from the G sharp[1] to the D sharp[2] in . The preparatory fifth-stop.

565. 

once and for all removes this evil.

Similarly:

Bruch, Ctº, G min. 1º Mov't.

566. 

Often the only thing left to do is to tip over the finger and take the fifth with the whole breadth of the first finger-joint as, for instance, in:

Bruch, Ctº, G min.

567. 

Schradieck, 24 Etudes, Nº 2

568. 

Sixths

Sixths are played with change of fingers or with *glissandi*. I myself prefer to change fingers in the lower positions and use *glissandi* in the upper ones. Successions of sixths are so unpleasant on the string instruments because in most cases they take for granted a moving over of the same finger, producing a hiatus which is filled by a foreign tone.

569. 

The above, therefore, if we listen carefully, really sounds as follows:

570. 

Although the small notes, owing to their minimal duration, are hardly audible, still the listener senses an inexplicable discomfort at the points where they occur. This evil, it is true, can be obviated by *glissandi*, yet in that case, especially in a slow tempo, the danger of "howling," of the slow, unmotived *portamenti*, arises. In my edition of *Paganini's* Twenty-four Caprices I have endeavored, in the well-known Etude in Sixths, No. 21, to allow *glissandi* and fingering to alternate with one another in a manner appropriate to the musical declamation:

Paganini, Caprice Nº 21

571. 

Major sixths at intervals of a minor second may be taken as follows without using the same finger:

Ernst, F♯ min. Ctº.

572. 

The same applies to minor sixths, in distances of major seconds:

573. 

A fingering for scales in sixths absolutely opposed to tradition, yet following the laws of logic, is presented in the following examples:

574. 

Brahms, Son. Op. 78, 1º Mov't.

575. 

Wieniawski, Caprice Nº 5

576. 

Pfitzner, Trio, Op. 8, 2º Mov't.

577. 

Chausson, Poëme

578. 

Paganini-Kreisler, I Palpiti

579. 

(A combination which is extremely effective and all too seldom employed in violin compositions.)

In addition we give a few examples of sixth-fingering to be used, especially in the *Reger* compositions:

Reger, Son. Op. 42 Nº 1

580. 

(the same)

581. 

(the same)

582. 

xths d ther ouble ops

583. 
(the same)

The very frequently occurring combination of sixths and other double-stops is important:

Rovelli, Etude Nº 5

584. 
Correct
Incorrect

585. 
Correct
(the same)
Incorrect

Bruch, Cto, G min. 1º Mov't.

586. 
Correct
Incorrect

Rode, Caprice Nº 18

587. 

Léonard, Cad. to Beethoven Cto.

588. 

Brahms, Cto, 3º Mov't.

589 

In chromatic *glissandi* in sixths, the first and second or second and third fingers are the most advantageous to use.

Wieniawski, "Faust" Fantasia

590. 

n- red ctaves

Octaves may be produced by means of an unchanging fingering (simple octaves), or a changing fingering (fingered octaves).

591. 

Simple octaves have the advantage of a homogeneous fingering and an unforced position of fingers and hand, and the *disadvantage* of continuous *glissandi.*

Fingered octaves call for changing fingerings, and the stretching of the fingers out of a fourth- into that of a fifth-position; yet the manner in which they are played reduces the number of *glissandi* by one half, and these not being played by the same fingers are far less noticeable.

There can be no doubt but that in the case of a player who absolutely controls both varieties of octaves, the fingered octaves are to be preferred because by using them the constant change of position is partly suppressed. For instance, in:

Mendelssohn, Cto, 1º Mov't.

592. 

the above passage, when fingered, may be played with far more sureness, or in:

Beethoven, Cto, 1º Mov't.

593. 

With simple octaves, four audible *glissandi;* and only three with fingered octaves. In the following:

Beethoven, Cto, 1º Mov't.

594. 

the annoying crossing—the leap into the uncertain—would be avoided.

If we take a knowledge of both kinds of octaves for granted (as explained in Part One of this work) the question still remains under which conditions they are to be applied in either case. The following eleven rules may be formulated on the basis of practical experience:

Plain or Fingered Octaves

a. Simple octaves produce an unfavorable effect principally as a result of constant change of position. In such case the partly substitution of fingered octaves for them seems desirable:

Ernst, Cto, in F♯ min.

595. 

At times, however, the change of position in broken octaves is only apparently necessary, and may be avoided with ease, as in:

Beethoven, Cto, 1º Mov't.

596. 

b In *ascending* diatonic scales, *fingered* octaves; in *descending* ones, *simple* octaves are in order:

Paganini, Caprice Nº 3

597. 

c. In *high* positions fingered octaves should be avoided:

Vieuxtemps, Cto, E maj. 1º Mov't.

598.

d. For chromatic scales and for half-tone intervals simple octaves always are the most appropriate:

Paganini, Caprice Nº 23

599.

e. Fingered octaves at intervals of a *minor* third are played on the same strings:

600.

f. Fingered octaves at intervals of a *major* third call for a change of string.

601.

g. Beginning with sixths all intervals may most advantageously be taken by means of fingered octaves in change of string:

602.

h. In fingered octaves the second finger may be used in connection with the open string at the beginning, but never in the middle of a passage (+).

603.

Correct
Incorrect

Ernst, Cto, F♯ min.

604.

Correct
Incorrect

i. Where fingered and simple octaves are mixed, which is necessary, in particular, as a consequence of numerous half-tones or when playing in high positions, the simple octaves never should be taken by the first and fourth fingers, but by first and third fingers, in order not to disturb the fifth-position of the hand.

Saint-Saëns, Cto, B min.

605.

Wieniawski, "Faust" Fantasia

606.

Furthermore, if only to avoid overtiring the hand, a necessary consequence of the uninterrupted use of fingered octaves, the player should try to mix both types as much as possible:

Paganini, Caprice Nº 23

607.

Schubert, Son. A maj. 3º Mov't.

608.

k. For simple octaves in a slow tempo and in high positions, the third finger should always be preferred to the fourth, because of the greater strength it possesses; besides, octaves taken in a high position with the fourth finger squeeze those fingers lying between into an unnatural position in the air.

In the following example the trill already indicates the previously mentioned use of the third finger:

Paganini, Caprice Nº 3

609.
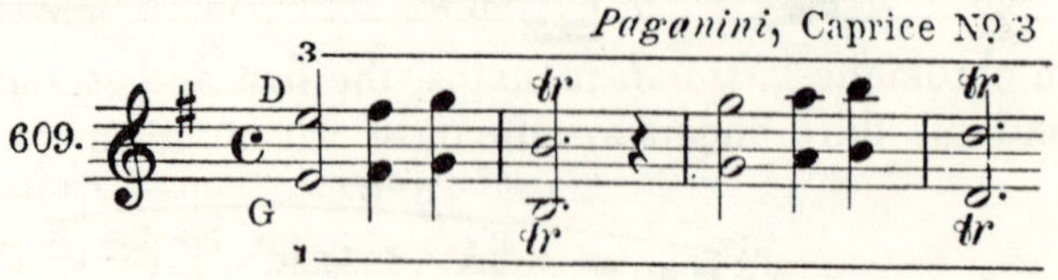

Reger, Op. 42 Nº 1

610.

l. The astounding rapidity and smoothness with which many violinists are able to play ascending series of notes in thirds or fingered octaves is due principally to the fact that their first and third fingers only leave the string in the change of *string,* but remain on it during the change of *position.* Similarly as in the case with sixths (see also p. 138), the *tempo* of the onward movement also plays a great part in simple octaves. Here, too, the *exclusive* use of springing or gliding change of position should be eschewed, and the manner in which the positions are connected should be adapted to the character of the phrase. This manner or way is most easily determined by playing the passage in single notes instead of octaves, whereupon the phrasing develops of itself, for instance:

S — Slow *portamento.*
R — Rapid *portamento.*

Ernst, Cto, F♯ min.

611.

(Cont'd column two)

Schubert-Wilhelmj, Ave Maria

612.

I will conclude with the fingerings I employ in the *Paganini* Caprice, No. 17:

613.

Paganini Caprice No. 17

ths

Tenths, as is generally known, can be produced in one way only.*

For this reason a discussion of their fingering would seem needless were it not for the fact that their combination with other intervals calls for mention. In such cases it is a question of *preparing* the *tenth*-position (i.e., position of a sixth) of the hand in order that the abnormal stretch which occurs, especially in the lower positions, does not have to be attempted without preparation:

614.

Correct
Incorrect

To conclude, a few other examples of preparation for tenths might be given:

Dont, Op. 35, Nº 7

615.

(the same)

616.

(the same)

617.

Dont, Op. 35, Nº 5

618.

Brahms, Cto, 1º Mov't.

619.

Dohnányi, Vln. Cto, 3º Mov't.

620.

* It is true that I have heard a young Hungarian violinist, *Nagy Jani* (who perished in 1922 as the result of an accident), play unobjectionable passages in tenths with the fingering 1-3, 2-4.

Chromatic Glissandi

Chromatic glissandi should be carried out preferably by the strongest, i.e., the third finger. If many violinists prefer the fourth finger it is usually as the result of years of habit, for instance:

Lalo, Symph. Espagnole, 4º Mov't.

621. 
chrom. gl.

The scale in this instance, gains in equality when the glissando is carried on to the half-position, and the very difficult transition in the glissandi to the ordinary chromatic scales is hereby rendered unnecessary.

Suk makes use of it in his Fantasy, Op. 24, in an interesting way:

Suk, Fantasia Op. 24

622. 

Trills

As a substitute for change of fingers in small chromatic passages in the high positions this procedure may also be employed.—In the *trill* the fingering is determined exclusively by individual capacity. The fourth finger is used only in case of need, and the first finger is usually dropped because it can only act together with the open string, something already inadvisable for tonal reasons. There remain the second and third fingers, of which the last seems to be the more appropriate, because the after-beat does not call for any gliding back. At all events, we must select that finger which is able to carry out the trill most perfectly and, if necessary, suffer the descending after-beat *glissando*, to be played as rapidly as possible, as a lesser and unavoidable evil. In the case of trills in connection with *changing double-stop* notes, should the second finger seem more appropriate than the third, a change of fingers may be made in an unobtrusive manner:

Leonard, Cad. to Beethoven Cto.

623. 

Wieniawski, Souvenir de Moscow

624. 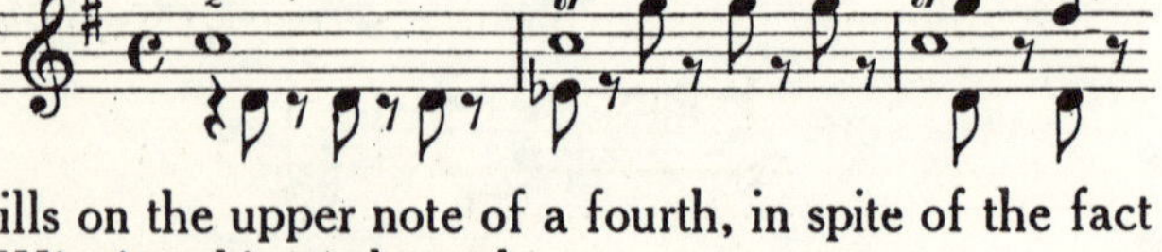

Trills on the upper note of a fourth, in spite of the fact that *Wieniawski* employs them:

625. 
(the same)

must be counted among the most unviolinistic combinations; the best one can do is to glide over them gracefully without laying stress on playing them exactly in tune. In the case of *fifths*, too, which appear in the middle of a chain of trills, the moving over of the finger which is trilling is avoided by change of finger:

626. 
Correct
Incorrect

Trills in Double-Stops, it is true, are of comparatively rare occurrence in violin literature, yet their study should not be neglected on this account, because with simple trills (*Kreutzer*, Etude, No. 36) as well as with double trills as in:

627. 

Similarly in:

628. 

or played in the form of scales, they supply one of the most interesting finger exercises we have at our disposal—though at the same time one of the most fatiguing physically.

Left-Hand Tremolo

The Left-Hand Tremolo as, for example, in *Paganini's* Caprice No. 6, or in *Kreisler's* Cadenza to *Tartini's* "Devil Trill" Sonata, is subject to the same laws as the trill, with the only difference that in the case of the former, tone-production is far more difficult, owing to the following reason:

Paganini, Caprice Nº 6

629. 

Here three different lengths of string are to be considered (open string, as well as the two notes of the third) hence a compromise among the three different points of contact between bow and strings is difficult to secure. This is the reason why in the tremolo in double-stops the tone so often "breaks." It is one of the most difficult of tonal problems, especially in the control of the *Kreisler* Cadenza to the "Devil's Trill" Sonata:

Tartini-Kreisler, Devil's Trill Sonata

630. 

It is best to practise and play those "short trill-tremolos" with as little bow as possible, strong pressure, and continued visual supervision of the points of contact. It is true that first of all specific left-hand problems must have been absolutely conquered, a result best secured by means of a preparatory exercise in which the tremolos are carried out slowly, without a separating pause, with several of them in the same stroke.*

Arti-icial Harmo-ics

Artificial Harmonics and their technique already have been discussed in detail (p. 48). Here we will call attention only to the following peculiarities. Since the natural harmonics:

631. 

at times do not "speak" easily, or do not sound at all, it is advisable to substitute for them corresponding artificial harmonics:

632. 

When a note does not speak clearly in a run in harmonics, the note, nine cases out of ten, will turn out to be a natural harmonic, especially when a steel E-string is used:

633. 
Paganini, C^to, 1º Mov't.

The above is far more certain than:

634. 

The same applies to:

635. 
Tschaikowsky C^to, 3º Mov't.
Correct
Incorrect

Furthermore the very high natural harmonics invariably sound too low, which, when the strings are out of tune, sometimes makes a difference of half a tone:

636. 
Saint-Saëns, Havanaise

Hence, the above might far better be played as follows:

637. 

or taken firmly, as in:

638. 
Ernst, C^to, F♯ min.

The fingerings for harmonics in double-stops offers a large choice of possibilities. A discussion of all the combinations possible would lead us too far afield, and I must confine myself again to calling attention to *Hoffmann's* "Schule der Flageolett-Technik" ("Technical School of Harmonics").—One would hardly believe that the fingering plays a certain part even in *left-hand pizzicati*, where it seems to be quite unmistakably indicated.

Left-Hand Pizzicati

639. 
Sarasate, Gipsy Airs

(The fingerings given do not refer to the note itself, but to the finger which plucks the string.) These pizzicati can only be played with a reasonable amount of security when the "plucking" finger is changed.

Chords

In *three- or four-note chords* as well, only one particular fingering resulting from the proportions of distance between the individual fingers is possible as a rule. Only in the case of three-note minor chords, which are in two different positions, does the fingering appear open to question:

640. 
Dont, Op. 35, Nº 11
Retain the chord

The second finger on D² is naturally better than the third, because it is easier to hold the hand in the second position, and stretch a half-tone down to the F sharp with the first finger, than to stretch a whole tone to the B with the fourth finger, from the first position up. In the following case:

641. 
not

the difficulty is overcome by arpeggiating the chords, through which time is gained to allow the second finger to move over. The straining of the hand necessitated by the fingering 1-3-2 is needless. Similarly:

642. 
Reger, Op. 42, Nº 1

643. 
(the same)

Enharmonic change in order to simplify fingering plays a great part in chords:

644. 
Joachim, Variations
Correct
Incorrect

In the case of chords it is extremely important that all the fingers be placed upon the strings *before* the bow-

* See Problems of Tone Production in Violin Playing by Carl Flesch (Carl Fischer).

attack, in order to prepare the chord, remembering that for this a certain amount of time—a slight pause—must be at the disposal of the player.

Broken Chords

Further, small figures may occasionally be *thought of* as being broken chords and thus taken, as for instance:

Dvořák, Trio, Op. 65, 2º Mov't.

645. 

Mendelssohn, Cto, 1º Mov't.

646. 

Brahms, Double Cto, 1º Mov't.

647. 

Dohnányi, Cto, 4º Mov't.

648. 

Expressive Fingering

The possibility of a simultaneous, preparatory and earlier dropping of several fingers upon the strings forms the preliminary conditions for an ideally smooth, frictionless change of string.

c. Fingering as a Means of Expression. In the preceding chapter we have considered the choice of fingerings primarily from the standpoint of strength-saving movements. We have endeavored to free ourselves from the visual notation, from the rigid adherence to a conception of a fixed place suggested to us by a definite note, and to establish the most convenient fingering in accordance with the rhythmic and dynamic factors.

This task was comparatively easy, for we had to follow a line of march definitely laid out, and were only compelled to take into account certain fixed circumstances established by the anatomical conformity of arm, hand and fingers. It is not difficult for the logically thinking student to establish the bad characteristics of a purely technical fingering, because they are visibly expressed in unnatural positions of the fingers or hand, and audibly in disagreeable tonal effects. In a run like the following, for instance:

Beethoven, Cto, 3º Mov't.

649. 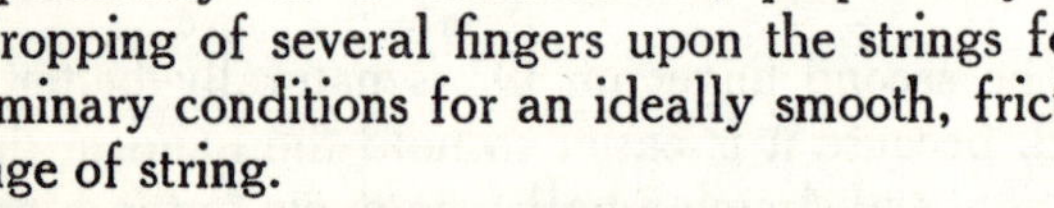

we soon learn that the transition from the third position to G^2 represents the most advantageous fingering in spite of the glissando in thirds. In the theme, however, on which this variation is based, technical considerations, on account of the comparatively slow tempo demanded, may hardly be regarded as applying:

(the same)

650. 

The finger-successions here possible may be counted by the hundred, and (the necessary technical ability being taken for granted) should first of all be determined by the player's individual good taste. When the latter is not to some degree influenced by established rules of an aesthetic kind, the danger of unchecked license lies near at hand. In general the personal taste is used as a mask for the latter. Now, it may be admitted that B is not necessarily going to like all that A regards as beautiful, and that both (from the standpoint of their individual mode of feeling) may be in the right. Yet this makes it all the more necessary to try to discover some skeleton of aesthetic principles around which each may drape the skin and flesh of his individual taste. In sequence the individual nature of these principles (in part already familiar to us) is illustrated by practical examples:

Rules for Portamenti

a. *Portamenti* based on an increased need of expression:

Schubert, Quartet D-min. 2º Mov't.

651. 

Beethoven, Cto, 2º Mov't.

652. 

Joachim, Hung. Cto, 2º Mov't.

653. 

Paganini-Wilhelmj, D-maj. Cto

654. 

b. *Unmotived Portamenti*:

Wieniawski, Cto, D-min. 1º Mov't.

655. 
instead of

Beethoven, Cto, 1º Mov't.

656. 
instead of

Mendelssohn, Cto, 1º Mov't.

657. 
instead of

658. 
Beethoven, Trio Op. 97 3º Mov't.
instead of

c. A portamento is the more effective the more *isolated* it appears and the less frequently it is employed. Under no condition should two or three *portamenti* succeed each other:

659. 
Mendelssohn, Cto, 2º Mov't.
Correct
Incorrect

A motive which frequently occurs is the following:

660. 
Correct
Incorrect

661. 
Wieniawski, D-min. Cto, 2º Mov't.
Correct
Incorrect

d. *Strongly emotional portamenti* should be executed by the same or by *adjacent* fingers (*L-portamento*):

662. 
Saint-Saëns, Rondo capriccioso
Correct
Incorrect

663. 
Dvořák, Trio Op. 65 3º Mov't.
Correct
Incorrect

664. 
Lalo, Symph-Espagnole, 4º Mov't.
Correct
Incorrect

e. *Portamenti weak in expression* are best executed by fingers lying further apart (*B-portamento*):

665. 
Spohr, Cto, D-min. 1º Mov't.
Correct
Incorrect

f. Change of position in an *ascending* line with the fingerings 4-1, 4-2, or 3-1; and descending with 1-4, 1-3, or 2-4, in *cantilene*, should be avoided:

666. 
Correct
Incorrect

g. With every change of position an *accent* is connected, more or less audible according to the player's skill, yet which never can be overcome completely. Hence the player should allow the accent, and with it the portamento, to fall by preference upon the strong beat of the measure:

667. 
Beethoven, Sonata C-min. 2º Mov't.
Correct
Incorrect

668. 
Sinding, Cto, A-maj. 2º Mov't.
Correct
Incorrect

h. For the same reason it is possible to underline a *crescendo* or some *accent* indicated by the composer, effectively, by means of a portamento.

669. 
Mendelssohn, Cto, 1º Mov'
Correct
Incorrect

Here the *D sharp* must unquestionably be regarded as the climax of the crescendo; and hence it would be altogether wrong to carry out the portamento on G, and thus give that note an importance to which it is not entitled. The same applies to *F sharp* in last measure.

i. *Long distances* on the fingerboard, so far as possible, should *not* be covered by the same finger, since in the case of stringed instruments the audibility of *all* medial degrees, lying between two notes far distant one from the other, makes a disagreeable impression:

670. 
Correct
Incorrect

j. Examples of *B-portamenti* (see p. 32).

671. 
Vieuxtemps, Cto, A-min.

672. 
Tartini, Sonata G-min.

673. 
Schumann, Fantasiestücke

k. Examples of *L-portamenti* (see p. 32).

674. 
Saint-Saëns, Cto, B-min. 2º Mov't.

Saint-Saëns, Havanaise

675. 

Lalo, Cto, F min.

676. 

l. Portamenti from the *open* strings upward should only be used with the greatest caution. In such cases, moreover, the gliding finger should by no means be placed abruptly on the string. Hence, in:

677.  not 

but the first finger is pushed *behind* the nut as a point of support, and the portamento thence carried out in the *B*- or the *L*-form.

m. Whole tone portamenti with the same finger, moving downward, in general produce a most unrefined effect:

Bruch, Cto, G min. 2º Mov't.

678. 
Correct
Incorrect

n. Portamenti in half-tones, in slower movements, which appear unjustified by the melodic line, are only permitted when they offer notable technical advantages without producing an unpleasant impression:

Beethoven, Cto, 1º Mov't.

679. 

(This glissando has the advantage of the firmly set, preparatory finger  ,

o. Stretches seem in order when *unnecessary* portamenti, especially when they follow each other without interruption, may be avoided (see p. 123).

Mendelssohn, Cto, 1º Mov't.

680. 
Correct
Incorrect

Take the third finger for E³ in order to prepare the extended position (of a sixth).

Nardini, Cto, E min. 2º Mov't.

681. 

Schumann, Sonata A min. 1º Movt.

682. 

d. Fingering and the Tone Colors. The choice of the string on which we wish to reproduce a musical phrase in accordance with the composer's intentions as well as our own personal feelings, closely approaches the art of registration in organ-playing. In both cases it is a question of tone color, with the difference, it is true, that the violinist has at his disposal only a few of these colors—but which, incidentally, may be mingled and transformed in infinite variety by means of dynamic differentiation. Yet just as each organist makes that application of the art of registration which is best adapted to his personal conception, so we shall never find two violinists who use the same tonal shading in rendering the same composition. Hence, in this connection, it seems even more difficult to set up any fixed rules than with regard to the *portamenti.* Yet even in this case we should not let the seeming impossibility prevent us from setting down a number of fundamental principles not based on personal views but on musical laws. Their net will not be so finely webbed as not to allow sufficient freedom for the play of individual expression.

Finge- ing an Tone Color.

a. The *choice of strings* should correspond, so far as possible, with the prescribed strength of tone, i.e., in *forte* we should prefer the E to the A-string, the A to the D-string, and the G to the D-string; while in *piano* we should prefer the A to the E-string, the D to the A-string, and the D to the G-string:

Beethoven, Kreutzer Sonata 1º Mov't.

683. 

Beethoven, Trio, Op.70 Nº 1 2º Mov't.

684. 

Here, despite the *piano,* the G-string is indicated, because the cello doubles this theme—a third lower, it is true—yet on the brightly radiant A-string, and the upper voice of the violin would be submerged on the faint D-string. Furthermore:

Beethoven, Sonata Op.30, Nº3, 3º Mov't.

685. 

(The *sfz* would sound too weak on the D-string.) The following appears daring yet unquestionably necessary:

Beethoven, Trio, Op.70 Nº 2 1º Mov't.

686. 

Similarly:

Dvořák, F min. Trio, 3º Movt.

687. 
A
G
f

D instead of A String

Nardini, Cto, E min. 2º Movt.

688. 
pp

Bach, E min. Sonata 2º Movt. *David*

689. 
D
pp

(Caused by the surprising modulation.)

Beethoven, Trio, Op. 70 Nº 1, 1º Movt.

690. 
A
D
f
p
più piano

Brahms, Trio Op. 8 3º Movt.

691. 
D

(In order not to cover the tone of the cello, which carries the theme)

Schubert, B maj. Trio 2º Movt.

A instead of E String

692. 
A
pp

(The E-string would sound too bright)

For *runs* in *forte*, the bright-sounding strings should be used as a matter of principle, and lower positions preferred to the higher ones:

Glazounow, Cto 1º Movt.

693. 
Correct
Incorrect

Mendelssohn Cto, 3º Movt.

694. 
Correct
E
A
Incorrect

Lalo, Symph. Espagnole 2º Movt.

695. 
Correct
E
A
Incorrect

the same 5º Movt.

696. 
Correct
E
A
Incorrect

(the same)

697. 
Correct
E
A
Incorrect

b. In the case of *echo effects*, every advantage is taken of the darker or lighter character of the strings.

Mozart, Cto, D maj. 3º Movt.

698. 
E
A
E
A
D
D
mf
pp

or the opposite:

Nardini, Cto, E min. 3º Movt.

699. 
A
E
p
f

c. Uniformly related phrases should be played whenever possible on the same string:

Schumann, Garden Melody

700. 
D
D

Beethoven, Cto, 1º Movt.

701. 
A

Brahms, Cto, 1º Movt.

702. 
A

Examples for the G-string are very numerous, for instance:

Reger, Op. 42 Nº 1. 1º Movt.

703. 

(the same) 2º Movt.

704. 
espress.
D.

At times, however, the homogeneity of the tone-color may be interrupted when the danger of playing out of tune becomes too great.

Brahms, Son. D min. 3º Movt.

705. 
G
D

Brahms, Son. A-maj. 3º Movt.

706. 
G
D

Tschaikowsky, Cto, 1º Movt.

707. 
G and D
D and A

d. The two outer strings, G and E, may be used up to the *end* of the fingerboard, but the two medial strings (especially in runs) sound well in runs only up to the *eighth position.*

708. 
Bruch, Cto, G min. 1º Mov't.
not the D String

The D-string in this instance sounds extremely weak.

e. Too long continued a use of the same string occasions *monotony*, which must be obviated by change of tone color:

709. 
Lalo, F min. Cto, 1º Mov't.

f. A new tone color should appear abruptly; it should not be robbed of its effect by a needless anticipatory use of the string involved:

710. 
Correct
Incorrect
Bruch, Cto, G min. 1º Mov't.

g. Using the *open* string in change of position for convenience's sake, at the risk of causing the tone color to deteriorate, is to be avoided. For example:

711. 
Correct
Incorrect
Mendelssohn, Cto, 1º Mov't.
sf

The basses of these broken chords imperatively call for the metallic tone of the G-string. In addition, change of finger on the same note as a means of securing increased intensity might be mentioned:

712. 
Bruch, Cto, G min. 1º Mov't.

713. 
(the same) 2º Mov't.

714. 
(the same)

In conclusion we might say that the conscious selection of a fingering which expresses one's individual feeling is essential to the expressive requirements of an artistic personality. Without claiming that there can be only one "best" fingering for every sequence of notes, I feel certain, nevertheless, that it is the duty of every thinking and emotional violinist to seek the most appropriate fingerings suitable for musical and personal needs, and to use them accordingly. The fingerings and bowings one uses, quite aside from any general technical ability, are an absolute criterion of violinistic culture. Tell me which fingers you use and I will tell you whose child you are in spirit!

e. The Bowings. As a rule the bowing is indicated by the composer in a manner which cannot be misunderstood, so that there is but little opportunity for the player's personal initiative to make itself felt. **Bowin**

In a run like the following, for example:

715. 
Wieniawski, Cto, D min. 1º Mov't.

the activity of the *right* arm can at the most differ with respect to the change of string (which also depends upon the left hand), while with regard to the *left*-hand fingering many combinations are possible. Hence, in making the choice of the most appropriate bow-stroke the subject of this division, we must first of all remember that our freedom of conclusion is very noticeably affected by the intentions the composer has expressed in his musical text.

Yet here the question obtrudes itself whether the prescribed marks of interpretation, so far as they are expressed in ties or (denoting short notes) in dots, really represent the manner in which the composer wishes to have his work played on the violin; or whether he does not merely intend that purely musical moments, which do not take into consideration the nature of the instrument, should be expressed. In many cases the ties indicated by the composer refer only to the phrasing and the indivisibility of a figure:

716. 
Beethoven, Son. Op. 30, Nº 3, 3º Mov't.
I
II

The tie prescribed by *Beethoven* (I) connects four notes, whereby the subsequent following *détaché* commences with an V and becomes extremely awkward.

The bow-stroke No. II therefore seems to be entirely justified, the more so since it in no wise impairs the rhythm of the phrase.

A second circumstance also deserves to be mentioned:

The eighteenth-century composers were acquainted only with the extremes when it came to bowing indications: the *tie* or the *dot*, slurred or short notes. Must it follow that in older musical compositions one should not use a broad *détaché?* Even at the present day distinguished composers pay little heed to the mechanics of bowing, because they know no more about them than what is conveyed in *Berlioz's* "Instrumentation," and that is none too much.* Hence, as regards the choice of the most appropriate bowing we should carefully seek to discover the composer's wishes; but we need respect them unconditionally only when they make allowance for the peculiarities of the instrument. When this is not the case, we may take the liberty of making certain changes, with the proviso that they do no injury to the composer's purely musical intentions.**

Let us examine in detail the application of the following bowings: the stroke *with the whole bow*, the *détaché*, the *martelé*, the *staccato*, the *mixed strokes*, the *springing bow*, the *thrown bow* (the *chords*). Hereby their momentary relation to the *division of the bow*, the *change of bow*, the *change of string*, the *up-bow* and *down-bow;* furthermore to *dynamics*, *agogics* and, on occasion, to *rhythm*, will be taken into account in so far as they have not yet been discussed in the proper sections dealing with Technique in General.

The *long-sustained, whole-bow stroke on a single note* (see p. 64). Spun notes (*sons filés*), seem to be called for where the musical declamation demands uninterrupted flow of sound without change of bow. An initial accent always calls for a down-bow, while for the  up-bow is quite as applicable. In the *piano* the possible duration of the bow-stroke is far greater than in the *forte:*

717. 

718. 

When several notes are to be taken in a whole-bow stroke (*legato*), the difficulties of change of string as well as changing the point of contact are added. Here one should remember, first of all, that upward change of string calls for a down-bow, and downward change of string for an up-bow.

719. 

for instance, would be impossible to produce with the V.

720. 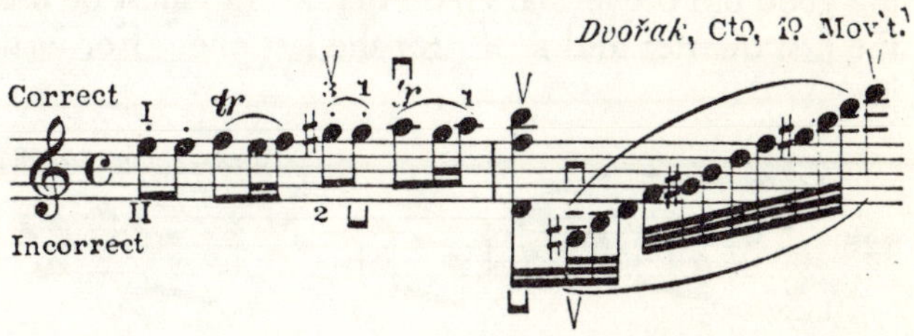

In Example 720 the bow-stroke, 1, involves noticeably less effort with up-bow in spite of the chord.

When *descending* change of string is mixed with *ascending* change of string, the majority decides:

721. 

The reason why the player so often fails in this sequence of notes in his incorrect division of the bow—the latter must occur in such a way that for those notes which are taken firmly, only one-quarter of the bow is used; while the harmonics, on the other hand, receive three-quarters of the bow.*

722. 

Here the down-bow is indicated for the eighth-notes, the up-bow, especially in the neighborhood of the nut, making too clumsy an effect.

When it is a question, however, of drawing the bow in a comparatively rapid and energetic manner, and when we are not interested in reducing the bow expenditure, the opposite occurs: we use the V with ascending change of string, and the ⊓ with descending change of string.

---

* One of the greatest among the young composers of our day once brought me a manuscript in which a > had been placed above the majority of the notes of a noble, quiet *cantilena*. His explanations made clear to me that he meant a *vibrato!*

** Still another frequently occurring example of a somewhat puzzling addition to existing methods of bowing-indication: when a pianist-composer writes  he invariably means  or  but not the *martelê-staccato* which he has inadvertently indicated.

---

* Incidentally it might be remarked that the tonal effect of this run as well as of similar ones (which in the majority of cases as a rule do not speak) will be incomparably more beautiful when played as regular broken triads, *without harmonics.*

Mendelssohn, Cto, 3º Mov't.

723. 

St. Saëns, Cto, B min. 1º Mov't.

724. 

In general, the violinist often unconsciously clings to the good old proverbial credo that a ⊓ must be used for the first quarter and a V for the last one. For instance, in:

Mendelssohn, Cto, 2º Mov't.

725. 
Correct
Incorrect

a <> with the fourth eighth-note as the climaxing point corresponds with the meaning of the phrase, hence a V logically should be used. Similarly in:

Suk, 4 Pieces, Nº 3

726. 
Correct
Incorrect

Beethoven, Romance G maj.

727. 
Correct
Incorrect

Bruch, Cto, G min. 1º Mov't.

728. 

The greater the number of notes we play on a single stroke the nearer the point of contact between bow and string approaches the bridge, which may endanger the tone quality. Hence, in these cases we should never hesitate to divide the stroke at the correct places:

Wieniawski, Ecole moderne Nº 2

729. 
Notation
Execution

If we can so arrange that change of bow coincides with change of strings or change of position, or, perhaps, with both, the smoothness of the passage-work is greatly enhanced thereby:

Saint-Saëns, III. Cto, 1º Mov't.

730. 

By this division the *glissando*  which produces so unpleasant an effect, may be avoided in three places, and becomes practically inaudible.

The *détaché* with the whole bow is taken into account especially when an energetically accentuated effect is desired. ***Détach***

However, when used in connection with *piano* or *mezzo-forte*, the breadth of the necessary movement would be sufficient to provoke a feeling of restlessness. Here partial strokes are more favorable:

Bruch, Cto, G min. 2º Mov't.

731. 
U.H.W.B.W.B.

Violinists inferior in musical culture have the habit of transferring the accent in syncopated bow strokes to the middle, instead of making it at the beginning:

Dvořák, Cto, 3º Mov't.

732. 
Correct
Incorrect

The *détaché*, when used as a partial bow-stroke, is best produced between the middle and the point. Frequently, however, when it is interrupted by a *whole-bow* stroke or a *legato*, it is played alternately with different parts of the bow, since otherwise a false accent might easily develop:

Mozart, Cto, D Maj. 3º Mov't.

733. 
Pt.
W.B.
Nut
Pt.
W.B.
Nut
W. B.

Beethoven, Trio Op. 70, Nº 2 1º Mov't.

734. 
Nut
W.B.
Tip
W.B.

Beethoven, Quart. Op. 72, 1º Mov't.

735. 
U.H.
Tip
U.H.
M.

When there is *no* danger, however, of a false accentuation, the use of the same division of the bow should be preferred because the tonal results at nut and point differ from each other in the case of most violinists. For example, in:

Brahms, Cto, 1º Mov't.

736. 
Nut
Pt.
Nut
Better: Nut
Nut
Nut

the exclusive use of the *lower half of* the bow is decidedly preferable to the mixed stroke, since double-stops at the point, in order to sound with the same power as at the nut, call for an outlay of strength many times greater.*

Détaché on the G-string is made by preference at the nut:

737. 
Sibelius, Cto, 1º Mov't.

738. 
Vieuxtemps, Cto, E maj. 1º Mov't.

For continuous, regular change between two strings, the middle of the bow first calls for consideration:

739. 
Dont, Op. 35 Nº 5

When we begin this etude with an V it turns into a bow-technique study of the most stubborn difficulty. The *détaché* with regular alternation between two strings is always begun with a ⊓ when the first note is on the lower string; but when the note with which one begins, lies on the upper string, then the V is indicated:

740.  741 

What should we do, however, when the following figure occurs in a composition which is to be performed?

742. 

We are confronted with the alternative of either regarding the awkwardness of the bow-stroke as something unavoidable, or of aiding ourselves by means of a slight alteration:

743. 

When the musical meaning of the figure is not thereby injured (something which can be decided only specifically in each case) this slight variation of the bow-stroke should be preferred to that originally indicated. In the case of regular change of string between more than two strings, the greatest *reduction* of bow-expenditure is necessary.

*During the last few years the following bowing has come more and more in favor:

736a 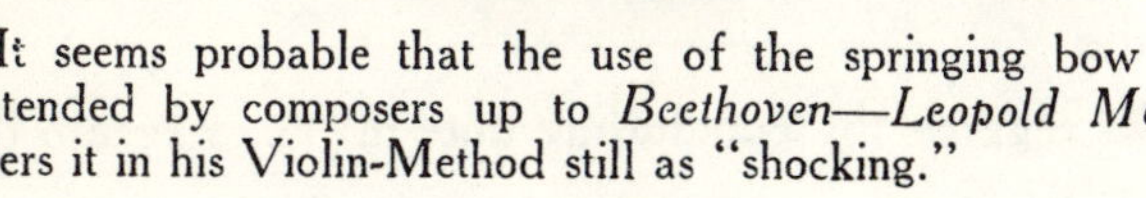 etc.

**It seems probable that the use of the springing bow was not intended by composers up to *Beethoven*—*Leopold Mozart* considers it in his Violin-Method still as "shocking."

744. 
Bach, Partita, E maj.

745. 
Viotti, Cto, A min. 1º Mov't.

The *more softly* the *détaché* is to sound, the closer the bow must approach the point—played piano in the middle it would soon change to a springing bow-stroke. Hence, for echo effects the springing bow seems indicated:

746. 
Détaché
Bach, Partita E maj.
Spring Bow

The player, especially in the case of *chamber music,* must take into consideration whether or not a series of detached notes should be played with the *détaché* or springing bow. The character of the composition in question alone should influence his decision:**

747. 
Détaché
Schumann, Piano Quintet 1º Mov't.
(the same) 3º Mov't.

748. 
Spring Bow

749. 
Mendelsshon, Trio Op.49, 1º Mov't.
Tip Dét.
M

750. 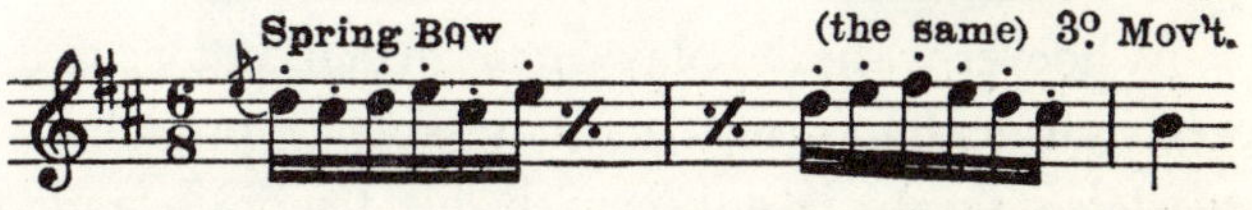
Spring Bow
(the same) 3º Mov't.

Martelé

Strict rhythm is the principal distinguishing mark of the *martelé.* From this point of view, we may judge whether, in the case of short notes in a slow tempo, the *martelé* or the thrown *spiccato* is to be used:

751. 
Martelé
Bach, Partita E maj.

752. 
Vieuxtemps, Cto, E maj. 1º Mov't.
Martelé

753. 
Vieuxtemps, Cto, A min.
Martelé

Martelé Staccato

In the case of short notes in a *rapid* tempo, a *martelé-staccato*, a thrown or springing bow-stroke must necessarily be substituted for the *martelé*.

Schumann, Quartet A min. 4º Mov't.

754. 

Thrown Bow at Nut *Beethoven*, Trio Op. 70 Nº 1 1º Mov't.

755. 

The bow division at the *end* of the *staccato* always is difficult. When it ends with a long note, or with a short note in the middle, there can be no question as to the division. However, when the bow should be at the nut at the beginning of the following stroke, one must try to produce the last staccato-notes in a way tonally unobjectionable at the lower half of the bow (which is so unfavorable for this bow-stroke) by means of a light, *flying* staccato combined with a tiny *ritardando*:

Vieuxtemps, Cto, E maj. 3º Mov't.

756. 

For passages of light and graceful character, a *flying* staccato should be substituted for a *firm one*.

Whoever wishes to play *Spohr's* compositions in a manner stylistically correct, must be able to produce a pure *martelé*-staccato in any conceivable tempo in a rhythmically correct manner:

Spohr, Cto, E min. 3º Mov't.

757. 

Spohr, Cto, D min. 2º Mov't.

758. 

Spohr, Gesangsscene

759. 

In pieces more of the virtuoso type it is immaterial whether the staccato be played exactly in tempo, or taken somewhat more rapidly and brilliantly:

Wieniawski, Polonaise A maj.

760. 

Vieuxtemps, Ballade and Polonaise.

761. 

When the staccato is combined with repeated change of string, the springing bow is often substituted for it, even by excellent staccato players, because of its difficulty. Nor are staccato runs in double-stops within the reach of all.

Wieniawski, Cto, D min. 3º Mov't.

762. 

Sibelius, Cto, 3º Mov't.

763. 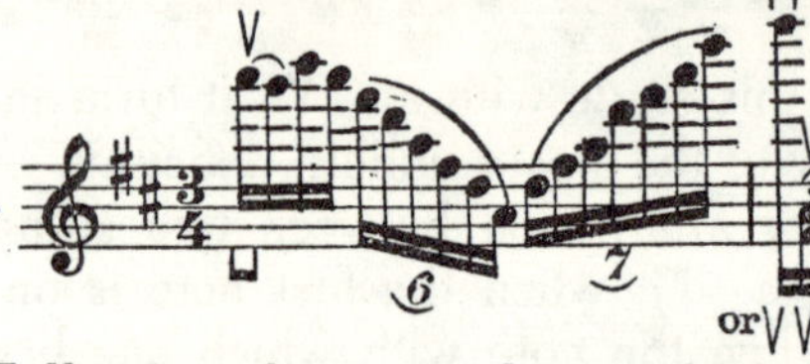

⊓ or V in Stacc[ato]

Following the same laws which hold good for the *legato*, it is executed more easily when ascending with the ⊓ and when descending with the V.

764. 

Among the most important moments of the ⊓ staccato must be counted the notes which precede or which conclude the staccato:

Wieniawski, Cto, D min. 1º Mov't

765. 

Here three possibilities are indicated for the bow-strokes *preceding* the staccato. We may play the two notes which precede the staccato with a ⊓ at the lower half of the bow, and immediately connect them with the staccato itself. Or, we may play the two notes with an V in the upper bow-half; or else we may choose the middle way—first the ⊓, then the first staccato note V and the remainder ⊓. In all three cases the difficulty consists in presenting the first staccato notes in as sharply detached a manner as possible; after which it is for the individual player to discover the best way to do so. For my own part I prefer the second manner, and I also know of cases where the staccato could not be successfully carried out until the place of the first ⊓ had been taken by the V.

As regards the concluding note in ⊓ staccato it must

always be played with a detached bow. Herein, and above all in the rise or fall of the tonal sequence, we find the criterion for the logical use of the V or ⊓ staccato, musically as well as technically.

Spohr, Cto, D min. 1º Mov't

766. 

Vieuxtemps, Cto, E maj. 3º Mov't.

767. 

Example 766 may be played about as successfully with the ⊓ as with the V staccato, since the sustained concluding note permits of an independent V.

In Example 767, on the contrary, the concluding note is conceived as being quite short, and hence would sound rather clumsy if played after a ⊓ staccato. For this reason the V staccato is unquestionably better.

The Springing Bow and Thrown Bow often alternate. The tempo, first of all, determines which is to be used:

Brahms, Cto, 1º Mov't.

768. 
Thrown Bow
Nut

(The thrown bow in the middle sounds too thin here, and the springing bow too superficial.)

From the above 3º Mov't.

769. 
Thrown Bow
Nut

Brahms, Trio Op. 8 2º Mov't.

770. 
M. Thrown Bow

Beethoven, Son. G maj. 1º Mov't.

771. 
Thrown Bow
M.

Vieuxtemps, Cto, D min. 4º Mov't.

772. 
Spring Bow

Haydn, Quartet D maj. 4º Mov't.

773. 
Spring Bow

Thrown and springing bowings mixed:

Beethoven, Trio, Op. 97 2º Mov't.

774. 
Spr.
Thr.
Spr.
Thr.

Beethoven, Trio, Op. 1, Nº 2 4º Mov't.

775. 
Spr.
Thr.
Spr.
Thr.

Beethoven, Son. Op. 30, Nº 3, 1º Mov't.

776. 

Here springing bows are mingled with springing staccati in order to allow the down-stroke to fall on the *sfz*.

With regard to the bow-division in the case of springing and thrown bows, in general, see p. 73. Some additional examples follow:

Sarasate, Zapateado.

777. 

Beethoven, Kreutzer Son. II. Var.

778. 
Piano
Viol.

Beethoven. Son. A maj. 1º Mov't.

778a 

Soft thrown-bow strokes:

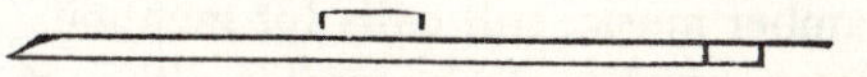

Beethoven, Romance F maj.

779. 

Bach, Chaconne

780. 
segue

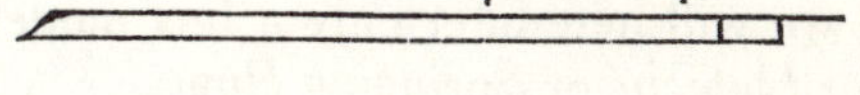

Suk, 4 Pieces, Burleske

781. 

Brahms, Cto, 3º Mov't.

782. 

That on occasion the rhythmic structure may be entirely distorted in consequence of a wrong choice of *bowing* is shown by the following **examples:**

Tschaikowski, Cto, 3o Movt.

783. 

Here the majority of violinists in direct opposition to the character of the theme use long ⊓ instead of short V when playing the eighth-note preceding the sixteenth, something which may very easily be avoided by using the bow-stroke indicated above.

When the thrown bow is combined with change of string in double-stops, it becomes one of the most difficult bowings to play in a tonally beautiful manner. When the thrown bow in this connection is beyond the player's technical ability, a short *détaché* between the middle and point may, on occasion, be substituted for it.

Bruch, G min. Cto, 3o Movt.

784. 

The substitution, as a matter of principle, of the short *martelé* at the point, for the thrown bow in solo playing and in chamber music, still calls for mention.

In passages of delicate character although of undeniable charm, this substituted bowing will scarcely suffice for the expression of increased energy and a clean-cut rhythm, quite aside from the fact that its use already calls for a double expenditure of strength and also for slow tempi.

Mixed Bowings

The use of *mixed* bowings, in the main, is determined by a division of the bow which ought to be tonally as well as musically free from objection. Out of the abundance of the very great number of the possible combinations available, we will here offer only a few model examples:

Legato+Détaché or *Springing Bow*:

Lalo, Symph. Espagnole 2o Movt.

785. 

Saint-Saëns, Cto, 3o Movt.

786. 

No more bow should be expended on the tied notes than upon each of the detached notes. Similarly in:

(the same)

787. 

Here, owing to the ascending change of string, so much bow is gained in the down-bow that the bow-stroke seems effortless; but the circumstances would change at once were the up-bow to be used. In:

788. 

on the other hand, an up-bow at the point is unquestionably indicated.

Bach, Cto, E maj. 3o Movt.

789. 

Bach, Son. G min. 4o Movt,

790. 

(the same)

791. 

Half-Bow + Détaché:

Beethoven, Quartet, Op. 59, 4o Movt.

792. 

Thrown Bow + Thrown Staccato. For the sake of equality the thrown bow is frequently mingled with the thrown staccato:

Beethoven, Sonata F maj. 4o Movt.

793. 

Brahms, Son. Op. 100, 1o Movt.

794. 

In general, the rule may be laid down that in the case of detached *triplet* figures the thrown *staccati* are used in practically every instance on the second and third notes of the triplet in order to avoid the clumsy V on the strong beat:

795. 

The same holds good for *two-part* rhythm, when, for instance, two eighth notes are to be tied, and two are to be played detached:

796. 
Bruch, Cto, G min. 3º Mov't.

Only a few know that thrown or springing *staccati* may be executed on two notes with far less effort when played with the ⊓ and thus transformed into *saltati*. For instance:

797. 
Glazounow, Cto.
instead of

The familiar rhythmic figure ♪. ♪ (*martelé* + *small détaché*), may be executed in different ways, in accordance with purely musical demands. The change of string has to *precede* the short notes:

798. 
Correct
Incorrect

The same applies during change of position:

799. 
Correct
Incorrect

800. 
Sibelius, Cto, 3º Mov't.
W.B.
Pt.
W.B.

If the return to the nut in the last eighth-note of each measure is too difficult for the player, the bow-stroke may be modified in the following manner:

801. 
(the same)

Similarly:

802. 
Schumann, Trio, D min. 2º Mov't.

or:

803. 
Paganini, Capr. Nº 11

804. 
Beethoven, Trio, Op. 97, 4º Mov't.
U.H.

805. 
Beethoven, Sonata F maj. 4º Mov't.

Reversed Chords

As chords in general and the avoidance of needlessly breaking them has already been treated in Part One of this work, the only remaining question is how chords are to be broken when thematic considerations forbid the natural break upward:

806. 
Bach, Chaconne

In breaking the chords in the usual manner the theme would sound as follows:

807. 
(the same)

Instead of:

808. 
(the same)

The only correct mode of execution from the thematic standpoint may be expressed in notation as follows:

809. 

Breaking of Chords

On the other hand, we have cases in which the breaking of the chords produces too unrhythmical an effect, and must be avoided under all circumstances.

810. 
Brahms, Cto, 1º Mov't.

Here the entire chord, not only its lower section, must fall on the first eighth of the measure.

Wrong Accents and Bow-Motion

In conclusion a few words might be said about the avoidance of false accents:

811. 
Correct
Beethoven, Romance G maj.
Incorrect

812. 
Correct
Mendelssohn, Cto, 1º Mov't.
Incorrect

Here we almost always hear a false accent, produced by the violent movement on the second quarter note (c). It would be well to weaken it indirectly by means of a *consciously* produced accent on the third beat of the measure. Similarly:

Bruch, Cto, G min. 3º Mov't.

813. 
Correct
Nut
Point
Point
Incorrect

Mozart, Cto, A maj. 1º Mov't.

814. 
Correct
Incorrect

In Example 815 the notes marked with an + in most cases are played with a sustained accent—to the decided detriment of the rhythmic structure peculiar to this theme:

815. *Mendelssohn,* Cto, 3º Mov't.

in the Siciliano rhythm, as in:

Tartini, Devil's Trill Sonata

816. 

or:

Saint-Saëns, Cto, B maj. 2º Mov't.

817. 

where there may be too much bow on the first sixteenth-note or not enough on the first eighth. This evil may be obviated by the following division of the bow:

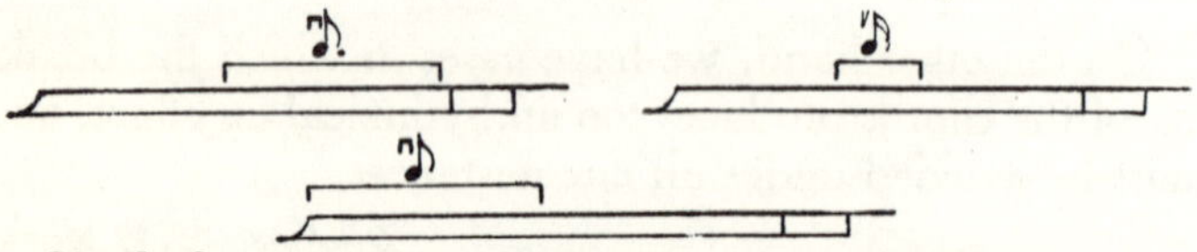

Similarly: *Lalo,* Symph. Espagnole, 5º Mov't.

818. 
I
II
III

Here, at I, only a little more than half the bow, instead of the whole bow, is used; at II one-quarter in the middle; and at III the upper half. In this way the usual unmusical accent at II may be avoided.

An instructive example of the dependence of musical phrasing upon the proper division of the bow is offered by the first theme in the last movement of *Mozart's* Concerto in A Major:

Mozart, Cto, A maj. 3º Mov't.

819. 
L.H.
W.B.
Point
W.B.

L.H.
W.B.
Point
W.B.
Nut
W.B.

Here, too, should be considered the avoidance of false accents in mixed bowings, where the same length of bow is alternately to be distributed among a differing number of notes (see also Examples 785 and 791).

Brahms, Piano-quartet, Op. 25, 1º Mov't.

820. 
Point

Tschaikowski, Cto, 1º Mov't.

821. 
Nut

Lalo, Symph. Espagnole 2º Mov't.

822. 
Point

Slightest expenditure of bow, no pressure upon the single notes, and above all greatest care in preventing false accents in general, are of prime importance here.

Lalo, Symph. Espagnole 2º Mov't.

823. 

Here, at the places marked +, only half the bow should be expended so that the middle can be used for the following bow-stroke:

Or in: (the same)

824. 
G

At + one should *not* play up to the nut (no matter how greatly tempted to do so because of the G-string), since in that case the succeeding *legato* would make too clumsy an effect. In the case of two voiced movements, when it is a question of decidedly emphasizing the theme at the expense of the purely harmonic or rhythmic meaning of the second voice, correct division of the bow plays a great part. For instance, in:

Bach, Son. A min. 3º Mov't.

825. 
I
II

at I, on the *melodic* E^1 about five-sixths of the bow-length should be expended, and the remainder on the isolated

* This bowing, extremely inconvenient in connection with double-stops, may be changed in the following manner without any hesitation:

Tschaikowski, Cto, 1º Mov't.

821 a. 

rhythmic C[1] (at II). Similarly in:

Bach, Chaconne

826.

The rhythm of the Chaconne is emphasized as follows: On the first eighth note value of each dotted quarter (I), three-quarters of the bow is used; and on the remaining two eighth-note values (II), only the last remaining quarter of the bow.

Chausson, Poëme

827.

At I (theme), three-quarters of the bow; at II (harmonic counterpoint), one-quarter of the entire bow is used.

Not until the most appropriate movement sequences in the form of the best fingerings and bowings have been established should we try to *learn* the composition by mastering its motoristic and spiritual contents.

actis-
s

4. Practice as a Means of Learning.

Our first consideration with regard to a composition (as has already been mentioned) is that of gaining an insight as to its content—to which end we must have recourse to its musical notation. Only gradually do we free ourselves from the notes, and may then speak of *knowing*. It is possible, as a matter of fact, that the performance of a composition from a musical standpoint may reveal the same advantages or disadvantages whether we play it from notes or not. Psychologically, however, the inner processes which here must be taken into consideration are fundamentally different. In consequence they will be considered in two distinct divisions: *Practice* and *Memory*. Before we pass to a discussion of the principles which should guide us in practicing, we must first establish the casual difference between making music for *practice purposes* and for *performance*.

Practice will always be a *conscious* activity, one consisting of a greater or lesser number of repetitions, by the aid of which we endeavor to master difficulties which stand in the way of a correct cycle of movement.

Performance, on the other hand, the reproduction of an art-work, the absolute making of music, delves into the very depths of our subconscious psychic life. One either *practices* or one *plays*. If both are done simultaneously, neither comes into its own.

To translate into practical terms: *while* one is reproducing a work as an entirety, the player must not concern himself with inadequately developed technical details. One may, however, make note of unsatisfactory details by marking them on the margin of the page, as subjects of study, for *future* unequivocal practice-activity.

Practice in itself is taught in two ways by pedagogically gifted teachers. Some recommend musical practice on a *logical*, others on a *mechanical* basis. In reality, a technically perfected performance can only result after the student has formed the right conception of the movements required for it, and then is able to find the proper transferring mechanism for them. An exaggerated preoccupation with one of these factors develops either intelligent bunglers or brainless acrobats. Most widespread is the unthinking mechanical repetition of separate note-sequences, sometimes accompanied by an extension of the practice-time to eight hours, a measure the destructive effects of which will be discussed later. An achievement so purely a matter of manual craftsmanship bears a desperate resemblance to specialized factory toil. Even performers of great natural talent who have strayed into this wrong track sooner or later have been ruined artistically, and sometimes physically and spiritually as well. They lose connection with the essential thing in music, technique becomes an end in itself, the springs of imagination run dry. Not until violin teachers collectively have come to realize that the development of the student's *ability to think logically* is one of their most important functions, and that the latter will learn more in half an hour of consciously directed study than in a week's mechanical practice; not until instead of uttering the commonplaces of judgment—good, bad, in tune, out of tune, tonally beautiful, clean-cut, unclear—they point out the road the student must follow in order to do better, not until then will the degenerate type produced by the eight-hour labor day disappear.

How should we begin learning a musical composition? The first step has been taken when teacher and pupil have a clear idea of the number and the kind of problems which have to be mastered. ***Division of Problems***

Dont, Op. 35, Nº 2

828.

Here the gaining of certain ends is the object in view:

Left hand,
Correct intonation
Lightness
Right hand, Springing bow

Each of these individual technical problems must be solved *apart* from the others occurring simultaneously, and by itself. Never should one attempt to master two technical problems at the same time. Should the student, even after this simplification and isolation, encounter a difficulty he cannot overcome, then a *hindrance in movement* exists. This must be discovered and done away with. There are violinists who find it impossible to play certain figures in spite of correct practice and a preceding analysis. The reason, in most cases, is a single hindrance, principally mechanical in character, which has escaped notice. For instance, in:

Beethoven, Cto, 1º Movt.

829. 

Here the hindrance consists in the simultaneous change of position and strings of the octave: 

On E[1] and E[2] the fingers must be placed upon the string without any preparation, something especially risky at this exposed point, since the fingers may easily slide off the string. (I aid myself by hardly raising my fingers from the strings between C sharp and E, and rather risking a pizzicato—well-nigh inaudible, however—with the fourth finger.) Technical hindrances as a rule occur at some very small division of the unsuccessful sequence of notes. To find such hindrances, to isolate and remedy them through means of suitable exercises is one of the most important problems of violin study.

Wieniawski, Ecole moderne, Etude Nº 2

830. 

First hindrance: change of position.

Simplified Manner of Practice

831. 

Second hindrance: change of string with the left hand.

Manner of Practice 832. 

Furthermore, it is not practical to study a difficult passage exclusively in its *original form.* The monotony of such a procedure causes fatigue; and the musical meaning of the section is lost to the player, which, in the end, may react injuriously on the impulsive directness of the interpretation.

Brahms, Cto, 1º Movt.

833. 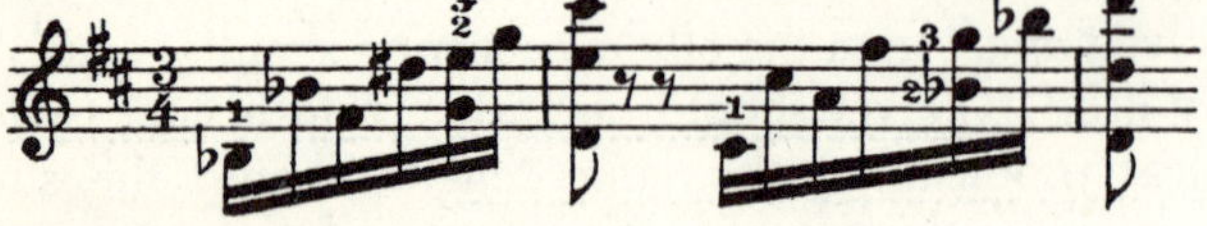

In order to achieve simultaneous, chord-like placing of the fingers on the string, practice like this:

834. 

Similarly in:

Vieuxtemps, Cto, E maj. 3º Movt.

835. 

The manner of practice for the left hand:

836. 

The student will find it advantageous at times to choose a mode of practice in which *difficulties are increased,* since later this makes the conquest of the real task seem far easier. The great artist should possess not only just the technique he actually needs, but a good deal more, in order thus to balance the hindrances which may result owing to deficiencies of mood. In the following examples we will transform *détaché* runs into *legato* runs, and *legato* passages into *chords*:

Wieniawski, Cto, D min. 3º Movt.

837. 
instead of

Dont, Op. 35, Nº 5

838. 

A more difficult execution for the left hand:

839. 

Slow Prac

All technical difficulties should be practiced slowly. The habit of practicing too rapidly carries with it the most varied disadvantages, such as: lack of exact *control* of *correct intonation;* a tendency toward indistinct playing; inability to *apply the mental brake* when necessary in consequence of lack of self-control, which unmistakably stamps all technical achievement with the seal of unequivocal insecurity. Experience teaches us that violinists who practice slowly are superior to others, at all events in a purely technical way. It is true that the advantages of slow practice are evident mainly on the concert platform —in a room the difference is less apparent. Yet when the individual in question has become psychically less capable of resistance owing to the excitement connected with public appearance, it becomes clear that he who has practiced slowly can rely upon his muscular instinct, memory, self-control and courage to a far higher degree than his colleague who has accustomed himself to practising rapidly.* On the other hand the advantage of practising slowly becomes apparent only when wrong notes are put

* *J. M. Grün* (1837-1915) might claim the merit of having been one of the first teachers to insist on the honest and conscientious study of technical difficulties.

right i.e. corrected without exception. If not, there remains only the disadvantage of the elimination of facility!

This by no means implies, however, that one must invariably and under all circumstances practice slowly. Slow practice secures the greatest possible correctness of intonation, while rapid practice furthers agility. Hence, in case we wish to learn a certain passage, we should first practise slowly, and afterward, in the tempo prescribed, since if we confine ourselves to slow practice exclusively, the lightness of our left-hand technique might suffer. The reverse, however, is still more injurious: favoring *brilliancy* at the expense of accuracy. This habit owes its existence to the fallacy that a "brilliant" run, that is, one played in a tempo more rapid than the one prescribed, produces a far greater effect upon the listener than an execution with an abundance of swing but in the original tempo. As a matter of fact, accuracy and sureness of intonation are qualities less frequently in evidence than exaggerated, necessarily inaccurate rapidity; every more or less cultured listener takes greater pleasure in hearing *each* note of a run distinctly than in listening to a blurred mixture, which at best may conclude with a pure *final* note. Far be it from me to recommend a limping, spiritless mode of playing. There is, however, a kind of spirit which does not exclude the retention of the correct tempo, while the hurrying which is a result of faulty practicing or of striving for effect may fall far short of doing justice to the composer's intentions. The following is a striking example:

Brahms, Cto, 3o Movt.

840.

Nearly all violinists play these runs too rapidly, the orchestra comes limping along after them, and the two-part rhythm which is so characteristic of this movement is destroyed. In order to exorcise this speed devil which possesses us all to a greater or lesser degree, I recommend the use of the accents indicated above, according to the principle of a brake applied to the finger movements by means of the bow (see p. 161).

This is the proper place to touch upon the importance of the note with which a run *concludes*. It is customary to remark, sarcastically, about violinists whose technique is uncertain, that only the first and last notes of their *bravura*-passages are audible. Quite aside from the fact that for the real violinist a clean-cut technique is a self-understood necessity, the last note of a run is decidedly more important than its medial notes. For the listener is hardly able to control the inner components of rapid note-sequences during their performance except with respect to their equality, and not until the advent of the *pause* which succeeds the *last* note does he find the fraction of time needed to form an opinion with regard to their purity. Hence apparent failure or success in playing a passage as a whole is intimately connected with the impression produced by the last note, and for this reason alone special attention should be paid to quality and pitch. The broken E major chord is most frequently sinned against in this connection:

841.

where the concluding harmonic E^4, which crowns the passage, so often is dropped, and merely because the fourth finger imitatively carries out the "in the air" movement of the bow in a reflex manner and never reaches the E^4.

The impeccable execution of technical difficulties in public performance demands a high degree of *self-control* in watching the degree of rapidity of the various movements. Then, too, every *technical* study should be regarded as a tonal study as well. We will endeavor to apply all these principles in several examples:

Examples of Logical Practice

Wieniawski, Cto, D min. 1o Movt.

842.

What is the nature of the technical problems to be mastered? In the left hand we have chords; and in the right a mixed bowing combined with change of string at the lower half of the bow. Let us begin with the study of the left hand, slowly practising the following figures without regard to the bowing:

843.

The fingers are to be placed simultaneously on the strings as demanded for the setting of the chord.

This mode of procedure allows us to examine and correct the exactness of intonation. Gradually speed is increased until the prescribed tempo has been reached. If the exactness of intonation is not what it should be, it is in most instances due to faulty *change of position*. In such case we should first of all repeat each change of position individually:

844.
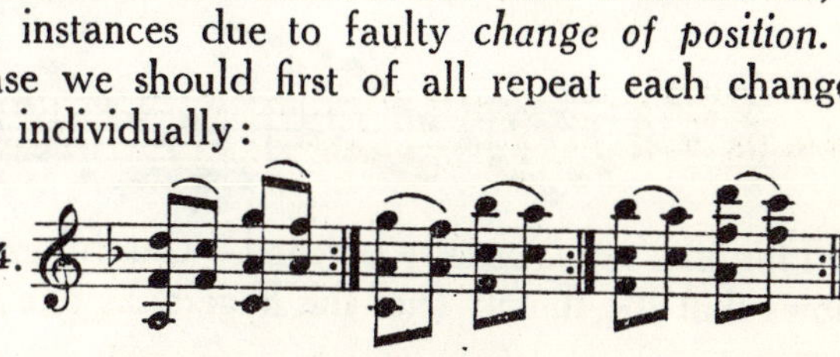

After securing favorable results a chord exercise may follow:

845. 

After a renewed removal of any hindrances which may have existed, the technical ability of the left hand may be regarded as satisfactory for its task. Let us now turn to the right arm. In accordance with our principle of not merging the study of two different difficulties, we assign a position of repose to the left hand, and isolate the movements of the right arm. If we allow open strings to take the place of the notes in the text, we obtain the following bow-stroke schedule:*

846. 

We may now take any etude in three note chords which may commend itself to us, and practice it with the preceding bow-stroke and with the same change of string, for instance: *Dont,* Op. 35, No 1

847. 

In a short time we will be in a position to control this bowing in a *tonally beautiful* manner. It is *only now* that we undertake to practice the run in its original form, something which after the preceding preparatory exercises, will only take a short space of time. Another example:

Saint-Saëns, Rondo Capriccioso

848. 

If we wish to isolate the left-hand difficulties in this case, we must first practice the entire passage legato.

It is true that this procedure means a decided increase in difficulty, since inequalities in change of string and position are far more apparent in *legato*:

(the same)

849. 

The speed is now increased gradually, and hindrances in change of position which may exist are done away with by means of special exercises, and *only then* may we also study the passage with a springing bow. Or: (the same)

850. 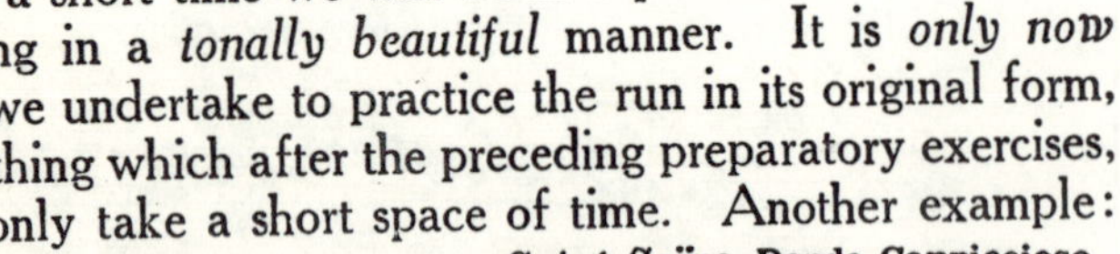

This final run is usually botched. Careful examination shows that the thumb (not the fingers, as one might believe) is to blame, because the placing of the thumb underneath the neck which prepares the ascent into the highest positions, with fingering *a*, is mingled with the upward movement of the lower arm. I avoid this difficulty by using fingering *b*. Remaining in the third position, I have sufficient time and leisure—owing to the use of the open E-string—to lay the thumb (ready to ascend) under the neck of the violin, and to carry out the figure with assurance. In view of this I am content to throw in the minor inconvenience of the leap across the A-string.

Saltati, too, should always first be studied in *legato,* since control of the left hand during the *saltando*-stroke is hardly possible.

Paganini, Cto, D maj.

851. 

Manner of practice

We will now turn to short and comparatively simple examples:

Beethoven, Cto, 3o Mov't.

852. 

Broken *triads* in slow tempo are among the note sequences most difficult to play in tune, especially when, as in connection with the preceding example, a rapid change of position (A^2-D^3) is combined with their performance.

The exercise  will not suffice here to give the student the necessary security, since it will not guarantee a correct position of the entire hand in the extended sixth position. The most serviceable manner of exercise would be the following:

853. 

The most difficult exercise in intonation in the entire range of violin literature is the short prelude to Paganini's etude in thirds:

Paganini, Caprice No 18

854. 

It should be played as rapidly as possible in order to render the inaccuracies, which can never be altogether overcome, less audible. Then there is:

*Theoretically, a mixed stroke between nut and middle, for the sake of tonal cleanness it is better played entirely in the middle.

Bach, Son. G min. Presto

855. 

It is no longer sufficient at first to study this composition *legato* and afterwards study the bowings marked. The player must also see to it that he keeps the tempo set at the beginning, and does not yield to an impulse to hurry, which may lead to a catastrophe.

Self-control is the watchword, something more easily recommended than followed. It is hard for a runner—on the fingerboard as on the street—to revert to a normal rate of progress once he is in full swing. Of what avail are all the good intentions in the world if the fingers do not obey? Now, it is a curious fact that it is easier to slow up the tempo of the *right* hand than that of the left, for example in a rapid *détaché,* because the movements of the left hand are far more complex than those of the right arm. With this knowledge as our point of departure we should try to influence the left hand indirectly by means of the right, that is, attempt to recall to reason the left hand which is galloping away, by means of "brake" accents.

(the same)

856. 

Many also employ the *metronome* for this purpose, yet this alien tempo controller is less efficacious and much more inartistic than the will-power of the artist himself. Similarly:

Mendelssohn, C^to^, 3º Mov't.

857. 

Wieniawski, Scherzo-Tarantelle

858. 

Paganini. C^to^, D maj.

859. 

(the same)

860. 

W. B. as a means of effecting a ritard.

Sarasate, Gipsy Airs

861. 

In this last broken G major triad even the most routined violinist is apt to develop a certain restlessness which betrays itself in "running away," and is the reason for such frequent failure. The corrective, the simplicity of which cannot be improved upon, consists in a slight bow accent on the B¹, which serves as a "brake." Another example follows:

Notation

Bruch, C^to^, G min. 1º Mov't.

862. 

Manner of Practice:

Here the moment of retardation rests upon the accent made on the *fourth* (instead of the first) note of the sextolet. Furthermore:

(the same)

863. 

The seemingly unconquerable inclination to hurry unduly in the preceding example is most effectively combated by a *broadening out* (even while playing in public) of the *first four notes* of every measure, whereby the repose necessary for the subsequent accents is gained. Quite as important as learning the "brake" accents, be it said, is "*unlearning*" them again in view of public performance; since otherwise a flavor of the school-room is apt to characterize the rendition, and stamp it with the hall-mark of inartistic mechanization. In Example 864 the difficulty lies mainly in the change of position.

Wieniawski, L'ecole moderne, Nº 2

864. 

The hindrances will be most thoroughly done away with by the use of the following *intermediary note* exercise:

865. 

In addition is is well to dwell somewhat *longer* on the notes used for change of position, in order to check up and improve for purposes of control and improvement:

866. 

Similar examples: *Vieuxtemps*, Cto, E maj. 1º Mov't.

867. 

Manner of practice:

868. 

869. 

Vieuxtemps, Cto, D min. 4º Mov't

870. 

Manner of practice: (The original notes on the E-string are to be played mutely.)

871. 

872. 

(The notes on the D-string are to be played mutely.)

When the finger, in spite of these retarding exercises, is unable to strike the distances between certain notes lying far apart one from the other, the *intermediary notes*, or notes between them, should be used as an aid. For example:

Paganini, Cto, 1º Mov't.

873. 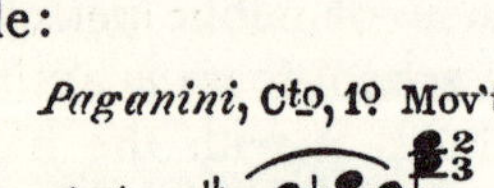 Manner of Practice 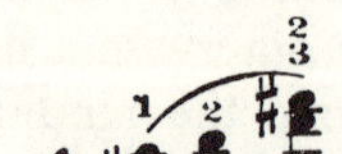

Brahms, Cto 1º Mov't

874. 

Manner of practice: At first an audible, later an *inaudible glissando* from B^2 to C^4:

875. 

Wieniawski, Scherzo Tarantelle

876. 

Manner of practice: 877. 

The same in the case of the following, justly dreaded figure:

Lalo, Symph. Espagnole 5º Mov't.

878. 

Manner of practice: 879. 

Bruch, Cto, G min. 3º Mov't.

880. 

Manner of practice with intermediate notes:

881. 

Rhythmic changes are recommendable for purposes of study when a more secure control, and possibilities of improvement are obtainable by their means (see p. 41).

Rhyt
mic
Chan
for
Pract
Pur-
poses

Ernst, Cto, F♯ min.

882. 

Manner of practice: A more extended resting on the first note after every change of position:

(the same)

883. 

Schradieck, Finger Exercises Book II

884. 

Manner of practice:

885. 

In order to lend more interest to practicing an extended run in *legato*, one should change the slurs in the following manner:

886. 

An admirable method of practice, and one all too little used is that of transposing small, very difficult figures in the circle of fifths, instead of employing more or less stultifying mechanical repetitions:

887 

Manner of practice:

888. 

In this connection a few other examples of bowing patterns might be given:

889. 

Pattern of string change:

890. 

Manner of practice: Using chord exercises (*Sevčik*, School of Bowing Technique, Book VI), as a foundation:

891. 

892. 

Pattern of string change: for example 892:

893. 

Manner of practice:

894. 

895. 

The individual character of this composition necessitates a very short and vigorous accentuation of the up-bow note, pieces of a general technical character may be used as preparatory study. The *bow scheme* is as follows:

896. 

Manner of practice in the system of scales (double-stops):

897. 

To resume: the technical combinations possible are so numerous that composers of etudes have been able to consider only an infinitesimal portion in their works. Hence, when studying a musical composition, we not infrequently have to invent exercises ourselves in order to master certain difficulties. In this connection, incidentally, we may draw on well-known etudes and also (in a somewhat altered form) on the system of scales. A few examples follow:

898. 

899. 

900. 

901. 

Beethoven, Kreutzer Son. 2º Mov't.

902. 

903. 

Beethoven, Cto, 3º Mov't.

904. 

Kreutzer, Etude No 5

905. 

Bach, Partita E maj.

906. 

Dont, Op. 35 Nº 1

907. 

Bruch, Cto, G min. 3º Mov't.

908. 

Dont, Op. 35 Nº 1

909. 

Paganini-Kreisler, Caprice Nº 20

910. 

Ševčik, School of Bowing, Book V

911. 

Schubert-Kreisler, Balletmusic from Rosamunde

912. 

Ševčik, School of Bowing Book V

913. 

Joachim, Hung. Cto, 1º Mov't

914. 

915. 

Brahms, Cto, 1º Mov't.

916. 

917. 

Paganini, Cto, 1º Mov't.

918. 

919. 

All that is essential with regard to the so-called *mute exercises* has already been said on p. 24. Their use as an extreme case might be justified in an example such as the following:

Mute Trai ing o Left Hanc

Joachim, Hung. Cto, 1º Mov't.

920. 

The dreaded difficulty of this passage lies less in the third or in the half-tone change of position than in the alternating stops by the third and fourth fingers:

921. 

The following seems a naturally indicated preparatory study in this connection:

922. 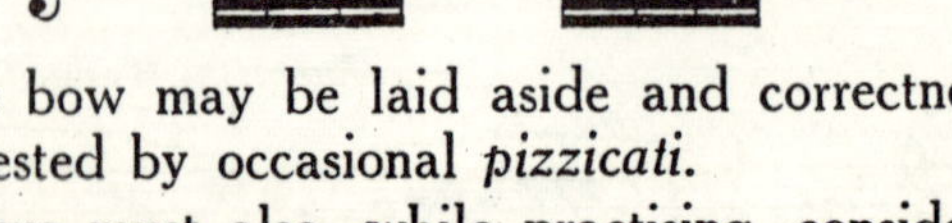

Here the bow may be laid aside and correctness of intonation tested by occasional *pizzicati*.

Finally, we must also, while practising, consider the purely tonal factor above all in connection with the use or elimination of the *vibrato*. Opinions in this respect differ widely. I myself find vibration on quite insignificant notes just as insupportable as a dry stringing together of cold sounds. The standard for a correct *practice*-tone should be that it is not unbearable to those who may be compelled to listen to it. One should not employ two different tone temperatures, a cold one for practicing and a warm one for performance. I am in favor of the consistent use of a pleasant sounding tone while practising, brought about by a very, very slight vibration, hardly visible or audible, which does not at all produce a *vibrato* effect, yet is enough to give the tone a certain amount of color. Thus, the tone still remains non-emotional (as it should remain so long as it is not used to express an emotion), yet makes a pleasant tonal impression. Violinists who accustom their ear and fingers to a dry practice-tone are in danger of finding that they are unable to produce a soulful tone just when they need it.

After the rules to be observed, as well as the auxiliary means at our disposal for the technical shaping-up of a musical composition have been discussed, we must turn our attention to those quite unserviceable means (not as yet mentioned) which are all too frequently employed with the same end in view. We will group them collectively under the general denomination of *unserviceable manners of practice.*

ong ys ctice

Unserviceable Manners of Practice. There are two ways of practising incorrectly: by raising some conception which may be correct enough in itself yet is quite *secondary*, to the dignity of a *main* principle; or by allowing one's manner of practice to be controlled by an absolutely *wrong* principle, the value of which is entirely imaginary. Common to both these main errors as well as to their variations, is a certain tendency to *exaggeration* which, at times, assumes a grotesque form. In the first group in this chamber of horrors the place of honor belongs to the terrible mania for breaking up a figure into lesser and very least components:

Goldmark, Cto, 1º Mov't.

923. 

Incorrect manner of practice:

924. 

whereas the sensible way of making the rhythmic change consists in shifting the slurs, without a repetition of the individual fragments (Example 886). A second fault, which also becomes a mania, consists in the choiceless, indeterminate use of *too slow* a tempo when practicing. When one hears a violinist practice the following run:

Beethoven, Romance, F maj.

925. 

in a tempo eight times too slow.

926. 

and in addition with a flinging down of the fingers so powerful that it suggests the drop of a waterfall, we may be certain that the person who practices in this fashion never will become the possessor of a light, fluent finger technique. This quite apart from the paralyzing monotony which after a time cannot help but characterize his playing. In the same way constant strong *accentuation* gives one's playing a certain pedantic quality, though the *occasional* use of accents by violinists who are inclined to nervous hurrying may have a beneficial effect. Similarly, the habitual use of the *metronome* should be avoided, since it nips in the bud any possibility of a *rubato* suggested by the player's fancy, and his whole manner of playing takes on a machine-made cast. Not without reason is it regarded as a reproach when an artist is said to play like a metronome.

Cantilenas

While the carrying-out of technically difficult works certainly takes for granted intensive study, *practising* (in the sense of manifold, immediate sequential repetition) of *cantilene*, the appropriate and expressive performance of which, in the first instance depends on inner feeling, should be eschewed absolutely. The repetition of an action, it is true, favors greater fluidity of the movements called for, yet at the same time dulls the sensations which accompany the action. Without directness and freshness, technically easily mastered note successions such as *cantilene* are void of all effect. When a violinist possesses a certain degree of general technique and the emotional content of a *cantilena* is clear to him, the use of the most appropriate form of movement in the shape of the most serviceable fingerings and bowings, as well as a knowledge of the musical importance of the phrase to be played, are enough to allow its content to be expressed.

In general a principle sound in itself, but which is exaggerated or used in the wrong place, is invariably harmful.

Exaggerated Repetition

In this category belongs the exaggerated *repetition* of individual figures. In my opinion the repetitions in succession of any run should not exceed a *dozen*, and then a short pause should be made between each, so that the player on every occasion may account to himself for any hindrance or imperfection which still remains and has to be overcome. It makes an out and out laughable impression when the person practicing charges the difficulty to be overcome in continually renewed, useless rushes, like a frenzied bull, without rhyme or reason, unable to vanquish it; while calm consideration, a weighing of the difficulty and logical repetition according to plan, would soon lead him to his goal.

Intermediary Notes

The determination of the *intermediary notes* in change of position, as we already know, is the most effectual means of securing a larger degree of manual certainty. Yet, alas, for the teacher who neglects to remind the student, again and again, that from the aesthetic point of view *audible* intermediate tones are among the ugliest blots the tonal picture can show! The violinist who practices in this manner as a matter of principle, soon will have forfeited all his ability to detect finer aesthetic differences, and above all will produce a variety of *portamenti* which, so to speak, develops into a cheap opportunity for transport from one position into another without meaning or charm.

Change of Fingering

The deliberate selection of especially *obstreperous* fingerings and bowings for practice purposes is injurious, when the technical portions of a *piece which is to be played* are used for this purpose. So long as the player occupies himself with *general* technical formulas, it seems reasonable if, on occasion, the difficulties to be overcome are artificially increased, in order that they may afterwards appear easier than originally written. In *applied technique*, however, one of the very chief ends we must attain is the discovery of the *least exerting* and most appropriate and most serviceable form of movement in the shape of the best fingerings and bowings. Parts of a piece, a living organism, to be performed, are too precious to be utilized as subjects for experiment. Besides, the employ of two different kinds of fingering or bowing, one fatiguing and the other effortless, would unquestionably be injurious by leading to chronic insecurity. Quite as dangerous for the collective presentation of a work of art seems to be the use of parts of pieces in the practice of *general* technical formulas, especially for bowings. Undoubtedly, the bowing

927.

grafted on the well-known passage in the *Beethoven* Concerto:

Beethoven, Ct°, 1° Mov't.

928.

will appear in greater perfection than before after it has been practised for a certain length of time; but unfortunately its musical meaning has been lost on the way. In purely technical training only musical images which are ***not*** intended or suited for public performance, hence are primarily exercises, should be used. It is, in truth, conceivable that the artist who, intellectually and technically, stands on a lofty plane, under the compulsion of certain necessities (as, for instance, lack of time), without doing violence to his collective artistic personality, may take the liberty of substituting the practice of difficult repertoire-passages for daily exercises of a general technical nature. Yet—*quod licet Jovi, non licet bovi.*

Abno- mal Meth- of Practi- ing

The examples of incorrect modes of practice hitherto given, at least possess in common a certain logic, though it be one founded on false premises. Yet there are also modes of practice which seem to have originated in an *abnormal* condition of mind. As a rule their unfortunate possessors treasure them as precious secrets, which their imaginations credit with the best results. This is the reason why only a comparatively small number of them are made public. It is almost inconceivable that there are violinists who practise the notes of a note-sequence in an *inverse* order. These very persons would probably say that an elocutionist was insane if he were to read a poem backward to its beginning for purposes of practice. Less absurd, yet equally injurious is the *reversal of the bow-stroke* for practice purposes. At a pinch I can understand a violinist's practising a *détaché* study with a correct and an incorrect bowing, although the utility of this complication appears open to question. To misuse a certain definite part of a *piece which is to be played* for such trifling, however, is senseless, because its consequence is insecurity of the bowing mechanism, which shows itself especially in public performance. In the same class belongs the entire *elimination* of the *thumb* during practice. No doubt, in the case of cramped contraction of the ball of the thumb, and rigid clamping of the violin-neck between forefinger and thumb, this procedure may have a beneficial effect. In general, however, the thumb support is such an extraordinarily important prerequisite for the dropping of the fingers, change of position and holding of the instrument, that we can dispense with it for any greater length of time as little as the lungs can do without oxygen—though holding one's breath for a longer period may, on occasion, have a strengthening effect on the lungs. The use of too *heavy a bow* when practicing calls for a warning, since on subsequent use of a light bow, unfamiliarity with the new weight proportions is apt to confuse.

Similarly the advantage of an exaggeratedly *high string position* for practice purposes is questionable. The possible advantage of the fingers being strengthened by means of the necessarily stronger and more penetrant finger-pressure seems illusory when compared with the disadvantage of an unnaturally increased bow-pressure. Playing *without a supporting cushion* in the case of long-necked violinists (especially if habitually accustomed to use a cushion) can be dangerous and may cause an arm affection due to over-exertion or, at the least, of a diminution of sureness in change of position.

In conclusion we shall touch upon a few hygienic rules which apply generally.

The Hygiene of Practice

giene
actice

1. When beginning one's daily exercises, while arm and fingers still are stiff and awkward from the nocturnal period of rest, in short, when one has not yet "found one's fingers," even the finest player will lack those tonal qualities which ordinarily are peculiar to him. It is a direct disadvantage to sensitive old Italian instruments to make use of them at this stage of practicing. The use of a *second violin* (when possible a copy of one's own concert instrument, with the same proportions) for the first daily exercise means taking a noticeable burden from the concert instrument, hence a sparing of its tonal qualities whereby its lease of life is positively extended for decades. (See p. 13.)

2. One must see to it that the *desk* of the *music-stand* is on a level with the eyes. A desk which is placed too low is apt to mislead the player, to make him hold the instrument too low, something very injurious to tone-production (a pencil should be attached to the stand itself).

3. To use violin exercises to warm *cold fingers* when beginning to practice means a loss of time. Many prefer to dip the hands into very hot water and to leave them there about a minute, by which means the warming-up process is carried out almost instantaneously. (*Kreisler.*)

4. Before beginning to work one should test the *strings*, using intervals of a minor *sixth*, to verify their purity of pitch with relation to each other. One should never practice on strings which are false, for in order to play in pitch they compel one to take the notes incorrectly with the fingers, or if one takes them correctly, to play out of tune—hence either the sense of hearing or the sureness of the hand is jeopardized.

5. Many violinists have the bad habit of drawing the bow across the open *strings* again and again, without any valid reason, as though they were permanently out of tune. This bad habit, indicative of an unsettled nature, is particularly objectionable because the concentration absolutely necessary while studying is continually interrupted.

6. At the beginning of the day's work the pitch of the instrument should be fixed by means of a tuning-fork or a properly tuned piano, since one's sense of hearing as well as the instrument itself suffers from changing pitch when the strings are differently tuned every day.

7. *Fingerings and bowings* should be written down clearly and neatly in the music. A printed page lacking neatness, fingerings crossed out, slurs and ties tangled up with one another, confuses the visual memory and very often is the cause of mistakes which again give rise to errors of memory. Every fingering which seems to be impracticable should not alone be struck out but, so far as possible, made *invisible.*

8. A *rest pause* of a quarter of an hour should be made after every hour of practice, during which time one should do something else, read, or even better, do nothing at all. Practice unbroken by pauses for several hours in succession is extremely injurious to one's power of concentration.

9. The external conditions under which the player practices should be as little fatiguing as possible. Therefore, during a longer practice period, one should not *stand* throughout the entire sessions. Works which are to be played *seated* should also be practiced in that position. (See p. 15.)

10. One should never practice near an *open window*. When the weather is bad it may injure the instrument and the strings, at all events it disturbs the neighbors and, on occasion, may lead to reprisals on the part of some neighboring radio owner.

11. One should not indulge one's self while practicing in clothes which are too comfortable (taking off one's collar, etc.), since on the concert-stage, on occasion, unaccustomed evening dress may have a very constricting effect.

12. When one's work is finished one should never neglect *cleaning* the instrument and bow from the day's accumulation of dust.

5. The Musical Memory

Memory

The matter of *learning* or *acquiring* which thus far has occupied our attention, consists among other things, in the purpose of fixing our technical and spiritual achievements in our memory. Scientific observation has proved that within the range of memory itself we have two very different predispositions: the *acoustic-motoristic* and the *visual* type. The violinist unquestionably belongs to the first type, that is, the musical impressions renew themselves within him principally in the form of sound and movement pictures; yet recollection of the printed music may also come to his aid. For our purposes, it is true, we must separate the acoustic from the motoristic conceptions. Hence we distinguish among:

1. The *acoustic.*
2. The *motoristic.*
3. The *visual memory.*

Conscious and Subconscious Memory

A good musical memory is nearly always *subconscious.* When *conscious* recollection and reflection interpose themselves, a hindrance arises. When the violinist wishes to account to himself for the carrying on of the melodic line or the technical execution of a series of notes immediately before he plays them, without exception a stoppage takes place at the moment of reflection. Whoever wishes to rely upon his memory must see to it that the course of movement (not the course of feeling) occurs automatically. The ideal interpreter should combine the highest subjectivity, immediacy and receptive freedom with a technical apparatus which is altogether subconscious and obedient to the slightest inward hint. The necessary movements are suggested by the printed page, furthermore by the fingerings and bowings indicated in it, the exact fixation of which is therefore absolutely essential. With regard to normal capacity we might remark that first of all, in the case of every violinist, there is only *one* "best" fingering and bowing, the one most in keeping with his technical disposition and his interpretative needs. Secondly, *accidental fingerings* and bowings not only fail to comply with the requirements already mentioned, but also make the technical accomplishment uncertain and dependent upon chance. Thirdly, the insertion and comprehension of the proper signs, and their recognition by the eye, can but be most beneficial for the memory picture which is to be retained. In order that the inward conception of a series of notes be really anchored in our consciousness, it is well to see its outward picture as often as possible. The oftener we play a piece from the printed page, the more often, besides the tone which we *hear* and the movement which we *feel*, will the notes which we *see* be visualized for us. And if, later, when we are playing by heart, we are able to dispense with it, we still will be able to recall its outward semblance. This *visual memory* is, unfortunately, an auxiliary the value of which in securing a reliable general musical memory is often underestimated. Most violinists believe in order to be sure of a piece they have memorized that they should play it as frequently as possible *without* music. For the reasons already given the direct opposite is the case. Violinists endowed with extraordinary memories often, after having played a piece from memory for a time, feel the need of taking up the notes again in order to refresh their faded recollections by means of the visible symbols of the notes. Those who do not do this are in danger of gradually unlearning a composition of which they formerly were sure, and even of forgetting it altogether.

Visual Memory

Study of a Piece

We already obtain a superficial view of the musical construction as well as the emotional content of a composition while noting its fingerings and bowings. As soon as this preliminary work has been done we must undertake to look at it in a purely musical way—*even before we have mastered it technically*—and should play the piece frequently with an accompanying instrument, usually the piano.

Generally speaking, it is a mistake to wish to master a piece *first* technically and *afterwards* musically.

Whoever studies the violin part of a work without being acquainted with its general harmonic construction suggests a Romeo who knows only the cues of his Juliet, without having ever seen her. A technical performance may be "correct" when it attains exact reproduction of the notes; but it can have meaning only when its presentation adapts itself to the character of the composition as a whole. Hence we must know where we are with regard to the structure and mood content of a tone-poem before we can begin its actual *technical* study.

This last, in first instance, calls for: *Segregation* of those portions (*cantilene*) which make no exacting demands on technical facility. Slow tonal successions possess great value as carriers of emotional effect, although technically considered they consist of simple, quite easily learned movements. How nonsensical it is to expend the same amount of time upon their practice as we would upon figures technically difficult, yet more or less negligible with regard to emotional content, has already been discussed.

Since the movement sequences in the left hand are more manifold than in the right, we will begin with the left hand. In so doing, certain quite definite, narrowly bounded technical hindrances will soon force themselves upon our attention; they call for separation and isolated practice. The same thing occurs again with regard to the right arm (schematic bowing exercise, etc.). This choice of movement sequences in need of improvement is continued until all hindrances have been eliminated. By this time, as a rule, the transformation of voluntary into involuntary movements has also taken place. For purposes of control the composition as a whole is then played with piano accompaniment, any inaccuracies which exist are corrected, and the piece (rational methods of practice having been taken for granted) will finally be firmly fixed in the mind as well as the fingers.* Now it must also become part of one's flesh and blood, by repeated repetition at longer intervals, still paying careful attention to every possibility of improvement. The step of public performance should be ventured upon only when the work has received its baptism of fire in familiar surroundings, in the presence of friendly auditors. Not until then will that feeling of security, of ability to rely upon one's technical apparatus, of fusion with the spiritual content which makes it possible for us to do our best, take possession of us.

Improvement of Mem

Now comes the question as to the steps to be taken when the student or we ourselves *cannot* manage to reproduce a work perfectly from memory. First discover which of the three types of memory has been neglected and must be accounted guilty. *Visual* mnemonic weakness will be indicated when we cannot recall the *printed* page; *acoustic mnemonic* weakness, again, is shown when we cannot *sing* the piece in question by heart. The most frequently occurring cause of stoppage of memory lies in the *defective mechanization of the movement processes*, usually as a result of incorrect practising. In this connection it is evident that often, when one type of memory gives out, another leaps into the breach to save the day, that, for instance, when the fingers fail to find the proven fingering the violinist's inner tonal conception will discover the right notes, though his fingerings may be wrong, and he must compel nerves and will to make a strong effort. Furthermore, it is a fact that when the player's acoustic and motoristic memory fails him, he unconsciously calls on his visual memory to aid him—he tries in spirit to reconstruct the printed page as a whole—like the drowning man who, in his last moment, sees his whole life pass before him with lightning-like rapidity. Thirdly and finally: When the player, whose excitement is natural, while reviewing a composition mentally, *before* the first public performance, feels that the thread of continuity has broken, there is only one thing for him to do: quickly take up his violin and allow his fingers, which fortunately do not think, to do their work automatically.

mory
r

Among the physical hindrances which oppose themselves to the realization of our artistic intentions, that of "*memory fear*" ranks first. In particular we have been *thinking in advance*, that is, the bad habit of unjustifiably visualizing the finger and bowing movements long *before* we come to a certain dreaded passage, which produces a condition of tormentful restlessness.

It happens, furthermore, in the case of violinists otherwise highly gifted, and in spite of correct study, that *stoppages* always recur at certain points, in the form of an *outbreak of fear*, or psychical impotence, against which the player should struggle bravely already in his younger years. A player who interrupts a performance before listeners because of sudden mnemonic weakness is like a soldier who flings down his weapons on the battlefield at the mere sight of the enemy. What in our profession as in that of the actor is colloquially known as "swimming" (faking), means nothing more or less than the faculty of saving one's self from destruction in a dangerous situation by presence of mind. Habitual stopping at the least unimportant disturbance of the mechanical apparatus merely indicates a combination of inner disheartedness and weakened will power. If the teacher does not combat this condition of mind with the necessary energy it may turn into a permanent disqualification, making public appearance impossible.

We have mentioned that subconsciousness of feeling as well as self-assurance with regard to technical constituent parts, represent the ideal condition for artistic interpretation (in contrast to conscious analysis during practice). Yet it must be observed that, given certain conditions, entirely conscious reflection and action become a necessity, even while playing in public. When, for example, the theme with each repetition modulates into another key, or individual measures are dropped, etc., then our memory must seek certain points of support:

Conscious Memorizing

929. 
4 times
Brahms, Cto, 3º Mov't.

930. 
2 times

+ begins with G double sharp and remains in F sharp major.

931. 
Dohnányi, Cto, 1º Mov't.

+ begins with G sharp and modulates to D major.

932. 
Dohnányi, Cto.

933. 
(the same)

934. 

935. 

936. 

937. 

938. 

939. 

Similarly, when it is a question of a series of variations. The *Bach Chaconne* is often, and rightly, divided for study purpose, in single variations. At times there are mnemonic stoppages with regard to the *sequence* of the variations. Here we aid ourselves when studying the individual variations by always beginning with the *close* of the preceding one. Changes in the leading of the thematic line also may be impressed on the memory by a *change of bowing.* For instance:

940. 941. 

The same holds good for *changing fingerings*:

942. 943. 

944. 

One of the most effective memory aids (not a mere technical facilitation) is the use of *similar fingerings* and bowings in *sequential* note successions:

945. 

946. 

947. 

948. 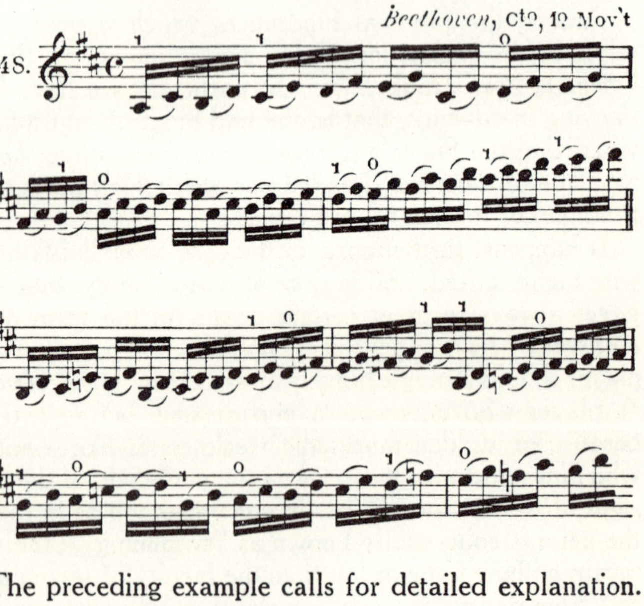

The preceding example calls for detailed explanation. Every solo violinist knows from experience that in the introduction of the *Beethoven* Violin Concerto the whole feeling of interpretative responsibility is, so to speak, concentrated to an almost oppressive degree, and stamps the greatly exposed passages in question as the most ticklish part of the entire work. Hence a fingering simple enough to exclude all possibility of error should be used for the broken thirds. This I secure by a practically complete elimination of the second position, substituting a primitive yet all the more secure alternation of the first and third positions.

Dont, Op. 35 No 2

949. 

(the same)

950. 

Tschaikowsky, Trio Op. 50 Fugue

951. 

Saint-Saëns, Cto, B min. 1o Mov't.

952. 

953. 

954. 

955. 

emov- g rors emory

In general, in the case of pupils who suffer from weak memory, and especially dread of it, I advise the following method: After the stoppage has occurred, I at once interrupt the pupil, we verify the mistake, and immediately begin to seek its cause together. In *cantilene* it usually is due to an incorrect carrying on of the motive when a modulatory crossroad has been reached (see p. 168). In purely technical figures, old, half-forgotten, discarded fingerings or bowings usually succeed in confusing the motoristic picture. Both conditions were hidden in the twilight of *subconsciousness*. They are now haled forth into the daylight of the conscious, logically analyzed and incorporated in the pupil's consciousness. From this moment on the error in question will not be repeated because we know its physic or motoristic cause. In this way all faults of memory which occur are tracked down until the inner conception has been cleansed, and is established in changeless clarity.

Conclusion

We have now come to the end of Book One (dealing with the acquisition of the technique of violin-playing) of our complete work. The *artistic realization*, which is the final end of our efforts; the *hindrances*, which oppose themselves to the realization of our loftiest artistic intentions, as well as the most practical mode of transmitting our experience in the form of vital *instruction* will form the subject of Book Two.

The present volume may be utilized from two different points of view. Firstly, it may be intensively studied as a whole, with comparison between new and hitherto existent opinions, in the course of which special effort should be made to rid one's self of many long-established and fondly cherished bad habits, which have installed themselves under the cloak of "*tradition.*"

Secondly, the book may be regarded as a *work of reference* in all cases in which doubts of any kind regarding the right mode of procedure may arise, whether in teacher or pupil. To this end a detailed *technical index* is intended to make it as easy as possible for those who use it to find that for which they are in search.

Only perfected mental and physical control of the separate disciplinary units, collectively known as technique, offers us a guarantee for the realization of our artistic intentions. The ability to carry out technically and to shape musically may be compared to man's bodily and mental activities. Just as the soul cannot develop freely unless the body be healthy, so our power of expression depends first of all on the type as well as the extent of our technical ability. It is this possession alone upon which the proud edifice of true art may be erected.

End of Book One

APPENDIX

Technical Index -- Index of Composers, Artists, etc.
Index of Music Examples
Illustrations

TECHNICAL INDEX

(The Numerals refer to the pages, the hyphens indicate the key-word.)

Accents during up-bow 95. Division of Bow for—64. Brake —161. Definition of—94. Three Varieties of—95. Pressure—68. —through the left-hand 95. Mechanics of the—68. —during *piano* 96. —as tonal studies 98. Unjustified initial—97, 155. Undesirable—96.

Accompanying Noises (*see also Tonal Defects*) in connection with Tone Production, 81, 82. —with three-toned chords 84. Neglect to do away with—86. Rattling or buzzing—87. Scratchy—88. —as caused by the Orchestra Attack 97. Whistling—127.

Applied Technic (see *Technic*).

Arm, The left—17. The right—50.

Arpeggios 62. Tied—+Thrown or Springing—79.

Attack 95. —without accent 96.—of the bow 96. Guiding lines for the—96. Orchestra—97. —during *piano* 96.

Beginners, Position playing of—26. Instruction for—5.

Body, Position of the—14. Movements of the—14.

Bow-Changes 58. Faulty—60. —at the Nut 59. Historic development of—59. Ideal—60.—at the tip 59.—through means of "stroke-continuation" 59. *Brilliancy* at expense of accuracy 159.

Bow Division. Importance of correct—156.

Bow-Hairs, Renewal of—14. Tightening of—53, 58, 88.

Bowing, General remarks, 51. Mechanics of—54. Preferable—for gaining certain tonal advantages 150.

Bow-Pressure 53, 58. Exaggerated—85. Insufficient—85.

Bow-Stick, Smoothing down edge of frog of—13. Properties of the—13, 88. Weight of the—13, 88. Division of weight of the—53.—with rubber winding at the frog 13. Shorter—13. Position of the—53, 57. Crooked —88. Trembling of the—88. (See also Bowing Varieties).

Bowing Varieties (see also *Bow-stroke, Detaché, Martelé, Legato, Staccato*) choice of—148, 153. Definition of the thrown—73, 76. Function of the small finger for the thrown—76. Mixed—78, 153. —prescribed by the composer 148. Short—68. Long—64. Unbuoyant—97. Buoyant—99. Springing—73. Thibaud's—80. Difference between long and short—68. Viotti's—72. Undulating—(see *Portato*).

Bow-Stroke, Direction of the—51. Faulty direction of the—57.

Bow-Stroke Exercises, schematic—160.

Bridge, Customary moving of the—13. Height of the—12. Rounding of the—12, 87. Thickness of the—12. Position of the—12, 88.

Change of String (left) 25. Stretching to avoid unnecessary—123.

Change of String (right). Intermittent—63. Mechanics of—61. Regular—during Détaché 151. Scheme of—163. Undulating and angular movements during—61.

Chinrest 16.

Chords. —Breaks 83, 154. Mechanics of Bow for—83. Fingering for—143. —during *forte* 92. Point of contact for—83. Breaking of the tone with—84.

Chromatic Scales (see *Scales*).

Combination Tones 22.

Crescendo 94. —with Up- or Down-bow 94.—through lifting of the Violin 94. Unjustified—96. Too rapid a —94.

Cushion 15.

Détaché 66, 150. Division of bow for—66. French—67. —at the Nut 66, 151. —with whole bow 66, 98, 99, 150. —with whole bow+Martelé+Thrown Bow 79. —+spun tone 78. Large, broad—66.—+Half-bow stroke 154. Short, small—67. Painful right arm hindrance while using the—and possible cure 67. Scratchy—67, 86. —+Legato 79, 154. Martelé+small— (Nut) 80. Martelé+small—(Tip) 79. Regular change of strings during—151. "Tossing" or "flinging" about of the wrist while playing—67. —or Springing Bow 151.—(Middle)+Springing Bow 80. Indistinct—86.—+Thrown Staccato 80.

Decrescendo 94. Mechanics of—94. —through lowering of the Violin 94. Unjustified—96.

Division of Bow for accents 64. —for avoiding faulty accents 156. General remarks 63. —for Détaché 66. —during Legato 65. —during Thrown and Rebounding bow 73, 154. —and Bowing Varieties 64.

Double-Stops in widely separated positions 83. Point of contact with—83. —in *Forte* 92. Breaking of the tone in—86. (See also Thirds, Fourths, Fifths, Sixths, Octaves, Tenths).

Down-Bow during forte 91. —during change of string 62. Repeated—78. (See also Up-bow).

Drum Stroke 75. Methods of practise 75.

Dryness of the Air 87.

Dynamic Faults 96.

Dynamics, General—90. (See also *forte, piano, crescendo, decrescendo, accent*).

Echo Effects, Fingering for—147. Spring bow for—151.

Enharmonic Changes 143.

Etude Material 114.

Exercises, Invention of original—163.

Expression, Transferring of—101.

Final Note of a passage 159.

Fifths, Fingering for—137. Broken—in slow tempo 137.

Fingering for chords 143. —in General 118. —as a means for expression 144. —for chromatic tonal passages 134. —for chromatic *glissandi* 142. —for tenths 141. —for echo effects 147. —through change of finger on the same note 129, 148. Similar—170. —in the same position 119. —and enharmonic changes 143. —and tone colors 146. —for artificial harmonics 143. —and change of position 127. —for octaves 139. —for *Portamenti* 144. —for playing on individual strings 147. —for fourths 136. —for fifths 137. —and choice of strings 146. —for chords of the seventh 132. —for sixths 138. —as technical means 119. —for thirds 135. —for scales 130. —for trills 142. Selection of either fourth finger or open string 120. —for broken thirds 132. —for broken triads 131. Simplified—for introduction of Beethoven's Violin Concerto 170.

Fingers (left hand) Setting of—18. *Pressure* of the—18, 29. *Fall* of the—18. Simultaneous setting of the—126. *Position* of the—17. *Holding down* of the—125. *Nails* of the—18. *Tips* of the—18, 103. *Stretching* of the—120. *Substitution* of the third for the *fourth*—117, 128. Special exercises for the fourth finger 118. Fourth—or open string 120. Pressing together of the —124. Exceptional use of one of the—124.

Fingers (*right hand*) (see also *holding of the bow and bowing*). Cold—167. Fourth or ring—54.

Fingerstroke, Significance of—58. Learning the—58. Mechanics of the—58.

Forte 90. —during down-bow 91. —with chords 92. Definition of—90. —with Double-stops 92. —with the spun tone 91. Various carrying powers of the—90. —during *Legato* 92. Two varieties of producing the —91.

Fourths, Fingering for—136.

Fundamental Movements of the Left Arm 23. —of the right arm 54.

General Technic (see *Technic*).

Glissando (See also *Portamento*, Change of position and intermediary note). Chromatic—42. Fingering for chromatic—142. Difference between—and *Portamento* 28. Avoiding of the—through change of bow 150.

Half-Bow Strokes+Détaché 154.

Hand Position (left) 17. —(right) 58. Some varieties of—58.

Harmonics, Learning the—48. Fingering for artificial—143. Artificial—48. Natural—47. Correct application of natural—47, 127. Improper use of natural—47, 126. Resounding of natural—48. Causes for failure of natural—48. Point of application in the case of—127.

Head, its position 16.

Holding the Bow, Three ways of—51. Participation of lower arm while—51. Learning the Russian manner of—52. Changing to the Russian manner of—52. Advantages of the Russian manner of—52.

Index Finger (left) Leaning of the—against neck of the violin 18.

Index Finger (right). Use of the—53.

Inflamed Neck 16.

Instrument (see also Violin) The—and its component parts 7.

Intermediary Note (see also *Change of Position, Glissando, Portamento*) Wrong—during change of position 29. Establishing the distance in position changes through means of the—27. Abuse of the—27. Its relativity 35. —as a means for practising 161.

Intonation 19. General remarks about—20. Bowing while correcting the—21. Influence of—on the purity of tone 103. Correction of the impure tone 20. Practical—studies for improvement of hearing 21. Impossibility of playing absolutely in tune 20. Quarter tones 22. Changing pitch of one and the same note 22.

Legato 65, 150. Division of bow during—65. —+Détaché 79, 154. —during Forte 92. Point of contact during—92. —+Springing Bow 154. —+Thrown staccato 79.

Martelé 68, 151. —+small Détaché (Nut) 80, 155. —small Détaché (Tip) 79, 155.

Memory, General remarks about—167. Similar (parallel) fingerings and bowings for support of the—170. Change of fingering and bowings for support of the—170. —Hindrances 169. —Control 169. Method of memorizing 168. Musical—168. Outbreak of fear 169. Visual—167. Weak—and remedy for same 171.

Methods of Practise, Increasing the difficulties of—158. Unserviceable—164.

Methods (System) of Study of former times 3.

Middle Finger (right hand) 54.

Mute, see Sordino.

Nut, Change of bow at the—59. Détaché at the—150. (See also *Bowing Varieties*.)

Octaves, Simple—with 1 and 4 fingers 44. Learning of fingered —43. —with fingering in scales and broken triads 43, 139. Tempo of the onward movement in connection with simple—140.

Ondulé, see *Portato*.

Open String, see *String* and *Finger*.

Over-Exertion 19.

Perspiration of the Fingers 19.

Phonograph Recording 18.

Piano 92. Attack during—96. —at the fingerboard 93. —through bending of the upper part of body toward the right 93. —with "shoulder pedal" 93. —at lower half of bow 93. —with diminished pressure 93. —during an accent 96.

Pizzicato (left hand) 49.

Pizzicato (right hand) 49.

Point of Contact between bow and strings 81. —with double-stops and chords 83. Establishing the—81. Visual control of the—82. Change of—81,82. —during *Legato* 92.

Portamento, Descending—33. Emotional value of the—30. —through means of accented half-tone 33. Accented—145. B—(gliding with the commencing finger) 30. L—(gliding with the ending finger) 30. Combination of the B and L—34. Choice between the B and L—32, 145. Ascending and descending—146. Impressiveness of the—32, 145. —with faulty increasing and decreasing tonal volume 34. Fingering for the—144. —through means of the same finger 145. Isolated—145. —from the open string 146. —to the open string 34. Rapid—34. Stretching to avoid the—123. Thibaud's—34. Predominance of the musical esthetic over the technical impulse of the—32. Inaudible intermediate note during the—32. Unmotived—144. Difference between—and Glissando 28. —in combination with Nuances 145. —through more distantly separated fingers 145. Choice of the executing finger for the—31, 144. —between separated bow strokes 33. —between two Harmonics 127.

Portato 73. Unjustified, habitual—97. —as a tonal exercise 85, 98.

Position Change 25. Descending—26. —through means of B or L Glissando 128. Ascending—27. Definition of the surety of—27. Wrong intermediate notes for—29. Establishing the distance through means of the intermediate note in—27. Fingering in—127. —on the strong beat 29, 128. —on half tones 29, 128. Mechanics of—26. Faulty use of intermediary notes during—27. Quick or slow—29. Stretches for avoiding unnecessary—123. Actual distance in—126. Needless —130. —through means of the same finger 28. —or change of string 130. Wide or close-lying—29. Avoiding—in broken octaves 139.

Position of the Legs 14. —while facing an audience 15.

Position Playing 25. —with Beginners 26. Its neglect 26.

Positions, Simultaneous use of two different—129. Half—121. Intermediary position 27. Relative value of marking the —118.

Practising, General remarks 104. —of the general left-hand technic 108. —of the general right-hand technic 108. —of applied technic 118. Examples of correct methods for—159. Doing away with mechanical hindrances while—157. —through means of different intermediary notes 161. —through means of "brake" accents 161. Fallacy of brilliant—159. Extracts of solo compositions as exercising material 166. —of cantilena movements 165. Continuous accentuation while—165. Elimination of the thumb while—166. —with exaggerated high string position 166. Hygiene of—105. Slow—158. —too slowly 165. Mechanical—157. —with a metronome 161, 165. —as a means for learning 157. —at the open window 167. —passages with reversal of the bow-stroks 166. —with rhythmic changes 161. —with too heavy a bow 166. Self-control while—159, 161. —self-invented Etudes 163. —while seated 15, 167. —the Scale System 108. —Mute exercises 24, 163. —transposition of difficult passages 163. Separation of technical problems while—157. Exaggerations while—105, 164. Changing of original version while—158. —with reversed bow-stroke 166. Exaggerated use of intermediary notes while—166. —with or without Vibrato 165. Exaggerated repetitions while—165. —as repetition 105.

Preface 3.

Pressure, see *Bow-Pressure.*

Pressure Accent 86.

Pressure Pause 68.

Printed Page. Clear and correct—167.

Realization, Definition of Artistic—6.

Relaxation of the motive apparatus 19.

Rest Periods while studying 167.

Rosin 14, 88.

Saltati 76. —+Thrown staccato +Legato 80.

Scales, Chromatic—42, 134. Chromatic Glissando—42. Chromatic—in Thirds 43. 136, Chromatic—in Octaves 43. Simple, diatonic—40, 130. —in simple octaves 44. —in fingered octaves 43. —in Sixths 44, 138. —in Thirds 42. See also Scale System.

Scale System (Flesch) 108. Methods for practising the—113. —in connection with applied tèchnic 113. —in connection with tonal exercises 113. —in connection with bowing exercises 113.

Sevčik's Study Works, Characteristics of—115. Methods for study of same 115.

Seventh Chords, broken—41. Fingering for broken—132. A rule for dominant or diminished—and explanation therefore 132.

Shoulderjoint 55.

Shoulderpedal 93.

Sixths, Fingering for—44, 138.

Sordino 103.

Spring Bow Stroke 73. Lifting of the little finger for—74. Bow division for—153. Détaché or—151. —in echo effects 151. Position of the stick in the—74. —+Legato 154. Methods of practising the—75. —through means of lower arm or wrist 74. Selection of most suitable part of bow for—74. —+Thrown Bow+Thrown Staccato 80.

Springing Arpeggios 76.

Spun Tone 61, 91. —+Détaché 78. —during forte 91. —+Staccato 79. "Mute"—98. —as a tonal study 98. —while interpreting 149.

Staccato during Down Bow, upper half,—during Down Bow lower half. 71, 152. Up or Down Bow—72. Significance of the—69. Mechanics of—69. Necessity of —77. Flying—77. Irregular—71. Normal learning of the—69. Martelé—69, 151. Springing—75. Stationery—78. Stiff—71. Concluding note of a—passage 152. —and division of Bow 152. —Corrections 70. Faulty cooperation between right arm and left hand for—72. Psychic hindrances in—71. Substitution of—through Springing Bow 152. Substitution of—through the Viotti stroke 72. —+Spun tone 79.

Stage Fright 89.

Stretching, its dangers 24. Forward and Backward—120. Unnecessary—124. —to avoid unnecessary position or string change 123. —to avoid *Portamenti* 146. Advantage of backward—122. Example of disagreeable —124.

Strings (see also Tone colors). Drawing (pulling out) of the—12. Simultaneous touching of two—with the bow 87. Whistling of the—86. Testing the purity of the—9, 167. Strength of the—9. Tuning of the—11, 167. Open—or 4th finger 120. Open—sounding an octave higher 41. Deterioration of tonal color through open—148. Covered D—9. Steel E—, their advantages and disadvantages 10, 87. Advisability of certain changes for tuning steel E—12. Measuring of the G—9. Rattling of the G—87.

Survey of the Work 6.

Syncopations, Wrong accentuation of—150.

Talent, Original—4.

Technic, Definition of general—6. Definition of Applied—6, 104. Fundamental forms of—of the left hand, 40. Fundamental forms of—of the right arm, 50.

Technic in General, see *Technic.*

Tenths 45. Fingering for—141.

Thirds, Method of learning—43. Chromatic scales in—43, 136. Fingering for—135. Fingering for broken—132. Problems of tonal purity with—43, 44. Scales in—42. Broken—42, 132.

Thrown Bow Stroke, 73, 77. Application of the—77. Selecting the most suitable part of the bow for the —77. Division of Bow for the—73, 153. —for double stops during change of string 154. Substitution of Martelé for the—154. —or Springing Bow 153. —+Thrown Staccato 154.

Thrown Stacato 77. —+Détaché 80. Substitution of Saltato for—154. —+Legato 79.

Thumb (left) Cramp-like contraction of the ball of the—19. Correct position of the—17. Lower position of the—17. Advance movement of the—27.

portato
martelé
staccato
dynamics
alla breve signe = ¢
agogic
ritard. (rallent.)
allargando
calando
tempo rubato 57 } 57

Read only a single technical point or idea
(148)(2) = 300] & understand well
(230)(2) = 460
760 and [illegible] 2+ yrs @ 1 col/day
Just to keep technique in intellect
Read only [illegible]

Trill, Definition of the—45. Fingering for the—141. ...ormal learning of the—45. Valuable study material for the—46. The inverted mordent 47. Chain—47. Goat's (Bocks)—47. Hindrances during the—46. —after-beats 47. —in double stop scale succession 142.

Tuning—11.

Up or Down Bow 149. —during *crescendo* 94. —during string transfers 62. —during staccato 72.

Up-Bow, with Accents, 95.

Upper Arm (left) see Arm.

Upper Arm (right) (see also Arm) Holding of the—55. Lifting movements of the—55. Horizontal movements of the—55.

Urstudien, their use 23, 108

Vibrato 35. Its continued use 40. Duties of the pedagog in connection with the—40. —as expression 101. Too broad (Wrist)—37. Its influence upon tone quality 35. Too close (Finger)—37. Possibility of learning the—37. Too high or too low—39. Indirect—and how obtained 39. Café and Moving Picture—39. Correction of too broad a—38. Correction of too close a—37. Correction of the stiff lower-arm—38. Cramped thumb pressure during—38. Probable cause of—impotence 38. Lack of need for the—38. Mechanics of the — 36. Subsequent — 39. Stiff lower arm — 37. Origin of the—36.

Violin, Purchase of a—8. Judging the tonal qualities of a—8. Firm holding of the—35. "Lined"—7. Size of the—7. Position of the—15. Italian—7. Opening of the—13. Care of the—9, 166. Direction in which—is held 15. Mute—103. *Second* or Practise—13, 166. Comparison between — 8. Diminishing the string pressure on the—9. (see also Instrument.)

Whole-Bow Stroke, see *Détaché* or *Spun* Tone.

Wrist (right) Problems of the—56. Horizontal—movement 56. "Tossing" or "flinging about" of the—for Détaché 67. Vertical—movements 57.

N1404

INDEX OF COMPOSERS, ARTISTS, ETC.

(The numbers refer to the respective pages.)

Alard, Delphin 114
Amati, Nicolo 16
Auer, *Leopold* 45, 51, 114
Bach, Johann Sebastian 11, 99, 170
Baillot, François 3, 8, 67, 110
Barmas, J. 19
Beethoven, L. van ... 10, 105, 113, 126, 132, 148, 166, 170
Benda, Franz 114
Bériot, Charles de 3, 4, 114
Berlioz, Hector 48, 149
Bloch, Josef 114
Bosse, Gustav 5
Brahms, Johannes 22, 45, 49, 63, 114
Bull, Ole 87
Capet, Lucien 3, 54, 65, 66
Caressa, Felix Albert 14
Cherubini, Luigi 8
Chopin, Frederic 114, 122
Dancla, Charles 114
Debussy, Claude 49
Dessoir, Max 5
Dont, Jakob 114, 115
Elman, Mischa 126
Enesco, Georges 18
Ernst, H. W. 6, 114, 115
Fiorillo, Federigo 3, 114, 115
Fischer, Carl, Inc. 114
Flesch, Carl 54, 89, 108, 115
Gaviniés, Pierre 3, 114
Grün, J. M. 158
Guarnerius, Joseph del Gésu 8, 16
Haba, J. 22
Hammig, W. H. 9
Hansen, Wilhelm 114
Heermann, Hugo 9
Hellmesberger, Josef, Senior 40, 81
Helmholtz, Hermann 20
Hill, William 14
Hoffmann, Max Heinrich Franz 48, 115, 143
v. d. Hoya, Amadeus 5
Hubay, Jenö 114
Jahn, Artur 3, 51
Jani, Nagy 141
Jarosy, Albert 118
Joachim, Josef 3, 40, 69, 101
Kayser, H. E. 3
Klingler, Karl 3, 17, 26, 27, 68
Kreisler, Fritz 4, 15, 91, 123, 142, 167
Kreutzer, Rodolphe ... 3, 4, 8, 46, 53, 56, 61, 114, 115, 142
Küchler, Ferdinand 5, 118
Lamoureux, Charles 12
Lange, Hans 11
Léonard, Hubert 3, 75
Liszt, Franz 114
Locatelli, Pietro 114, 132
Lolly, Antonio 48
Lombardini, Signora 22
Maggini, G. P. 7
Mahler, Gustav 4
Marsick, M. P. 17, 66
Massart, Lambert 56
Mayseder, Joseph 114
Mendelssohn-Bartholdy, Felix 77
Möllendorf, C. von 22
Mozart, Wolfgang A. 156
Nikisch, Artur 47
Paganini, Nicolo, 9, 11, 48, 67, 79, 100, 106, 114, 115, 123, 138, 141, 142
Petri, Henri 114
Prume, François 75, 114
Pugno, Raul 104
Reger, Max 138
Rivarde, Achille 37, 38
Rode, Pierre 3, 4, 8, 21, 114, 115
Rovelli, Pietro 114
Sarasate, Pablo de 18, 40, 47, 69, 81
Sauret, Emile 114, 115
Sauzay, Eugene 22, 110, 115
Savart, Felix 8
Scholz, H. 102
Schott, (B. Schott's, Söhne) 9
Schradieck, Henry 115
Schumann, Robert 49, 100, 114
Sevčik, Otokar, 4, 26, 41, 46, 47, 48, 50, 63, 78, 108, 114, 115, 116, 117, 126, 163
Sitt, Hans 114
Sivori, Camillo 40, 114
Spiering, Theodor 114
Spohr, Ludwig 3, 4, 48, 72, 114, 115, 152
Steinhausen, Friedrich A. 3, 53, 54
Stradivarius, Antonius 8, 16
Suk, Josef 142
Tartini, Giuseppe 22, 142
Thibaud, Jacques 18, 34, 55, 80
Thomson, César 19
Togni, Felix 114
Tourte aíne 13
Vidal, L. A. 8
Vieuxtemps, Henri 4, 114, 115
Viotti, G. B. 4, 72
Vuillaume, I. B. 7
Weininger, H. 102
Wieniawski, Henri 51, 114, 115, 142
Wilhelmj, August 11, 122
Ysaÿe, Eugene 30, 54, 101, 124

INDEX OF MUSIC EXAMPLES

(The numerals refer to successive order of the music examples.)

BACH. *Chaconne.* 2, 2a, 326, 781, 806, 807, 808, 809, 826.
A-Minor Partita. 161, 825.
B-Minor Partita. 546.
E-Major Partita. 153, 744, 746, 751, 906.
E-Minor Sonata. (David High School). 360, 689.
G-Minor Partita. 211, 277, 278, 790, 791, 855, 856, 889.
Concerto (E-Major). 276, 789.

BACH-WILHELMJ. *Aria.* 276a, 288, 718.

BAZZINI. *Ronde des Lutins.* 245.

BEETHOVEN. *Violin Concerto Op. 61.* 29, 30, 164, 171, 228, 252, 305, 319, 320, 329, 335, 349, 364, 397, 429, 435, 439, 449, 513, 514, 593, 594, 596, 649, 650, 652, 656, 679, 701, 829, 852, 887, 904, 928, 948.
Cadenza to Violin Concerto by Léonard 588, 623.
Piano Trio, Op. 70, No. 1. 755.
Piano Trio, Op. 70, No. 2. 225, 684, 686, 690, 734.
Piano Trio, G-Major, Op. 1, No. 2. 244, 775
Piano Trio, Op. 97. 318, 658, 774, 804.
Quartet, Op. 18. 290.
Quartet Op. 59, No. 1. 292.
Quartet Op. 59, No. 3. 792.
Quartet Op. 74. 735.
Quartet Op. 95. 284.
Quartet Op. 127. 275.
Romance (F-Major). 215, 270, 780, 925.
Romance (G-Major). 371, 727, 811.
Sonata (A-Major). 214, 779.
Sonata (A-Minor). 262.
Sonata (F-Major). 213, 793, 805.
Sonata, Op. 30, No. 2. 667.
Sonata, Op. 30, No. 3 (G-Major). 346, 685, 716, 771, 776.
Sonata, Op. 47 (Kreutzer Sonata). 233, 237, 337, 338, 339, 340, 341, 342, 683, 778, 902.

BRAHMS. *Double Concerto (Violin and Cello) Op. 102.* 647.
Piano Quartet, Op. 25. 162, 820.
Sonata, Op. 78. 416, 575.
Sonata, Op. 100, (A-Major). 706, 794.
Sonata, Op. 108 (D-Minor). 510, 705.
Trio, Op. 8. 380, 414, 440, 691, 722, 770.
Trio, Op. 101 (C-Minor). 557.
Trio, B-Major. 462.
Violin Concerto, Op. 77. 293, 399, 400, 401, 417, 431, 453, 465, 467, 468, 469, 471, 472, 473, 554, 589, 619, 702, 736, 768, 782, 810, 833, 840, 874, 875, 898, 916, 917, 929.

BRAHMS-JOACHIM. *Hungarian Dance, No. 1.* 374.
Hungarian Dance, No. 9. 372.

BRUCH (Max). *Concerto D-Minor, Op. 44.* 547.
Concerto G-Minor, Op. 26. 6, 7, 15, 16, 17, 77½, 271, 350, 361, 411, 412, 421, 422, 436, 566, 567, 586, 678, 708, 710, 712, 713, 714, 728, 731, 784, 796, 813, 862, 863, 880, 908.

CHAUSSON. *Poëme.* 402, 559, 578, 827 947.

CHOPIN-WILHELMJ. *Nocturne, Op. 27, No. 2.* 377, 378, 537.

CORELLI-LÉONARD. *La Folia.* 388.

DOHNÁNYI (Ernst von). *Violin Concerto, Op. 24.* 133, 133a, 160, 174, 363, 555, 563, 620, 648, 931, 932, 933, 934, 935, 936, 937, 938, 939.

DONT. *Caprice, Op. 35, No. 1.* 381, 847, 894, 907, 909.
No. 2. 425, 426, 456, 828, 949, 950.
No. 3. 482.
No. 4. 483.
No. 5. 382, 392, 618, 739, 838.
No. 7. 391, 615, 616, 617.
No. 11. 393, 394, 640.
No. 12. 481, 545.
No. 16. 282.

DVOŘÁK. *Dumky Trio.* 217.
Mazurka, Op. 49. 413.
Trio, Op. 65 (F-Minor). 279, 415, 455, 464, 645, 663, 687.
Violin Concerto, Op. 53. 720, 732.

ERNST. *Airs Hongrois.* 296, 463.
Concerto, Op. 23 (F♯ Minor). 274, 385, 386, 387, 460, 497, 572, 595, 604, 611, 638, 882.

FRANCK (César). *Sonata.* 169.

FRANCOEUR-KREISLER. *Rigaudon.* 344, 345.

GLAZOUNOW. *Violin Concerto, Op. 32.* 420, 521, 693, 797.

GOLDMARK. *Violin Concerto, Op. 28.* 886, 923.

HANDEL. *Sonata, D-Major.* 366.

HAYDN. *Quartet, D-Major.* 773.

JOACHIM. *Cadenza to Paganini Concerto.* 541.
Hungarian Concerto. 430, 542, 653, 892, 914, 920.
Variations. 365, 644.

KORNGOLD. *Suite Op. 11, No. 1.* 418, 419.
Suite Op. 11, No. 2. 944.

KREISLER. *Ballet-Music from Schubert's Rosamunde.* 912.
Caprice Viennois. 543, 544.

KREUTZER. *Etude No. 2.* 170, 173, 176, 177, 178, 179, 188, 189, 190, 191, 199, 200, 201, 202, 203, 220, 231, 232, 238, 239, 240, 241, 242, 246, 247, 248, 264, 265, 267, 317.
Etude No. 3. 20.
Etude No. 4. 180, 181, 182, 183, 226.
Etude No. 5. 321, 322, 323, 324, 905.
Etude No. 6. 152.
Etude No. 7. 146, 221a.
Etude No. 12. 398.
Etude No. 13. 121.
Etude No. 26. 151.
Etude No. 38. 125a.

LALO. *Concerto F-Minor.* 272, 676, 709.
Symphonie Espagnole. 137, 389, 390, 438, 445, 621, 664, 695, 696, 697, 785, 818, 822, 823, 824, 878, 946.

LEONARD. *Cadenza to Beethoven Violin Concerto.* 588, 623.

MENDELSSOHN. *Concerto, Op. 64.* 60, 64, 128, 165, 221, 230, 295, 348, 362, 427, 432, 433, 441, 454, 470, 517, 519, 592, 646, 657, 659, 669, 680, 694, 711, 723, 725, 812, 815, 857.
Piano Trio, Op. 49. 749, 750.

MOZART. *Concerto (A-Major).* 273, 814, 819.
Concerto (D-Major). 216, 286, 448, 698, 733.
Sonata (E-Minor). 212.

NARDINI. *Concerto E-Minor.* 287, 681, 688, 699.

PAGANINI. *Cadenza to Concerto, by Joachim.* 541.
Caprice, No. 1. 224, 629.
Caprice, No. 3. 597, 609.
Caprice, No. 5. 205.
Caprice, No. 11. 803.
Caprice, No. 12. 280.
Caprice, No. 17. 613.
Caprice, No. 18. 854.
Caprice, No. 21. 571.
Caprice, No. 23. 599, 607.
Caprice, No. 24. 142.
Concerto D-Major. 3, 459, 539, 549, 633, 654 (Wilhelmj), 851, 859, 860, 873, 918.
Moses Fantasia. 496.
Perpetuum Mobile. 194, 198.
Witches Dance. 139.

PAGANINI-KREISLER. *Caprice No. 20.* 370, 910.
I Palpiti. 579.

PIERNÉ. *Serenade.* 129.

PFITZNER. *Trio, Op. 8.* 577.

PUGNANI-KREISLER. *Prelude and Allegro.* 167, 428.

REGER (Max). *Sonata for Solo Violin, Op. 42, No. 1.* 4, 367, 368, 383, 444, 446, 447, 474, 475, 476, 477, 478, 479, 480, 560, 562, 580, 581, 582, 583, 610, 642, 643, 703, 704, 942, 943.

RODE. *Etude No. 3.* 281.
Etude No. 5. 163.
Etude No. 12. 306.
Etude No. 18. 587.

ROVELLI. *Etude No. 5.* 584, 595.

SARASATE. *Gipsy Airs.* 639, 861.
La Muniera. 257.
Spanish Dance No. 8. 540.
Zapateado. 138, 777.

SCHNABEL, ARTHUR. *Sonata for Violin Solo.* 409.

SCHRADIECK. *24 Etudes, No. 2.* 568.
From Exercises Book II. 884, 885.

SCHUBERT. *Rondo brillante.* 283.
Quartet, D Minor. 651.
Sonata, Op. 169, A Major. 608.
Trio (B Major). 243, 692.

SCHUBERT-KREISLER. *Ballet Music from Rosamunde.* 912.

SCHUBERT-WILHELMJ. *Ave Maria.* 612.

SCHUMANN. *Fantasiestücke.* 673.
Garden Melody. 700.
Piano Quintet. 747, 748.
Piano Trio, D Minor. 802.
Quartet, A Minor. 754.
Sonata, A Minor. 682.

SEVČIK. *School of Bowing, Book V.* 911, 913.
School of Violin Technique, Book 3, No. 7. 19.
System of Scales; Sequence of Broken Triads; Scales in Octaves, Thirds, Sixths, etc., according to Sevčik. 327.

SIBELIUS. *Violin Concerto.* 737, 763, 800, 801.

SINDING.. *Violin Concerto, A-Major.* 466, 564, 565, 668.

SMETANA. *String Quartet, E-Minor.* 130.

SPOHR.. *Concerto (Gesangsscene).* 74, 759.
Concerto, D-Minor. 373, 434, 665, 758, 766.
Concerto, E-Minor. 757.
Concerto, No. 9. 717.

ST. SAËNS. *3d Concerto (B-Minor), Op. 61.* 166, 168, 223, 297, 437, 461, 605, 674, 724, 730, 786, 787, 788, 817, 952, 953, 954, 955.

SUK. *Burleske (Four Pieces).* 781.
Fantasia, Op. 24. 622.
Op. 17, No. 1. 443.
Op. 17, No. 3. 726, 940, 941.

TARTINI. *Sonata G-Minor.* 672.
Sonata (Devil's Trill). 816.

TARTINI-KREISLER. *Devil's Trill Sonata.* 630.

TSCHAIKOWSKY. *Sérénade Melancholique, Op. 26.* 62.
Trio, Op. 50 (Fugue). 951.
Violin Concerto, Op. 35. 403, 552, 635, 707, 783, 821, 821½, 900.

VIEUXTEMPS. *Ballade and Polonaise.* 197, 761.
Concerto A-Minor. 172, 229, 289, 451, 671, 753.
Concerto D-Minor. 500, 772, 870.
Concerto E-Major. 197, 511, 598, 738, 752, 756, 767, 835, 867.
Fantaisie Caprice. 218.

VIOTTI.. *Concerto No. 22 (A-Minor).* 154, 745.

WIENIAWSKI. *Concerto, D-Minor, Op. 22.* 61, 134, 135, 136, 655, 661, 715, 762, 765, 837, 842, 843.
Caprice, No. 4. 499.
Caprice, No. 5. 576.
Ecole Moderne, No. 1. 204.
Ecole Moderne, No. 2. 719, 729, 830, 864, 866.
Faust Fantasia. 208, 590, 606.
Légende. 369.
Polonaise (A-Major). 222, 760.
Scherzo-Tarantelle. 294, 858, 876, 895.
Souvenir de Moscow. 624, 625.

ILLUSTRATIONS

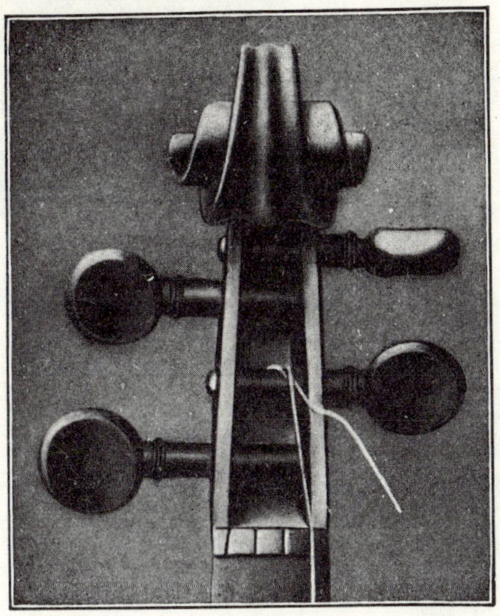

Illustration 1.
Mounting of a string.
The extreme end of the string is firmly fastened.
(Page 11.)

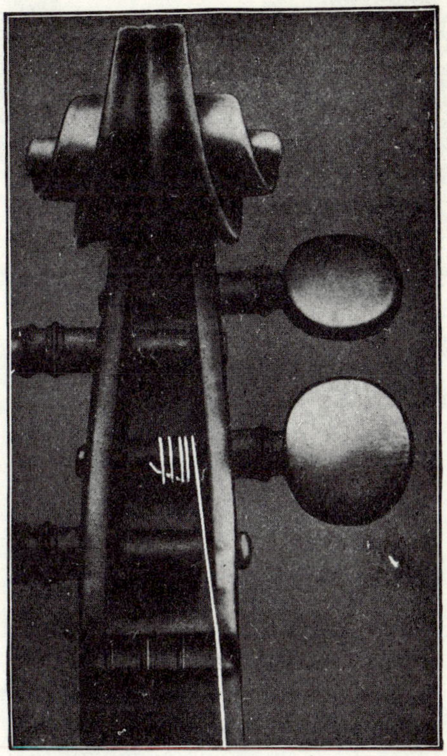

Illustration 2.
Mounting of a string.
The string is rolled around peg.
(Page 11.)

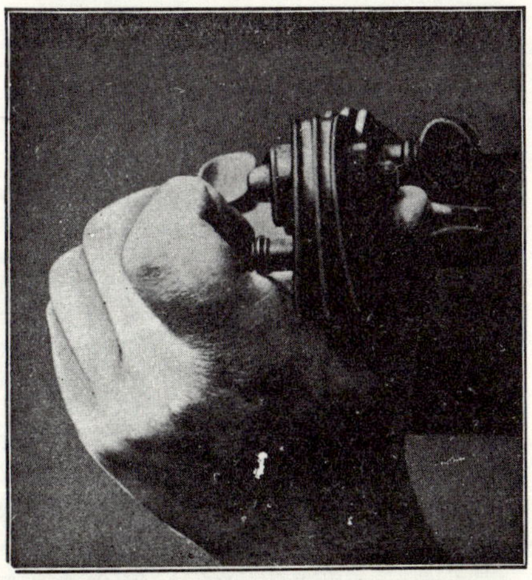

Illustration 3.
Tuning of the A- or E-String.
The index-finger tunes, the thumb provides the counter-pressure.
(Page 11.)

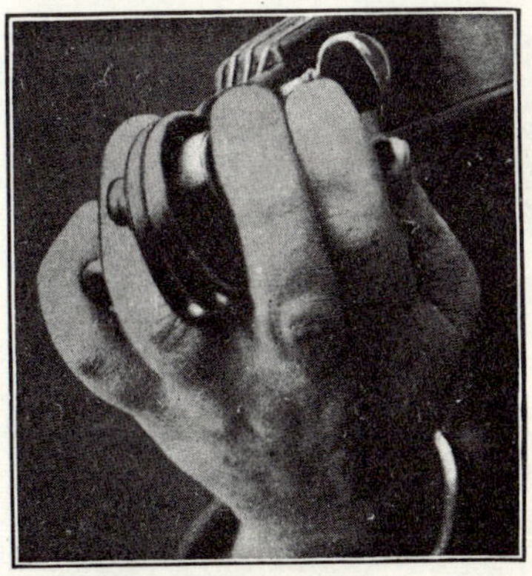

Illustration 4.
Tuning of the D- or G-String.
Thumb and index-fingers tune, ring and little fingers provide the counter-pressure.
(Page 11.)

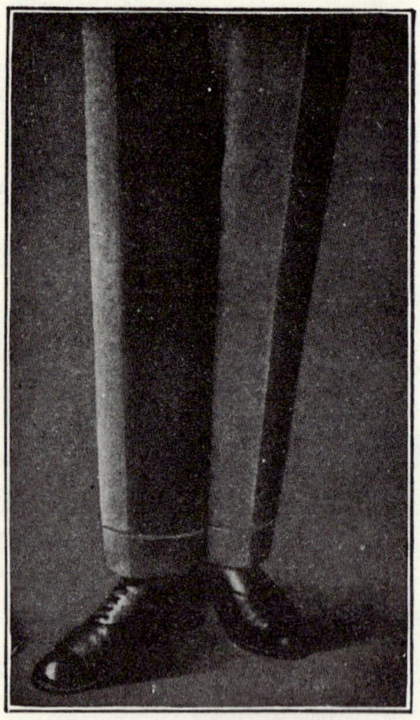

Illustration 5.
Rectangular Leg-position.
(Page 14.)

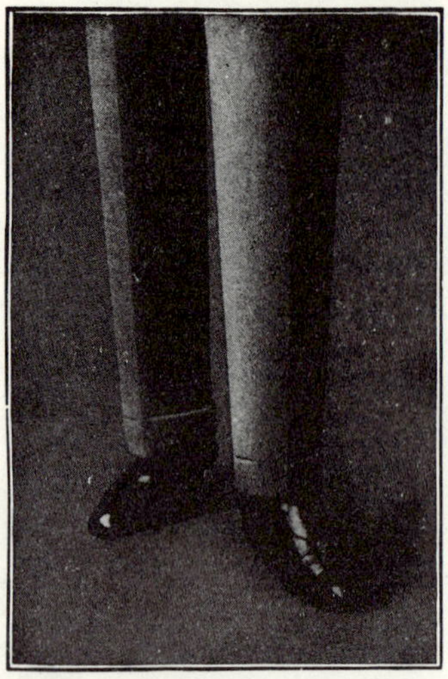

Illustration 6.
Acutangular Leg-position.
(Page 14.)

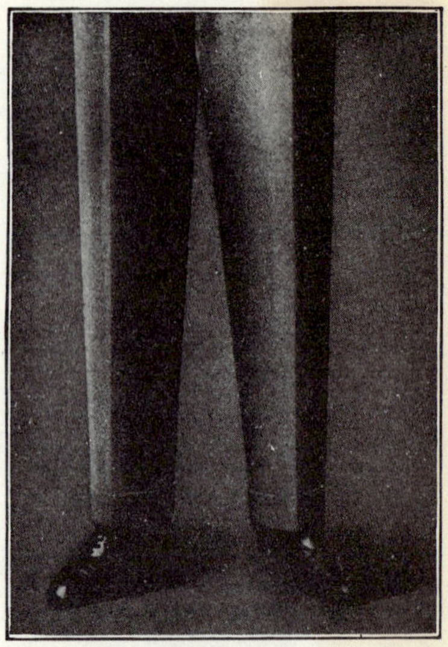

Illustration 7.
Spread or Straddling Leg-position.
(Page. 14.)

Illustration 8.
Correct direction in which the Violin should be held.
(Page 15.)

Illustration 9.
Cushion. Too slanting a position of the Violin owing to too large a cushion.
(Page 15.)

Illustration 10.
Cushion. Correct position of the Violin with a cushion, the size of which is suitable for the length of player's neck.
(Page 15.)

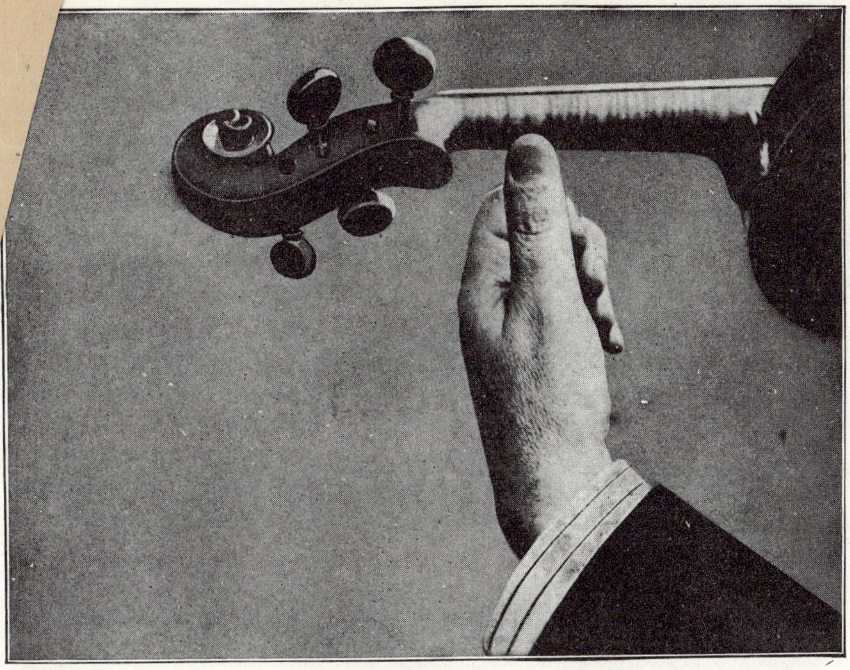

Illustration 11.
Thumb Position (left).
Establishing the natural proportion of the thumb to the neck of the Violin (Marsick).
(Page 17.)

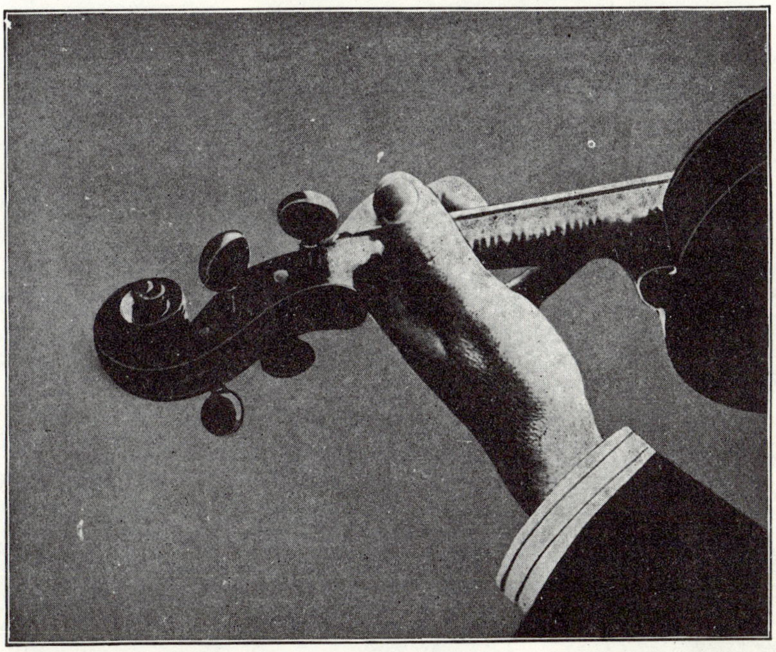

Illustration 12.
Thumb Position (left).
The correct position of the thumb.
(Page 17.)

Octaves in Sevcik, Pt IV, "Octaves," is good for this thumb position in up & down shifting

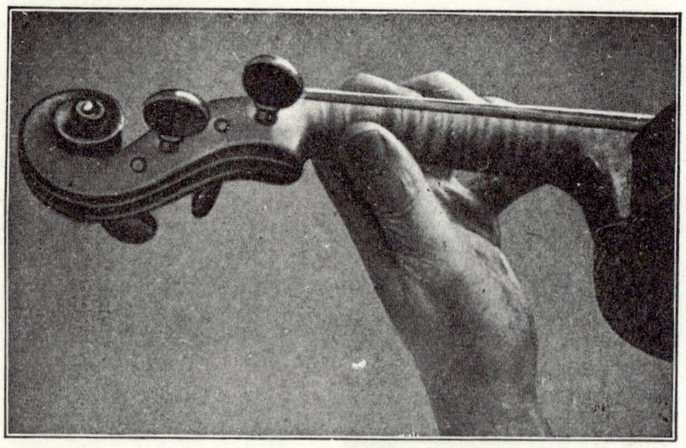

Illustration 13.
Thumb-position from below.
(Page 17.)

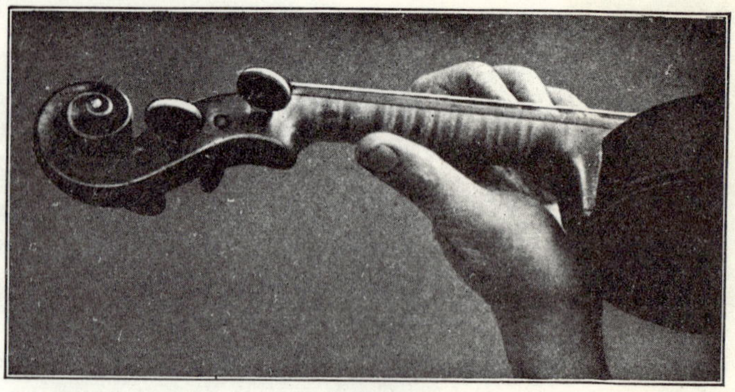

Illustration 13a.
Thumb-position in the III or IV Position before descending into the lower, or ascending into the upper positions.
(Page 18.)

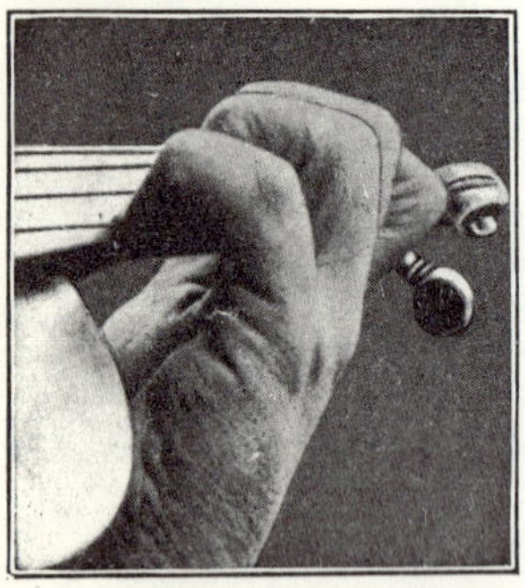

Illustration 14.
Exaggerated curving of the fingers.
(Page 18.)

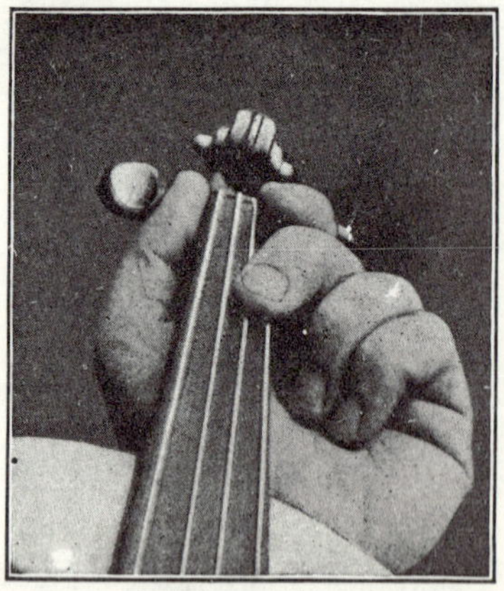

Illustration 15.
Vibrato Exercise by Rivarde.
(Page 37.)

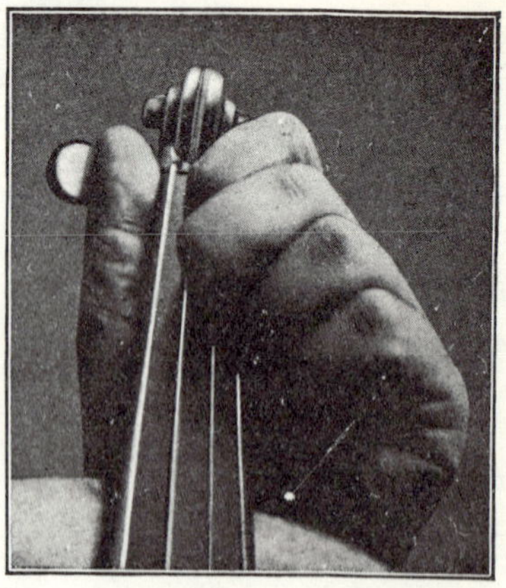

Illustration 16.
Vibrato Exercise by Rivarde.
(Page 37.)

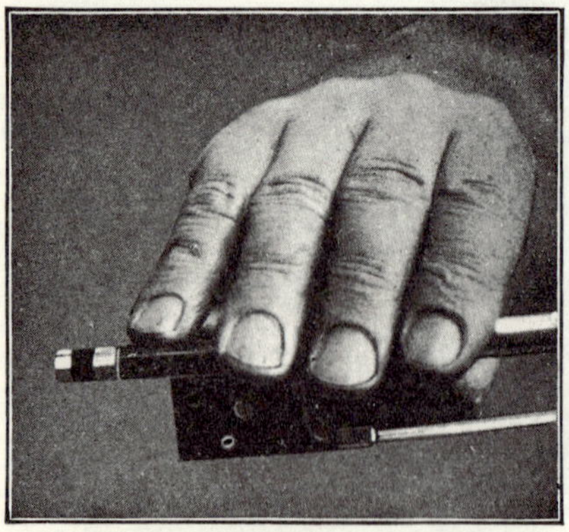

Illustration 17.
Old (German) Method of holding the Bow.
(Page 51.)

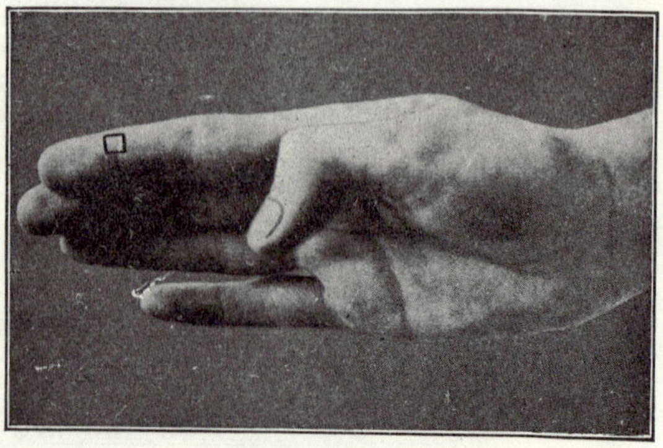

Illustration 17a.
Point of contact between Index finger and stick of the bow with the older (German) method of holding the bow.
(Page 51.)

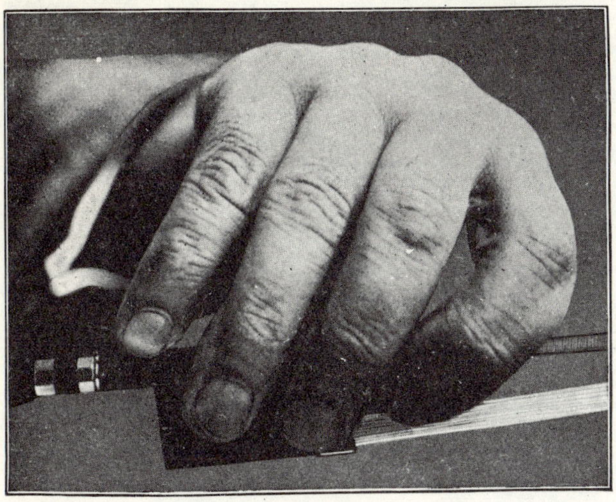

Illustration 18.
Newer (Franco-Belgian) manner of holding the bow.
(Page 51.)

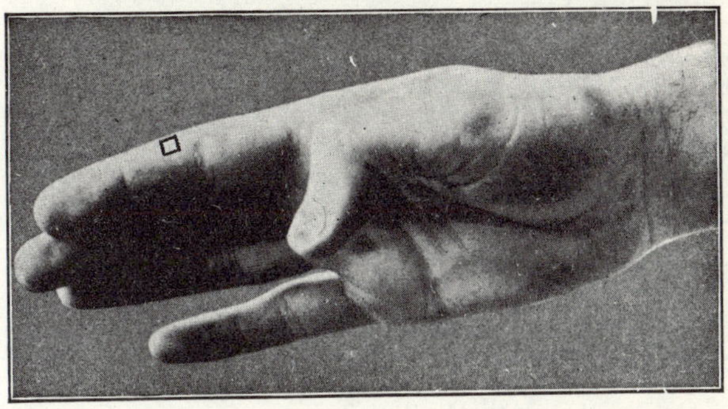

Illustration 18a.
Point of contact between index-finger and stick of the bow; modern (Franco-Belgian) method of holding the bow.
(Page 51.)

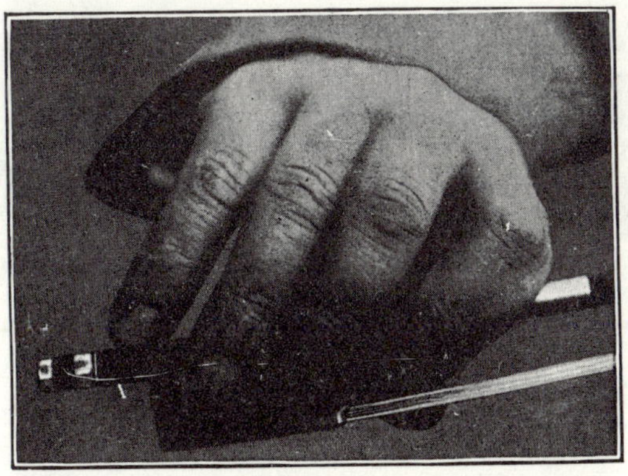

Illustration 19.
Newest (Russian) method of holding the bow (Auer).
(Page 51.)

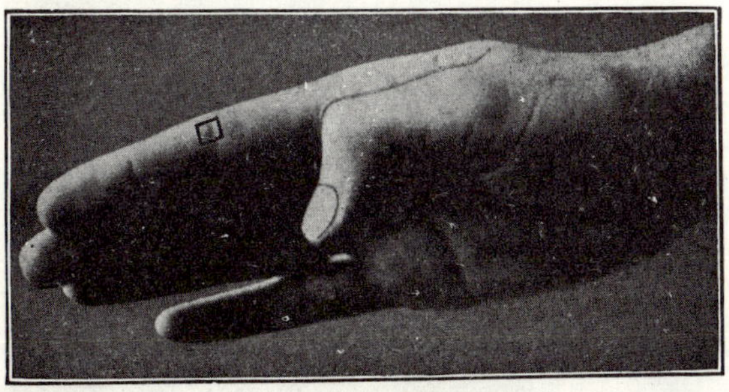

Illustration 19a.
Point of contact between index-finger and stick of the bow; newest (Russian) method of holding the bow.
(Page 51.)

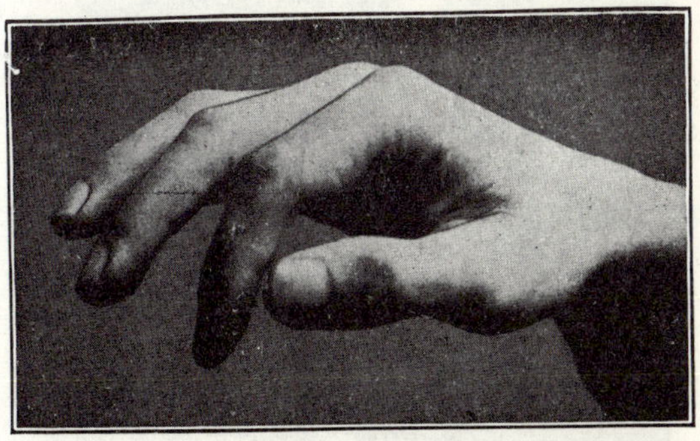

Illustration 19b.
Turning of the lower arm as employed with the older (German) method of holding the bow.
(Page 51.)

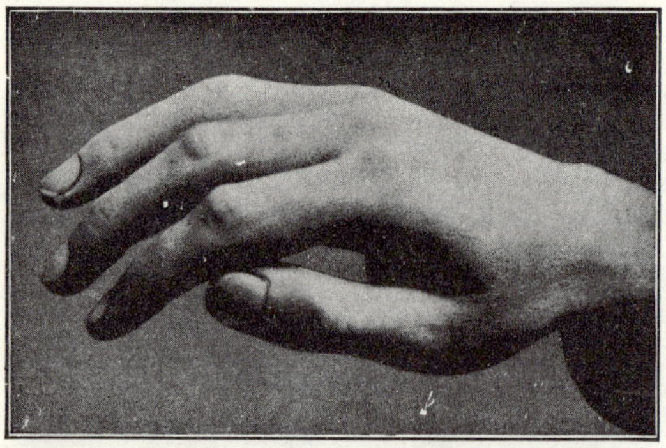

Illustration 20.
Turn of lower arm for new method (Franco-Belgian) of holding the bow.
(Page 51.)

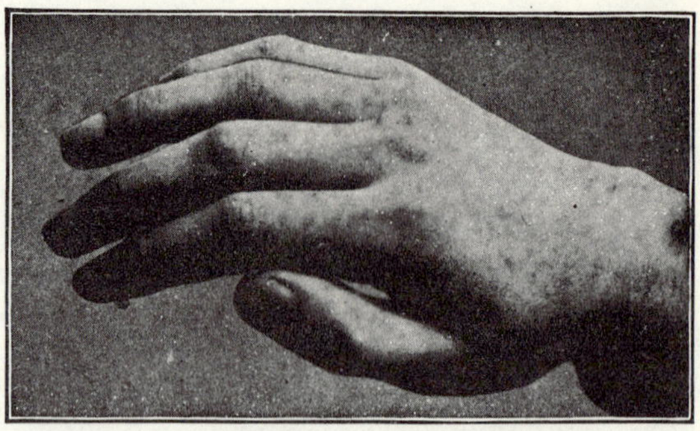

Illustration 21.
Turn of lower arm for newest (Russian) method of holding the bow.
(Page 51.)

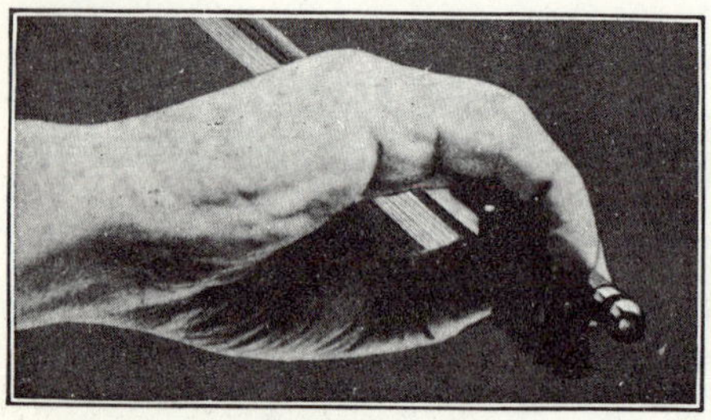

Illustration 22.
Correct position of little finger on the stick.
(Page 54.)

to be used at nut, not at pt unless bow to be raised (thrown stroke)

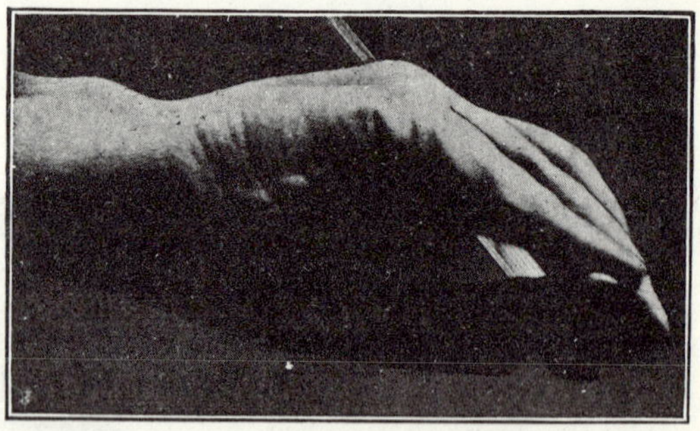

Illustration 23.
Incorrect (flat, stretched) position of little finger on the stick.
(Page 54.)

Illustration 24.
Upper arm pressed against body; nut.
(Page 55.)

Illustration 25.
Upper arm pressed against body; tip.
(Page 55.)

Illustration 26.
Upper arm held too high.
(Page 55.)

Illustration 27.
Right angle between hand and lower arm with lowered upper arm; nut.
(Pages 55 and 58.)

hand level
lower arm level
" " Lowered
" " lifted
wrist = strt. line
" = rt ∠
hand sloping

Illustration 28.
Straight line between hand and lower arm, correct holding of upper arm; nut.
(Pages 55 and 58.)

Upper arm in plane of string on which bow now is resting

Illustration 30.
Wrist too high with downward slope of hand; tip.
(Page 58.)

Illustration 29.
Wrist too high with downward slope of hand; nut.
(Page 58.)

Illustration 31.
The wrist dropping downward (too low) and the hand raised; tip.
(Page 58.)

Illustration 32.
Hand and lower arm in a straight line; tip.
(Page 58.)

Illustration 35.
Shoulder pedal—high drawn shoulder.
(Page 93.)

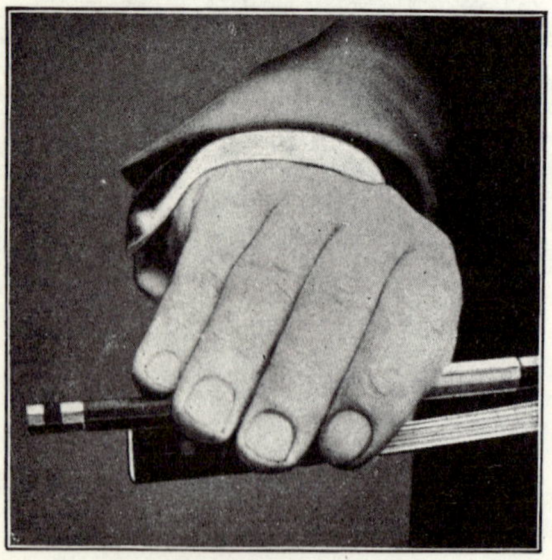

Illustration 33.
Fingerstroke—Stretching of the fingers.
(Page 58.)

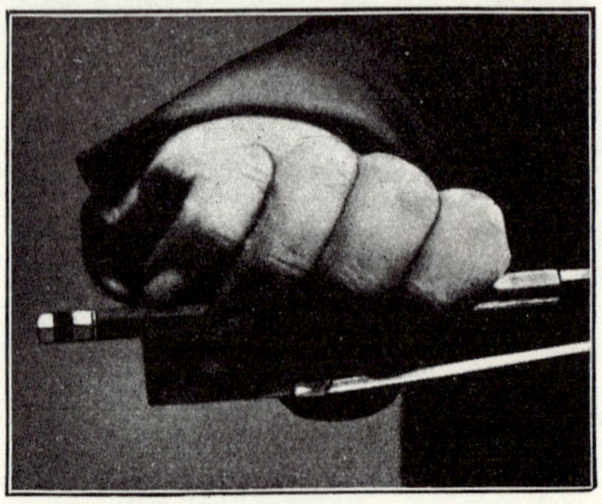

Illustration 34.
Fingerstroke—Curving of the fingers.
(Page 58.)